THE SINATRA CLUB

THE SINATRA CLUB

My Life Inside the New York Mafia

SAL POLISI

and Steve Dougherty

GALLERY BOOKS

New York London Toronto Sydney New Delhi

G

Gallery Books
A Division of Simon & Schuster, Inc.
1230 Avenue of the Americas
New York, NY 10020

Copyright © 2012 by Sal Polisi

All rights reserved, including the right to reproduce this book or portions thereof in any form whatsoever. For information address Gallery Books Subsidiary Rights Department, 1230 Avenue of the Americas, New York, NY 10020

First Gallery Books hardcover edition July 2012

GALLERY BOOKS and colophon are registered trademarks of Simon & Schuster, Inc.

For information about special discounts for bulk purchases, please contact Simon & Schuster Special Sales at 1-866-506-1949 or business@simonandschuster.com.

The Simon & Schuster Speakers Bureau can bring authors to your live event. For more information or to book an event contact the Simon & Schuster Speakers Bureau at 1-866-248-3049 or visit our website at www.simonspeakers.com.

Designed by Davina Mock-Maniscalco

Manufactured in the United States of America

10 9 8 7 6 5 4 3 2 1

Library of Congress Cataloging-in-Publication Data

Polisi, Salvatore, 1945–
  The Sinatra Club / by Sal Polisi and Steve Dougherty.
     p. cm.
  1. Polisi, Salvatore, 1945– 2. Mafia—New York (State)—New York—Biography.
  3. Organized crime—New York (State)—New York—Biography. 4. Gambling and crime—New York (State)—New York—Biography. I. Dougherty, Steve, 1948–
  II. Title.
  HV6452.N7P65 2012
  364.1092—dc23
  [B]
                                                                    2012000610

ISBN 978-1-4516-4287-2

ISBN 978-1-4516-4291-9 (ebook)

Such was the rule of the sanctuary. A candidate for the priesthood could only succeed to office by slaying the priest, and having slain him, he retained the office till he was himself slain by a stronger or a craftier. The post which he held by this precarious tenure carried with it the title of king; but surely no crowned head ever lay uneasier, or was visited by more evil dreams, than his.

—Sir James George Frazer, *The Golden Bough*, 1922

To my sister, Rose Marie, who died at twenty-one in 1965. I loved her dearly.

—Sal Polisi

To my father, Dick Dougherty (1920–2008), a lifelong news-paperman who despised in equal measure wiseguys and the public officials who let them get away with murder.

And to Ray Filiberti, a proud Italian who loathed the glorification of the Mob and cheers its fall.

—Steve Dougherty

⩍ THE SETTING ⩍

The Sinatra Club. The after-hours gambling joint I ran in Ozone Park, Queens, New York, from 1971, when that Life of ours was in its glory, to 1974, when death took over and we all started on the long highway to hell.

⩍ CAST OF CHARACTERS ⩍

MY FAMILY TIES

Frank Polisi. My father. He bootlegged whiskey with his brother Tony for Joe Profaci's gang during Prohibition but left that Life for honest work in the legitimate world.

Rose Belviso. My mother. She was a former showgirl who hoofed it out of my life when I was two years old. She split because she loved the Life.

Rose Marie Polisi. My beloved sister and guardian angel. She urged me to find happiness in the legitimate world; it didn't do her any good and I didn't listen.

Tony Polisi. My uncle, a flamboyant gambler and Profaci-Colombo Family gangster in whose footsteps I gladly followed into a career of crime.

Angela Polisi. The sweet and caring woman who made the biggest mistake of her life when she married me and became the last thing a woman like her should ever be—a Mob wife.

Sal Jr. and Joseph Polisi. Angela's and my two sons, the kids I neglected to live the Life.

Jane Parker. The beautiful, wild-hearted whore who became my *goomada* and mistress. When our lust turned to love, my two worlds—the criminal Life I shared with Jane and my home life with Angela—collided. The results weren't pretty.

Ronald "Foxy" Jerothe. No relation, but he was my brother in crime. The Fox would get trapped in a blood feud that—like the Life itself—became a dance with death.

COLOMBOS

Dominic Cataldo. My boss, business partner, and mentor in the Colombo Family.

Ervolino Cataldo. Dom's grandmother, a bootlegger and loan shark who groomed her son and grandson to become gangsters.

Sammy Cataldo. Dom's father. He grew up with my father and uncle, and became a made man and capo in the Profaci Family.

Joseph "Joey" Cataldo. Dom's younger brother, who was only peripherally involved in Mob business. He was my good friend and godfather to my younger son, Joseph.

Louise Anastasia Cataldo. Joey's wife and godmother to my son Joseph. She was the niece of the powerful Brooklyn waterfront boss Tough Tony Anastasio and of Albert Anastasia, the Mob godfather who was murdered in the Park Sheraton Hotel's Grazie barbershop in 1957.

Joe "the Wop" Cataldo. Dom's cousin and a powerful Mob figure who ran Family-owned casinos in Havana in the '50s. His ties with Jack Ruby—both in Cuba and as the Dallas mobster and strip club owner's contact in New York—ensnared him in the Warren Commission investigation into the Kennedy assassination.

Joe Profaci. One of the original godfathers of the New York Mob's Five Families. He was also a legitimate businessman who owned the Mama Mia company, the largest olive oil–importing business in the United States.

Joe Colombo. Profaci's underboss, who was installed as head of the Family by Carlo Gambino in 1965. In 1970, Colombo led the so-called Italian civil rights movement that culminated with a rally in Columbus Circle that drew more than fifty thousand supporters.

The Gallo Brothers. Larry, Crazy Joe, and Albert "Kid Blast" Gallo were Profaci Family soldiers who, along with gang mate Carmine "Snake" Persico, formed the "Barbershop Quartet" that carried out the contract to assassinate Albert Anastasia in 1957. Four years later, the four launched a rebellion against Profaci that resulted in the bloody decade-long power struggle known as the Gallo Wars.

Carmine Persico. He got his nickname "the Snake" when he switched sides in the Gallo Wars. He later led the Colombo Family faction that included my boss, Dominic Cataldo.

Freddie "No Nose" DeLucia. A Profaci-Colombo hit man who was in on a botched hit during the Gallo Wars that became the model for a famous scene in the film *Godfather II*. He helped school me when Dom first brought me into the Colombo Family.

Pegleg Brancato. Dominic Cataldo's boss and a Colombo Family capo who became temporary boss of the Family in the early 1970s.

Jackie Donnelly. Dominic's business and crime partner. His friendship with a corrupt Irish State Supreme Court judge gave us something priceless that *could* be bought—justice.

Eddie Pravato and Joe Dellamura. Career bank robbers and close friends of my uncle Tony's. They taught me all I needed to know about how to empty a jug.

GAMBINOS

John "Johnny Boy" Gotti. The charismatic Gambino soldier who became my friend and who rose to be the most famous boss in the Mafia.

Gene Gotti. John's younger brother. Genie introduced me to Fox Jerothe, the young Gambino soldier who would become my best friend.

Carlo Gambino. Godfather of the largest and wealthiest of the Five Families. He ruled the Commission, the Mob's board of directors, and until his death in 1976 was the single most powerful Mafia don in the nation.

Charlie Fatico. A longtime Anastasia-Gambino Family capo who ran the Family's largest crew from his headquarters, the Bergin Hunt and Fish Club in Ozone Park.

Neil Dellacroce. Carlo Gambino's underboss and heir apparent. He ran operations at the Family's Ravenite Social Club on Mulberry Street in Little Italy.

Manny Gambino. Carlo Gambino's nephew. He ran a Family loan-sharking business and hung out with his mistress at a favorite haunt of mine.

Angelo "Quack" Ruggiero. John Gotti's wing man, a nephew of Neil Dellacroce.

Willie Boy Johnson. Son of a full-blooded Mohawk and a Sicilian mother, he was one of the Bergin crew's most feared and loyal warriors.

John and Charles Carneglia. Brothers who formed a dandy two-man hit squad—John whacked guys and Charles vanished them.

Tony "Roach" Rampino. A scary hit man who was a great guy to have on your side in a softball game.

Paul Castellano. Carlo Gambino's first cousin, brother-in-law, and successor. He would be locked in a lethal power struggle with John Gotti.

Dave Iacovetti. A Gambino capo who ran Family operations in Florida and was close friends with the patron saint of the Sinatra Club—Old Blue Eyes himself. Dave befriended me in prison and taught me things about the Life that led to my salvation.

FRIENDS OF OURS

Mike "the Mouthpiece" Coiro. A former cop and Waterfront Commission investigator who flipped to our side and became a well-connected Mob lawyer. One of the Sinatra Club's best customers, he represented Dom and me as well as John Gotti and other Bergin crew members and friends of ours like Jimmy Burke and Henry Hill.

Roy Cohn. A longtime acquaintance of Mike Coiro, he was the famous attorney who made his name prosecuting the Rosenbergs and his fortune representing mobsters like Carlo Gambino and John Gotti.

Tommy "Two Guns" DeSimone. Fox and my hijacking partner and the notorious killer immortalized by Joe Pesci in Martin Scorsese's *Good-Fellas*. Long-simmering tensions between Fox and Tommy would one day explode in violence.

Jimmy Burke. The murderous Irish businessman who elevated truck hijacking to a fine art. He was the best—and winningest—card player at the Sinatra Club. Robert De Niro played a character based on him in *GoodFellas*.

Henry Hill. Like Tommy and Jimmy, he was connected to the Lucchese Family. Ray Liotta played him in *GoodFellas*, which was based on *Wiseguy*, Nick Pileggi's best seller about Henry.

Paul Vario. The Lucchese Family capo who got a taste of everything Tommy, Jimmy, and Henry stole.

MOB NEMESES

Diane Giacalone. An Ozone Park girl who grew up to become an assistant U.S. attorney. Her investigation of an armored car heist by a couple of thugs who stole cars for me put her on a trail that led to a Brooklyn courthouse where she prosecuted John Gotti, by then boss of the Gambino Family, for racketeering in 1986.

John Gleeson. Giacalone's assistant in Gotti's 1986 trail. He got a second crack at the Teflon Don six years later as lead prosecutor in the case that proved that the New York Mob wasn't too big to fail after all.

Remo Franceschini. That once rarest of beasts, an honest cop. He went after the Mob back in the days when most of his brethren in blue were either out to lunch or on the take.

Dan Russo and Ed McDonald. Eight years after the Mob's protector, FBI director J. Edgar Hoover, died and the feds declared open season on the Families, these two flipped Henry Hill and got him in the Witness Protection Program. After that it was easy to see that the Mob was a sinking ship—all you had to do was count the rats.

Prologue

WE WERE AT A joint called the Fireplace in Ozone Park, Queens, when I first heard Johnny Boy's name. It was the summer of 1968, not long after Bobby Kennedy got whacked. I knew better than to ask my boss, Dominic, who I was with that night and who was a hit man himself, about Bobby, but I assumed it was a Mob job like his brother. Nobody ever heard of any of the Families using an Arab button man, but crazier shit happened that year. Race riots, student riots, police riots, whole cities on fire, Chicago cops busting heads on TV—it looked like the whole country was going up in flames. Maybe that's why it seemed like pyromaniacs named all the Mob joints we hung out in back then.

The Fireplace had a cage over the bar with a couple of go-go dancers shaking it to Steppenwolf's "Born to Be Wild" and "Good Lovin'" by the Rascals. They didn't normally play hippie music in there, but the Rascals were Italians, and "Born to Be Wild" was a great song to crank up after a score.

Dom was busy telling a story about a guy in our crew named "Big Funzi" Tarricone. Funzi was with the Colombo Family, like us. Everybody called him Funzi because his name was Alphonse; they called him *Big* Funzi because what else can you call a guy who is six foot four? Funzi was a gorilla, but not exactly what you'd call a high-wattage kind of guy.

The year before, my uncle Tony and another friend of ours named Sonny were going away for bank robbery. Before Sonny went in, he sold one of his Cadillacs. "Funzi gets a call and he's told that Sonny's got car trouble," Dom says. "Funzi goes, 'So find a mechanic.' He's not bein' a smart-ass. He really thinks you got car trouble, get a mechanic. Turns out the dealership Sonny sold his car to did what dealers do: They turned around and sold it to somebody else. Trouble is the car salesman tells the new buyer to have the Caddy swept for bugs because it belonged to 'a hoodlum named Sonny Franzese.' No shit. He calls Sonny a hoodlum. The dumb prick doesn't know that the buyer is connected. The buyer makes a call, and next thing, Big Funzi's on his way to give the used-car salesman a talking-to. Funz was hanging out with a couple of Gambino guys from Fatico's crew that day. So he takes these two bruisers with him—the Indian, Willie Boy, and this kid Johnny Boy, who thinks he's Al Capone—he does his shylock work with a baseball bat. That fuckin' salesman had to sell cars from a wheelchair after that."

A week later, Dom and I were at the Flame, another bar named in honor of the wiseguy's favorite problem solver—arson. The Flame was a Gambino joint on the Brooklyn-Queens line, and some of that Family's guys were in there. Dom pointed out one of them and said that's the guy who's got the swing like Capone, Johnny Boy. From where I stood at the bar, I couldn't make out much about him except that he looked like a typical tough guy with linebacker shoulders and his hair swept up and back like a hood from the '50s. The next I heard he was in the can on a federal rap for hijacking. After that, nothing; if his name came up, I didn't notice. I didn't give Johnny Boy a second thought.

In the summer of '68 I was twenty-three and already a career criminal with an arrest record dating back to high school, but I was still a rookie outfielder with the Colombo Family. A few years would pass before I earned my Mob name, Sally Ubatz—Crazy Sally. Ubatz is Brooklynese for *upazzo*, "crazy" in Italian.

How I got it is a wild story I'll get to later. But back then, if Dominic or anybody else told me that this guy Johnny Boy, a low-level Gambino with a Capone fixation, would one day not only become boss of that Family and the most powerful Mafia leader in the country but would also rewrite the history of the Mob and become world famous in the process, I would have thought they were the ones who were *upazzo*.

I would have known for sure if anybody had predicted that when Johnny Boy skyrocketed to power and flamed out in equally spectacular fashion, I would have a front-row seat and that he and I would be bound together in a personal drama, one that began the day he got out of prison in 1972 and didn't end until thirty years later, when he was back in stir for life but where he met an early death instead.

———————

I got to know John Gotti four years after that night at the Flame. That's when he started hanging out at the Sinatra Club, the new gambling joint in Ozone Park I owned with the Cataldos, Dominic and his little brother Joey.

John and I spent a lot of time together because we both had a big-time jones for gambling. Even though he loved playing cards, he was a lousy poker player and he hardly ever hit a winner at the track—but he was great at board games. John and me and Foxy Jerothe—a young guy who'd been with John since he was a kid and who became my best friend and crime partner—used to spend hours playing at my club and at the Gambinos' own place nearby, the Bergin Hunt and Fish Club. We played marathon games of Scrabble and Monopoly. We bet on those games, and John won a lot of them. He was pretty good at chess too. Once we got to know each other, Johnny and I hung out together outside my club and our other regular haunts. We went to the track, we went to ball games and barbeques, we played softball at his crew's annual picnics. When our kids got older, they played on the same Pop Warner football teams.

Despite the fact that Johnny and I were with different Families, we planned scores together. That's something that would never have happened in the old days, but thanks in part to the Sinatra Club, the strict lines between Mob Families were beginning to blur. The club was a place where guys from all the different Families hung out together regularly, another thing that the bosses never would have allowed just a few years earlier.

John and I talked a lot about the Mob and how it was in the old days and how things were changing. He grew up in the same neighborhood where I was born—in East New York, Brooklyn. That's where John's heroes Al Capone and Albert Anastasia were from and where the Murder Incorporated headquarters—Midnight Rose's candy store—was. John loved all the stories about the Mob in those days, and I was full of them thanks to my uncle Tony. Uncle Tony was an old-school gangster who came up under Joe Profaci, and he raised me on his stories about what it was like running booze during Prohibition and how guys like Profaci and Lucky Luciano and Frank Costello and, before all of them, Arnold Rothstein, the guy who fixed the World Series, ruled New York and lived like kings.

John and I both grew up with the same dream to become part of that world my uncle Tony told me about when I was a kid. John was five years older than me and already a soldier in his Gambino capo Charlie Fatico's crew. I was twenty-six by then and still trying to prove myself. But we both had the same goal—to join the brotherhood of hoodlums and become made members of our respective Mafia Families.

By any measure of the New York Mob's wealth and power and popularity, it was at an all-time high when John Gotti and I became friends in 1972. That was a watershed year, when a new generation of Mob leaders began their ascendancy and the old structures that had been in place for decades began to crumble. It was a year of big changes, not the least of which was the public's perception of the Mob's might and influence. That happened in large part thanks to *The Godfather*, which was released that March. Every connected guy alive loved that movie because it turned us into romantic heroes. Women all over town wanted to bang a gangster once they saw it. My best friend, Fox Jerothe, and our hijacking partner Tommy DeSimone and I saw the picture together that spring. We left the theater so juiced up, we went out and committed a major felony in celebration of the Life we'd just seen played out on the big screen.

Most legitimate people had no idea how big and powerful the Mob really was until they saw that film or read the best-selling novel by Mario Puzo that it was based on. The year before the movie came out, another book—Gay Talese's *Honor Thy Father*, about Joe Bananas, the boss of the Bonanno Family—laid out the true facts behind the fiction.

"We're bigger than U.S. Steel." That's one of the lines everybody remembered from *The Godfather.* The guy who says it is the film's Meyer Lansky character, Hyman Roth. Lansky was the Jewish gangster who was the brains behind Lucky Luciano, the Mafia's *capo di tutti capi* in the old days. What Lansky actually said was—in a bugged conversation with his wife—"We're bigger than General Motors."

Truth was, the Mob was bigger than both those outfits put together, along with most of the rest of the Top Ten Fortune 500 at the time. According to Talese, the American Mafia—including twenty-four Families scattered around the country, with the five centered in New York City by far the richest and strongest—was raking in $40 billion a year by the early '70s. That was more than the earnings of General Motors, U.S. Steel, Standard Oil, Chrysler, Ford, IBM, AT&T, RCA, and General Electric *combined.*

The Mob wasn't just big business—it was the biggest business in America. And like its legit corporate cousins today, it operated with little or no government regulation and paid zero taxes.

The only fees the Mob paid on all its profit came in the form of payoffs to friends of the Families in high places and low. It took some hefty sums to grease all the politicians and government officials, judges, lawyers, prosecutors, police brass, investigators, detectives, and cops on the job who were also on the take.

But thanks to the greed and corruption of the same people taxpayers paid to serve and protect them, the Mafia's enormous gang of criminals were able to commit the most brazen acts of thievery and violence imaginable—from back-alley serial killings to public executions, including the most blatant whacking of all time, the assassination of a president—and get rich in the process. The so-called good guys gave us the greatest gift any small-time hoodlum or Mafia don could ask for: They let us get away with it.

———————

In 1972, no Mafia CEO reaped more of the rewards or presided over a larger empire and ruled it more ruthlessly than the man Johnny Boy Gotti would one day succeed.

If the movie's producers had set out to portray the *real* godfather, they never would have cast Marlon Brando as Don Corleone. They would have found an obscure character actor nobody ever heard of to play Carlo Gambino, a short and unintimidating seventy-year-old man who looked like he couldn't fight his way out of the old folks' home.

Despite all his wealth and power, the Gambino Family father was modest and unassuming in every way. Unlike some of his predecessors who lived in lavish party palace penthouses overlooking Central Park and country estates that were like feudal manors, Gambino resided with his wife and kids in a tiny-for-a-crime-lord house on an average-size lot on an ordinary cul-de-sac in the nothing-special middle-class town of Massapequa, New York, off Sunrise Highway, a few miles east of Jones Beach Parkway. Every day he was driven from his modest home to his modest office in a nondescript brick building on Ocean Parkway in South Brooklyn, in a car no Caddy- or Lincoln-loving wiseguy would be caught dead in—a fucking Oldsmobile.

If you happened to see Gambino on the street, you'd never give him a second look. His only distinguishing features were his bent beak nose and the little porkpie hat and enigmatic Mona Lisa smile he always wore. Joe Bonanno wrote that Gambino was "a squirrel of a man, a servile and cringing individual."[1] Of course he waited until Gambino was already safely tucked away in his grave before he said it out loud in a book.

For a penniless illegal immigrant who washed ashore in 1921 at age nineteen, Gambino did all right for himself. By 1972 he commanded an army of four thousand made men and associates; he ran a business enterprise whose holdings rivaled those of any modern-day hedge fund; his earnings from the waterfront shipping, air freight, trucking, construction, garment, and waste disposal industries and the unions under his control rivaled the enormous cash flow funneled to him by the twenty-four capos who ran the Gambino Family's gambling, loan-sharking, and extortion operations, and whose street crews carried out the robberies, inflicted the beatings, and committed the murders and other crimes that

[1] Joseph Bonanno, *A Man of Honor: The Autobiography of Joseph Bonanno.* St. Martin's Press, New York, 2003.

made headlines. But thanks to the protection provided by public servants, little if any punishment resulted for the perps.

The Gambino criminal enterprise that became more profitable than all the rest was narcotics. Despite what Brando's Don Corleone said about the drug trade being too dirty a business for bosses who ran their Families by strict codes of honor and respect, the real godfather started importing heroin into the United States by the freighter load in 1948; that's when he and Lucky Luciano established the Turkey-to-Sicily-to-Marseilles-to-New-York smuggling operation known as the French Connection.

Throughout the following decade, demand for hard drugs was pretty much limited to lowlifes, bohemians, and ghetto-crushed blacks. That changed in the 1960s when the Vietnam War created a mass market for the stuff. By 1972, more than fifty-five thousand American kids had been killed, a quarter of a million wounded, and countless survivors had been so severely traumatized that they were happy to pay $100 for a gram of smack to kill the pain.

The Mob hadn't seen a cash cow like it since 1933 when Prohibition ended. Booze was a golden fountain of cash and goodwill. It was the ultimate crime, the perfect illegal business. The product was a magic elixir that everybody wanted. There was no top to the demand; the Mob controlled the entire supply, paid off the cops to reduce the risk, and kept all the profits. Plus, everybody—the legitimate public, their elected officials, and even the cops—loved bootleggers because they kept the beer taps flowing and their liquor cabinets full.

Prohibition was the golden goose that made the Mob. Narcotics was the poison that killed it. Legitimate slobs wanted no part of soul-killers like heroin. You never saw Bogart or Cagney or Edward G. make a movie about the glamorous life of drug traffickers. Pushers were the worst kind of scum, and they brought the worst kind of heat—the kind that couldn't be bought. That's why Gambino and the rest of the dons distributed the product from the French Connection pipeline through surrogate non-Mafia gangs—and why they kept their involvement in trafficking a secret from all but the very top echelon of their own Families.

The bosses never shared their profits with the guys in the bottom tiers of the Family hierarchy. The Mob was a trickle-up organization; all cash flowed up from the street crews to the capos and from there to the top guys and, finally, to the boss, never the other way around. The Mob's CEOs figured that the less the rank and file knew about the wealth that was not trickling down to them, the better.

In 1956, Congress passed legislation establishing mandatory sentences of twenty years in prison, with no chance of parole, for anyone convicted of selling narcotics. That's when the bosses got panicky. They realized that when faced with the prospect of spending a third of their adult lifetime in the paint, even their most loyal soldiers would forget their vows of silence—*omertà*—and turn rat on their Fathers.

The next year, the Commission, the national crime organization's board of directors, called an emergency meeting of Mob leaders from across the country to discuss the new drug-sentencing law. They held the big sit-down in the town of Apalachin, New York, near Binghamton. Carlo Gambino, the Commission's newest member thanks to his whacking of his own godfather, Albert Anastasia, in a celebrated hit a few weeks before, proposed a simple solution to the problems posed by the feds' new narcotics laws: capital punishment—Mob style.

This meant that any made member of a Family caught dealing drugs would be executed by lethal injection—he'd get a bullet right in the coconut.

At the time of the Apalachin conference, narcotics weren't even on the average Mob soldier's radar. But fifteen years later they were—and big time. I know because that's when I got into the *babania* trade myself. And as soon as I went all in, the government upped the ante. The Dangerous Drug Acts of 1972 included mandatory sentencing provisions that meant if I got caught dealing just four ounces of the stuff—a fraction of the kilos we were moving—I'd be looking at twenty-five years to life in prison.

When that happened, Carlo Gambino, who by then was the most powerful don on the Commission, countered with a mandatory sentencing act of his own: From now on, he decreed, not only made guys but anybody even vaguely associated with any Mob Family who dealt the smack got the whack. (The dons themselves as well as top lieutenants involved in the godfathers' own huge drug-importing business were of course excluded.)

On top of that, Gambino announced a new Mafia Code of Honor: It was the responsibility of middle management—Family captains and crew chiefs—to locate and confront any and all drug-dealing underlings and act accordingly. Failure to do so meant the violator's superior faced the same mandatory sentence—execution without trial. Thanks to the diminutive Don Carlo's brilliant use of force and persuasion, Gambino not only ran the Commission and the Mob's entire national organization; he was, by the time our story begins, the de facto boss of all the other New York Families except one—my own, the Colombos.

By means of marriage (Lucchese), muscle (Bonanno), and *morte* (Genovese), Gambino had installed puppet bosses beholden to him in each of those three Families. The fourth Family, the Colombos, formerly run by my uncle Tony's old don, Joe Profaci, and torn apart by a bloody civil war fought between a rebel faction led by the Gallo brothers and family loyalists led by Carmine "the Snake" Persico, had caused terrible problems for Gambino and the entire New York Mob for more than a decade.

Gambino thought he had solved them and ended the so-called Gallo Wars by installing Joe Colombo in 1965. But even after Larry Gallo's death and his brother Joe's imprisonment, the bloodshed continued intermittently until 1969, when two friends of my boss Dominic were rubbed out in what everybody thought was the war's final skirmish.

But then, in the spring of 1971, Crazy Joe Gallo came home from prison, and that's when tensions began to build until it looked like there was going to be all-out war all over again.

———

There were other forces at work in 1972 that made Gambino's position of wealth and power—and that of the Mob itself—not quite as unassailable as it seemed. The whole country was about to go through major convulsions that nobody foresaw when a crew of bungling burglars blew the Watergate break-in that June. For the Mob, the seemingly unrelated event that caused a catastrophe happened a month before the fiasco at the Watergate, in May 1972, when J. Edgar Hoover croaked.

People can be forgiven for assuming that the death of the famous G-man who had run the FBI for the past half century would have caused rejoicing in the Families. But the truth was that J. Edgar Hoover, the Justice Department's chief crime fighter, was the best friend the Mafia ever had. Hoover's ties to the Mob went back decades, and that was the main reason why the Families prospered the way they did for so long without the feds doing squat about it. The nation's top cop was closely associated with two of the Mob's most prominent players: Frank Costello, who used his knowledge of Hoover's secret gambling addiction and his closeted life as a homosexual to intimidate and control him; and Roy Cohn, the infamous Mob lawyer who helped Hoover wage war on Communists and the Left instead of on Cohn's clients, who were a far more real danger to the republic than any civil rights leader or peace demonstrator ever was.

Throughout the decades he ran the bureau, Hoover insisted publicly that the Mafia was a bugaboo that didn't exist. Privately, when his agents presented him with solid proof that it not only existed but in fact was the engine that drove 99 percent of organized criminal activity in the United States, he suppressed the reports and shitcanned the agents who filed them.

Instead of going after the Mob and its honchos, Hoover chased headlines and the bank robbers and kidnappers and mad bombers who made them. Those were the bad guys Hoover put on his famous Ten Most Wanted lists—never the mobsters who committed more serial killings and torture murders and stole more money and abused the laws of the land far more brazenly than lone gun freelancers like John Dillinger and Machine Gun Kelly possibly could.

When the Kennedy brothers got in office and ordered Hoover to go after the Mob, the FBI finally turned up the heat. But Hoover's brief and belated war on the Mafia ended with one genius hit in Dallas. And when J. Edgar led the Warren Commission investigation into the Kennedy assassination, he suppressed all evidence that pointed to the true culprits behind the plot.

Before he died on May 2, 1972, Hoover performed one last service for the Mafia. He instructed Roy Cohn to deliver a deathbed warning to Cohn's client Carlo Gambino. There was, Cohn told the godfather immediately after Hoover's demise, a rat in the Gambino Family's largest crew. An unnamed source inside Charlie Fatico's Bergin Hunt and Fish Club had been feeding information directly to Hoover since 1966. As long as J. Edgar was on the job, the top secret "director's-eyes-only" reports filed by the rat's contact agent were placed where they could do no harm—in Hoover's office shredder. The FBI's new director was sure to see to it that the Bergin spy ratted in vain no longer—which meant serious trouble ahead for Don Carlo Gambino, his Family's entire organization, and the New York Mob itself.

There was something more about the death of the Mob's Great Protector that must have kept the lights burning late in Massapequa. The year before Hoover died, Congress passed a law specifically calibrated to destroy the Mafia. The Racketeer Influenced and Corrupt Organizations Act was diabolically simple: It basically made it a crime to run a Mob Family. Carlo Gambino recognized that the RICO Act was more than a sick joke—the lawyer who came up with it named it after Rico Bandello, every Mob guy's favorite movie gangster played by Edward G. Robinson in *Little Caesar*. Gambino knew that RICO meant it was open season on the Mob, and without Hoover's shield to protect him the government would finally go after the country's real public enemy number 1—Don Carlo Gambino himself.

With threats looming all around—from government regulators on the outside and from his own wiseguys within—Gambino purged the ranks of deadwood, dealers, and traitors. He also began to lay the groundwork for a total reorganization of the Mob's Family structure. The first step was to find new blood to replace the old. To do so he spread the word that he would soon reopen his Family's membership rolls to proven young men who would take the place of its aged or eliminated made members.

But pinning buttons on worthy new soldiers was easier said than done. The sad fact was that the talent pool was running dry. The city that once teemed with native and first-generation Italians had turned into a melting pot full of mutts. Gambino could still find guys who were 100 percent Italian but few who were steeped in the traditions of the ancient secret societies of Sicily or the old-school Family values of their Americanized offspring, the New York Mob.

One who did honor the old customs and traditions and who eventually caught Gambino's eye was my friend Johnny Boy Gotti.

––––––––––

I was always a street guy. I was into robbing and stealing and gambling and loan sharking. I wasn't involved in the big-money sit-downs, the labor racketeering and construction company shakedowns, the Garment District and garbage and cement company kickbacks. As for the Mob's control of the Teamsters, all I did was hijack the trucks.

For guys like me and Fox, my blood brother and crime partner, the thing we loved about being in that life was the action, the excitement. All we wanted was the chance to pull robberies, heists, and hijackings. We were in it for the money, sure. But it was the danger, the thrills that made the life of crime something special. Talk about a rush? Forget about it. There's no rush like pulling a robbery. It's like sex. I couldn't get enough.

A guy like John Gotti was different. He was far more ambitious than me and Fox. He wasn't in it just for the rush and the riches. He wanted the power and the glory.

John Gotti's tragedy, if you can call it that, was that he was born too late for the old-school gangster crown that he craved. He began his rise as the Mob was beginning to crumble; by the time he got to the top, the bottom had dropped out.

From the beginning, John was charismatic and smart. He just wasn't cut out to be godfather. Once he became boss, he drove the bus right off the bridge. Or maybe it was the bus that drove him. Either way, I watched him go.

Here's how it all happened.

PART ONE

PART ONE

CHAPTER ONE

A Star Is Born

JANUARY 1972

HE MADE HIS ENTRANCE on a frigid night about three weeks after New Year's. He was dressed like a street guy in a leather jacket, but he walked and talked like a king. And he got treated like one. Even my boss, Little Dom Cataldo, showed him respect that first night. "Wait 'til you meet this guy," my new friend Foxy Jerothe had told me. "Johnny's a real gangster."

I hadn't seen John Gotti since that summer in the Flame. He was thirty-one now, but he still wore his hair swept back '50s style like most of us did back then. He had thick sideburns, and his widow's peak was more pronounced that it had been in '68; it looked like he was combing it into a fall in front like Dion, but that might just have been the way his hair grew.

I remembered he looked like a linebacker when I saw him three years before, but now he was bulked up from pumping prison iron and was built more powerful, like a nose guard or a tackle; he had a barrel chest with massive shoulders and thick arms, kind of like Rocky Marciano, only better looking.

He didn't need the expensive silk suits and the Chesterfield coats he took to wearing later to make an impression. He walked into the club like there was a force field around him; he had that kind of charisma, a presence that commanded instant respect. It was strange. You could tell by looking at him that he didn't have two nickels to rub together, but guys were drawn to him. He had a kind of body language, a swagger that everybody liked.

It was like Fox said: He was a gangster's gangster.

Johnny was barely out of the cuffs and leg chains when he arrived. He'd been bused in from Lewisburg, the federal penitentiary in Pennsylvania, and processed out at the West Street lockup that afternoon. Before he went home to see his wife and kids, he checked in with his Gambino Family boss at the Bergin Hunt and Fish Club, about ten blocks away from our joint on Atlantic Avenue in Ozone Park. The Bergin was the new headquarters of Charlie Fatico, boss of the largest and strongest crews in Don Carlo Gambino's entire organization. Charlie had a couple hundred soldiers under him; he was number three in the Family behind Neil Dellacroce, Don Carlo's underboss and heir apparent who worked out of the Ravenite Social Club in Little Italy.

After his welcome home sit-down with Charlie, Gotti went to spend some time with his other family, his wife, Victoria, and their five children. Itching for some action after three years in the cement, John got one of his guys to pick him up and bring him over to the Sinatra Club, where his crew from the Bergin—along with made guys and associate members of Dom and my Colombo Family and even some Luccheses from Paul Vario's crew in Brooklyn—were gathered to greet him.

All five of the Families that made up the New York Mob were as touchy about their turf as Indian tribes in the Old West. Guys from different Families didn't work together without permission from their bosses, and as a rule they didn't hang out at each other's social clubs. The exceptions were the floating craps and card games that most of the bosses ran on certain nights of the week that were open to all connected guys.

Because the Sinatra Club was a gambling joint owned and run by Colombos in a part of Queens where the Gambinos and Luccheses also operated, Dom had to get permission to open from the bosses. Before a hand was dealt, he had sit-downs with Pegleg Brancato, who was acting boss of our Family, Paulie Vario, and Charlie Fatico. All three gave their blessing, though Charlie made sure that we wouldn't open on Fridays and compete with his weekly craps game.

The Bergin guys were regulars from the first night we opened two months before. We had a tight connection with Fatico and his brother, Danny, because Dom and my mouthpiece, Mike Coiro, represented them and a bunch of their guys, including John Gotti and his brother Genie.

Mike was there that night, and he was one of the first guys Johnny embraced when he arrived—I would have hugged the Mouthpiece too if he'd done for me what he did for Johnny. Gotti had been looking at more than twenty years for three hijackings and a kidnap count for making off with one truck with the driver still in it. Mike had magic connections in the Queens courthouse, where he got one of John's cases dismissed outright; a federal judge threw out the second case after Mike pointed out that the FBI used illegal wiretaps; and in the one case John ended up doing time for, Mike got the sentence knocked down from eight years to thirty months.

Then John lucked out again. Instead of getting sent to Atlanta or some other hard-core federal pen, he got assigned to Lewisburg, which was run like the courthouse in Queens—the Mob owned everybody from the warden to the prison priest. John made the best of his time at Lewisburg just like I would later; he ate steaks, drank scotch, and pumped iron; he also made connections on the prison's Mafia-only cellblock with some very top guys like Carmine Galante, the boss of the Bonanno Family, and Jimmy Hoffa, the Mobbed-up Teamsters boss who knew every major Mob leader in the country. John came out of prison like a rough-neck prince; glory awaited once he got some grooming . . . and if he could survive the deadly leadership tests that lay ahead.

Mike the Mouthpiece got a lot of congratulatory slaps on the back that night from Johnny's guys, and he loved every minute of it. Mike was a very sharp—and sharp-looking—lawyer. He was tall and lean, with dark wavy hair. He looked like the actor Jerry Orbach. He always had a big smile and an infectious personality. He was a married, middle-aged attorney, but he'd been representing gangsters so long he thought he was one himself. He loved gambling, strong scotch, and forbidden pussy, all of which he found at the Sinatra Club, where he was a regular even on nights when we weren't throwing a welcome home party for one of his clients.

Another guy John greeted like a long-lost brother was Foxy, the young Gambino who'd been coming to the club since the night we opened and who'd become my crime partner. The Fox idolized Gotti; he couldn't stop talking about him. The whole time I knew Fox, I never heard him say a word against John Gotti. I really think he thought of him as god-like. Fox and John both grew up on the same streets in East New York where my grandfather owned a bar and where my family lived when I was born. Fox was a fatherless sixteen-year-old high school dropout running with John's old street gang, the Rockaway Boys, when John was in his mid-twenties and starting out with Fatico's crew, which operated out of Albert Anastasia's old East New York headquarters, the Club, in those days.

John must have seen something of himself in Fox because he took the kid under his wing and showed him the ropes. He had Fox play the outfield for him on jobs, working as lookout and helping out at Charlie Fatico's drop unloading swag off trucks that John and his crew jacked. John loved Fox like a kid brother, and Fox would do anything for him, including kill, which he vowed he'd do in a heartbeat even though it wouldn't get him his button. Fox couldn't be a made guy because he was a mutt—half Italian, part Irish, and part whatever.

Even though he could never be a full-fledged mafioso, Fox was a val-ued member of the Bergin crew; he had already got his bump up and was pulling action scores by the time we met and started working together.

Soon after Gotti's homecoming, Fox and I would be teamed with another Sinatra Club regular to form the New York Mob's first Three-Families hijacking crew.

The third man was Tommy "Two Guns" DeSimone, the Lucchese Family killer who would become famous twenty years later when Joe Pesci played a character based on him in Martin Scorsese's *GoodFellas*.

Tommy was from my neighborhood in Ozone Park; he went to high school with my wife, Angela, and I'd known him to say hello to for years. In *GoodFellas*, Pesci got Tommy's weird, almost schizo personality dead on, but not his look. Tommy was tall and trim and a really handsome guy—he looked like Errol Flynn. He was one of the few connected guys I ever knew with a mustache. I don't know how he carried it off—or why his own boss, Paul Vario, didn't make him shave it—but it worked for him.

Tommy had ADD and ADHD; whatever other deficit disorder you can think of, he had it. Put that together with a guy who liked to drink and snort coke, had a violent, hair-trigger temper, and never left home without at least two guns in his belt, and you hoped you weren't around when he flew into one of his rages.

Part of Tommy's problem was that he had a large-size chip on his shoulder. He came from a long line of mobsters: His grandfather and uncle were both bosses in the Los Angeles Family, and two of his older brothers were connected to the Gambinos in New York; one was a rat who got whacked for it. Having a rat in the family made Tommy very eager to prove himself.

Most of the time he was a blast to be around. He was funny as hell and was always up for wild times. He had an upbeat personality but with a real downside; he'd be smiling and laughing one second, and he'd pull the trigger the next.

Once Fox and I teamed up with Tommy, the three of us became pretty good friends. But from the beginning there were underlying tensions between Tommy and Fox, who was with the Gambinos, the Family Tommy's brother ratted on. But their differences were personal and went deeper and, just like the vendettas that tore apart the ancient secret societies of Sicily, their feud would start over a woman.

———

Two gorillas paying homage to John Gotti that night at the Sinatra Club were his right-hand man and best friend since they were kids, Angelo Ruggiero and Willie Boy Johnson, another Rockaways graduate who started out with Fatico at the same time John did.

Between the two of them, Fat Angelo and Willie Boy outweighed King Kong. Ange was a 280-pound behemoth with a pudgy face and a permanent scowl that made him look like a big lethal baby. He had a face that would scare the rattles off a snake.

Ange also had a nasty temper and he was a brutal killer, but that didn't mean he wasn't fun to be around. He was funny as hell and had all kinds of weird mannerisms. I always got a kick out of him and so did a lot of guys. They called him Quack because he was pigeon-toed and walked like a duck. Years later they called him that for reasons that weren't so funny.

Ange had a lot going for him. Besides riding John Gotti's rising star, he had a connection at the very top of the Gambino hierarchy—his uncle was Neil Dellacroce, second in command under Carlo Gambino and presumed to be the Family's next godfather. Ange also had another blood relative who was going places. His brother Sal, who got pinched with Johnny Boy back in 1963 for stealing an Avis rental car, would soon become one of the wealthiest gangsters in New York City.

Gorilla number two had even more muscle than Angelo but none of his connections. Willie Boy Johnson was six feet and 250 pounds of bad trouble. You could tell by looking at his hands. He had the words LOVE and HATE tattooed on his knuckles, like Robert Mitchum in *Night of the Hunter*. Willie Boy's tats looked like jailhouse handiwork performed by a drunk who did the carving with a broken liquor bottle.

Willie Boy was five years older than Johnny Boy, ten years older than me; he came up doing freelance muscle work for Fatico back when Anastasia was still boss. He'd been a loyal Gambino soldier ever since, but, like Fox, he could never become a made member of the Family. Willie Boy was only half Italian. His father was an ironworker who built skyscrapers; he was also a real native New Yorker—a full-blooded Mohawk Indian. His people were living in this country before Columbus became the first Italian to come over on a boat.

Willie Boy's real name was Wilfred or some shit like that. Guys called him Half-Breed behind his back. If they were smart, they called him Mr. Johnson to his face.

Willie Boy didn't seem to have a nerve ending in his body. When he was playing cards, he sat still as a rock. That's why guys figured he had the brains of one. But Willie Boy had a lot more going on than anyone knew.

Another one of Johnny's friends from the old neighborhood, John Carneglia, was there to greet him that night. John and his younger brother Charles came up stealing cars for Charlie Fatico. In later years they would make their own fortune in the hot-car business. Brother John would make his bones as a button man, one of the top hitters in the Family. Charles would do his own fair share of killings, but his skill at vanishing bodies in tubs of acid so there was no earthly trace left of the victims made him the go-to guy after a whacking for all the crews in the Gambino Family.

Every thug in the club used a baseball bat at one time or another to bust a deadbeat's skull or kneecaps—or balls. But Tony Roach, Johnny Boy's driver, was the only one who could crush a softball two city blocks like he did every year at Charlie Fatico's Fourth of July barbeque and fireworks picnic. Tony was a gifted athlete, but that's not what you'd think if you ran into him in a dark alley—or even a brightly lit one. Tony was scarier than your worst dream of what a hit man looks like. He was a tall and skinny Frankenstein's monster. He didn't stand; he hulked. He had sunken cheeks and sunken eyes, and his skin was scarred from chicken pox or some shit he had when he was a kid. His head looked like a skull; he looked like the walking dead. He killed a lot of guys. Getting whacked is bad enough, but when the last thing you see in life is a face like Tony's, you wish you were never born to begin with.

Jimmy Burke and Henry Hill were two more of Mike Coiro's clients who became regulars at the Sinatra Club, along with their friend Tommy D. Like Tommy, they were first immortalized in Nick Pileggi's fantastic book about Henry, *Wiseguy*, the book Scorsese based *GoodFellas* on. In the movie, as everybody knows, Jimmy was played by Robert De Niro, and Ray Liotta made Henry Hill probably the most famous New York City gangster who ever lived to tell about it.

I first met Jimmy Burke the previous summer when I played outfield on one of Dominic Cataldo's hijacking scores and we used his warehouse for the drop. He and Tommy were coming into the club since we opened, and Henry sometimes came along with them.

Jimmy Burke was probably the smartest connected guy I ever knew. And he was far and away the best cardplayer who ever sat down for a game at the Sinatra Club. A lot of players count cards; they remember every card that's played. Any guy who has a memory like that is a good player. And we had a lot of very good players at the club.

Jimmy counted cards as well, and he had a calculator mind, but what made him a great player was that he read people. He watched the other players' facial expressions and mannerisms as close as he watched what cards they played; he could study a guy and figure out his character and then could predict how he was going to play his hand.

When we finally sat down to play that night, Jimmy discovered that the man of the hour, John Gotti, the future king of New York who would become boss of the largest, wealthiest, and most powerful Mafia Family in America, had a fatal flaw.

Most private Mob clubs in those days were dingy, dark, depressing holes-in-the-wall. They were usually furnished with cast-off tables and chairs contributed by the waste management side of the Family. The artwork was always the same—color photos of the pope and the only two famous guys from Hoboken you ever heard of: Frank Sinatra and Jimmy Roselli.

Our joint was different. It looked more like something you'd find in the South Seas than in South Queens. We had fishnets draped from the ceilings and walls and hung with dried starfish and cork buoys. Travel posters from Tahiti and other South Pacific isles decorated the walls. Chinese lanterns strung throughout the club gave the place a year-round holiday feel.

Bamboo partitions separated the main room from the bathroom, storage area, and makeshift kitchen counter in the back that we used to stash food we brought in from outside. Up front was the bar and lounge area where guys could sit in cushioned chairs and drink, shoot the shit, and play Sinatra songs on the red-and-silver Wurlitzer jukebox that stood against the wall by the bar. The juke held fifty singles and a hundred songs; three plays for a quarter.

Guys pumped in lots of coins while they waited for a seat at one of the felt-top casino-regulation-size poker tables. If they had business they had to attend to, there was an old oak wood phone booth with a pay phone at the rear of the club that we used in the daytime to run our sports book and other gambling operations.

We meant no offense to Frankie and Jimmy or to the pope, but we decorated the walls with blown-up photos and wall posters of some other Italian heroes, like Joe DiMaggio and Rocky Graziano; we had a couple of famous Italian villains too—Mussolini and Al Capone. Displaying photos of non-Italian celebrities is unheard of in any Mob joint. But when guys complained about the half dozen color photos of my favorite blond goddess on the wall behind the bar, I had to remind them that Marilyn Monroe was married to an Italian saint, DiMaggio.

Guys didn't know what to make of the framed print I bought special and hung by the poker tables for good luck. It was a painting of a gorgeous nude by Salvador Dalí. Mob guys aren't big on art to begin with—never mind surrealist art. They looked at the big red rose that grew out of the girl's neck and figured the painting was typical strangeness from a guy everybody called Sally Ubatz. None of the guys knew why the painting had special meaning for me. I hung it up there in memory of my sister Rose Marie—my guardian angel.

Another woman who was important in my life was named after the heavenly angels, but I never asked my wife Angela what she thought of the painting or about the way I decorated the place. She wouldn't know what to say if I did, because she never stepped foot inside the Sinatra Club. No woman ever did, and that includes the two hookers I booked every night the club was open; their pleasures were a perk we provided our high rollers—gratis. It was one of the little extras we offered that guys couldn't find in any other Mob joint and gambling den. The hookers helped make the Sinatra Club something special, like the jukebox and the travel posters and the Dalí painting—only hotter. But the club wasn't a brothel; all tricks were turned off premises. Guys who wanted something else to play with between hands had to drive a few blocks to a nearby motel where I put the girls up on game nights.

The Sinatra Club was off-limits to wives, girlfriends, and mistresses—even mine. As far as I know, none of the guys who wet their wicks at the motel—or, later, at the secret splash pad I set up in an apartment walking distance from the club—told their wives or girlfriends about the hookers. I sure as hell didn't tell *my* wife. Like all Mob wives, Angela depended on my lies so she didn't have to face the truth, which was that, like all Mob guys I knew—save one—I cheated on her every chance I got.

As for my mistress, Jane, I didn't have to lie to her about the hookers—she was a whore herself and a madam; she provided the girls I booked for the club. I paid her for the girls, but I didn't pay Jane for sex. That's because we were in love. It was a sweet arrangement, but looking back maybe I should have kept things on a professional level. Hookers don't get jealous, but lovers do. And when things went too far between us, Jane did what jealous lovers do—she lashed out at her rival. And like so many things in that upside-down world of ours, our relationships were reversed and the other woman was my wife. And when my wife and my mistress locked horns, Angela fought like the devil and it was Jane who got bloodied.

That first night John came into the club, we had two poker tables—one up front for nickel-and-dime games that brought in a lot of semi-legit blue-collar guys from the neighborhood, and a high-stakes table farther back. We were serving deli sandwiches, beer, and wine, and we were still playing with plastic chips and store-bought Tally-Ho and Bee decks. We didn't become a real first-class joint until a month later when we made John a partner. He brought in so many high rollers from every crew in the city we started calling it the All-Families Social Club.

When that happened, the Sinatra Club became so popular we had twice as many guys waiting for seats than we had playing. So I ordered a third custom-built table from a company in Toronto. We stocked the bar with brandy and champagne and top-shelf liquor, brought in hot catered meals from the Villa Russo and other local Italian restaurants the guys liked, and replaced the cheapies with real fourteen-gram chips like they used in Vegas and decks of plastic-coated Kem cards that I bought by the gross direct from the manufacturer.

After two years and seven months playing cards for cigarettes in the can, Johnny was eager for a cash game. But before he sat in on one, Dominic walked him to the back room for a sit-down. They were in there long enough for the rest of us to play a few hands.

Johnny showed Dominic a lot of respect from the minute he came into the club. Dominic wasn't a made guy, but Johnny treated him like he was. Dominic—his Mob name was Little Dom, even though he was average height, maybe an inch or two shorter than Gotti—had been in on some hits for Carmine Persico's faction during the civil war that split our Family in the 1960s. Dom had earned his button, and everybody knew he would get it as soon as the Commission opened up the books and the Families could swear in new members again. Dom was also five years older than him, and that's another reason why Johnny was so deferential—in the beginning, anyway.

Dom had done enough time himself to know that three years off the streets had left John Gotti broke. He also knew that John was a strong earner and that he would make good on a loan. So Dom did for his Gambino friend what Charlie Fatico did for out-of-Family members who were regulars at his weekly games—he extended Johnny a line of credit good for a couple of thousand.

Within a few hours, most of Johnny's stake and a couple thousand more that he borrowed from the house was part of the huge pile of chips stacked on the table in front of Jimmy Burke.

You'll never find a connected guy who's not a devoted gambler—the Mob's lifeblood flowed from gambling and loan sharking. Whether we bet on horses or sports or dice or cards, gambling was like breathing for Mob guys—we couldn't live without it.

That's not to say everybody was good at it. Most Mob guys were chronic losers, and a lot of those who weren't were mediocre at best.

There were plenty of good players but only a few really gifted card sharks like Jimmy Burke. There were also a whole lot of degenerate gamblers, guys who, the more they lost, the more they kept at it until it broke them. The gambling bug infected them and made them sick. Degenerate gamblers were like junkies who couldn't stay high; they kept right on shooting up the shit that was killing them.

Johnny Boy was like that. It took me a few more nights playing seven-card stud with John at the Sinatra Club before I realized that for all the charisma and power that he exuded and the respect he got from everyone he met, he was also one of the worst cardplayers I ever met.

But Jimmy Burke had Johnny Boy pegged from the very first hands John played. Once Gotti took a look at his bottom cards, he was fucking William Tell. When he thought he had a winner, he started running his fingers through his hair. Late in the hand, if his cards still looked strong, he got so eager to raise the bet he was practically yanking his hair out by the fistful.

It got comical once he lit up a cigar. Johnny always smoked De Nobilis, and when he had a winning hand, it stood straight up, proud as a pecker in a whorehouse. When he held a loser, his lip went limp and the stogie drooped down.

But giving away his hands wasn't Johnny's biggest problem. Two things that made him a truly terrible cardplayer were that he always thought the next card would make him a winner, and he could not stand to be bluffed. Either because he didn't think anybody would dare pull one over on him or because he was too proud to be made a fool of, he always stayed in as long as possible and he always bet big in hopes of knocking the other players out. The result was that all of his chips ended up in the stacks of another player's winnings, usually Jimmy Burke's if he was in the game.

As big a loser as Johnny was that first night at the Sinatra Club, he was an equally soreheaded one. When a pot went to the other guy, his face turned red and the veins in his forehead popped like his brains were about to spurt all over the table. He'd throw down his cards and then grab them up again and rip them with his teeth. That was his thing. I saw him do that time and again over the years. He ruined a lot of perfectly good decks that way. He ripped them with his chompers or crumpled them in his fist and threw them across the room.

By the time we got a fresh deck, he was calmed down and ready to play again. He loved gambling so much he couldn't wait for the next deal. I guess he figured his luck was about to change.

It never did, and years later, it would be his undoing.

———————

Everybody has an Achilles' heel, but the only guy I knew who got even a taste of the kind of fame and glory that kick-ass Greek warrior won before one lousy flaw tripped him up was John Gotti. He was no true tragic figure, obviously—nobody weeps for a man who is as greedy and vicious as he is ambitious and who doles out contracts on guys like betting slips at the track. But to us who were in that Life back then, who watched him come from nothing and achieve great wealth and power and fame, all because he had the balls to grab it when he had the chance, he *was* a kind of hero.

Johnny Boy's rise was really something to see. Just a couple of months after his first night at the Sinatra Club, he was running Charlie Fatico's entire gambling and loan shark operation, a job no corporate mortgage banker could handle even if, like the song says, he robbed people with a gun instead of a fountain pen. Before the year was out, he was acting boss of Charlie's crew and answering directly to Neil Dellacroce and Don Carlo Gambino himself.

Johnny's career took off like a rocket and, in one way, at least, the Sinatra Club was his launching pad. A Mob war erupted that spring and summer, the worst the city had seen since the bloody Castellammarese War of 1930–1931. This war in fact turned far more dangerous than that one when, in August, innocent civilians were murdered in the crossfire at a Midtown Manhattan restaurant during the dinner rush.

The public and official outcry caused a crisis that threatened the entire New York Mob. Desperate to end the war, Carlo Gambino decided that the only way to save the Five Families was to dissolve them and blend the New York gangs into One Big Family.

To test his vision of the Mob of the future, Don Carlo gave his Family's rising young Turk a challenge. Johnny had told the boss all about the Sinatra Club—that it was a joint venture owned and operated by Colombos and Gambinos, and so many guys from crews all over hung out there that we called it the All-Families Social Club. Gambino told Johnny to start using his partnership in the club to make it a proving ground for cooperation among all the Families. That meant setting up a score that all five of the bosses could profit from. If any of his plans backfired, it would be Johnny's head that would roll.

Because Fox, Tommy, and I had gotten approval from our three bosses to pull scores together, John asked me to start looking for a heist big enough for five guys to work and splashy enough that all the Families would gladly quit fighting long enough to split the spoils. John's idea was that while they were at it, the bosses might learn that the benefits reaped from peaceful cooperation beat the hell out of the damages everybody was suffering because of the war.

I'm going to tell you all about how the Five-Families Heist went down. I'm also going to fill you in on how I was practically raised from birth to become a mobster. But first, let me talk about a chain of events that began the spring before John Gotti got out of prison and ended in the fall with me getting into a Wild West–style shoot-out with a New York City police officer—think *High Noon*, except when the lawman got the drop on me, I aimed a speeding Corvette right at his balls. Thanks to Mike Coiro, that incident resulted in a surprising and historic win for the bad guys in the eternal war between cops and robbers.

It was also the inciting incident that led to the opening, on Thanksgiving weekend 1971, of the Sinatra Club.

CHAPTER TWO

The Geriatric Twins

SPRING 1971

I TURNED TWENTY-SIX THE DAY before May Day. My second son would be born before the month was out, and I was at a crossroads in my life.

I made my living as a professional gambler and a loan shark. That meant I lent money at exorbitant interest to losers at Ozone Park's own Aqueduct Racetrack and beat the crap out of them when they welshed or didn't pay the weekly compounded interest—the vig— on a timely basis.

In the past three years, I had been busted for bookmaking so many times I lost count. There were more than a dozen at least that were logged on to my rap sheet along with arrests for robbery, burglary, forgery, assault, gun possession, and—my bread and butter when I was a kid—auto theft. I never did any real jail time for any of it; the charges were always dropped or forgotten. The reason for that is that I was connected.

Because I had a Family legacy thanks to my uncle Tony—and also because my business partner and boss, Dominic Cataldo, ran one of its top crews—I was an associated member of the Colombo Family.

Dom and I ran our gambling operation; I was also the collector and the muscle. But I wasn't in on the real action, the big scores that Dom and his crime partner, an Irish guy named Jackie Donnelly, pulled with Dom's crew. I played outfield on a few hijackings, driving the follow-up car, babysitting the hostages, unloading trucks, and sorting the swag, but

I never got in on the planning and rehearsals, which were almost as much of a blast as the takedown itself. That was the best part, the actual hijacking, when you stick a gun in the driver's face and steal his truck. But Dom didn't think I was ready to work up front—I had to sit in the car and watch him and Jackie have all the fun.

I was an excitement junkie; I wanted in on the scores. I wanted to move up, and to do that I had to prove to Dominic that I was a serious heist guy and not content to play outfield the rest of my life. It was time for me to step up to the plate and show him what I could do.

I made an okay living from the gambling operation—enough that Angela did not have to work and could stay home with our three-year-old son, Sal Jr. But with another kid on the way, we would be just getting by financially. I had a little money saved but not enough to carry the family over if I got busted or, worse, ended up in the hospital— or in the ground.

We were living in the house Angela grew up in, in Ozone Park, right next door to her parents, who owned a bar in the neighborhood, the Parkside.

I was like every other family man in the neighborhood— except that I had no driver's license even though I owned two cars. Those cars and everything else I owned, including our house, were in somebody else's name, either my wife's or her mother's or father's. I didn't pay taxes, I didn't vote, and none of the guns in my arsenal were registered.

Becoming a father—even the second time around—sets a man to thinking about the future, about his career and what he wants out of life.

My long-term goal was to become a made member of the Colombo Family.

Short term I needed to impress my boss so I could get in on the real action and the exciting adventures of the gangster life that I'd dreamed of since I was a kid on my uncle Tony's knee.

More immediately, I needed money so I could provide for my growing family.

What I didn't need was a book to tell me what to do when my wife was expecting.

I knew exactly what I was going to do. It was something that would solve both of my short-term goals and, ultimately, put me on a path to getting my button.

I was going to rob a bank.

And I knew just the guys who could help me do it.

———————

The Geriatric Twins were two old-time bank robbers I'd known for years. They were friends of my uncle Tony, and when I was a teenage kid they used to hang out at the Diamond Horseshoe Lounge, which was the bar inside the Aqueduct Motor Inn, the motel Tony owned near the racetrack.

Uncle Tony, who was the father I wish I'd had and my idol growing up, was a bank robber himself. He was a professional gangster connected to the Profaci-Colombo Family practically his whole life, but he was also a very successful independent operator. He was a bookmaker and loan shark, a bootlegger, a speakeasy and nightclub owner, a wartime black marketeer, and a postwar building contractor. But his two great loves in the Life were gambling and robbing banks.

His motel doubled as a hideout for his Colombo Family friend Sonny Franzese's gang of bank robbers as well as for the Twins—Eddie Pravato and Joe Dellamura.

Eddie and Joe were both in their late fifties but looked a lot older—Dominic called them the Geriatric Twins because they had spent so much time in prison they were pretty decrepit by the time Dom met them. When they had nowhere else to go after a stretch in stir, Uncle Tony used to put them up at the motel.

Also, because they were in the can and off the streets for half their adult lives, neither of them ever learned how to drive. Which is why when I looked them up a couple of weeks before my birthday and asked if they'd be interested in pulling a job, they jumped at the chance. They were both eager because Uncle Tony, who used to help them set up their scores and provided transportation, was away himself in prison for a bank job he pulled with Sonny back in 1967, doing the one and only stretch he ever served.

Eddie and Joe were knocking off banks back during the Depression,

around the time Bonnie and Clyde and John Dillinger were in the headlines. They were both in Alcatraz in 1963, the year they closed down the
famous prison in San Francisco Bay. They and twenty-five other hard-core
convicts were the last to leave the Rock. All the old cons were transferred
out to other federal pens. Eddie and Joe both finished their time at Atlanta.

Joe was a unique character. He was older and taller and a far better dresser than Eddie, a little guy who must have been born wearing
a Hawaiian shirt and a straw porkpie. He looked like a caricature of a
track gambler. Joe was more like my uncle; he wore tailored suits and the
finest European imported clothing. He was debonair and handsome, and
must have been the dashing outlaw in his day. He had a deep, gravelly
voice and steel-blue eyes; he was funny and charming. He loved women,
whiskey, and music.

And pulling jobs.

Joe was proud to be a bank robber. It was his great talent and passion, and he made a career out of it. Uncle Tony told me that on jobs,
Joe carried a small sawed-off shotgun that he could conceal in the folds
of his overcoat. He would very calmly walk into the bank and pull out his
shotgun. He would position himself near the front door with his blaster
pointed at the guard and ready in the event a customer entered during
the heist. Then he would be the last man out; he always let his partners
go ahead, covering for them like the hero in a World War II movie.

Joe looked back at prison like it was an even trade, the price you paid
to have the time of your life when you weren't locked up. He told me
that during the Depression, he traveled all across the country and did
nothing but pull bank jobs. He used to hit one after another until he got
caught. Then he would take a plea and do five to eight years. His longest
sentence was out in Nevada, where he got twenty years but they let him
out for good behavior after only three. He had no regrets, he said, but
he'd had his fill of prison.

Growing up, my uncle used to talk all the time about Willie Sutton,
the great "Gentleman Bandit." Legend has it that when a reporter asked
Sutton why he robbed banks, he said because "That's where the money
is." Sutton claimed he didn't really say that, but he *did* say he was like
Robin Hood—only he stole from the rich and kept it for himself.

Tony told me that Sutton robbed more than a hundred banks, stole more than $2 million, and never once killed anybody. He didn't have to, my uncle said, because he was smart; he planned everything out, and during the robbery he remained cool and calm. He kept his head and nobody got hurt.

They called him the Gentleman because he was always sharp-dressed and polite. His victims always said how charming he was. I loved Tony's stories, and when I was little I told him I wanted to be a bank robber when I grew up. Tony didn't laugh. He said, "When you do, remember Willie Sutton—be a gentleman."

I thought I knew everything there was to know about the Gentleman Bandit, until Joe Dellamura told me that he met Willie Sutton in prison. Joe said something I had not heard before, that Sutton never carried a loaded gun. In all those stickups, he never had any slugs in the chamber. That made Willie Sutton all the more cool to me—but not to Joe.

Playing the bluff wasn't Joe's style. He said that every time he carried his sawed-off into a bank, he was prepared to use it if he had to.

And that was true now more than ever, he said. He'd seen enough of the inside for one lifetime; he was too old to take another long stretch in prison.

He said if things got hot while we were doing our piece of work, he'd shoot his way out—or die trying.

Joe came along when we cased banks the week before, but at the last minute we had to find a third man. Joe was ill with something that gave him an awful rib-rattling cough. Whatever it was, it must have been hurting him bad because eager as he was to get in on the heist, he begged off. But before he did, he and Eddie gave me a crash course in the fine art of emptying a jug.

That's what those guys called a bank. It was an Italian thing; back in the old country, people stashed their savings in a jug. To Joe and Eddie, a bank was just a really big jug stuffed with a whole lot of cash.

Anybody who robs banks today has to be seriously *upazzo*. Pull one job and your MO is in the database, your picture is on the Internet, and your video is on YouTube. If you get away with more than a couple, you get ratted out by your neighbors the second their favorite real-crime show cuts to commercials.

It was a whole other ball game back then. There was no Internet and no security cameras covering every inch of the bank and all the entrances. There was usually one lousy security camera trained on the tellers' windows, and it took fuzzy out-of-focus single-shot black-and-white pictures that nobody would recognize if your mug happened to turn up on a wanted poster at the post office.

There were no thick Plexiglas shields encasing the tellers' booths end to end; there was just a nice flat open counter no higher than your rib cage—bank counters were almost the exact same height as the vaulting dummies I used to work out on in football practice in high school and on the indoor obstacle course when I was in Marine boot camp on Parris Island.

Another thing about banks then, which isn't so true today—they were stuffed to the rafters with cash. Credit cards were just coming into use—the jug we ended up hitting was a branch of the first bank in the country that issued plastic. All banks used real live tellers; there were no ATMs that allowed customers to get cash or deposit money without even going inside. There was no direct deposit. Everybody, from the boss to the kid in the mail room, had to go to the bank to cash his paycheck.

And all that loot was fairly easy pickings. All you needed was a dream—and a heater. "Just show 'em the gun," Eddie Pravato said. "Everybody in the bank will be scared shitless—they'll remember nothin'."

Joe and Eddie and I cased a bunch of banks. One was in a shopping center with all kinds of foot and car traffic. The second was at a busy intersection in a downtown business district. Location wasn't the only strike against it. Inside we found a young uniformed security guard on duty who looked like the gung-ho jarheads I knew in the Marines before I was lucky enough to get drummed out. "You don't want anybody you can't outrun or knock on his ass," Joe said. "There are plenty of bank managers who pay their grandfathers to stand around and be bored all day. Make sure you pick one of those."

There was really no need to check the floor plan in more than one bank. "That's the beauty of 'em," Eddie said. "All banks are the same bank. In Queens or in Kentucky, they're all exactly alike."

It was true. Every jug in the country was set up the same—with tellers behind a long counter and loan officers and the manager's desk behind a low-gated partition—and they all ran according to the same schedule. They all opened at 9:00 and closed at 3:00, except on Fridays, when some stayed open a few hours longer to accommodate the long lines of people cashing their paychecks.

That's why the big payroll deliveries were on Thursday afternoons and Friday mornings—with another on Monday morning to replenish the cash that went out Friday and to cash checks for people who couldn't get there before the bank closed on payday.

Payrolls were always delivered by armored cars. Two guards always walked in together, one either carrying the cash in canvas bags or pushing it on a hand cart, the other carrying the weight—sometimes a shotgun, usually a Smith & Wesson held at his side and pointed at the floor.

There was a system. The guards walked the money into the gated area, and the bank manager signed for it and placed it on the countertop. The head teller unsealed the money and distributed it to the tellers. Each teller clipped the bottom bill under a trip wire; if the bill was moved, it set off the alarms.

Before we made a final decision on which bank to hit—or even knew for sure who would be the third man—we designed our plan.

First off, it was my job to get two hot cars, big four-doors with V-8 engines. (That's one of the things we always had over the cops regardless of what kind of heist we were working—eight cylinders under the hood. They drove sixes. No matter how much they souped them up, we always outpowered the police.)

I would park one of the hotskis, the switch car, a few blocks away. The second one we'd drive to the bank and use for the getaway.

We'd hit the bank early, clocking our arrival for five minutes after the armored truck left, giving the head teller enough time to distribute the cash but before a lot of legitimate customers came in with their pay-checks to take out some for themselves.

Because Joe couldn't make it, Eddie would man the shotgun and the third man would take Eddie's usual place as point man. That was the trickiest part of a bank heist. The point man entered first and asked to see the bank manager while his partners waited outside. He had to be very cool and calm, just another ordinary legitimate slob who wants to talk about a loan or open an account, but he needs to talk to the manager to be sure he wants to do business in that particular branch.

Then, once he's seated at the manager's desk, the point man would quietly tell the manager that the bank is about to be robbed and the manager needs to sit right where he is and don't move. To make sure he does as he's told, the point man would slip his own Smith & Wesson out of his jacket and coolly rest it on his lap for the manager to see. That's the signal for the action team to rush the bank.

From then on, the third man would have to keep a close eye on the second hand of his watch. From the moment Eddie and I entered, we'd have exactly ninety seconds to grab the cash and get out of there. (That didn't sound like enough time to make a deposit, much less withdraw all cash on hand, but I kept my doubts to myself.)

At the first tick of the ninety-second clock, it was my turn—and that's when the real fun began.

———

The jug we picked was the Franklin National Bank on Horace Hard-ing Boulevard in Queens. The headquarters of the bank was across the line in Nassau County. The Franklin National had branches all over the country and was one of the biggest banks in the United States. Three years later, it would become the most infamous bank in the country, and not because we hit the Queens branch. *Why* we got the green light from the bosses to hit the Franklin National is what made it famous.

We chose it in the first place because it was perfect for us. It was in a free-standing building, which meant it had no neighboring businesses full of workers looking out the windows at what was going on next door. It was surrounded by parking lots, so customers had to drive to get there.

There would be no legitimate slobs wandering in off the street and, if it came down to it, if there was trouble with any witnesses on the way out, we had a guy in a Queens detective squad who could trace their license plate numbers for us. Also, it was close by an underpass of the Long Island Expressway, which runs parallel to Horace Harding Boulevard. That underpass would give us a quick and easy getaway.

We had cased a couple of other banks with sweet setups, but there was something else about the Franklin National that made it all the more ripe.

Because I was with Dominic, I needed his blessing to pull the score. And I couldn't wait to ask him for it, since I wanted him to see that I wasn't content doling out cash at the track and busting deadbeats' knees day in and day out. I knew I'd have to give up a piece of my take to him and to his boss, Pegleg Brancato, and I'd have to give a taste to Mike Coiro, our mouthpiece. Mike didn't charge us anything when he handled one of our cases; in exchange he got a little bite of everything we earned. And Mike did such good work for us, we were all happy to pay.

Normally the bosses didn't approve of bank robbery because it's a federal crime. And it was the one major crime that the FBI was really good at investigating. And why shouldn't they be? Busting bank robbers who were usually the big stars on Hoover's Ten Most Wanted list earned promotions for the agents, and each bust made the bureau look good in the public's eyes.

With heist guys like Dom, and most guys in the Family rank and file, bank robbers got a lot of respect because they had balls. Bank robbery was an action score; you had to be smart in the planning and quick in the execution. You'd be surprised how many guys in the Mob avoided real action, who never used a gun because they were afraid to look their victim in the eye. They'd rather sit back and let another guy take the risk by doing the dangerous dirty work.

So I knew Dom would have no problem with my bank score. He liked that I was trying to make something of myself. He was my mentor, and he wanted me to do good and he said so.

What surprised me was what he said about the bank we were targeting. The word had only recently come down that the Commission was declaring open season on the Franklin National. It turned out our plan to rob it was nothing compared to what the Families had in store for it. The bosses were cooperating with the Italian Mafia to take over the bank and blow it out like it was some pizza joint the owner gave up to cover a gambling debt.

Michele Sindona, the Italian Mob's high-finance wizard, orchestrated the whole thing. Three years after he got control of the bank, the Franklin National collapsed and caused one of the biggest banking scandals of all time. When it did, it exposed the Mob's ties to the Vatican Bank and to the highest reaches of corporate America and the Nixon administration.

But before Sindona bought the bank, he wanted to bring the price down. And there was nothing like a sudden rash of bank robberies to encourage the current owners to sell. So crews in all the Families were told to do their bank robbing at the nearest Franklin National branch. And we were only too happy to oblige.

The guy Eddie and Joe lined up to be the third man on our job was somebody I knew, a Colombo named Joe Vitale. He was about ten years older than me and a very experienced bank robber. They used to call Vitale the Jesse James of the East. He was a big, strapping Italian, six feet tall and two hundred pounds, and very good at what he did. I knew that he was smart and he'd be a good point man. But I also knew that he was a junkie—a guy hooked on heroin was the last person you wanted on a score. Partnering on a heist meant putting your life in the other guy's hands and vice versa. When you've got a smack fiend for a partner, you could both end up dead. But Eddie and Joe vouched for Vitale. They said he was clean and up for the job. I had no choice but to believe them.

I managed to heist two great cars, both Chevys with big eight-cylinder engines. On the night before the score, I parked the switch car on a residential street a few blocks from the underpass on the other side of the LIE.

We hit the bank on Monday, May 3. It was a beautiful spring day, sunny and warm.

I wanted to look sharp for my first bank heist, so I wore my best white turtleneck knit shirt and pleated Italian trousers. I had bought the most realistic-looking rug and fake mustache that I could find. I wore rubber-soled shoes so I'd be sure to get good traction on the bank floors.

I picked up Eddie and Vitale in the second hotski and drove to the bank. Vitale was cool, and that made me feel better. If he'd been sweating and nervous, or nodding out, I'd have postponed the job until we found somebody else.

We had clocked the armored truck, and it drove past us going in the opposite direction as we approached the bank. I pulled into the parking lot out front and backed into a slot so I was pointed directly at the entrance to the bank. As soon as I parked, Vitale got out and walked inside. Like all banks, it was brightly lit so there was not much reflection on the glass entrance; the whole scene inside was framed like the stage of a Broadway theater.

When I saw Vitale being escorted through the gate and shown to the manager's desk, Eddie and I got out and ambled toward the entrance. Eddie stopped to tie his shoe. While I waited for him, I watched for Joe's signal. I couldn't see the security guard and supposed he must be right inside the door to my right.

When I saw Vitale reach his right hand into his jacket, Eddie pulled up his bandanna and we rushed inside.

As soon as we did, I looked to my immediate right. No security guard.

Eddie was a little guy, but he looked ten feet tall when he pulled the sawed-off out of his coat and pumped it. "Freeze!" he shouted. "This is a holdup. Nobody move, nobody gets hurt!"

That was my cue.

I didn't even glance at Vitale as I sprinted toward the bank counter. I was already springing up and my feet were off the ground when I slapped the countertop with both hands and swung from the hips; my momentum carried me right over the counter—a perfect ten-point vault. It was like flying. It was also the greatest feeling in the world. I pulled my gun with my right hand and with the other I snatched the plastic grocery bag that was hanging out of my back pocket; it had the I ♥ NY logo printed on it big letters.

That's when things started to get fucked up.

The head teller just stood there in front of me, frozen with fear, staring at my gun. She was so scared, she pissed herself. It was running down her leg. I was standing there dumbstruck, staring at the puddle spreading out on the floor at her feet when somebody banged into me from behind. I whirled around expecting the security guard. It was Eddie, who got jumpy when he saw that the head teller wasn't moving quick enough. I didn't have to tell Eddie to cool it. He was staring at the puddle too and didn't know what to do.

At that moment, I swear I heard Uncle Tony's voice. *Be a gentleman!*

I told the lady nobody was going to get hurt, and she should step aside. "Please," I added. She finally did, and Eddie went back and took up his position by the door. I started scooping out the drawers, careful to leave the bottom bill untouched, and began stuffing fistfuls of cash in the bag.

I got to the last teller in line, but before I could clean out her drawer, I heard Vitale shout, "Go!"

We had lost time because of the head teller, and it cost us all the sweet cash in that last drawer.

I hopped up on the counter ass first, swung around, and slid to the floor. The adrenaline was pumping so hard I had to tell myself to walk slow. Eddie was there, back against the wall just inside the door, alert and sweeping the room with his shotgun, still waiting for a security guard to show. He never did. Either he was on an ill-timed break that would probably get him fired or the Franklin National felt so secure they didn't have a guard. Because we hadn't wanted to be seen inside casing the bank before we hit it, we had no way of knowing there would be such a convenient breach of security.

Joe Vitale was already out the door, with me right behind him; Eddie backed out after me. Except for his momentary case of nerves, Eddie played Joe Dellamura's part just fine that morning.

I couldn't believe we were in and out of there in a minute and a half;

throughout it felt like time stopped dead. But once we got outside and into the hotski, everything happened fast. Vitale dove in and laid across the backseat, Eddie knelt down under the dash, and I drove, so it looked like there was only one person in the car when the cops would be looking for three.

I drove at normal speed to the underpass. We crossed under the LIE, drove three blocks and took the first right after we passed the switch car. I parked around the corner so nobody saw us leave one car and get in the other. I drove carefully back to Vitale's house, where we split the take—25 g's, a nice load of fruit for ninety seconds' work even without the contents of that last drawer. My end was a third of that, a little less after I gave Dom and Pegleg and the Mouthpiece their tastes. Seven grand was not bad, especially when you consider that in 1971 you could buy a new car with all the trimmings for $2,800 and a whole house for less than $20,000.

I felt like I really was on top of the world as we counted the money and talked over the heist and how it went down.

Nobody said anything about Eddie's bandanna slipping down when he crashed into me. Because we never even noticed when it did.

CHAPTER THREE

Off to the Races

COMING OFF THAT SCORE, I was high as a kite. Now I knew what Sinatra felt like when he walked offstage after a killer concert. When I drove away from Vitale's with seven grand in my pocket, the adrenaline was still pumping strong enough to fly me to the moon. Guys like Dominic came down after a score by hitting the nearest bar. A lot of guys I knew in that Life handled the crime rush by not coming down at all—they popped pills, snorted coke, and got as high as they could get.

Me, I didn't drink more than I could handle and I hardly ever did coke and never touched the harder stuff. I didn't even smoke cigarettes.

But there was one drug I was a fiend for—sex.

Just like rock stars, gangsters had groupies, but they weren't waiting outside the bank to give you a blow job like backstage fans at a rock concert. Our groupies were whores and you had to go to them.

So two hours after I vaulted over the counter at the Franklin National, I was rolling around in bed with two blond hookers at a small basement brothel in Rego Park, a ten-minute drive from my house in Ozone Park. It was my first time at that place, but I'd heard they had some really nice, very hot, and very skilled entertainers. I heard right.

Both those girls were really something special, and we spent most of the afternoon getting it on and drinking champagne and laughing and telling stories in between. The girls told me they worked for a madam who had another place in Manhattan where I could find them when they weren't in Rego Park. They said the other girls working there were pretty and friendly and that if I wanted they would get the hostess of the Rego Park place to call the Manhattan location and get my name on their preferred list. I told them please do, and I promised to look them up the next time I was in the city.

I felt calmed down and about as content as a man can feel when I left the whorehouse and drove home for dinner with my wife.

Sex for me was food—I couldn't live without it and I was a glutton. If I got laid three times a day, I'd have to settle for blow jobs in between. I wanted sex whenever I could get it and wherever—except at home.

Angela and I got married on my birthday, April 30, 1967. I'd say we celebrated our fourth anniversary a few days before the bank heist, but for her it had to be more like a day of mourning. I never hit my wife, but I abused the shit out of her with my total neglect. Our marriage bed was ice-cold. She could count the number of times we made love in the three years since our first son was born—and she could do it on the one hand she'd slap the shit out of me with if I was with her.

But violence wasn't in Angela's nature. She was sweet and kind and loving—and resigned to the fact that I was a lousy husband and a cheat. I think she was like a lot of Mob wives, who knew their husbands weren't always out all night doing crimes. They knew but they didn't want to know the real score.

Every Italian mobster I knew in those days—except one—had girls on the side or was an out-and-out whoremonger like me who banged his own wife only on special occasions. I think it had something to do with being Catholic and raised in fucked-up homes where our fathers were the same way—they didn't touch their wives once they had kids because then the women they married were mothers and nobody wants to be a motherfucker. It's shitty to say, but that's the way it was.

Looking back, I'm ashamed of the way I treated Angela. She deserved way better than what she got. She gave us two great kids and I'll love her forever for that. But that doesn't change what I was. I was an animal. I felt no shame, no guilt, no nothing. I was too obsessed with having sex with anybody but her to care how she felt about it.

I had a stock line I used whenever my wife asked me where I was going or why I was out all night: "I got business—and it's none of yours."

Later on, when I had a steady mistress and I wouldn't be home for days on end, Angela came straight out and said she knew exactly what was going on and that I should drop the charade and stop pretending.

"You're going to do what you're doing and I can't stop that," she said. "But if you ever shove it in my face and embarrass and humiliate me, I'm taking the kids and you'll never see us again."

That arrangement worked until the day my infidelities were indeed shoved in Angela's face—by my mistress herself. But that's another story we'll get to later.

That night after the Franklin National job, I went out with Dominic and his kid brother, Joey. We had a very quiet celebration, just the three of us. I knew better than to start bragging about my first bank robbery. Not just because everybody's got ears and there was a market for tips you could feed the feds, but also because I wanted Dom to respect me as a serious heist guy, not some wannabe who never would be if I shot off my mouth about what a ballsy gunman I was.

I told Dom about the heist and how it went down when I gave him his taste that evening at Club 93, a Colombo bar in Ozone Park where we kept a little office that we used in our gambling operation. Later, when Joey joined us, we made a toast to the Geriatric Twins and to my bright future, and that was about it.

We didn't talk more about the heist because Joey wasn't in the Life. But I knew that night that Dom was looking at me with new respect. I also knew that one bank robbery wasn't enough to make me a full-fledged member of his crew. I would have to prove myself in more action heists.

In the meantime, it was back to business as usual.

The next morning I reported for duty at Dom's grandmother's house in East New York, which was the headquarters of our gambling operation.

Dom's grandmother Ervolino Cataldo was a trip and a half. She was like Ma Jarrett in *White Heat.* She raised her sons and grandsons to be "Top of the world, Ma" gangsters like James Cagney in the movie.

The Cataldos were a crime Family unto themselves. Ervolino started out as a bootlegger, and she was still running a shylock business forty years later when I met her. Her son Sammy, Dom's father, was a capo in the Profaci Family and a good friend of my uncle Tony. One of Dom's cousins was Joe "the Wop" Cataldo, a real heavy hitter who ran casinos for the Mob when the Families owned Havana before Fidel Castro put them out of business. He also owned clubs in Manhattan and booked hookers and strippers in out-of-town Mob joints like one of his old Havana cronies, Jack Ruby, ran in Dallas.

Dominic was groomed from childhood for a life of crime. Take one look at him and you knew what he was—a New York City gangster.

Unless he was on a score, he was always dressed like he was ready to spend New Year's Eve at the Rainbow Room. Whether he was pushing money with me at the track in the afternoon, playing cards in an after-hours joint late at night, or even hunting in the woods upstate or playing softball on the Fourth of July, he was always done up in threads that were brand-new and expensive: Italian leather shoes, dark silk trousers and shirt and, except when he was shooting deer or fielding a grounder—or burying a body at Boot Hill, his upstate dumping ground—a tailored jacket. Everything he wore was of the highest quality, which meant his duds were imported from Europe.

Dom liked to have his hair styled and his nails manicured every day. He wore diamond jewelry, a pinkie ring, and an eighteen-karat Baume et Mercier watch with a solid gold band. He carried his money on a clip, $100 bills on the outside, smaller bills folded under.

And he was movie star handsome. He looked like John Garfield in *Body and Soul,* brooding, dangerous. He had wavy hair, a broad forehead, deep-set eyes. He was cold and calculating, smart as hell, and he could charm a snake. He spoke fluent Italian. He always drank Johnnie Walker scotch, smoked Camel straights, and loved talking about gangster movies; he adored Bogart and Cagney and Edward G. Robinson, all the old-time Hollywood tough guys.

Dom's brother Joey was the black sheep of the Cataldo family because he *wasn't* a career criminal. Which is kind of surprising considering his upbringing and the fact that he was married to Mob royalty. His wife Louise's maiden name was Anastasia, and one of her uncles was Tough Tony Anastasio,[2] the old boss of the Brooklyn waterfront, which was an even bigger cash cow for the Mob than JFK Airport later became. When Tough Tony died in 1963, thousands of longshoremen lined the streets of Brooklyn to watch his funeral procession; it took fifty limousines to carry all the dignitaries and fifteen more just for the flowers. Another uncle of Louise's was Albert Anastasia, the Family father who ran Murder Incorporated in the 1930s and who got clipped at the Park Sheraton barbershop by the Gallo brothers and Carmine Persico in 1957.

Despite the Family connections, Joey only dabbled in the criminal life. He had a little shylock business on the side, but he wasn't connected to the Colombos except through his brother, who looked out for him and took care of any of Joey's loan shark customers who made the mistake of pushing him around. Because of that, the cops identified Joey as a wiseguy, but he was basically legit.

Dom was ten years older than me, but Joey was my age and we became pretty close. Until Foxy became my crime partner and I started spending almost all my time with him, Joey was my best friend. He was also my *compare*. He and Louise had agreed to stand as godparents to Angela and my new baby, who was due at the end of May. If it was a girl we were going to name her Louise; a boy would be named Joseph. In any Italian family, there is a very close bond between you and the person who agrees to be your child's *compare*—godfather—or *comare*—godmother. They vow to take care of your kid if something happens to you. In Mob families, it was even more important because the chances of a premature death were pretty good.

———————

By the spring of 1971, Dom and I had been in business together for four years, and we had an established routine just like ordinary legitimate

———————

[2] Born Anastasia, Tough Tony changed the spelling of his family name to differentiate himself from his infamous brother, Albert Anastasia.

slobs who punch a clock every day. We took horse and sports action starting at 10:00 in the morning at Ervolino's house in East New York. She made a sweet setup for us in her basement, which was all nicely finished and fixed up with couches, tables, comfortable chairs, and three phone lines that she got one of her shylock customers who worked for Ma Bell to run in free of charge. We needed all three to take the bets we were booking.

The day after the Franklin National job, we worked taking action as usual at Ervolino's until it was time to get back to Ozone Park for the first race at Aqueduct where we did our loaning. (All sharking was done off premises.)

We worked out of Ervolino's throughout the racing season, which was year-round. When it moved from Aqueduct to Belmont in June and July, we attended the races there too, but on-premises loaning wasn't as big a business at that track, which catered to a much smaller, more high-end crowd. In August, when the season moved upstate to Saratoga, we took action from all the long-distance gamblers back home. The rest of the time we were at Aqueduct, the Big A, where the real action was. That's where all the blue-collar racing fanatics played the horses. The track held seventeen thousand people, and they used to pack the place in those days.

For me, Aqueduct was like a second home because I'd been going there since I was four and five years old with Uncle Tony. There were no phones at the track because the authorities didn't want gamblers using them to call their bookies. So all the Mob crews had people out there every day for every race. Each crew carved out its own little piece of the clubhouse. The Gambinos from the Bergin were set up around the corner from the main escalator. We set up shop at one of the racetrack bars. Dominic and I were there every day to push money—making shylock loans to the gamblers when they went broke. There were no ATMs at that time. We were it, standing there with bankrolls, doling out cash to those in need.

If the Mob guys working the track didn't have enough in their own bankroll to loan out, their bosses did; they'd borrow from a capo at 1 percent and loan it out at 5.

It was gravy. All you had to worry about was the cops and the Pinks.

The cops were busting us all the time, but thanks to everybody's favorite lawyer Mike Coiro, that was more of a pain in the ass than anything else. It was the Pinks you had to look out for. Pinkerton was the detective agency that had contracts to work all the tracks in New York. Before the Internet era, all they had to go on was what was in the KG book, a roster of Known Gamblers with photos. If your picture was in the book, they wouldn't let you in the track. Luckily Dominic had one of the Pink brass in his pocket. He pulled our pictures from the KG book whenever the NYPD sent over our mug shots.

Gambling and loan sharking were the Mob's bread and butter. Guys used to say they went together like beer and peanuts—the more you ate the more you drank. Likewise, the more you gambled, the more you borrowed. And the more you borrowed, the more you had to pay back at 5 percent vig paid weekly.

Everything we did flowed from gambling, our lifeblood. Degenerate gamblers were our number one source for heists. If guys couldn't meet their nut every week, they'd become tipsters, paying their debts by offering information and assistance instead of cash. They tipped us off to high-value shipments coming into JFK that we could hijack; and inventory—maybe they'd forget to lock up at closing time at their business, or they'd tell us when a competitor's payroll was delivered. They'd tell us about diamond and gold deliveries in Manhattan's famous Diamond District, who was the courier and when and where to hit him. It was the choice of either that or getting their legs broken.

Gambling was still going strong in 1971, but the writing was on the wall. That was the year the first Off-Track Betting parlor opened in New York. Add to that the slow death of numbers running, which used to bring in millions every week for all the Families; it had taken a huge hit back in 1967 when New York State started running its own numbers game. There were still plenty of people, especially old-timers, who played the neighborhood numbers, but enough legitimate slobs were into Lotto that we knew our share would die off sooner or later.

But later on, when Resorts International opened in Atlantic City and legalized casino gambling started on the East Coast, that was the death knell for a big part of the Mob's business. We no longer had a monopoly on gambling. Luckily, the shylock business lived on because degenerate gamblers are a gift that never stops giving—it doesn't matter if it's legal or illegal, they still lose.

After the last race of the day at 5:30 our work wasn't done. We moved our operations from Aqueduct north twenty-two blocks to Club 93, at the corner of Woodhaven Boulevard and Atlantic Avenue, which was a quarter mile from where I lived. The bar was owned by an Italian guy named Fat Mike who was a friend of Dom's and rented us the little office in the back. That office was our bank—it's where customers who owed us knew they could find us when it was time to meet their loan officers.

The 93 was a tiny but classic bar right at the corner with one wall on Atlantic and the other on Woodhaven and a double entrance in the middle. It was a Colombos-only joint, and all the gamblers and thieves and robbers connected to the Family hung out in there—it was Eddie Pravato's favorite bar. You could enter and leave through one of two doors, one facing Atlantic and the other the Boulevard. So if the cops were staking out the place on one side, you could slip out through the other—or use the side entrance at the back.

Tommy DeSimone's ex-wife, Anjelica, tended the bar in Club 93. She was a loud and brassy babe who loved to mix it up with the guys and break their balls. Angie didn't care if a hood had twenty hits on his belt—she didn't take shit from anybody.

She knew every bar trick in the book and bet on them all. But her favorite gamble of all was racing for "regies." Guys used to drag-race on Atlantic Avenue and the starting line was right outside the door of Club 93. When they raced for regies, the bet was their car—the loser had to sign over his registration to whoever beat him to the finish line, two blocks down. Angie had a killer 1963 big-block Chevy Super Sport that she raced against all comers.

I never heard of Angie losing a street drag, and I know she never lost a regies race because she parked that '63 Chevy right out front for all to see. But that didn't stop me from breaking *her* balls.

"Wait 'til I get my hands on the right set of wheels," I told her. "I'll blow your doors off and *I'll* be parking that big-block bastard outside."

"Bring it on, Sally!" Angie said.

In a few months, I would do just that.

That night after our business was finished and we were alone in the back office, Dom told me that he was going out of town the next month and that I'd be running things on my own for a few weeks. Ervolino was in her eighties, and Dom said she wanted to see Sicily one more time before she croaked. She was born over there and hadn't been back since she came over as a girl at the turn of the century. In all the time she lived in the States, Ervolino never learned to speak English. Dom said she was excited as hell to get back to the old country where nobody else did either.

Then he turned serious. He said that he talked to Eddie Pravato, and he was proud of the way I handled myself at the Franklin jug the day before. He liked that I gave Pegleg and Mike the Mouthpiece a taste of my take; that showed I had learned everything he taught me about the right way to do things. He said that when he got back from Italy there would be more up-front action work for me. In the meantime, he was trusting me to keep the business here running smooth.

Dom said he was going to combine business with pleasure and take his crime partner Jackie Donnelly along with him and his grandmother on their trip to Sicily.

"I won't say more about it now," he said. "But we have something very big cooking, and when it pops, it's going to change the way we do things. It's not going to happen anytime soon but before the year's out. It's big, Sally, and I want you to be a part of it."

CHAPTER FOUR

A Hot Summer in the City

WHEN I WAS A kid, my uncle Tony told me that the old-time Italians used to call New York City *Il Vulcano*—the Volcano—because even when things were quiet, there were always rumblings of violence under the surface.

The biggest eruption of the New York volcano that Uncle Tony remembered happened in the early 1930s, during the Castellammarese War, when Lucky Luciano rubbed out the old Mustache Petes and set up the Five-Families structure and the Commission to run the nationwide Mafia crime syndicate. It was mostly quiet for the next twenty-five years, until 1957, when two of the biggest Family bosses—Frank Costello, who was forced into retirement by a bullet in the head, and Albert Anastasia, who unlike Costello didn't survive to read *his* pink slip—were eliminated in power grabs orchestrated by Vito Genovese and Carlo Gambino.

Four years after that, the Volcano erupted again in the decade-long Gallo Wars. Uncle Tony used to say that the Gallo Brothers—Larry, Crazy Joe, and their kid brother Albert,[3] or "Kid Blast"—were "a bunch of clowns with big balls." That's because instead of just whacking their boss, Joe Profaci, and taking over his Family, they came up with a *upazzo* scheme to kidnap him and his top guys, including Joe Colombo.

---

[3] Albert is the Anglicized version of his given name, Umberto, which was also the Gallos' brothers' father's name.

The Gallos and their accomplice, Carmine Persico, rounded up all Profaci's top leadership, but the boss himself escaped the net, and once he negotiated the hostages' release, he put out contracts on all the rebels. Persico saw the light and switched sides and became the loyalist general in charge of wiping out the Gallos. Guys in his own crew called Persico "Junior," but after he turned on the Gallos everybody else called him the Snake.

The long civil war that followed that botched kidnapping ended finally in 1969.

But now, two years later, with Joe Colombo's position as boss of our Family shaky to begin with and Crazy Joe Gallo fresh out of prison—he was released a month before Eddie Pravato and I emptied the Franklin National jug—and swearing revenge against Colombo and Persico, it looked like the Volcano was getting ready to blow sky-high all over again.

An outbreak of a new and bloody war posed dangers to all the Families, but there was something almost comical about the two main adversaries, Crazy Joe Gallo and Joe Colombo, who was a boss who got no respect, even from most guys in his own Family.

A lot of *upazzo* business was going on in the country in 1971. You had astronauts playing golf on the moon, convicts taking guards prisoner at Attica, Indians occupying Alcatraz, and the government operating horse-betting parlors. But none of them were as off the rails as the comedy show starring the two Joes.

On the one hand you had the well-known don of a Mafia Family going on the *Dick Cavett Show* to promote his Italian-American Civil Rights League and swearing there was no such thing as the Italian Mafia and whining about how unfair it was that people said there was. Colombo's "civil rights" campaign was a scam to begin with, because its sole purpose was to take the heat off Joe Colombo himself.

And it was a joke to hear Colombo compared to Martin Luther King Jr., because he was no doubt as big a racist as every other Mob guy in New York. I can say that because I was a bigot too. The only time any mobsters attended civil rights rallies in the '60s was to protest *against* integration. A lot of it had to do with the fact that blacks were moving into the old neighborhoods and driving out the Italians. Even Fox, who was as fair-minded as anybody I knew in that Life, was a member of SPONGE when he was a teenager. That was a pro-segregation group in New York. SPONGE stood for—I shit you not—the Society for the Prevention of Negroes Getting Everything.

On the other hand you had Crazy Joe Gallo. Here was another guy who I had trouble believing was a friend of the black man. When he was in Attica, he had supposedly gotten tight with a lot of black inmates. After his release he put the word on the street that he was going to lead a crew of black wiseguys in a war against Colombo if the boss didn't redress his grievances.

Gallo was a colorful guy and the press loved him. Back in the '60s, *Life* magazine did a big photo spread about him and his brothers and their headquarters on President Street in Red Hook, Brooklyn. Crazy Joey used to keep a lion in the basement of his clubhouse, and he liked to walk around the neighborhood with it on a leash. There was a midget in his crew named Mondo. Joey told reporters that Mondo was his body-guard.

As soon as Gallo got out of the joint, the newspapers treated him like a celebrity. He was in the gossip columns, hanging out with famous actors and musicians and comedians; he dated models. He told reporters he was working on his memoirs. He shot off his mouth about all kinds of shit—he was supposedly reading Camus and Sartre; he said he had even taken up painting. He was an *artiste*, not a thug. But he sure sounded like one when he made noises about getting rid of Joe Colombo and taking over the Family.

It later came out that he wasn't bluffing. In May, Gallo sent a team to kidnap the boss—just like he and his brothers tried and failed to kidnap Joe Profaci ten years before. The knuckleheaded plan didn't work any better the second time around.

Even though Colombo's "movement" was a crock, enough people bought it that more than fifty thousand supporters turned out for his Italian Unity Day rally in Columbus Circle in 1970.

Now the boss was planning a second Unity Day rally, scheduled for Monday, June 28, 1971. Throughout the spring there were flyers all over the city promoting the rally. Joe Colombo himself was going to speak, and local television stations were all going to be there, covering it live.

Dom and I were Colombos, but nobody in his crew or any of the guys we knew had anything good to say about the boss. We were all with Carmine Persico, the powerful Colombo capo who had a lot of influence in the Family even though he was in prison. The Snake was one guy I'd never want to mess with. He made headlines way back in 1950 when he was seventeen years old and was arrested for killing a guy in a street gang fight. He was a made guy in the Profaci Family before he turned twenty-five. During the civil war, the Gallos trapped him in a can't-miss crossfire. Persico was shot five or six times. In the ambulance on the way to the hospital, he woke up and spit out a bullet that had got lodged in his teeth.

Carmine Persico was one tough motherfucker, and if it came to war between guys loyal to Colombo and Gallo's crew, I'd put my money on the Snake to come out on top whichever way the war went.

I knew that Dominic felt the same way.

As the date of the rally approached, Club 93 and other businesses in Ozone Park refused to put up rally posters or wear the Unity buttons Colombo's people passed out all over the city. And word began to spread among all the Families that this year's rally wasn't going to be like the year before. Carlo Gambino, who put Colombo in as Family boss back in the '60s and who tolerated the Unity Day rally in 1970, ordered that all Gambino guys, including workers in unions his Family controlled, which meant all the longshoremen and Teamsters, were supposed to stay away. Shopkeepers in Little Italy who put up signs advertising the rally were told to take them down. People who bought Unity buttons at fundraisers the year before weren't seen wearing them this time around.

In early June, right after my second son, Joseph, was born, Dominic left on his trip to Italy with Ervolino and Jackie Donnelly.

Before they left, Dom told me to be sure to stay away from Columbus Circle on June 28.

———

According to the papers, Joe Colombo was in the middle of the crowd at the Unity rally that Monday afternoon, working his way to the speakers' platform and pressing flesh like a veteran politician, when a beautiful and shapely black woman wearing an Afro and showing off mile-long legs in a miniskirt greeted him.

"Hello, Joe," she said.

When Colombo turned and saw her, he must have thought this civil rights leader bit had benefits he never dreamed of.

"Hi ya," Colombo said. Those were the only words he spoke at the rally that day. The next thing anybody knew, the black guy the beauty had arrived with, a filmmaker with press credentials and an expensive movie camera, dropped to one knee and aimed something at Colombo that was not a Bolex. He got off three shots at point-blank range.

As the boss hit the ground, a Colombo bodyguard and a bunch of cops jumped on the shooter. When they cleared everybody away, Colombo was alive but out of commission for good, his would-be assassin was dead, his bodyguard had vanished—and so had the shooter's beautiful accomplice. She was never identified and remains unknown to this day.

———

I did like Dom said and stayed away from the boss's rally. I'm glad I did, but I wish I had been home and in front of the TV when it happened. Instead I was out on the playground by our house, messing around with three-year-old Sal Jr.

When I got home, I found out that I had just missed a historic event: a Mob hit, live on local TV. The attempted assassination of Joe Colombo in front of ten thousand eyewitnesses attending his second annual Italian Unity Day rally was not the first Mob hit ever televised, of course. The first occurred on Sunday, November 24, 1963, in Dallas. But that's another story.

———

In the days after the shooting in Columbus Circle, there was little question in the press or in the public's mind about who was behind the hit on Joe Colombo, who was in a coma and would never recover from his wounds, living in a vegetative state until his death in 1978. The very next morning after the shooting, the *Daily News* ran a picture of the black gunman—identified as Jerome Johnson, a nobody street hustler who had "patsy" written all over him—right next to one of Joey Gallo. The caption under Gallo's photo said that he had recruited black gangsters in prison. They might as well have said he pulled the trigger.

As for the Colombo bodyguard who plugged his boss's shooter, the papers said he was unidentified, but it was easy to assume that he played Jack Ruby's part in the assassination. I assumed like everybody else that it was Gallo who hired Johnson and got the bodyguard to flip on his boss.

I also assumed that war would begin as soon as Persico gave the word from prison. My attitude at the prospect of gang warfare in the streets of New York? Like Angie at the 93 said, "Bring it on."

It wasn't just that I was young and stupid enough to think that a war would be fun and exciting. I did. But I also knew that when the shooting started and I got in on a few hits, I'd win my button in no time. And as soon as the Commission reopened the books, all my dreams would come true and I'd be a made member of the Colombo Family—or whatever it was now going to become.

———————

Dom returned from Italy a little while after our boss got it at what wiseguys were calling "Colombo Circle." He didn't say much about the hit except that he heard the news when he was in France. When I asked him what he was doing there, that I thought he was going to Italy, he changed the subject.

He was so stoked about whatever business he and Jackie were cooking up overseas that he didn't seem the least bit concerned about the outbreak of Gallo Wars II. That made me think that maybe one of the rumors I heard was true—that it wasn't Joey Gallo at all; it was Carlo Gambino who was behind the Colombo hit and that he and Persico had come to some kind of understanding. I knew better than to ask Dom about it since I was basically still a wannabe, and even though Dom and I were close, I hadn't fully gained his trust. I knew I probably wouldn't until I was a full-fledged buttoned-up Family man.

Dominic told me not to worry about a war because there wasn't going to be one. He said he needed me now to focus on business. He said he wanted to crank things up and generate as much cash as possible before the year was out.

So as things turned out, the Volcano didn't blow after all—not that year, anyway. I didn't make my bones that summer when the war failed to materialize. But I did manage to make my rep during the uneasy peace that settled over the city.

With the racing season now under way at Belmont and our gambling business slowed somewhat, Dom was out of pocket a lot of the time that summer, pulling scores with Jackie. I was worried that my success at the Franklin National would fade fast from his memory, so I got together with the Geriatric Twins to plan another heist. Once we came up with a target and clocked the jug and ironed out the details, I took it to Dom. He gave me the nod right away. He even said he liked that I didn't wait around for an assignment. "If you wanna earn in this Life," he said, "you gotta be a fuckin' self-starter." I felt like I was in first-year Mob Business School and I just got an A.

For my second piece of work, Joe Dellamura was back to health and I got to work with the master. And this time the score went without a hitch. We hit the First National City Bank on Francis Lewis Boulevard in Bayside, Queens. Eddie worked point and strolled in and had a nice meeting with the bank manager, Joe D pulled out his sawed-off and told everybody to freeze, and the judges would have given me another perfect ten for my performance in the counter-vaulting event.

We walked out of there with three times as much as we scored at the Franklin—$77,000. After I gave a nice taste to Mike Coiro and kicked up a big bite to Pegleg Brancato, who was serving as acting Family boss while Junior Persico waited in the wings for the Commission to make him don, I brought an envelope with $2,000 in it to give to Dominic.

He refused it. He said I was like family and he didn't feel right about taking tribute. I took that at first to mean he still didn't think I was ready to move up. But the next thing he said made my day. "We're developing that new operation I told you about, and it's going to keep Jackie and me busy until we get it up and running. I want you to come along with us on our next score because I think it's going to be the last one Jackie and I can work for a while. You're going to be doing the planning, working up front, and taking care of the back end. I want you to come along so you can meet the King, the guy who makes it all happen."

I left Dom's place on top of the world that day because now I was in. I knew that at last Dominic considered me a serious heist guy. He was bringing me into his crew and I was finally going to get to see some real action.

The score went down a few weeks later. I went along with Dom and Jackie Donnelly a couple of mornings when they clocked a garment truck from Kennedy Airport into the Garment District in Manhattan. They included me in the planning from beginning to end. When they hit the truck a few days later, I still had to play outfield while they had all the up-front action. But Dom made it clear that while I watched from the follow car I was supposed to study his and Jackie's every move as they jumped the cab and commandeered the truck. Then, after I dropped off the driver, I drove back to the drop in Queens.

I expected Dom to tell me to help unload the truck and sort the merch; instead, he took me into the warehouse office to meet the King. Dom had told me everything about the guy except his name. He said he was a true entrepreneur, a fence who moved more swag than Macy's. Dom said they called him the King because he was the biggest operator in the city. He got away with everything he did because he had all the cops in Queens in his pocket.

That day Dom took me to the King's office and introduced me to Jimmy Burke.

I took home only a few hundred from that score—the usual out-fielder's pay. But I still had most of my 25 g's from the job with the Geri-atric Twins, and I wanted to spend some cash to celebrate my new status as a full member of Dominic's crew.

I made my first visit to the Manhattan brothel that the girls in Rego Park had told me about. It was a first-class apartment in the East 30s off Park Avenue. That's where I first met Lisa, a truly gorgeous whore with a heart full of the same kind of lust for sex that I had. We really hit it off. It was the beginning of a very fruitful friendship that led to love—between me and her madam.

Right after I enjoyed an evening of R&R with Lisa, I found a contractor and hired him to put in a swimming pool behind our house in Ozone Park.

Then I went out shopping for a new car, a little gift to myself for a bank heist well done.

———————

One cloud of trouble floated over that summer. It was right around the time I had my on-the-job hijack training with Dom and Jackie. Aqueduct and Belmont were closed while the racing season was going on in Saratoga, but Dom and I were still running our gambling and loan-sharking business. I was on my way to check in at Club 93 one day when I spotted a couple of fedoras driving slow in a sedan on Woodhaven Boulevard. I knew they were feds because only FBI guys wore hats and suits and ties in that neighborhood in August.

Then I saw who they were tailing. It was Eddie Pravato, wearing one of his Hawaiian shirts and walking his dog Petey on the sidewalk. When he got to the end of the block, he walked into the 93 and the sedan pulled to the curb twenty yards back from the entrance.

I kept driving and found a pay phone. I called the club and told Eddie to get the fuck out of there and use the Atlantic Avenue side exit. There were feds right outside the door.

When I picked him up a few minutes later on Atlantic, Eddie said he wasn't all that concerned. The feds had been hassling him all his life.

I told Eddie I had a bad feeling that they weren't tailing him just because he was a known offender with a whole string of bank robberies on his record, but that we had slipped up somehow on one of our own jobs.

We ran down both scores but didn't see any obvious tells. But just to be safe, Eddie got out of town later that same day.

I put it out of my mind, figuring it was like Eddie said. Even if the heat was on him for the Franklin job or our second one in Bayside, it was only because he was just one of many likely suspects.

Then in September I saw another carload of fedoras parked by the playground around the corner from my house where I was helping coach my wife's kid brother Lenny's Lynvet Pop Warner football team, the Browns. I knew Eddie had been staying somewhere in the neighborhood when he went on the lam, and I knew they weren't after me since unlike Eddie I was not a known bank robber and my name wouldn't be in any of the feds' suspects files. Just to make sure, I made a point of walking past their car with my brother-in-law on the way home after practice. They didn't seem to pay any attention to us, but still, they were a little too close to home for my liking.

Anyway, I didn't lose any sleep over a couple of feds nosing around. I had too many good things going on. And one of them went faster than a speeding bullet.

———————

The car I ended up buying was the hottest street dragster I ever owned. It was a 1961 Corvette, with a fresh coat of Porsche paint—silver, the color of coin. I paid $2,000 for it and planned to sink another $3,000 into it to soup it up.

The car was ten years old but cherry. It came with the standard 283-cubic-inch V-8 Chevy engine they bolted in on the assembly line. That's a powerful engine in a two-seater, and this Vette's had been re-furbished so it was a fast car to begin with.

But I didn't just want to go fast. I wanted to go faster than God. Speed was right up there with crime and sex in my book, and I wanted all I could get.

Before I took it in to the speed shop, I wanted to see what it could do as is.

I had the tank loaded with racing fuel. Then I drove over to the 93 that night to see if Angie was up for a challenge.

I told her I didn't want to risk my new car against her big-block Chevy, so this wouldn't be a race for regies. I said that partly to con her into thinking for sure that she could beat me but also because I didn't know what the Vette would do and I sure as hell didn't want to lose it the day after I bought it.

Angie went out and looked over my car and came back in, pretty sure she could take me. I knew that because of the bet we made. She was always busting my chops about the flashy jewelry I wore in those days, and the way she used to go on about the diamond-studded money clip I carried, I knew she coveted it.

So I said if she wins, she gets the clip.

She said, "The money clip and the cash in it."

"Okay," I said. "If I win, you give up something personal too—a blow job."

Angie laughed at that. "Sure I'll blow you," she said, "*away.*"

Angie was a great broad; she swore like a trucker and she looked like one too.

"Not me," I said. "I win, you give head to whoever I say."

"You're on, motherfucker!"

We agreed on a midnight run. I hung out at the bar, nursing a beer or two, and Angie pumped up the crowd and all the guys made side bets right up until race time. Before we went out, I said we should sweeten the pot and each put up $100, winner take all. She told me to fuck off. "I like your hundred right where it is—in the clip."

The whole bar emptied out onto the sidewalk at midnight. We got a couple of barflies to flag us. One old fella stood at the finish line at 87th Street, about five hundred yards up Atlantic Avenue. The other guy stood between us and dropped the bar towel. We both got off to a great start, but I was still winding the Vette out in first when I heard Angie shift into second. I knew I had her then. I popped it into second and jumped out in front of her. I was a full car length ahead when I shifted into third and shot across the finish line, the toothless old drunk standing grinning at the curb and waving his bar rag up and down like it was the checkered flag at Daytona.

Back in the bar, the losers paid up their side bets and guys demanded to know, "Who gets the blow job?"

"Yeah, who's it gonna be, wiseass?" Angie said.

I let her off the hook.

"Eddie Pravato," I said.

CHAPTER FIVE

Shoot-out on Atlantic Avenue

MONDAY, OCTOBER 4, 1971

I PICKED UP THE VETTE from the speed shop that afternoon. When the guy who owned the place popped the hood, I was almost blinded by the chrome. The damn thing looked like it could power a Saturn rocket to the moon. His mechanics had replaced the manufacturer's 283 with a brand-new 327 high-performance Chevy engine, the biggest hot rod racing mill the Vette could carry. They customized it with an Edelbrock manifold and dual high-performance Holley carburetors—the kind they used to juice the engines of B-52s during World War II and that NASCAR still uses today. Once I pumped ten gallons of Sunoco 260 with special additives into the tank, that fuel would explode like nitro when it shot through the Holleys.

As a final touch, they bolted on a new set of wide ovals, custom tires that doubled the traction and gave you a few extra square feet of rubber to burn; the tires increased the speed and screamed like a virgin at a Roman orgy when you dragged.

All gangsters are gearheads and speed junkies, so the first thing I did when I got the Vette out of the shop, I drove over to Club 93 to show it off.

It was a warm and sunny fall afternoon, but I knew I'd find Dom at the 93. Monday was the day all our customers came in to settle up the weekend action and lay bets for *Monday Night Football* before kickoff at 9:00.

I pulled up outside and announced my arrival by revving the engine and letting it roar. Somebody opened the door, saw it was me, and got Dom to come take a look. Jackie Donnelly was with him, and even though it was 3:00 in the afternoon they were both dressed like it was Friday night and they had dates with a couple of stews.

Dom was a good-looking guy, but Jackie was the real lady-killer. He was taller than Dom, a little over six feet, with sandy hair and ice-cold blue eyes, and he was fit as hell from hiking and roughing it in the woods. Jackie was the only real outdoorsman I knew in the Mob. He liked to hunt and fish and climb mountains and go camping. We all used to go hunting upstate and shoot deer, but we wore city clothes and got in the car and drove back to Queens afterward. Jackie dressed like a hunter, and he liked to stay out there and build a campfire and sleep under the stars and all that shit.

But when he was in the city, Jackie looked and acted like a real gangster, even though he wasn't Italian and everybody called him Beansie because he liked that shit Irish food. Jackie was also a gearhead, and he and Dom got me to pop the hood and they admired my new racing mill. When I said I'd give them a little show, they did what gangsters do— they bet on it.

"That's a lotta car for the kid," Jackie said. "Fifty says he stalls off the line."

"You're on," said Dom.

I didn't take it personally. Dom and Jackie both had ridden with me enough to know I was good behind the wheel. And I knew those two guys would bet on their grandmothers' next breath. Still, I wanted to show Jackie that $50 saying I'd choke was a dumb bet.

As I was about to get in the car, Dom stood there on the sidewalk with one hand in his jacket pocket, Edward G. style. "Look, you mug," he said, "don't blow it, see?"

I couldn't tell if that was his trigger finger, or the barrel of his real piece in his pocket.

———

Looking back on what happened that day, it's bewildering and frightening and sickening to know that I did what I did without a thought of the consequences or of the safety of all the innocent people in that busy intersection, the children walking home from schools that had just let out, the shoppers and couples and old folks out for a stroll on that beautiful afternoon.

All I can say is I was oblivious; we all were. We lived in our own world, separate and superior we thought to the workaday world. We existed in a parallel universe, a different dimension from the legitimate slobs all around us. That's what we called the squares, the ordinary working stiffs, the average Joes who lived quiet nervous lives because they didn't have the balls to live large. Back then, Dom and Jackie and me, everybody in that Life, we saw ourselves as superheroes. We had special powers because we did something no legitimate slob ever dared do—we said fuck Death. We believed in life with no tomorrow. Once you decided you didn't give a fuck about anything, that every day was your last day, you were set free. And all you could say to the ordinary mortals in the legitimate world was:

Look the fuck out.

———————

Dom and Jackie and a couple more Colombos with highball glasses in their hands were on the sidewalk cheering me on when I climbed in the Vette, fired her up, and let her roar. The radio, tuned to WABC as always, was on full blast but I couldn't hear it over that 327.

I revved it until the needle hit 6,000 rpm. Then I popped the clutch and stomped the gas, and those wide ovals burned two-hundred-foot stripes of rubber down the middle of Atlantic Avenue. That engine was so powerful I could feel the g-force pin me to the seat. I got it up to seventy, took my foot off the gas, and downshifted to forty; then when I got it to around thirty-five miles an hour, I tried a trick I saw in a Bond movie and was taught by a guy I shipped out with in the Marines.

Atlantic Avenue wasn't a divided highway in those days, just four wide, open lanes. Normally at that time of day it would be full of traffic, but for those few minutes there was nobody behind me and no traffic coming at me for a couple of blocks ahead. At 90th Street, I pushed in the clutch and shifted to neutral, slammed on the brakes, yanked up on the emergency brake, and spun the wheel hard as I could to the left. The brakes locked, the car spun a one-eighty, and I was stopped dead in a black cloud of burned rubber and facing back the way I came. It must've looked like God reached down, snatched the car up, and set it back down like a kid with a toy at a slot car track.

I let out a whoop, revved the engine, and left another hundred feet of wide oval tire on Atlantic Avenue. I was going to do the Bond spin again, right in front of the club this time to blow the guys' minds. But when I got close I saw Jackie and Dom waving their arms and pointing toward Woodhaven. I thought they wanted to see if I could make the light at the intersection.

I gunned it, and as soon as I did I saw the cop.

This crazy motherfucker was standing out in the left lanes of the intersection in combat stance, feet spread, two hands stretched out front, elbows locked, and a service revolver pointed right at my windshield.

For the hell of it, I thought I'd give him a scare, let this cop know it wasn't too smart going mano a mano with him in nothing but a badge and me in a two-ton, seventy-mile-an-hour steel missile aimed right at his balls.

The light was still green. I jerked the wheel just enough to make the cop shit his blues. I straightened the wheel and blew past him, laughing my ass off. I downshifted as I passed him, and as I did, I heard two explosions, like blasting caps. I thought, *Shit, I must've blown the transmission.* I wasn't even thinking about the cop; I was pissed that I'd have to take the Vette back to the shop the same day I picked it up.

I went through the intersection and pulled the car over about sixty feet on the far side of it, just beyond the Woodhaven overpass. As I got out of the car, I felt something at the back of my neck. I reached to touch it and realized there was blood running down the back of my shirt. I must have been in shock, but all I thought at that moment was, *He just shot me in the fucking back! I'm gonna kill this guy.*

I started running toward him, furious. I saw Dominic out in the street, punching and wrestling with the cop. Dom had his hands on the cop's throat and the cop was wildly waving his service revolver. Jackie pulled Dom off, and the cop managed to back up against a chain-link fence under the overpass. He was pointing the gun at me and shouting, "Get down! Get on the ground! Get on the ground or I'll shoot you again!"

I just stood there staring stupidly at the cop, turning to hear what Dominic was saying. "Do it, Sally. Get down. This guy is out of control."

I don't know if I fell or what, but the next thing I knew I was lying on my back. There was blood soaking my shirt, and for the first time I saw there was a crowd of schoolkids on the sidewalks and I heard the cop on the radio, shouting police code: "10-13! 10-13! Woodhaven and Atlantic. 10-13!"

A 10-13 meant there was an officer under attack and needing assistance. A 10-13 was code for, *I'm fucked.*

Lying there in the middle of Atlantic Avenue, I must have blacked out for a minute. When I came to, there were red lights flashing and black-and-white cop cars everywhere and dozens of people standing around, gawking, trying to see what was going on. I wondered too. Then I realized that the guy laid out there bleeding in the street was me.

I tried to raise my right arm and felt a sharp pain, like somebody came along and stabbed me and left the knife in my back. I moved my foot and raised my knee to ease the pain, and I thought about Lee Marvin dying at the end of *The Killers*, the color version where he's just plugged Ronald Reagan and he's shot in the gut himself and he's in the suburbs dripping blood on the green lawn and sprawled on the black driveway of a tract house in his silver sharkskin suit. I thought, *If I'm gonna die, die cool like Lee Marvin.*

CHAPTER SIX

It's a Helluva Town

WAS IN AND OUT of consciousness, and most of what I remember was the jolts of pain that brought me to.

I was yanked from the pavement to my feet and my arms were pulled behind my back and a set of cuffs was cranked on my wrists.

I was dragged by two cops, one on each side, and they hauled me right past the idling ambulance and shoved me in the back of a squad car. I saw Dom standing up against the fence in handcuffs, waiting for his own ride with the boys in blue.

The cops had the siren on, but they stopped at every light, and the storefronts and apartment buildings we drove past didn't even blur; it felt like we were going about ten miles an hour.

"How you doing back there, wiseguy?" The cop riding shotgun was turned in his seat and poking me with his nightstick. "Feel good? Glad to hear it!" I thought, *That's where that comes from.* Cops had been calling us wiseguys for so long we called ourselves that now.

"Don't touch that man!" We were outside the hospital, and a big Irish police captain pulled up behind us in a squad car, jumped out, and started barking at an ER doctor who was having a tug-of-war with the cops—me the monkey in the middle as they tried to put me on a gurney. "This is our prisoner. Our men will handle him."

I woke up on a hospital bed as a nasty-assed cop yanked my right arm and cuffed me to the metal bar in the headboard. And again when an ER doc tried to help me sit up but the cuffed arm prevented it. He lifted my legs and swung me around so I sat up on the side of the bed. He and an orderly cut away my T-shirt, which was stuck to my back with coagulated blood. The doc poked around the upper left side of my back and said there was a single bullet hole just below the shoulder. I told him there were two shots. He repeated there was a single wound.

Orderlies wheeled the gurney into an elevator and I rode up to be X-rayed.

I woke up from a nightmare in a private room. The door was open and a big cop was standing there looking at me like he wanted to make sure the doctor standing next to my bed didn't do anything that might keep me from a slow and agonizing death.

The doc was holding a set of X-rays. "The bullet did not hit any major organs or arteries, which is why you're not dead," he said. "Normally I would tell you that's the good news. But in your case, I can't really say that."

"Try, Doc," I said.

"If the bullet had hit you about one-one-hundredth of an inch to the right, it would have smashed the vertebrae and severed the spinal cord, and if you lived, which is doubtful, you would have been paralyzed for life."

"A vegetable, right?"

"Not brain-dead—paralyzed. You'd be fully aware that you had no use of your arms, legs, or anything else. You'd maybe wish you were brain-dead. But that's not the case. The bullet did not sever the spinal cord."

"So that's good news."

"Except that the bullet is lodged under your spinal column and we don't know how to get it out."

"Get outta here."

"That's exactly what I'm going to do," said my doctor, the comedian. "But first we're going to knock you out with a painkiller and give you massive doses of penicillin to prevent infection. Then we're going to leave you here for a couple of days until the swelling goes down. Then maybe we'll have some idea what to do next."

"Great, Doc. Thanks loads."

The painkiller did what he said it would; I was out for most of the next two days.

I dreamed I was playing chicken in my prize supercustomized 1961 silver Corvette with the 327 high-performance engine. It was *Rebel Without a Cause* come true, and Natalie Wood herself was cheering me on. I dreamed I raced that car right over the cliff.

Natalie wasn't at my bedside when I woke up late Wednesday afternoon—but my wife was. So was Mike Coiro. The Mouthpiece was wearing the happy mask. Angela looked like she was watching a tragedy and it was me.

"There's the kid," Mike said when I opened my eyes.

Angela didn't say a word. She looked at me with her bloodshot eyes and sat down on a chair against the wall.

"I only got a second, kid," Mike said. "I just wanted to tell you ya got nothing to worry about."

"Oh yeah?" I said. The cop at the door, the IV drip in my arm, the handcuffs chaining me to the bed, and a doctor who doesn't know how to get the bullet in my back out made me think different.

"What'd they do with Dom?" I wanted to know. Dominic probably hadn't been thinking about the fact that he was still on parole when he beat the shit out of that cop. It looked like my best chance of working alongside him now would be cleaning toilets on Rikers Island.

"Don't worry about Dom. He's going to be fine and so are you. Once they get that bullet out, we'll go to court and answer the charges against you," he said.

"What would those be exactly—besides making a U-turn in the middle of an intersection?"

"I told you, you got nothin' to worry about."

"Just for the hell of it, then, what am I looking at here?"

"Let's see," Mike said, "attempted murder, reckless endangerment, reckless driving, and . . . oh, yeah, driving without a license."

"You gotta be shittin' me!"

"It happens when you don't even have a learner's permit."

"I mean attempted murder, for Chrissakes!"

Mike smiled. "Like I said, don't worry about it. You're in good hands, kid!"

"What about Dom?" I repeated.

"How many times do I have to tell you? He's got the same representation you do, so he's got nothing to worry about either."

"What's he booked for?"

"Felony assault of a police officer and federal parole violations," the Mouthpiece said, with no more concern than if I'd asked him what Dom was wearing and he replied, "Shoes and a shirt."

Mike had a word with the cop outside the door about my handcuffs before he left. The cuffs stayed on, but I never saw that cop on duty at the hospital after that night.

"This is what it's going to be like, isn't it?" Angela said once we were alone in the room. She wasn't crying anymore. She didn't seem even a little bit sympathetic as she looked at me lying there with a bullet under my spine. Her look was more along the lines of pure disgust. "I should have known from the beginning, but I fell for your bullshit. You're going to be a good provider, you said. You'll keep us safe, you said. Well, how the fuck are you going to do that when you try to run over a cop with a car that's more important to you than your own wife and kids? Look at you. You look like the cop ran over you."

"Aw, c'mon, baby," I said, reaching for her hand. "Let me live." That was a line that always made her roll her eyes, maybe give me an elbow and say "Fuck you," but I'd know she was laughing inside and that despite everything, she loved me.

Not that night.

"I'm glad you're okay, Sal," Angela said as she got up and gave me a kiss on the forehead. Her lips felt as warm as ice. "But only because I didn't want to have to go home and tell Little Sal and the baby any different. I'll be back when you're better, and I'll bring the boys and Mom and Louise. I'll play the good wifey and bring you some hot food. You look like you could use it. You look like shit."

"Don't forget the sausage and peppers," I said. She flipped me the bird and walked out.

I was busting her chops, but what she said gave me a lot of dark depressing thoughts about the shit hole I'd dug for myself. Here I was, twenty-six years old, and just when I'm about to get my bump up to the big time, I go and fuck it up. I was going to prison for attempted murder of a cop and my boss was probably going up with me. I'd be gone who knew how many years, leaving my wife to fend for herself and our son and newborn baby. Without me earning, what the fuck was she going to do now? As my family's breadwinner and as the Family's new recruit, I was a big fat bust.

The next morning the doctors examined me and decided the swelling had gone down enough that they could cut me open. My doc and a couple of specialists gathered around the bed with me on my stomach and bare assed; they discussed what to do next. It sounded like they were making it up as they went along. Because that's exactly what they were doing.

Somebody stuck a needle in my back and pumped in some local anesthetic. A minute later I felt a tingling sensation when my doc stuck his finger in my bullet hole.

"We're both lucky it's not my ass up there," I said.

The hole was high on my back to the left of the spinal column. He told the specialists he originally planned to go right in through there, follow the path the bullet made, and pluck that sucker out. "But then we'd be groping blind," he said for my benefit. He said it would be "like trying to get a golf ball out from under a bushel without moving the bushel." I didn't play golf, but I got the picture. Only instead of the ball under a bushel, I pictured it under the third rail at the 86th Street A train stop. One slip of the scalpel and the whole system goes down.

One of the specialists suggested they cut a hole through my shoulder on the opposite side from where the bullet hole was. He said by going in from the right they could get a better angle and dig out the bullet that way.

That's what they decided to do.

Once they wheeled me into surgery and stuck the mask on my face, I was out before I could count backward past ninety-seven.

The operation was supposed to last an hour. Seven hours after they wheeled me in, they wheeled me out. They got the bullet, but it took a lot more probing and digging than they thought it would. By the time they were finished scraping and snipping and severing and reattaching and sewing, my right arm was two inches shorter than it was the last time I put on a shirt. I had nightmares after that where my arm wasn't long enough to reach my schvantz.

I slept around the clock after the surgery, and when I woke up, it was my left arm that was cuffed to the bed, because my right wouldn't reach that far anymore, I figured. The doctors said I'd have to wait a day or two before I had any visitors. But that didn't stop Mike Coiro from finding a way in to see me.

There was a new cop on duty, and this time Mike said something to him on the way into my room. This cop walked in right behind Mike and, without a word, he unlocked the cuff from my wrist and left it there hanging from the headboard bar. It stayed there the rest of the time I was in the hospital, but it was never clamped around either of my wrists after that.

The Mouthpiece definitely had a way with words—and a knack for putting a few bucks in the right hands.

Mike had started out as a cop, but he wasn't like most cops. He joined the force after he graduated from college with a degree in prelaw. He left the NYPD after a few years and became an investigator for the Waterfront Commission, the agency set up by the City of New York to investigate corruption on the docks back when Louise Cataldo's uncle Tough Tony ran them. In the '50s, the Waterfront Commission held hearings just like the ones in *On the Waterfront* that Brando's character Terry Malloy testifies before. Brando was a big disappointment in that movie. He made turning rat look good.

Mike Coiro was such a crack investigator that the commission's top lawyer talked him into getting a law degree. When Mike graduated, he worked alongside his old boss. But Mike was a smart guy, and it wasn't long before he saw he could have a brighter future with the guys he was prosecuting than with the guys doing the prosecuting.

One of the first cases Mike worked for the Mob was Dominic Catal-do's federal beef for stock fraud and possession of counterfeit bonds back in '65. Mike negotiated a plea and Dom was out of prison in less than twenty months.

I knew Mike could work magic. He'd done it enough for me in the past. But I couldn't figure out why he was acting like he just hit the number when he came to see me the day after I got out of surgery.

"We got the cops right where we want 'em," Mike said, rubbing his hands together like the villain in a silent movie.

"How do you figure that?"

"The DA's already backing away from reckless endangerment, and there's no way they can prove felony assault."

"They've got a hundred witnesses who saw me nearly take out that cop."

"Look at it this way," Mike said. "What's more dangerous? A skilled driver who does an illegal U-turn or a rookie cop who fires two shots in a crowded intersection? We have witnesses who will testify that this cop was out of control. Two gunshots. One's a miss. Only a miracle saves some innocent bystander from getting clipped by that stray bullet. The cop's other shot hits the driver of a speeding car. Lucky for those inno-cent people that the driver wasn't killed instantly, or there would have been an unguided missile blasting onto the sidewalk. That cop has only the skill of the driver to thank for the fact that he didn't lose control of that car and smash into a bus stop or crosswalk crowded with schoolchil-dren and elderly people.

"Instead, the driver is shot in the back, and the bullet comes within a hair of paralyzing him for life. Yet he somehow manages to brake and steer the car to the curb and park it safely without harming a soul."

Mike was addressing me like he would a jury.

"We have laws in this city, kid. We can't have cops shooting people for a traffic violation. It is legal for a New York City police officer to discharge a weapon only during the commission of a felony crime. The use of deadly force to prevent the escape of a suspect in a misdemeanor is forbidden in New York and in every other jurisdiction in this country.

Illegal U-turns do not constitute felony crime; nor does speeding. If you aimed your car at the cop with the intention of hitting him, he would have shot you in the face, not in the back."

To hear Mike tell it, I was beginning to sound like the hero instead of the chump.

"So what's it all mean, Counselor?"

"Are you fucking kidding me? It means we're gonna sue the shit out of the City of New York."

The next day, Angela came as promised with the kids. She also brought her mother and Louise Cataldo and Joey. They all came in carrying trays of food—my mother-in-law's famous homemade ravioli, meatballs, baked ziti, and my favorite, sausage and peppers. Joey brought pastries and best wishes from his brother.

Mike had got Dominic out on bail, but because he was a known felon, he wasn't allowed anywhere near my hospital room.

"He told me to tell you when you get out of here he's going to give you a big fat kiss, you crazy bastard," Joey said.

That got my spirits up in a big way. Ever since I saw Dom in cuffs at the intersection, I thought my days with the Colombo Family were over. Now that Mike was going to sue the city, I guessed Dom looked at it like a big score for the crew. Shit, I'd give him the whole cash settlement if it'd make him happy. But that wasn't going to change his parole violation and his cop assault charges. I didn't find out why Dom was so jazzed on me until I finally got out of the hospital.

The family hung around for a couple of hours until it was time to take baby Joseph home for his nap. Joey Cataldo told his wife to go on ahead. "I'm going to stay and keep Sally company," he said. "I don't want him to get lonely while he's laid up."

I didn't get the joke until Big Funzi showed up with a cute little blonde I'd been banging in tow for a get-well visit. I was in no shape for a real screw, but she could find other ways to cheer me up. Joey and Funzi hung around and the four of us played gin rummy, and then the guys left long enough for me and the blonde to have a little fun before Funz came back and gave her a ride home.

The next day the doctors told me I had to stay another week, possibly two, until they were sure the wound was healing and no infection set in. But thanks to the little blonde, bed rest took on a whole new meaning.

Whoever Mike Coiro greased was coming through in a big way. Not only did the duty cops leave the handcuffs alone, word came down from somewhere that I was allowed unlimited visits. The cops assigned to my door let me close it anytime I had visitors and never complained about the noise when I had a party, which was practically every night. Usually it was Joey and Funzi and my girlfriend; they'd bring wine and food, and we played gin rummy and brisc—that's an old Italian card game played with a forty-card deck. The guys would hang out, and at the end of the night make themselves scarce long enough for the blonde to nurse me with a blow job. Then either Joey or Funz would come back up to take her home.

It says something about what it was like to be in the Life back in those days. Most people want nothing to do with a world where you can end up in prison or get whacked. But here I was, shot in the back by a cop, a hair from death and under twenty-four-hour guard, but I have only good memories of being in the hospital. Same thing when I went to prison three years later. I met a lot of great people. I learned a lot when I was inside and I came out a better criminal. Inside or out, being a gangster in those days was the best job in the world.

I did get some bad news, though. Mike Coiro found out that the cops impounded my car. My beautiful '61 Corvette was locked up at the Whitestone police pound. I never got to drive it again. After that, whenever I wanted a new Corvette, I stole one.

Two weeks after I got shot, I was discharged from the hospital. Two NYPD captains and two sergeants took me into custody that morning and escorted me to Queens police headquarters on Yellowstone Boulevard. I was booked for the attempted assault of a police officer and reckless driving. The cops who brought me in were happy to see a wiseguy get what was coming to him. They sure weren't acting like the fix was in. And when they took my fingerprints and put me in a holding cell, I wasn't so sure myself.

At 2:00 that afternoon I was standing before a judge in the Queens courthouse. Mike Coiro represented me at the arraignment and my bail bondsman was there along with Dominic Cataldo and Jackie Donnelly.

After I posted $25,000 bail, I couldn't wait to get outside. It was still warm in mid-October, and when I stepped outside I had a rush like you feel on the first day of spring. We all walked over to the Greek diner across from the courthouse where we'd always go after we were booked on gambling charges. We sat in a big booth in the back, and Mike told me not to worry about the charges.

"They're just going through the motions," he said. "Believe me, that cop will go on trial before you ever will. He had no right to shoot you. They know it and we know it. They also don't want to be any part of a lawsuit that they know they'll not only lose, but it will embarrass the hell out of them. We've got 'em over a barrel. Once we get them to dismiss Dominic's charges, we'll get yours thrown out too."

"This is going to pay off for us in a big way," Dominic said. "Mike is gonna handle everything and we're going to end up with the kind of connections we've always talked about. Not only the cops, but the DA too. Mike's always had his people in the courthouse, but this is going to take things to a new level of cooperation.

"And it's all because of you and your stunt with the Vette, you crazy-ass motherfucker. That's why we call him Sally Ubatz, Mike. This crazy kid is going to make us the best-connected crew in the city."

Dom had called me Sally Ubatz since we got to know each other. But after word got around about my shoot-out on Atlantic Avenue with the cop and the deal that came out of it, everybody called me that. That's when it became my Mob name. It got so if you knocked on the door of every Mob joint in the city and asked for Sal Polisi, nobody would know who the fuck you were talking about. I was Sally Ubatz, Crazy Sally, or just plain Ubatz from then on.

Our mouthpiece won a delay until after the New Year. In the end, it turned out just like he predicted. The cops agreed to drop the charges against Dominic and me, and we agreed not to sue the city for my pain and suffering, considerable as it was—if you don't count the blow jobs.

As for the cop who shot me, he was given a medal for bravery and promoted for risking his life to stop a dangerous criminal from causing injury and possibly even death to an untold number of innocent civilians, right?

In Disneyland maybe.

Not in New York.

Instead of being hailed as the hero, the cop was made the goat for endangering the citizenry by discharging his firearm without due cause. He was reassigned somewhere and never seen again on the streets of Queens.

Me? I was rewarded, not with a plaque but with a promise of full membership in Dominic Cataldo's crew, soon to be one of the richest and most envied in the city. That meant I was on a fast track to become a made member of the Colombo Family. On top of that, Dominic was about to make me an offer that promised riches beyond my most *upazzo* dreams.

Like they say in the song, it's a helluva town.

CHAPTER SEVEN

Getting Hooked Up

NOVEMBER 1, 1971

FELT FEDORAS WERE BACK in style, but I wasn't any happier seeing them now than I was last summer.

And this time the two hats didn't stay in their car and watch the Browns, my eleven-year-old nephew's peewee football team practice. They got out of their Fairlane and gumshoed it right across the field to where I was standing on the sidelines.

It was my first day out of the house since I got sprung from the hospital and a full month since the day I got shot. I had a drainage tube stuck in my back that had to be emptied every day, and I had to go back to the hospital every week for the next month to have both the bullet wound and the surgical wound checked for infection.

I told Dom I could still make my collections, but I couldn't go out with the crew on heists like we had talked about. He said forget about it. Funzi or one of the other guys would cover my collections. And as for the heists, he said the operation he and Jackie Donnelly were working on was going to bring in more cash than if I hit two trucks a day for the rest of my life.

Dom's exaggerations and my curiosity about his big-money operation aside, I knew I didn't have to worry about job security. But then the feds showed up at Lenny's son's practice. And I had to wonder what Dom would say if he found out I had FBI heat on me.

What these two wanted was no big surprise. They were looking for

Eddie Pravato and it was about the Franklin National Bank job last May.

"So what do you want from me?" I said. "I don't know anyone by that name."

"Mr. Pravato is a known associate of your father."

"I don't think so. My father is a carpenter. He lives out in Bay Shore. Go ask him yourself."

"Your father is a bank robber and he is in federal custody in Danbury, Connecticut."

"That's my uncle's address, not my father's."

"Are you Salvatore Polisi?"

"I am. And so is my cousin."

I let them muddle that one out for themselves. Uncle Tony had a son who was also named Sal. He was my first cousin. He was five years older than me and was not in the Life. He wasn't even in the city. He was living down in Florida.

It was ironic but not so funny that they came looking for the wrong Sal Polisi and found the right one.

"Do you not know this man?"

One of the agents held up an old mug shot of Eddie. It must have been twenty years old, at least. Eddie had all his hair and it didn't look dyed like it was now.

"No," I agreed, "I do not."

"That's too bad," the second agent said. "There's a reward for information leading to this man's arrest. Hear anything, let us know and we'll see you get the money."

"You clowns are funny," I said. "You better get back to the circus."

When the feds left, the Browns' coach, who was also commissioner of Lenny's Pop Warner League, jogged over to have a chat.

I played football in high school and I couldn't wait until my kids were old enough so I could teach them the game. I'd volunteered to assist Lenny's coach at the beginning of the season, and he welcomed the help. I was happy to be out there that day because I had missed a whole month of games and practices, but I knew the coach wasn't coming over to welcome me back and ask me to show the kids my blocking techniques.

After the shoot-out on Atlantic Avenue, all my neighbors and even my own wife thought I was a fucking wild man. The coach was no different.

"Sal," he said, "the story was in all the papers. Everybody knows you tried to kill that cop." What could I say? I didn't argue the point. I just shut up and let him talk. "Now you've got the FBI questioning you at our kids' game for God's sake. A lot of our dads are cops; we've got probation officers, corrections officers, firemen. It's nothing personal and I'm sorry, but maybe it would be better if you didn't coach the rest of the season. I hope you understand."

"Oh, sure, yeah, no problem," I said. I was disappointed. But I was also depressed at the prospect of spending another four weeks at home on the couch.

Not long after that, I got a call one boring Sunday afternoon from Dominic. He said he'd pick me up in half an hour, he wanted to show me something. I was so stir crazy I showered and got dressed like I was getting ready for a date.

I knew what he wanted to show me as soon as he drove up in it. A brand-new 1972 Cadillac Fleetwood, the seventieth anniversary model that had more trimmings than Santa Claus's tree. It was a three-ton monster with a 472 engine under the hood and leather seats big enough to fit the Dallas Cowboys cheerleading squad in the back with room to spare. The car listed for $11,000, and all the extras, from the tilting steering wheel to the remote control trunk and push-button power everything, must have set him back another thou at least.

But the car wasn't all Dom had to show me. We drove out to Valley Stream, where he showed me his other new purchase—a white Dutch Colonial on a block where they could have filmed *Ozzie and Harriet*. Or *Godfather Knows Best*.

Valley Stream was the suburbs of Long Island, a different world from the one Dom grew up in East New York. It was across the city line in Nassau County. Dom didn't say much, he just showed me the house and told me he paid cash for it. He said Jackie Donnelly bought a new house in Valley Stream too. Jackie also had a new Cadillac, he said.

On the drive back into Queens, Dom started to tell me how he and Jackie suddenly became happy suburban homeowners. But first he made me swear a blood oath.

"Sally, I'm about to tell you something big, something that'll change your life, but first you got to swear. What I tell you stays here between us; it goes nowhere."

"Sure, Dom, yeah."

"I'm talking about a secret you got to keep for life, otherwise you're dead. And I'm dead, *capisce?*"

"What is it?"

"You got to swear, Sally. You got to swear on the lives of your children."

Between Italians, swearing on your kids was the most sacred oath you could make. It was symbolic but a very serious blood oath. In the Mob, women and children were safe, no matter what a connected guy's crimes. The worst they'd do was punish the family by making a guy disappear, so there's no proper burial. But the Mob wasn't into taking it out on the wife and kids. If I got whacked—well, I'd like to think Angela and the kids wouldn't be happy about it. But they wouldn't be killed if I broke my promise to Dom. I sure as shit would, but they weren't to be touched. The oath was more about me vowing I would never betray Dominic. And I'd be a dead man if I did.

"I swear," I said.

Dom waited until we got to Club 93 to lay it out. The bar was closed on Sunday afternoons and Dom let us in with his keys. He poured us a couple of glasses of scotch and we sat at the bar.

Dom started by telling me about *The French Connection.* The movie came out the week I got shot. "The movie is based on a real drug bust back in the early '60s," he said. "It makes it look like they busted 'em and that was it. But in reality it was a Mob operation that's been going strong for twenty years." He said that in the movie the heroin was hidden in the rocker panels of a Lincoln Continental. In the real case, Dom said, they packed two hundred pounds of smack in the wheel housings of a 1960 Buick Invicta that they shipped over on the ocean liner SS *United States.*

Then he gave me the background about how the real French Connection was a joint venture between the Sicilian Mob and the American Mob. He said the Sicilians got the poppies in Turkey, refined them into junk in Sicily, and exported it to New York from Marseilles. That's why they called it the French Connection, Dom said, because the ships sailed from France.

Now, he said, there was a whole new kind of French Connection. There were guys in Marseilles who got their stuff from the Arabs direct and refined it themselves; their product was better, purer than the Sicilians', who stepped on it—cut it with milk sugar and quinine—before it even got to the States. The French guys bypassed the Sicilians and shipped their product to the United States. Their main customers were black gangs up in Harlem and in the Bronx. Now, Dom said, they were expanding their market and they wanted to find new contacts outside the black neighborhoods.

Dom said that was the reason he took Jackie along when he visited Sicily with Ervolino. They dropped her off in San Cataldo and went on up to France, where they negotiated a deal with the Marseilles heroin manufacturers.

Dom and Jackie got a pay-on-arrival deal where they would buy it at a prearranged price of $50,000 per kilo of pure, uncut junk that would sell as is for $150,000 in New York. The selling price varied all the time; it might be $180,000 at the moment, but they still paid 50 g's. A few years later when supplies dried up and demand increased, the price would skyrocket as high as $240,000 per kilo in New York.

And that's without stepping on it. They could turn that one kilo into two and still have grade A product to sell wholesale. One kilo is 2.2 pounds, 35 ounces, 980 grams. The street price for a gram was around $100. A distributor could step on one ounce and turn it into six. His dealers bought those ounces and stepped on them again and sold them as grams. "All the way down the line," Dom said, "every guy triples his investment."

The way Dom envisioned it, he and Jackie could reinvest their profits, and in no time at all they would be buying shipments of thirty, forty, fifty kilos at a time. Triple an initial investment of $2.5 million for a shipment of fifty k's and you're talking Carlo Gambino money. It didn't take a genius to figure out why he and the other godfathers would put a bullet in your brain if you got caught. And it didn't take me more than those few minutes at the bar to know that cash like Dom was talking about sure as hell made it worth the risk.

Until that day I'd never given the narcotics business a thought, but just like that, I was in it all the way.

Dom said he was bringing me in on "sales and risk management." He would sell me kilos at cost, and I could deal them however I wanted.

My other duties were going to prove trickier. The most obvious part of my job was simple, Dom said: Keep my mouth shut and make sure nobody, none of the guys in our crew or any Colombo crew or any other Family, finds out what we're doing, and for sure not Pegleg or Persico or anybody in top management of the Colombos. Dom didn't have to tell me to not say a word to anybody in the legitimate world, including Angela or anyone else in my other family.

The real problem, Dom said, and the key to our success if we solved it, was how to hide the money.

Dom and Jackie had already bought and sold their first shipment— dear Grandma Ervolino staked them the 50 g's. They covered their tracks before they even got the junk by inflating the tribute they paid to Pegleg on every score they pulled down since they got back from Italy. They were letting Pegleg think that they were scoring two and three times what they really were. That way they didn't have to explain where they got the money to buy their new Cadillacs and new houses out in Valley Stream.

Going forward, Dom said, a year of hijacks wouldn't account for all the cash coming in.

"What we need is a cover," Dom said, "a business enterprise that's big enough to explain some of our profits—not all of them; we'd need to start our own Disneyland to do that. Just big enough that nobody asks questions when you buy a new car or start wiping your ass with $100 bills. We could start a restaurant, but we might as well call it the Money Laundry 'cause that's why wiseguys get in the restaurant business in the first place.

"Then I thought instead of starting a new business, why not expand the one we got?" Dom lifted his glass like he was toasting the barroom. "We got a nice little operation going here with Fat Mike, but we need a place of our own. We need something bigger, something flashy, a private joint that gets talked about and that's not just a Colombo joint but a place where guys from any Family can get a drink, play cards, shoot craps, and hang out and have fun."

"You're talking about what—an after-hours bar, a gambling joint, or a social club?" I asked.

"All three. It should be like a social club, only we're not registered. We're a private club that opens at night after all the social clubs and Family bars are closed. And we run it like Charlie Fatico's crap game— it's open to anybody who knows about it. We have high-stakes poker games and craps games that once word gets out, everybody's gonna want to get in on."

"There's no joint like that in the city. The bosses would never allow it."

"You find the place and set it up. I'll get the okay."

"So we move our operation over there," I said, liking the idea the more I thought about it. "We'll still run our book and take action at Ervolino's, and guys will come in at night to settle up at the new place. We'll give guys something to do besides down a shot, make a bet, and leave like they do here. Maybe we'll even line up hookers that guys can go out and bang between games."

"Now you're talking, Sally. I want you and my brother to run it. I don't want Joe involved with the *babania* himself, but this is a way I can cut him in on the new business. Start looking for a place."

Just a few days after that I was walking over to Al's Candy Store, a little neighborhood place on Atlantic Avenue near 87th Street where I used to get treats for my kids. Two doors down there was a small shoe repair, and between them was a vacant store with a For Rent sign in the window. It said to call the shoe repair for details. I knew the old Italian cobbler who owned it. I used the pay phone in the candy store and called. The old man told me to meet him out front the next morning.

I got there early and waited out front. It was a single-story building with no front window, which was doubly promising because nobody could see in from the street and we wouldn't have to worry about upstairs neighbors. Plus, both businesses on either side closed at 5:00 and neither of them was open at all on Sundays.

When the cobbler arrived, he told me the space had been used as a paper drop for the *Long Island Press*, a daily newspaper that circulated in Queens as well as farther out east on the island. Trucks used to drop the papers off at the store and newspaper boys would pick them up for delivery.

The landlord opened the place and showed me around. It wasn't much to look at. The walls were mostly bare and the ceiling was unfinished, just a bunch of bare pipes and bundles of wiring and insulation hanging down. But the room was deep and rectangular, and there was room enough for what we wanted—we could fit a bar in there, two or three poker tables, and have room left over for a lounge area, where guys could sit and drink while they waited for a chair to open in one of the games. There were even a few nice touches, a bamboo partition across the back and fishnets on one wall with cork buoys that gave the place a nautical look. I guessed there had been a Polynesian restaurant in there before the newspaper took it over. There was a back room that could be used as a kitchen, and a toilet and sink off that.

There was a steel door at the back that could be rigged for emergency exits if unwanted visitors came through the front. And best of all, there was a classic old oak wood phone booth with a working pay phone in one corner, perfect for running a sports book. I thought, *Jesus, we hit the jackpot.*

In broken English, the old guy said that the rent was $75 a month, plus a $100 deposit. I gave him $400 cash on the spot for four months in advance. He didn't require a lease and utilities were included, so I didn't have to sign anything or give a name. He said I should leave the rent on the first of the month with Al at the candy store, then gave me two keys and said, "It's all yours."

We shook hands and he asked me what kind of business I was going to open.

I kind of wished I could tell him that his little place was going to become the hottest gambling joint in New York and every big-time gang-ster in the city was going to be clamoring to get in.

Instead, I told him I was in advertising.

Dom's brother Joey and I spent a solid week fixing the place up. Joey had a day job and spent a lot more time with his family and less time gam-ing than I ever did. Between his domestic life, his shifts on the docks, and his little shylock business, he didn't have a lot of time to work at the club.

But I knew I was going to be spending a lot of late nights and long afternoons at our new place, and I wanted to make it comfortable and colorful. I kept the nautical decor and added to it. I got new fishnets to replace the raggedy old ones and I found more buoys and dried starfish to hang in the netting. I strung the Chinese lanterns and hung the photos and posters and my Dalí painting of the nude with the head of a rose. I found some antique oak wine casks that I used to build the bar. I got some nice wooden bar stools and tavern chairs, a sofa, and some easy chairs. I hung beaded curtains on the walls and bought a pair of casino-worthy felt-covered poker tables.

Before we were finished getting the place ready for gaming, we moved our gambling operation to the new joint. One night when Dom and Jackie were in there settling up with some of our customers, I called a burglar friend of mine, Victor. He was a big tough guy with more balls than brains. But he could boost the clock from Grand Central if you asked nice.

I told Victor that the club needed music and to go out and get me the best Wurlitzer jukebox he could find. The next day he told me he and his heist partner hit a Polish bar in Richmond Hill, the next town over from our place in Ozone Park. "We glommed a real nice juke for you," he said.

Victor hauled the box in that night. It was a beauty, a Statesman model that held fifty 45s, three plays for a quarter. The only thing wrong with it was that all the records were Polish. The only name I recognized was Bobby Vinton. I gave Victor $40 and told him to go out the next day and buy some real records by Sinatra and Dean Martin and Dion and the Belmonts. "None of this Bobby Vinton shit. Italians only."

He came back with boxes of records. He had practically every forty-five Sinatra ever released. Once we had the juke stocked with decent music, we were ready for business. We knew if we provided good catered food and stocked cigars and top-shelf booze, gamblers would flock to the place.

We were shooting to have out first games on the last Sunday in November, Thanksgiving weekend, 1971. We would be unlicensed and completely illegal, of course. We didn't register with the city like the real Mob social clubs had to do, which meant we could open when we wanted and we could lock our doors and admit whoever we saw fit. We didn't have a liquor license or approval from the community board. We were going to be an after-hours criminal gambling club, plain and simple. The club would have no sign on the door. And so far, we didn't even have a name.

Once we got that juke, the joint was ready to jump. We had Frankie on the box, the bar was stocked with Johnnie and Jack. Now all we needed were some Jills.

When it came to making rules for La Cosa Nostra clubhouses, mobsters were more Our Gang than Our Thing. The Bergin, like all Mob social clubs, was strictly a boys' club: No Girls Allowed. My club was going to be traditional in that sense. It was going to be a clubhouse for boys . . . but with girls on the side. I told Dominic it was sound business practice to provide entertainment. If some of the guys wanted company, we should be able to provide it.

Make no mistake, we weren't in the brothel business—it wasn't that kind of joint. The entertainment we would provide would be strictly off premises.

It wasn't that guys didn't want women around; they just didn't want any outsiders period. That was understandable. Our club was going to be like all social clubs, which means it was all about crime. When you went to a Mob club, you were either on your way to or from committing a crime. Once you got there, you wanted to talk about past ones or plan new ones. Usually, you did both. And if you went to a club to gamble, that was a crime in itself. So it stood to reason that you wanted a place where you could hang out with your friends and not have to watch your mouth the whole time.

We weren't like a legitimate nightclub or bar with a reputation to uphold in the community. We *wanted* bad guys to hang out in our club. We *invited* the criminal element. We didn't want only made guys or connected guys to come; we hoped and expected every hood and hard-core heist guy within a twenty-mile radius to come to our place. We were an equal opportunity gambling joint—made guys, connected guys, wannabes were all welcome—and we were already putting out the word to every sneak thief, paperhanger, booster, bank robber, and midnight burglar we knew. Dom had already invited everybody from the Bergin and the Luccheses from Paul Vario's crew in Brooklyn.

We were opening a place where guys could feel right at home, where they could gamble and drink and smoke cigars in peace. We were going to keep it guys only, but we were going to present something extra that no other social club in the city offered.

I was already on the lookout for a permanent setup, a two-bedroom apartment in the neighborhood with a locked room that I could use in the daytime for our secret business, where I could clean and bag my kilos and store some of Dom's. On nights we had games at the club, a couple of hookers could use the living room and the second bedroom to entertain our customers.

But in the meantime, I knew a little motel in Howard Beach, a ten-minute drive from the club. The place was owned by a guy with the Colombos who gave me a standing deal on a room there.

And I knew just who I wanted to put in there. In that first week after I rented the club space, I drove in to Manhattan and talked my hooker friend Lisa into giving me her madam's phone number. Lisa said the woman was a mystery. None of the girls knew her name or where she lived. They all called her J.P. She gave me the madam's answering service number but made me promise not to tell her where I got it.

I called and left the number of the pay phone at the club. I kept calling and never got a call back. Finally, just a few days before Thanksgiving, the phone rang. It was a woman with a slight Southern accent. But she wasn't sugary and playful like one of the hookers at the Rego Park place who was from Dixie. The madam spoke softly, but she wanted answers. She wanted to know who I was and why I left twelve messages and how I got her number. I told her I couldn't tell her that;

I said I had a business proposition I wanted to discuss with her, that I had visited two very well-run establishments she might know. I named the hostess at each one, and said she could check me out with them. She said she would do that. Then she told me the name of a hotel I'd never heard of in Midtown. "Don't bother going if you're lying," she said. "Because I won't."

The hotel was tiny and smelled like big bucks. The lobby was empty. I arrived fifteen minutes early and ordered a scotch at the bar. I sat at a small round table in the lobby and kept my eye on the entrance. At a few minutes before we were supposed to meet at 10:00, I heard the rhythmic clicking of high heels on the polished marble floor behind me. I turned to see a tall blonde who looked like she just left a *Vogue* photo shoot. Her hair was long and wavy like Rita Hayworth's; she had brown eyes, pale skin, and legs like I couldn't believe. She wore a tight black turtleneck dress and no stockings. She didn't need any. I looked at her legs and I could feel her skin with my eyes. The way she looked in the light was like she was a power plant that produced sexual energy.

I stood up and told her my name was Sal. She looked me up and down, glanced around like she'd come to the wrong place, then walked over and sat across from me. "Call me J.P.," she said. I smiled. She waited. I could smell her perfume; it was sweet like gardenias.

She stared at me like she was looking through me. I liked the way I was dressed. I felt her eyes on my dark imported Italian jacket, my silk shirt, my favorite Piaget watch with the eighteen-karat band. I felt self-conscious. She stared at my manicure and then she started to smile but it ended up a smirk. I was wearing my favorite ring on my left pinkie— a big silver initial ring with *SP* written in diamonds. I got the feeling she thought it was a little much. I found out later she liked diamonds all right. She just liked them better when she was the one wearing them.

"What is it you want, Sal?" Her words clicked off her tongue cold as ice cubes. My blood was boiling hot.

"Look," I said, all business, "I have a poker game out in Queens. We need two nice-looking, clean-cut girls every Sunday night. How much?"

"One hundred each in advance. No kinky stuff. No bondage, no three-ways, no Greek. You pay the cab fare to and from." (I had no clue what Greek was. I found out later she meant no anal sex, but whatever she said was fine by me.)

I whipped out my bankroll and counted out eleven $20 bills.

She collected the money and stood up to leave.

"Hey," I said, "can I get you a drink? Do you want to get a bite to eat?"

"I don't think so," she said.

She turned and walked away, back through the lobby the way she came in. She moved like a lioness. I never saw anything like it, and I swore right then and there I was going to make that cat woman purr.

CHAPTER EIGHT

Birth of a Nation

Sunday, November 28, 1971

*T**HEY GOT AWAY WITH IT.***

My uncle Tony always used to say those were the most beautiful words in the English language. I wish he could have been there for the opening night at my club because all anybody wanted to talk about was D. B. Cooper, the instant folk hero who got away with the perfect crime. On the night before Thanksgiving, just a few days before we opened, Cooper hijacked a Northwest Airlines flight from Portland, Oregon, to Seattle. He said he had a bomb and demanded $200,000 cash. The plane landed at Seattle, they delivered the cash, and the plane took off again. Then Cooper pulled the most spectacular getaway of all time: He parachuted out of the plane somewhere over Washington and disappeared, nearly a quarter of a mil richer. Everybody there that night—but also all of us who were in that Life—had a new hero that Thanksgiving. And the club had a patron saint.

Thanks to Dom putting out the word, we had a full house. There were only two tables then, and we had seven guys at each one and more guys standing at the bar and smoking cigars, waiting for open seats.

Dom and Jackie and I were there, of course, and Dom's brother Joey. There were a couple other Colombos, and Dom invited guys he knew from the Bergin—Gene Gotti and some other guys I didn't know. Roundy, a Bonanno, was there, and Jimmy Burke, and maybe a couple of other Luccheses from Paul Vario's crew.

I got in a game at the front table with Roundy and Genie and a young guy from the Bergin they called Fox. Everybody was talking about D. B. Cooper getting away with two hundred grand.

"That's a lotta fruit," Fox said.

A little later, Roundy was about to deal a hand. Roundy got his name because you could roll him down the block; he was three hundred pounds of round and just about as tall, maybe five foot five, as he was wide. You wouldn't know it to look at him, but he was a sharp businessman; he was high up in the Bonanno Family and ran a very strong gambling operation in Maspeth. Roundy had the smarts and he liked to show them off by playing brain teasers.

While he was shuffling the deck, he made us a side bet. "A double sawbuck to the guy who tells me what all odd numbers between one and twenty add up to," he said. "Guess wrong, I win. Guess right, you get what's in the pot." Roundy slapped a $20 bill on the table. "You got twenty seconds."

Me and Fox were the only ones that took the bet. The rest of the guys sat there and stared.

Roundy started counting seconds backward: twenty, nineteen, eighteen . . .

I was jotting numbers on a newspaper—1,3, 5, 7, 9 . . . —and adding them as I went. I got as far as 25 when Fox said, "Ninety-nine."

"You got it," Roundy said, and the kid scooped up the three twenties.

"How the fuck?" Genie said. I wanted to know the same thing.

"Just sit back nice and dopey," Fox said, "and the numbers add themselves."

"Bullshit," Genie said. "You musta knowed the answer already."

"Yeah?" the kid said with a big smile.

None of us was exactly MIT material, but Fox looked like a regular math whiz. He was also quick and funny and had balls. That's a combination you didn't find in a lot of Mob guys. He didn't look like the other hoods at the table, either. He wasn't a greaser; he was a clean-cut, good-looking kid. He was probably only a year or two younger than me, but right off I saw him as young, maybe because he combed his hair down like a collegiate guy.

Most guys in that Life made a point of looking tough, glowering and scowling and trying to look as hard as possible. Fox seemed open and friendly. In that Life, you had to figure there was a blade behind every smile, but this kid wasn't looking for an opening. That was my first impression, anyway. He seemed like a guy I'd like to get to know.

Playing cards is one of the best ways I know to read a person. What I saw that night impressed me. I learned more about Fox after the last hand. I was dealing. It came down to him and me. He had a full house with queens. I beat him with a full house with aces.

After the game broke up, Gene Gotti introduced us. "Sally," he said, "I want you two to meet. This guy here is the Fox. This is a very special guy." We went to the bar and I poured us a couple of drinks.

Fox was about my height, muscular, trim, sharp looking in tailored clothes. I realized as we stood at the bar that head to toe he was in matching shades of blue, from his turquoise shirt to his blue suede shoes.

"You got a specialty?" I asked him, like we were two salesmen meeting at a convention.

"Heists," he said. "Payroll trucks. What about you?"

"Banks," I said.

"I'm not into that."

A lot of guys weren't. I didn't try to change his mind—not that night, anyway. "I'm into making money," I said.

"I noticed," Fox said. "Odds were against you coming up with that last ace."

"Yeah, that was something," I agreed.

"The odds were out of this world, astronomical."

"Is that so?"

"It's amazing when you think about it," he said. "Four aces in the deck and you're showing one and you already got one in the hole. The only card you could have beat me with was another ace, and there it is, right when you need it."

"Whattya know about that?"

"I don't want to even think how that ace got there."

"You don't, huh," was all I could think to say.

"It was nice and dopey that card just happens to appear like that," Fox said.

He said it with a smile—it was a smile that said he knew I knew something I was never going to admit to.

Fox had that same smile the very last time I saw him, years later.

The next day, I was at the club settling up Sunday football bets and all our action from the week before and taking bets on *Monday Night Football*. The phone rang as I was finishing up.

"Sally, it's Genie's friend, Fox, the guy you had the dopey luck with last night. Someday you'll tell me the secret of your success."

"What can I tell ya?"

"I need a favor you might thank me for. I've got a date with a stewardess, and she has a high-flyin' friend you might like to get to know."

"Oh yeah? What color's her hair?"

"Why?"

"I like blondes."

"Well that's just dopey, because I like brunettes."

We agreed to meet after the football game.

Fox picked me up at the club at around midnight, and we drove up to a restaurant in Forest Hills, which was about halfway between LaGuardia and JFK. The place was called Sebastian's, and it was owned by a Gambino guy Fox knew named Tommy Argo. He was also a friend of Dominic Cataldo's.

As soon as we got there and went inside, we ran into Argo, who was right there at the door talking to a tall, skinny guy. Argo himself was about five foot five and a nasty piece of work. He wore a rug, and his specialty was torturing guys with a blade. We stopped to pay our respects.

Fox told me later that the tall guy with Argo at the door was Manny Gambino, the nephew of Don Carlo. After that first night, Fox and I saw Manny practically every time we went into Sebastian's—and we went there a lot because it was near the hotels where all the airline stewardesses stayed. The airlines had a policy in those days: They hired hot women only.

By the time I got back from the men's room, Fox was sitting in a banquette at the back with two women, one brunette, one blond, and both stylish and very pretty. Fox made the introductions.

"Ladies," he said, "this is Sal. Sal's my business associate. We're in finance . . . and romance."

The brunette's name was Bonnie; she had long wavy hair, big hoop earrings, and big full lips; her friend Cheryl looked like she stepped out of a Clairol ad with her big bouncy blond curls.

It wasn't hard to tell that these stews had a thing for gangsters. They were sitting in a row, with Fox in the middle. When I came up, Bonnie cuddled close to Fox while Cheryl slid over and reached across the table, shook my hand, and patted the seat by her side.

I slid in next to her. She put one hand on my arm and stretched her fingers wide across my biceps. She purred like a hungry cat. "Foxy says you'll show me your gun if I'm a good girl."

The waiter came by and the ladies ordered martinis; Fox had a scotch and I got a bourbon.

Bonnie talked like Marilyn Monroe, breathing her words. "When are you going to take us out on your boat, Foxy?"

"We'll go now and watch the sun come up over Sheepshead Bay."

"I have to work tomorrow," Bonnie said, and pretended to pout.

"Me too," said Cheryl. She moved her hand from my arm to my thigh. Then she whispered in my ear, "Let's get rid of this holster, shall we?" The words felt wet and warm as they rolled off her tongue. She unbuckled my belt, and by the way Fox and Bonnie were huddled together, I guessed they were playing the same game we were.

Nobody said much for the next twenty minutes or so. We sipped our drinks and Cheryl's head disappeared below the table for a while and when she came up, Bonnie disappeared. While she was out of sight, Fox grinned.

"You can tell me, Sally," he said. "Where'd that dopey ace come from?"

Fox and me, we hit it off right from the beginning. I think both of us knew we were going to be friends. We got along so good we wanted to see what it would be like working together. The trouble with that was we were in different Families. Two guys from two different Families working together was unheard of in those days.

So we knew we would have to take it to our bosses—me to Dom and Fox to Gene Gotti, who was Fox's acting crew boss until Gene's brother Johnny Boy got out of the joint. Then they would have to have sit-downs with their bosses, Pegleg and Charlie Fatico, to get it cleared.

If the top guys approved, it would be a first. As far as I know there had never been a two-Family crime team before. What we were asking permission to do was like braves from competing tribes going on the war-path together. We knew our own chiefs were more likely to say "Forget about it!" than "Go for it!" but we thought, what the fuck? What have we got to lose?

So when both Dom and Genie came back and gave us the okay, it was a big deal. Dom said it was all about the green. If Fox and I pull a few scores and we do the right thing, meaning Pegleg and Fatico each gets his bite, then everybody's happy and we're in business. "If not," Dom said, "*Salut.* Find another partner."

Dom downplayed it like it was no big thing, but the fact that Pegleg and Fatico would green-light a Gambino and a Colombo partnering up together meant there was a whole new level of cooperation between the two Families. It also made me think that just maybe those rumors that the Joe Colombo hit was orchestrated by Snake Persico and Carlo Gambino, the power behind all the Family thrones, might be true.

As soon as we got the word, Fox and I got together to organize our first heist. I got a tip from a deadbeat shylock customer about a shipment of men's suits headed for a May Brothers warehouse for distribution to department stores on Long Island. We decided to hit it ten days before Christmas.

Our target was a twenty-two-foot garment truck, big and boxy and riding low when it passed us, and we followed it onto the Van Wyck Expressway. If Fat Nick was right, it was weighed down by $20,000 worth of merchandise hanging in the caboose.

Fat Nick got his name from eating too much of his own product. He had a roach coach out at the airport; he sold all the Danishes he couldn't eat and, while he was at it, he kept his eyes and ears open for anything that might get him off the hook to his shylock—me.

Fat Nick was a gambler with a string of bad luck. He was already into Dom and me for about $2,000 before he started losing at our new, still unnamed gambling club. Like most tipsters, Fat Nick lied when he thought he could get away with it. The going rate for a tip that panned out was 10 percent; on a 20 g score, that meant his loan would be paid once we pulled this job, and he could start digging himself a brand-new hole. But that wasn't enough for Fat Nick. He told me he got the tip from a guy at the airport that he had to grease, so he asked for 15 percent instead of the usual 10. I knew there was no guy at the airport. Nick spotted the truck himself; he clocked it from his catering truck as it came and went through the cargo gates. I guess he figured on paying me off and having another $500 to play with.

I didn't argue the 5 percent. I'd give him 15 percent, all right—15 of half of whatever we actually sold the swag for. That's the way it worked with tipsters. We had no respect for them—nobody in the Life, the real hoodlums, respected them, because they had no balls. They saw themselves as criminals, but they weren't really; they wanted the winnings but were afraid to get in the race. Fat Nick was like that. But he was in for a little surprise.

Nick never got any closer than the front seat of his roach coach to a real score before. I told him he was our outfielder and we were taking him with us on the job.

"You mean to watch?" he asked.

"This ain't no peep show," I said. "You want your fifteen percent, you're doing fifteen percent of the work."

We sat there at the entrance ramp to the Van Wyck Expressway and waited. Nick ID'd it soon enough—a rigid-rig GMC truck with a cab up front and a garage-type door in back that slid up.

I saw that truck pass us, and I felt like an outlaw in an old western. Instead of carrying dollars to Dodge, this stage was packed with cheesy threads bound for the suburban shopping malls of Nassau County. "Let's hit it, boys!" I said.

Fox was behind the wheel. He put it in gear and looked at me with a cockeyed grin I'd never seen before but would see many times again. "Ma name's *Buck*!" he said in a crazy Brooklyn hillbilly accent. "Ah'm from Kin-*tuck*! And I don't give a *fuck*!"

Fox gunned it, and the hotski spit gravel and did a little fishtail as we pulled onto the ramp. I turned around, and Fat Nick was scared stupid in the backseat.

Fox got us up the ramp and into traffic on the expressway, and we spotted the truck a little ways ahead. We hung back at a safe distance as it drove north and then exited onto Sunrise Highway. We followed a few miles east, waited until there wasn't much traffic, and then passed and got in the lane in front of the truck. We didn't cut it off or anything. It was broad daylight. We just waited until we came to a traffic light and the truck stopped behind us.

Fox and I got out of the car nice and easy and walked back, signaling and smiling at the driver like we didn't want to waste his time but we needed directions. He rolled down his window, and Fox hopped up on the running board and stuck a gun in his face. I climbed up and opened the passenger door. Fox had the other door open and shoved the driver aside. "Move over, goddamn it!" Fox must have kicked the driver's feet off the pedals. I felt the truck lurch and stall.

Fat Nick was still in the back of the hotski, turned around and looking through the window, bug-eyed.

Fox put the truck in neutral and turned the ignition. Nothing.

"What's the matter?" I said.

"It won't fuckin' start, that's what's the matter."

"What's your name?" I jabbed the driver in the ribs with the barrel of my Walther.

"Pappo."

"Pappo? What kinda name is Pappo?"

"My kind of name."

"Why won't the truck start?"

"Is trick."

"Yeah, I'll give you a trick." I pulled the gun out of his ribs and stuck it in his ear. "Start this fuckin' truck and no tricks, or I'll blow your head off."

"You take the gun out of my ear, I start truck."

"Don't fuck with me, Pappy!"

"Pappo."

"Cut the crappo, Pappo," Fox said. "If you don't start this fucker, you're gonna get your head shot off and we're gonna leave your brains here in the middle of Sunrise Highway—and a truckload of swag along with 'em."

"You want me to start, you got to let me out."

"You got some big Puerto Rican balls," I said.

I climbed out of the cab and stuck the gun in my belt. Pappo hopped out after me. Now, I thought, we're fucked. We've got a stolen car sitting at the intersection on Sunrise Highway with nobody behind the wheel, just Fat Nick pulling his pud in the backseat. I looked at Nick and didn't say a word. I just stared at him and thought, *What the fuck are you doing?* He read my mind and started to climb into the front seat. Two hundred fifty pounds of Nick squeezing between the bucket seats of a Chevy Super Sport must have been a sight, but I couldn't stick around to watch.

Pappo didn't pull any bullshit. He just walked to the back of the truck like he'd been hijacked a million times and the truck always stalled out. I followed him with my gun hidden under my shirt. None of the innocent motorists honking at the truck stopped in the right lane could see it, but any slipup, my balls got shot off. I waved the cars around us, making like I'm the Good Samaritan stopped to help a truck driver in distress.

Pappo's got a toolbox welded to the frame. He gets out a screwdriver, walks around to the front of the truck, opens the hood, gives Fox the high sign, and *varoom*, we're good to go.

Now, anybody watching has got to wonder why the truck driver in distress is fixing the truck and some wiseguy in a blue sharkskin suit with matching shoes is up in the cab behind the wheel. They've got to wonder more when I take Pappo by the arm and shove him in the backseat of the Super Sport like I'm pissed off, which I am because he's a defiant son of a bitch.

I clapped the cuffs on Pappo, and I was about to go back to the truck and ride with Fox to the drop as planned, when I see that Fat Nick is turned around in the driver's seat and staring at Pappo like he's a grenade about to go off. Nick is so terrified, his whole body's shaking like the bowlful of fat that it is.

I had drilled him on what to do with the driver, but now I realized he didn't hear a word I said. He was no more capable of playing the outfield than Mickey Mantle with broken legs. I signaled Fox that he would have to take the truck from here on his own. I walked around to the driver's side, opened the door, and Fat Nick heaved himself over to the shotgun seat.

While all this was happening, the legitimate slobs sitting in traffic behind us were still honking their horns impatiently but otherwise didn't react at all to the crime they were witnessing. I guessed that they were in such a hurry to get back to their miserable jobs after lunch that they didn't give a shit about a strong-arm robbery in broad daylight on Sunrise Highway.

Whatever the reason, nobody stopped us, nobody followed us, nobody batted an eye as I drove east a ways on Sunrise, took a left, and looped around and headed back in toward the city. Fox was right behind me until I made my turn. He didn't want Pappo to catch on, so he kept driving east on Sunrise until we were out of sight. Then he made his turns and drove the truck to the drop.

I was so pissed off at Fat Nick that I thought about just kicking him out of the car and leaving him at the side of the road. Instead I dropped him off at the A train stop near the airport and told him he better find some other way to pay his loan off because he wasn't getting any tipster fee and if he didn't get his vig in on time it was goodbye knees for Fat Nick.

Pappo and me, we had a whole afternoon to kill. I knew it would take a few hours for Fox to get the swag unloaded at Charlie Fatico's drop and ditch the truck. We didn't want to let Pappo go until the truck was empty and wiped clean, and Fox had dumped it.

After I dropped off Fat Nick, I took Pappo's wallet, uncuffed him, and made him drive while I rode shotgun. I told him I knew where he lived and where he worked. If he got any bright ideas about fingering us, he'd be dead before the next Puerto Rican Day parade.

It was a cold, clear day in December. We went for a long drive, Pappo and me. We drove up around Flushing, past Shea Stadium. Pappo said he was a Mets fan. I told him I was a Yankees fan but I made a pile of dough off the Miracle Mets in '69 . . . not because I bet on them but because my customers all bet against them.

Cruising with Pappo that day, I got to kind of like him. He was a ballsy little guy. Dom had taught me to always drop a hostage driver in a strange neighborhood where he wouldn't know where to go for help. Most drivers were white, and we dropped them in Bedford-Stuyvesant or Harlem or some other predominantly black neighborhood. Since Pappo was Puerto Rican, I had him drive back over the Nassau line and let him out there in the middle of suburbia. Before he got out of the car, I wrote down the info off his driver's license and gave him his wallet. Then instead of giving him the usual $50 to help him remember to forget what I looked like, I gave him $100.

By the time I ditched the hotski follow car and got back to the club, Fox was there waiting for me.

"How'd it go?" I said.

"It didn't."

"Whattya mean it didn't?"

"You gotta take me back to the drop."

"What for?"

"I thought we played it nice and stupid, but we didn't. We were too smart."

"What the fuck you talking about?"

Fox got in and explained as we drove. "The truck we jacked was an IDC."

"What's that?"

"International Dress Carriers."

"So what's the problem? We stole dresses instead of suits?"

"IDC is a trucking company."

"Yeah, I got that. So?"

"It's one of the biggest trucking companies in the Garment District."

"Uh-oh. I'm beginning to not like the sound of this."

"You got it. IDC is connected. And guess who to? Tommy fucking Gambino."

Meaning Don Carlo's oldest son. Tommy Gambino practically

owned the Garment District, running it like Tough Tony Anastasio used to run the docks.

"Mr. Fatico said we can hit any truck we want . . . just not any IDC truck."

"Don't fuckin' tell me."

"Yeah."

"We gotta unsteal the truck we just stole?"

"It's the law, Sally."

So the first score by the first-ever Colombo-Gambino crime team ended up a bust. To spare Charlie Fatico the embarrassment of having to explain to Tommy Gambino why one of his own guys, together with a member of another Family no less, hijacked one of his trucks, Fox and I picked up the stolen truck at the drop and drove it back out to Long Island that night and parked it—still packed with $20,000 worth of polyester—at the May Brothers warehouse where it was supposed to go in the first place.

We made Pappo's delivery for him, just a little late.

And Pappo came out ahead in more ways than one. That C-note I gave him was the only fruit anybody picked on that heist.

For Fox and me, the May Brothers score that wasn't at least proved to be a learning experience. And what we learned was that we could work together and we didn't freak out when things went wrong. We made a good team. And that made us eager to set up another score—one that might actually end with some fruit in our baskets.

But because it was getting close to Christmas and I was still busy fixing up the club and—unknown to Fox—finding a secret location to conduct Dom's and my drug business—we decided to put off our next piece of work until after the New Year.

The apartment I found was on 80th Street and Liberty Avenue in Ozone Park, a ten-minute walk from the club at 88th Street and Atlantic Avenue. It was a roomy two-bedroom that I rented from a wiseguy named Bankie Fagenti, who was close friends with John Carneglia, one of the Bergin guys who hung out at the club.

I moved in the week before Christmas and got it all set it up so the girls J.P. sent over could entertain guests on gaming nights at the club. I planned to bring my own girlfriends up there too, and I promised Mike Coiro that he could use it—the Mouthpiece had developed a taste for threesomes that didn't include his wife, and he was too well known around town to frequent hotels. I still felt like I owed Mike for the miracle he worked for me back in October. I was only too happy to oblige him the use of my secret hideaway.

I installed a steel door with a lock on the smaller bedroom. That's where I conducted our secret business. It was the one part of my life that I didn't tell my new goombah Fox a word about.

Our gambling nights at the club were only beginning to catch on, but the business that they served as our cover for was already booming. Dom and Jackie had received a second shipment, and they were rolling in so much cash that Jackie spent something like $20,000 on Christmas presents that year. He also began a family tradition of giving his kids dozens of teddy bears. The tykes never knew it, but he was using the teddy bears as a cash stash—there were 10 or 20 g's sewn up inside each stuffed animal.

I stored Dom and Jackie's kilos in the locked room. At first they did the work themselves, but soon I was helping them break up the bricks and divide them into ounces and step on them, turning each ounce into six or seven. The quinine itself was addictive, and that gave our product a brand; the junkies itched for our top-shelf stuff. But it was nasty work cutting and weighing and bagging. You had to wear surgical gloves and a mask because you'd get loaded just handling the stuff.

Dom's original estimate of the kind of money I could make was no lie. I paid him about $3,000 for one ounce of pure. I stepped on it and turned that one ounce into seven or eight. My dealer paid $4,200 per ounce for street-ready junk. All I had to do was sell eight ounces per week and I was grossing more than $32,000 on a $3,000 investment.

That kind of money turned Christmas into a very jolly season that year.

———————

Maybe it was because of the holidays and guys were home with their wives and kids, but we had a dead slow Sunday just before Christmas. There were some locals, legitimate working stiffs from the neighborhood playing a nickel-and-dime game at the front table, but when it looked like there wouldn't be enough high-stakes players for a game in the back, Roundy, who was in there every night we'd been open, got on the pay phone and started making some calls.

I was helping the bartender, Steve, stock the fridge with beer and soda when I heard Roundy on the phone, telling somebody about the game.

"Yeah, you know, you been there, that poker joint on Atlantic with the jukebox. Yeah, that's right, the club with all the Sinatra."

"The Sinatra! That's it," I said to Steve. "That's what we'll call the joint: the Sinatra Club!"

I had been calling the place the Coop in honor of D. B. Cooper, but Dom said that was a chickenshit name. "This ain't no henhouse," he said.

The Coop never caught on, but right away the Sinatra Club did.

It was just a few weeks after that, in January 1972, when Johnny Boy Gotti came marching home. In the years to come, John would rock the whole world. But the night he swaggered into the Sinatra Club changed my life.

It was the moment I felt like I'd been waiting for since the day I was born.

PART TWO

CHAPTER NINE

Motherless Child

I WAS BORN THE DAY Adolf Hitler shot himself, on April 30, 1945. I read somewhere he used a Walther, my favorite weapon. There was a guy they should have contracted the Mob to whack. Red Levine would have been just the button man for the job; he was the Murder Incorporated hit artist who refused to work on Jewish holidays.

My grandfather, Salvatore Polisi, was twenty years old when he arrived in Brooklyn from Naples in 1900. He found work right away digging sewers. Pretty soon he had his own company. He did well enough to buy a restaurant and bar in East New York, at Elton and Glenmore. My family was still living there above the bar when I was born.

Ervolino Cataldo and her family lived right around the corner from my grandparents, and her son Sammy grew up with my uncle Tony Polisi, who was born in 1909, and my father, Frank, who was born in 1912, the year the *Titanic* went down. Their mother, my grandmother, died in 1925 when she gave birth to the last of her five children, my aunt Marie. Like all the girls in the family, she became a musician.

During the decade after Prohibition started in 1920, all the little nickel-and-dime Irish, Jewish, and Italian gangs in New York became big business. They had huge operations running booze and an army of guys to protect their business, which was importing and bottling beer and liquor and distributing it all across the city. All the smart young guys who later ran the New York Families started as bootleggers. My uncle Tony told me that Frank Costello had a fleet of bulletproof speedboats that he used to bring in the booze from Canada. Joe Kennedy, JFK's father, was Costello's partner.

One of the biggest bootleggers in Brooklyn was Joe Profaci, who took over his Sicilian gang by whacking his boss in 1928. That same year, my nineteen-year-old uncle Tony and my father, who was only fifteen, went to work for Profaci, running whiskey from Profaci's boats in Jamaica Bay. They partnered up with their friend Sammy Cataldo and used horse-drawn wagons to transport the booze.

In 1929, the year of the stock market crash, my uncle opened a speakeasy in Brooklyn, where he sold Profaci's bootlegged booze. He became a big-time gambler and learned Yiddish from hanging out with all the Jewish gamblers and gangsters. He got into running craps games and card games and numbers. After prohibition ended in 1933, he turned it into a legit nightclub, a glitzy place with bands and beautiful Vegas-style dancers.

While Tony got deeper into that life, my father got out and became a carpenter. When they were kids, though, my father was wild. He used to hang out with Sammy Cataldo in the funeral home his parents owned. Frank used to win bets by climbing into the coffins and playing dead when customers came in to check out the merchandise. A lot of the old bootleggers owned funeral homes because they were a good way to dispose of the bodies of competitors; they built secret bottom compartments into their coffins and buried victims along with the legitimate stiffs up top.

Uncle Tony was the first in the family to move out of Brooklyn to Ozone Park, which was a new suburb in what was considered the countryside in those days. The developer who named it thought it would remind people of refreshing ocean breezes that came in off Jamaica Bay. That struck me funny when I found out that ozone is also a form of air pollution.

Tony got married in 1939, and when the war started he got into the black market. Everything was rationed, and for the Mob it was like Prohibition all over again. Instead of hijacking trucks full of booze, they hijacked trucks full of sugar and coffee and cigarettes and gasoline. They stole ration cards or counterfeited them, and those were as good as cash.

My grandfather's restaurant in East New York was a big neighborhood hangout. There was a beer garden connected to the restaurant where the Cataldos and everybody in the neighborhood came to eat and drink and dance.

That's where my father met my mother, Rose Belviso. She was from the neighborhood, but at the time they met in the early 1940s, she was a showgirl at Tony's nightclub. Before that she had been a dancer with the Rockettes at Radio City Music Hall. My mother was full Italian, but she dyed her hair blond. I think that's why I've always loved blondes. When I got older, Uncle Tony told me that she was beautiful, with long dancer's legs, and that she had a real vivacious, upbeat personality. He also said that her family was connected to one of the oldest East New York gangs, the same one Al Capone came up in.

Frank and Rose got married, and in 1943 my sister was born and named after our mother. Two years later I was born, but my identical twin brother didn't make it. I don't remember how old I was when I was told that my mother gave birth to twins and that something went wrong and my brother died. As soon as I found about it, I started having dreams about my twin and I became convinced that he was haunting me. I bugged my father until he told me what happened.

Throughout my mother's pregnancy, she had no idea she was carrying twins. There were no ultrasounds back then, and I'm not sure that she even saw a doctor before she arrived at the hospital to have her baby.

My father said I was born late at night after a long and difficult labor. My mother was knocked out on drugs and the doctor who delivered me got the job done and left the room. He also left my twin in the womb. Nobody realized it until hours later when my mother started hemorrhaging. That's when a nurse discovered the other baby, but it was too late; he was already dead. My father said it was just bad luck. "The war was still going on and all the good doctors were overseas or in hospitals here taking care of wounded soldiers. Your mother had a lousy doctor, that's all."

I was able to pry that out of him, but I never got any details from him or anybody else about exactly what happened between him and my mother.

To this day I don't know why she walked out on him and left me and my sister and never saw either of us again. But from what I know about my father and what I've heard about her, I'm sure that the main reason she walked out in the middle of a snowstorm in 1947 and never came back was that she was like Uncle Tony and me. She loved the Life.

My sister Rose Marie was four and I was two when our mother took off. Tony said he heard she went down to Florida. I used to fantasize that she went down there to hook up with Al Capone. If she did, she was out of luck because he died down there in Miami the year she left home.

My mother was gone before I was old enough to remember what she looked like. I can't remember the sound of her voice or the color of her eyes. The only picture I have of her is one where you can't really see her face; she's at a family picnic at the beach, and she's standing over a baby carriage that has me in it. My father got rid of all photos of her and anything else that reminded him of her. He never talked about her, and he smacked me if I ever said her name.

Besides the little my sister could remember, that she was pretty and smelled like gardenias, all I really know about my mother is what I heard from my uncle Tony.

And from the way he talked about her, I used to get the feeling that they were together at some point, either before my mother married my father or after. When I got to be about ten, I began to think that Tony was my real father. Maybe I just wished he was. But I've never really been sure he wasn't.

Two years after my mother vanished, my father remarried. My stepmother was Sicilian. Her father sold fresh-killed chickens. My first memory of her was her swooping up a chicken from the coop behind her family's house and slitting its throat. She stood there and held it by the feet while I watched bright red blood shoot out from its neck like it was coming out of a fire hose.

I was ring bearer at their wedding. My sister was a gifted musician and she played piano at the reception. Seven months later, we moved to Farmingdale, on Long Island, where my father bought a brand-new three-bedroom house. I think he got a deal, thanks to his brother, Tony. Farmingdale was the suburbs and it was during the big postwar housing boom. The Mob was making a fortune in construction, building Levittown and all the big tract housing developments.

The same year we moved, Uncle Tony got into home construction big-time. He bought a sand and gravel business in East Farmingdale half a mile from our house. We called it the Sand Pit. By the time I was in kindergarten, I could walk to the Sand Pit and hang out with my uncle. He ran a craps game in the gravel company office.

When he was the shooter, I got to blow on the dice. Sometimes he took me to games in Brooklyn, where they shot craps on the floor of a big vacant warehouse. He was so sharp and quick—when he wasn't throwing the dice, he was laying the odds and raking in the money. He used to let me hold all the dollar bills when he was fading bettors. It was very exciting being a little kid among all those gangsters; they looked like giants to me.

Tony got rich in land development and speculation. He and his partners bought properties at public auctions. Tony would write a check on a bank in the Bahamas on an account with no balance. The float—the time that elapsed between writing the check and when it hit the offshore bank—gave him enough time to sell the property to speculators and make good on the check. Tony's partners were Jewish, and they loved him because he spoke Yiddish.

I used to spend a lot of time with my uncle because I hated being at home. My father and stepmother had a son of their own, Joe. It didn't take long to figure out that my stepmother treated Rose and me different than she treated Joe. I didn't blame Joe. I blamed her for being unfair.

She constantly scolded Rose and me. She kept a list of what we did, and when my father got home from work she'd tell him and he'd punish us. Rose got sent to her room. Me, he'd beat with a belt. Frank would whip me on the legs and ass for ten minutes, then send me to my room. When I cried, he beat me longer. My sister used to come to my room to console me.

When I got older, he stopped sending me to my room after a beating.

Instead he put me down in the basement and chained me to a pipe and left me there, like he was punishing a dog.

I loved Rose and hated my stepmother, who was jealous of my sister for being beautiful and talented. Rose was a real knockout like our mother, only she didn't dye her hair. She had big dark eyes and long black hair. Rose was a child prodigy. Two of our aunts were piano teachers; our aunt Caroline taught Van Cliburn when he was a teenager at Juilliard. Rose performed at a piano recital at Carnegie Hall when she was four years old.

The first crime I ever pulled was stealing. I stole candy kisses from the corner store and gave them to my sister because she loved chocolate.

Every day my stepmother sent me to the store to buy bread, milk, and a pack of Camels. I never smoked in my life because I hated the smell of her cigarettes. She counted every penny in change when I got back. Sometimes Rose would give me a quarter to buy her some candy while I was at the store. My stepmother took it away from her even though Rose paid for it. After that I started stealing chocolate kisses and Hershey bars on a regular basis for my sister.

I was a baseball fan for as long as I can remember. One of the few good times I had with my father was following baseball in the papers together. We were both big Yankees fans. He used to tell me about seeing Babe Ruth play in the '20s. He took me to Yankee Stadium once so I could see Mickey Mantle play.

I collected a lot of baseball cards, and Tony showed me how to get more from other kids. He taught me how to flip a card so that it always landed faceup. My friends and I would flip cards for hours; if you won, you got the other guy's card. I made sure to keep every Mickey Mantle card I won. I had a whole stack of his rookie cards—Topps #311. In mint condition, those cards are worth 50 grand each today.

I lost a lot of my cards because my stepmother took them to punish me. If she was mad about something, she'd search my room when I was at school and dump the cards in the trash. My sister pulled them out when she saw them in the garbage, but most of the time they were gone for good. I started to hide my favorite cards, like Mantle and Yogi Berra, in my sister's room.

Sometimes I got a beating from my father just because I was spending so much time with Uncle Tony. Tony liked to take me to an old-time Italian social club back in East New York. I remember gamblers there smoking cigars and listening to the race results from the track at Saratoga. I liked to watch when a big guy counted out bills to Tony and he carefully rearranged them and put some in his pants pocket and the other half in his inside coat pocket.

That place was the Elkin Italian American Social Club. It was at the corner of Pitkin Avenue and Elton Street, which is how it got its official name, but everybody called it the Club. It was the headquarters of Albert Anastasia back then, in the late 1940s.

When I was four or five and I rode around with Uncle Tony, he taught me the names and makes and years of all the cars. When I got so I knew them all, he'd park outside the Club and set me on the hood of his Cadillac. There'd be five or six guys there, all gamblers and gangsters, and Tony invited them to try to stump me. Any car that drove by, one of them pointed to it. If I got it right, Tony collected from each of the guys. Once in a while Tony squeezed my arm or leg. That meant I was supposed to get it wrong to keep the guys hooked.

During horse-racing season, Tony spent practically every afternoon at Aqueduct Racetrack. As many times as he took me with him, it was always exciting; it was like being with Jimmy Cagney or Edward G. Robinson or a gangster from central casting. He wore double-breasted suits and always had a handkerchief stuck in the top pocket. He always had pockets full of cash, and we would travel in his new Cadillac, because that was the only kind of car he ever had. Once I remember he had a luxury model with a gadget I never saw before or since—a fifth wheel mounted on a vertical axle, like an airplane landing gear. He used it to parallel park; it was like the car parked itself.

Once in a while, it would just be me and Uncle Tony, but most times he had a beautiful blonde with him, who he always introduced as his new bookkeeper. He had a lot of bookkeepers.

When I got older and he took me to the track, he turned every trip into a learning experience. He taught me all about handicapping horses and how to bracket a race. "You don't have to bet a winner to be a winner," he used to say.

I was always lousy at school, but I got a great education in crime.

I remember the stories about famous robberies and outlaws and gangsters that I heard growing up like other kids remember fairy tales. When I was real little, even my father told me stories about Jesse James and Billy the Kid. As I got older, it was gangsters instead of cowboys, but the heroes were still the bad guys. When I first heard about Al Capone, he seemed like Robin Hood to me. Tony told me how Capone was ten years older than him and that before he left for Chicago around 1920, he made his reputation as a teenager in an East New York street gang just like John Gotti would four decades later.

I loved hearing stories about Babe Ruth and the 1927 Yankees Murderers Row, but my uncle's stories about Murder Incorporated were even better.

On one of our trips to the old neighborhood in Brooklyn when I was nine or ten, Tony pointed out the corner where Midnight Rose's candy store used to be. It was walking distance from the Club at Pitkin Avenue and Elton Street. I had heard so much about it I felt like a Davy Crockett fan getting to see the Alamo for the first time. The candy store was where the Murder Incorporated gang of mostly Jewish hit men hung out and got their assignments. They were freelance button men, and the Families used them to do hits so they couldn't be traced back to the bosses. When the bosses needed somebody whacked, they called Midnight Rose's. The button men took the calls on the pay phones at the back of the store. Tony said they went out on hits like they were delivering candy.

Tony knew a lot of those guys from his bootlegging days and from his nightclub and from just hanging out in the neighborhood. One of Uncle Tony's friends was Bugsy Goldstein. He was one of the Murder Inc. guys who was ratted out by Kid Twist Reles—the hit man immortalized as the Canary Who Sang But Couldn't Fly after he got tossed out a hotel window in Coney Island where the cops were holding him on the night before he was supposed to testify against Albert Anastasia. Bugsy and three other Murder Inc. members fried in Old Sparky, the electric chair at Sing Sing. Bugsy was asked at his sentencing if he had anything to say. Tony said that Bugsy just smiled and said, "Judge, I would like to piss on your leg."

Tony said the whole neighborhood went into mourning when Bugsy got the chair. His brothers Joe and Mutt Goldstein still lived in East New York when I was a kid, and Tony introduced me to them.

Tony was full of stories about famous gangsters like Owney Madden, the Irish boss who owned the Cotton Club, and Mad Dog Coll, who got machine-gunned while he was making a call in a pay phone booth in a drugstore on West 23rd Street in Chelsea.

Tony's personal favorite was Arnold Rothstein, who he said was known as the Brain and was the greatest gambler that ever lived. Two years after he fixed the 1919 World Series, he won the all-time high payout at Aqueduct, $850,000—in 1921 dollars! Tony said Rothstein dressed sharp like a gangster should and he died like a gangster should. He was gunned down in 1928 in front of the same hotel where Anastasia got it twenty-nine years later. He lived for two days and the cops grilled him as he lay in his hospital bed. He died without telling the cops who shot him.

I also loved Tony's stories about the old Mustache Petes, Joe "the Boss" Masseria and Sal "Little Caesar" Maranzano. During the Castellammarese War, they used to ride around town in armor-plated Cadillacs with bulletproof windows and machine guns mounted on tripods. Both bosses got double-crossed by Lucky Luciano, who set up Masseria to get whacked on Tax Day, April 15, 1931, at a seafood restaurant in Coney Island—when Luciano got up to go to the bathroom, that was the signal for the hit men to strike—and five months later Luciano sent a squad of hitters disguised as IRS agents to shoot Little Caesar in his office in the Grand Central Building.

Lucky Luciano wasn't known for his sense of humor but it was pretty funny that he used the IRS ruse to get Maranzano just a few weeks before another Mob big, Al Capone, got put out of business by the taxman—he was convicted for tax evasion that October.

Uncle Tony once drove me into the city to show me the building where Little Caesar got whacked—it's the gold-tinted landmark now known as the Helmsley Building, which straddles Park Avenue at 46th Street directly in front of Grand Central Station.

He also drove us past the Waldorf-Astoria, where Luciano lived; the

Park Sheraton on Seventh Avenue, where Rothstein and Anastasia got shot, and down Central Park West where Frank Costello lived in a lavish penthouse apartment and where he got shot in the lobby by Vince "the Chin" Gigante.

Tony said Costello was the most powerful godfather in the country in the 1940s and '50s and had every politician in New York in his pocket, including Paul O'Dwyer, who was mayor when I was born. "The politicians were all Irish," Tony said, "but the Italians owned them."

Most of Tony's stories were about gangsters and godfathers, but he also liked telling me about famous crimes like the Great Brinks Robbery in 1950 and the 1934 Rubel Ice Company heist in Brooklyn. That was one of my favorites, and I made my uncle tell it over and over. He described how the robbers dressed up like bums and one was disguised as a peddler. When the armored truck came to pick up the cash, the peddler pulled two Tommy guns out of his pushcart and the bums had shotguns hidden in the rags they were wearing. The best part of the story was the end. "They made off with half a million in cash," Uncle Tony said. "They got away clean and they never got caught."

Best of all were Tony's stories about the big bank robbers like John Dillinger. Tony told me how he was famous for vaulting over bank counters like a runner on an obstacle course; that's when I told him that's what I wanted to do when I grew up—be a bank robber.

When I got old enough to read the paper myself, I followed the news about the Mob as avidly as I read the Yankees box scores every morning. But there was one Mob hit that I read about in the paper when I was eleven or twelve that left a lousy feeling in the pit of my stomach. It was about a famous nationally syndicated newspaper columnist named Victor Riesel, who started a crusade against Mob control of labor unions like the Teamsters. The bosses wanted to shut him up, but Uncle Tony told me that it was against the rules to whack a newspaperman because of the heat it brought down on the Mob. So instead of popping him one in the head, the hit man threw acid in his face. The acid burned the guy's eyes out and he was blinded for life. Even though I always rooted for the Mob like it was my home team, I thought that was a cheap shot, like a dirty spikes-up slide that ends a player's career.

Eighteen years later when I was in prison, I got to know the guy who ordered that hit. Johnny Dio[4] was an old time mobster and a truly vicious guy. I made the mistake of owing him a favor when I got out of the joint. The payback was a piece of work that was as dirty as the hit Dio ordered on Victor Riesel—only it was worse because I was the guy who had to carry it out.

---

[4] John Dioguardi.

CHAPTER TEN

Teenage Untouchable

WHEN I WAS FOURTEEN and about to start high school, we moved to Bay Shore, on the south shore of Long Island. I hated to go because it meant I wouldn't be seeing as much of my Uncle Tony.

It was 1959, the year *The Untouchables* started on TV. I thought it was the greatest show ever because it was about Al Capone and the Chicago Mob. Me and all my friends watched that show and we booed Eliot Ness and rooted for Capone and his second in command, Frank Nitti. There was a voice-over narration at the beginning of every episode that made it seem as urgent as that day's headlines.

The fast-talking narrator was Walter Winchell, a famous radio and newspaper gossip columnist who Uncle Tony used to tell me about. Winchell used to broadcast his show from the Stork Club, the famous Manhattan nightspot where Frank Costello and all the big-name gangsters hung out, along with Winchell's showbiz friends and powerful people like J. Edgar Hoover.

Tony said it was common knowledge in the Mob that Hoover was a degenerate gambler who was into the Mob for big money. Winchell was friends with both Costello and Hoover, and the Mob boss used him to pass along gambling tips to the FBI director.

When I started high school in the fall of 1959, I wanted to play freshman football, but my father tried to stop me because as usual my grades were barely passing. I tried out anyway and got on the starting team as a halfback. I did really well, but my parents never came to see me play. It was embarrassing because all the other kids' parents were there even though their sons were only getting in for a few plays late in the game.

Summers I worked for my uncle's construction company, building houses on the north shore of Long Island. Tony was busy running his gambling operation. Often he'd take me with him when he made his rounds in Brooklyn and school me in the arts of bookmaking and loansharking.

I learned my biggest lesson when I was sixteen. I had stolen a couple of cars. It was easy back then before power locks and car alarms. Most cars had a little vent called a butterfly window. You could jimmy it open or just smash it, and reach in and unlock the car. Cars were so easy to break into that a lot of people just left them unlocked so the window wouldn't get smashed. To start the ignition, all you needed was a wire and a couple of alligator clips. My first hotski was a 1949 Pontiac that I sold for $20. Mostly what I got from it was excitement and a feeling of power and independence.

I did a lot of shoplifting too. There was no security system in most stores; usually just a round mirror up in the corner and maybe a big old fat guy who could never catch you unless he got you right in the store. Outside you could outrun him easy.

Some kids I knew did home burglaries, but I didn't like that so much. Sneaking around in somebody's house when nobody was home wasn't much of a challenge. Also it was too personal; it felt creepy. But mostly I didn't like it because it wasn't that exciting. There was nothing to it.

The first job I did for hire, I hot-wired a '59 Chevy for an older kid and his father who ran a stolen-parts garage on Sunrise Highway. His father paid me $60; I gave $20 to my sister and blew the rest at Islip Speedway, watching the drag races. That was the first real money I made stealing; it was the beginning of my life of crime.

But the lesson came later when the same kid got me to help him break into a speed shop owned by a guy named Dirty Al. The kid's last name was Crock, which should have told me something. At Dirty Al's, I did the dirty work—broke in through a bathroom window and handed out a bunch of race parts that the kid said his father would pay $500 to $1,000 for. We filled the kid's car with carburetors, manifolds, distributors, and dragster specialty parts that were worth way more than that. Crock's father helped us unload and he gave me a roll of cash. I got home and counted the money—three $20s wrapped around fifty $1 bills—$400 to $600 less than promised. I called the kid, and he said his dad had more money for me; I just had to wait a few days.

I did. I was home that Saturday about to go outside and mow the lawn when two guys in suits rang the doorbell. "Salvatore Polisi," one said, "we have a warrant for your arrest."

My stepmother stood there watching while the cops cuffed me and took me away. A neighbor was out in her front yard with a garden hose, starring at the cops putting me in the back of their car. The cops grilled me for two hours, trying to get me to admit that I broke into the speed shop. I denied everything. It turned out old man Crock out was on parole and the kid ratted me out to keep his father from going back to prison. The kid told the cops it was my idea to rob Dirty Al's in the first place and that it was me who sold the stolen parts.

My father came down to the station right after they took my fingerprints. He walked in and slapped me across the face. I was charged with burglary. My father got a bondsman to bail me out that night. I was grounded for a month and my stepmother walked around with a satisfied I-told-you-he-was-no-good smile.

A few days later, Uncle Tony dropped by with his newest bookkeeper, a blonde who looked just like Marilyn Monroe—she was like my secret sex fantasy in the flesh, right there at the dining room table. My sister had called my uncle and told him about the trouble I was in.

"Frank," Tony said, handing a lawyer's business card to my father, "when Sally goes to court next week, this mouthpiece here, Goldberg, will be there to represent him. The charge will be reduced and the complainant, this guy Dirty Al, he won't even show up."

My father didn't say much. Uncle Tony gave me a wink.

My sister drove me to court the next week and it went just like Tony said it would. Dirty Al was a no-show and the case was dropped. Some friend of my uncle's had paid Dirty Al a visit.

That was my first lesson in the Golden Rule of the Mob: *You got to know who to take care of.*

That was 1961, an exciting time. JFK was the youngest, most popular president since FDR; Roger Maris beat the Babe's record and hit sixty-one home runs, *The Untouchables* was on TV, movies like *Psycho* and *West Side Story* were out, and the Gallo Wars were raging on the news.

Another story in the papers was about the CIA's Bay of Pigs invasion of Cuba. My uncle told me that was the government doing the Mob a favor so they could get Castro out and put Lucky Luciano and Frank Costello's man Meyer Lansky back in.

I stayed out of trouble playing football on the varsity team during my sophomore year, but I flunked my classes and had to repeat. That June my sister graduated with honors and enrolled at junior college. She got a full-time job making enough money that she gave me her car, a 1947 Chevy she'd bought with her own money two years earlier. Our stepmother charged her $20 a week to park it at the house.

Rose moved out and got a place of her own. She let me stay there anytime I was fighting with our stepmother, which was all the time, so I was practically living at her apartment when school started in 1962.

That was the year my movie love, Marilyn Monroe, died. Also the father of my uncle Tony's Family, the olive oil king Joe Profaci, croaked. When I left for school every morning I watched the skies for bombers. It was during the Cuban missile crisis. They said World War III was going to start any minute.

When I finally made it to my junior year, I got kicked off the football team for drinking beer.

I passed all my classes somehow, but when I got to my eighteenth birthday in 1963, I decided fuck it. I quit school and moved out of the house.

My sister encouraged me to find a legitimate job and stay out of trouble.

Instead I enlisted in the Marine Corps.

CHAPTER ELEVEN

Crime of the Century

NOVEMBER 22, 1963

THE BUGLE CALL TO quarters came at an odd time—early on a Friday afternoon when we were in the middle of a training exercise on amphibious landings. I had finished basic at Parris Island, South Carolina. I was now at the end of an eight-week advanced-training program at Camp Lejeune.

We hurried back to barracks, got into formation, and stood at attention.

Our executive officer didn't start out with any of the usual introductory remarks. He just read a statement from a piece of paper he held in his hands: "The commander in chief of the armed forces, President Kennedy, has been shot in Dallas."

A little while later we got the word: Kennedy was dead.

We were restricted to barracks for the rest of the day and the base was put on full alert. Our gunnery sergeant called a special meeting and told us to be prepared to move out at a moment's notice. We didn't get any news from the outside. There were rumors that Castro had Kennedy killed and that the Russians were behind it and they were going to invade the country.

For me and the guys I knew on the base, it was a scary time. We were just green kids, eighteen and nineteen years old. We weren't ready to fight World War III. We all had the same sick feeling. It felt personal, like a death in the family, like Kennedy was a guy we all knew. We felt bewildered, like something momentous and very bad had happened and things were never going to be the same again and there was nothing you could do about it. You just had to wait and see what came next. I remember thinking people must have felt this way when they heard about Pearl Harbor.

I went into some kind of state of shock. I couldn't stop thinking about my dead twin brother and my mother, who all my life had been as good as dead. I felt numb and disconnected from the rest of the guys in the barracks, from everybody on the base and from the world outside. It was an almost overwhelming feeling of being alone.

I think it was like that for everybody who was alive when it happened. In ways I think the whole country suffered a kind of post-traumatic breakdown. They always say it was the end of innocence in America, but it was really the beginning of a mass mental depression.

The president of the United States was a guy everyone adored because he was young and bright as hell, and he had a beautiful wife and two cute little kids. He was the American dream come true and he got his brains splattered on a sunny afternoon down south. If that's not enough to shock the whole country and sink it right into depression, I don't know what is.

The Kennedy killing was like death knocked on the door and walked in and took over. After Dallas, death owned the 1960s.

People are still obsessed by the assassination fifty years later and that's because the crime was never really solved. The Warren Commission said Oswald did it and that was that, case closed. But a whole lot of people didn't buy it. They couldn't really believe little Lee Harvey did it all alone, not when every other assassination of a head of state, from Julius Caesar to Abraham Lincoln, was a group effort, a plot, or a conspiracy of some kind.

Plus, there were so many holes in the official story you could drive a Peterbilt truck with a forty-foot trailer through every one of them. Everybody I knew thought the single-bullet theory and all the rest of it was bullshit, but nobody could figure out what really happened. The Kennedy assassination was like an unsolved murder where the family gets no closure; with Kennedy, the whole country got none.

Whodunit was a mystery to me like everybody else. It wasn't until I got into the Life that I figured out what every connected guy with half a brain knew all along: The Kennedy assassination was a clip job—a Mob hit, pure and simple.

All it took to convince me—once I got to know the Mob from the inside and met plenty of guys who did hits—was the picture of Jack Ruby plugging Oswald. From his porkpie hat and dark suit to the .38 in his hand, he looked like a button man out of the old gangster movies, plus the guy owned a strip joint. You can't find a better job description of a Mob guy than that one.

Then when I found out that a cousin of Dominic's everybody called Joe the Wop and who ran Mobbed-up casinos in Havana in the '50s was questioned by Warren Commission investigators a month after the assassination when his number turned up in Jack Ruby's phone records— that cinched it for me.

Once I knew for sure that Ruby was connected, it all made sense. I felt like a fool for not seeing it before. The Mob wanted Kennedy dead for whatever reason and they set Oswald up. He was the patsy just like he said he was. Then Ruby shut him up just like Joe Colombo's body- guard put one in the black patsy who shot Colombo eight years later.

Don't believe it? Read two books by Selwyn Raab, the *New York Times* investigative reporter who covered the Mob for twenty years— *Mob Lawyer* and *Five Families*.[5]

Both are smart, solidly researched histories that are page-turners for anybody interested in knowing what really went down in Dallas in 1963. Raab lays out all the background—about how two powerful Fam- ily bosses down south who sat on the Commission, Santo Trafficante in Tampa and Carlos Marcello in New Orleans, wanted Kennedy dead in order to stop his brother Bobby, the attorney general, from going after them and the rest of the bosses, and how J. Edgar Hoover wrapped up the investigation into the assassination in a single month and ramrod- ded the Oswald-acted-alone bullshit by the Warren Commission in order

---

[5] Selwyn Raab, *Five Families: The Rise, Decline, and Resurgence of America's Most Powerful Mafia Empires.* St. Martin's Press, 2005. (See Chapter 15, "The Ring of Truth" pp. 139–154.) Frank Ragano and Selwyn Raab, *Mob Lawyer.* Charles Scribner's Sons, 1994.

to protect the real perps. The books are filled with mind-blowers about how the assassination went down and why, and I won't repeat them all now.

Here are some of the highlights of the Greatest Mob Story Never Told:

• Lee Harvey Oswald's uncle, Charles "Dutz" Murret, was a bookie and soldier in Carlos Marcello's New Orleans Family. During most of the year prior to the assassination, Oswald lived at his uncle's house in New Orleans.

• One of the most prominent Mafia bosses targeted by Bobby Kennedy, Marcello vowed vengeance, telling friends that the best way to neutralize RFK was by killing the president. A Marcello business associate later testified to Congressional investigators that in September 1962, Marcello " 'clearly stated that he was going to arrange to have President Kennedy murdered in some way,' and that someone outside of the Mafia would be manipulated to carry out the actual crime."

• That "someone," Raab strongly suggests, was Oswald, a former Marine trained in intelligence who previously defected to the Soviet Union, then returned a few years later, no questions asked; in 1962 and '63 he was in New Orleans where he lived with his Mobbed-up uncle while associating with both pro- and anti-Castro Cuban exiles, as well as shadowy figures in the intelligence community. My money says Oswald was involved in counterintelligence; he infiltrated radical groups as a mole, and when he got whiff of a plot to kill Kennedy, he took the bait to spy but got set up to take the fall instead.

• At the same that Oswald was nosing around extremist groups in New Orleans, Raab states, Marcello's close friend and fellow Commission member Santo Trafficante was working directly with the CIA and Cuban exile groups in Florida to get Castro out of Havana and the Mob back in.

• Jack Ruby, who claimed he killed Oswald in a patriotic fit of passion, worked for Trafficante in Cuba in the 1950s. He was a Mob bagman who carried illicit cash from Havana to the United States, where it was distributed among the Families. Ruby's home base in the United States was in Dallas, where the top crime boss was Jon Civillo, who was also the underboss of Carlos Marcello, whose Family's territory extended from New Orleans to Dallas. The favorite hangout and de facto headquarters of the made men in Civillo's gang was Ruby's strip joint, the Carousel Club. (The club was located close enough to Dealey Plaza, where Kennedy was shot, to see it from the sixth floor of the Texas Book Depository.)

• When Congress reopened the investigation into the assassination in 1976 (a radically edited and watered-down version of their report was made public in 1979 while the rest of their findings remain classified to this day), investigators learned that Hoover ordered FBI surveillance tapes of Mob leaders discussing the need to whack Kennedy to be destroyed, and he suppressed other evidence and overlooked testimony pointing to the Mob.

• In July 1963, as Teamsters boss Jimmy Hoffa faced charges brought by Bobby Kennedy that would ultimately send him to prison, Hoffa instructed his lawyer, Frank Ragano,[6] "to relay an urgent demand to Santo Trafficante and Carlos Marcello," Raab writes. "'The time has come for your friend [Trafficante] and Carlos to get rid of him, kill that son-of-a-bitch John Kennedy.'" Ragano, thinking it was some kind of not-funny joke, delivered the message to the two bosses when he met with them the next day in New Orleans. "The two mobsters stared back in icy silence," Raab writes.

---

[6] Ragano, Raab's *Mob Lawyer* co-author, also represented Trafficante and was a confidant of Marcello's.

• Minutes after he got news of the assassination, Hoffa telephoned Ragano. "Did you hear the good news?" Hoffa exclaimed. Three days later, Hoffa and Ragano were in a meeting when "Hoffa pulled Ragano aside. 'I told you they could do it,' Hoffa whispered. 'I'll never forget what Carlos and Santo did for me.'"

• On the night of the assassination, Trafficante celebrated in a Tampa restaurant with his lawyer, Ragano. "We'll make money out of this and maybe go back to Cuba," he said.

• In March 1987, four days before Trafficante died, Ragano picked the ailing boss up at his home and took him for a last drive on Tampa's Bayshore Boulevard. "Speaking to Ragano in Sicilian as he often did, Trafficante grumbled: 'Goddamn Bobby. I think Carlos fucked up in getting rid of Giovanni—maybe it should have been Bobby.' To Ragano's astonishment, Trafficante added: 'We shouldn't have killed Giovanni. We should have killed Bobby.' Ragano knew that 'Giovanni' was John Kennedy."

Even after I got into the Life and became convinced that Kennedy got whacked by the Mob, I never talked to Dominic or anybody else about it. Any Mob hit was like that—if you knew anything about it, you kept that shit to yourself. It was something I knew better than to ask even Uncle Tony about. So I don't know what he thought about the Kennedy hit. But whether he approved or not, he would have to give the mobsters who pulled it off his highest accolade:

They got away with it.

The Kennedy assassination was like a death knell in America, and it was for me too. Just like the decade that followed was a nightmare for the whole country, my life went to shit soon after that bright day in Dallas.

CHAPTER TWELVE

The Eve of Destruction

MY FOUR-YEAR HITCH IN the Marines started to feel a lot longer when I went home on my first furlough in February 1964. That's when Uncle Tony told me about his big new project: He was building a motel right next door to Aqueduct Racetrack. The motel would have forty rooms for out-of-town players to stay in during racing season. He was putting in a fancy nightclub with a horseshoe bar and a first-rate kitchen. I didn't let on to Tony but when he described his gamblers' paradise all I could picture was a dozen or so Marilyn Monroe lookalikes crowded around his horseshoe bar and me in a bad-luck Marines barracks somewhere at the other end of the world.

The other big news that greeted me that visit also made me feel like life was going on without me. My sister, Rose Marie, told me about a guy she met, Will, and that she loved him. Because he had been married once and was divorced, our father refused to give his blessing for them to marry.

Rose told me that they were going to elope, which they did soon after I reported back to duty.

I was in the middle of the Atlantic Ocean the next fall when I got a telegram from Uncle Tony saying that Rose Marie had a baby boy on Thanksgiving day. I was on board the USS *Boxer* with the Third Marines, headed for exercises in Barcelona, Spain. I planned to celebrate the birth of my nephew when we put in at the Canary Islands the first week in December.

Before we put to shore, the ship held a smoker. It was a boxing and wrestling tournament, Marines versus Sailors. I had done some wrestling in high school, so I was chosen as the middleweight. One of the marine boxers was Robert Lozada, who made the 1968 Olympics team. He knocked out the helpless sailor in the second round. I won my match with a double-leg takedown; I dropped to my knees, grabbed both of my opponent's legs, lifted him off his feet, and dropped him down on his back, pinning him.

When we put in at the Canary Islands, I was in the last group allowed ashore. I stayed on the ship the first day of liberty. I was down in my bunk when I decided to go up on deck to catch some rays. As I climbed a steep narrow stairway, I lost my breath and felt an excruciating pain in my chest. Then I blacked out.

I woke up in the ship's hospital. The medical officer told me I was going to be airlifted by helicopter and flown to Madrid for emergency surgery. He said the sac around my heart was swollen with fluid. A nurse shot me up with Demerol, and I came to in a hospital in Madrid. A cardiologist from New York was flown in to perform a pericardial tap. He stuck a needle in my chest and drained the fluid. When I came out of anesthesia, my father was in my hospital room.

"The Marine Corps flew me here," he explained. "The telegram said a priest was giving you last rites."

It was the first time in my life my father was there for me. Even so, I knew he never would have come if Uncle Sam didn't foot the bill for his flight.

A week later I was flown back to the States. The doctors said I'd have to stay in the hospital for at least a month. Before I got too depressed about that they told me that after a review by the Naval Medical Board and the Marine Corps' evaluation team, I was probably going to be honorably discharged from the Marines. Then they gave me even better news: The hospital they were sending me to was St. Albans Naval Hospital in Queens, a five-minute drive from my sister's house.

Rose and Will visited me a few days after I got to St. Albans. They showed me pictures of my nephew. My sister asked me if I'd be William's godfather. I told her nothing would make me happier. The bad news was that our father refused to even see his own grandson. Will was an ex-con, but he'd gone straight and Rose loved him. I told her that was good enough for me. Before she left, she mentioned that she had had some problems during her labor and she was on medication for something to do with her pancreas.

Uncle Tony came to the hospital with his new "bookkeeper," Kitty, who I immediately had a crush on. When he left, Tony slipped a crisp $100 bill under my pillow and said if I got the discharge, he had a job for me at the new motel, the Aqueduct Motor Inn, which he said was almost ready for its grand opening.

All the other patients in the hospital were old World War II Marine vets. They were full of great stories about the battles of Tarawa, Guadalcanal, Iwo Jima, and Midway. One of the best storytellers was an Irish guy everybody called Gunny O. He was wounded when a Japanese bullet pierced his heart. It was a miracle he survived, he said, but a curse that he was still in the hospital twenty years later.

I was being treated with steroids to increase my appetite and build my strength. But the prednisone they gave me was a powerful form of steroid with one nasty side effect: it creates feelings of heavy-duty hostility. One day I got into it with a male nurse who started hassling me when I was bored and walking around the ward. I ignored him when he told me to get back to my bed. He crossed the room and got right in my face. "Private, I said return to your bed *now!*"

I did something stupid. I punched him in the face.

"Call the MPs," he screamed.

Five minutes later, three MPs in full gear dragged me to the psycho ward on the top floor of the hospital. I was shot up with something. When I woke up, I was alone in a padded cell, strapped up in a straitjacket.

There were a lot of scary guys on the psycho ward, shell-shocked World War II vets who would never get out of there. I was afraid the same thing was going to happen to me. For hours I didn't stop struggling and hollering, "Let me outta here!"

After a few days, a civilian psychiatrist showed up and sat in on my evaluation. The Marine psychiatrists wanted to keep me on the ward as a violent paranoiac. The civilian doc got them to agree that if I stayed calm for two days, and didn't yell and scream like I'd been doing, they would send me back to the cardiac ward.

You'll never guess how that civilian shrink happened to be there. Yep, Uncle Tony; he came to visit, and when he found out they had me locked up in the psycho ward, he contacted the psychiatrist who happened to be a distant relation I'd never heard of before.

After the evaluation session, Tony was allowed a five-minute visit. Before he left, he whispered in my ear, "Be smart, play their game, in the long run you're gonna win."

As always, Tony was right. I played it cool and kept my mouth shut; after a couple of days, they returned me to the cardiac ward.

The guys there cheered me when I walked in because I punched the nurse. It turned out they hated the guy. He'd been hassling them all for years.

In March, six months after I was stricken with pericarditis, the doctors announced that all trace of infection was gone. I was taken off medication in April. They kept me in the hospital for observation for a couple of weeks, and I was called before the Marine Medical Evaluation Board.

They pronounced that I was to receive an honorable discharge from service for medical reasons.

I couldn't believe it when they said it was not because of the heart infection. I was unfit for duty because I had violent emotional problems; I was an unstable personality. Because I slugged the nurse and kicked and screamed when they put me in a straitjacket.

I was shocked and embarrassed and angry. How dare they say I'm psycho?!

Little did I know that being a certified nutcase was the best thing that ever happened to me.

Once I got into a life of crime, I found out that the shrinks had given me a get-out-of-jail-free card.

The psycho discharge paid off in other ways too—I received monthly disability checks for the next twenty years.

And right at the time I was discharged, the Pentagon started shipping Marines by the boatload to Vietnam to get shot and killed. That was one insanity I was glad to have no part of.

Eventually I learned how to *act* crazy when it served my purposes. I was on a Randle Patrick McMurphy trip years before Jack Nicholson played the character in *Cuckoo's Nest*.

My first few weeks of freedom were a blast. The rest of the year was the worst time of my life.

I started work at Uncle Tony's motel. He named the bar the Diamond Horseshoe Lounge. He poured a polyurethane floor and embedded silver dollars in it. Everyone who came in the place walked on plastic clouds of money. Which was fitting, because Tony's lounge was a heaven for thieves.

The first night I went into the Diamond Horseshoe, Tony had a torch singer named Anne entertaining the only customers—a group of guys sitting at the back of the club. The lights were low and I didn't get a good look, but Tony later told me who they were. Eventually I got to know all of them pretty well.

It was Sonny Franzese's crew. Sonny was around my uncle's age. He and Tony were friends since back in the '40s. He had been a capo under Joe Profaci, and Joe Colombo made him underboss when he took over. He was a classic gangster: handsome and sharp dressed and bad as they come.

The other guys were Whitey Florio, Sonny's right hand, and his two henchmen, Johnny Irish Matera and Red Crabbe. Those two guys pulled off the big Harbor Island Spa score in Florida the next year. Another guy, who became one of my good friends, Funzi Tarricone, was in on that job. Funzi hit the hotel's safe-deposit boxes with a sledge and chisel. They gave each box a couple of whacks, and if it didn't open, they moved on to the next. They got half a million out of the boxes.

One guest thought he was lucky because Funzi couldn't bang open his box. But when the feds did an inventory, this guy had a box full of money he couldn't explain. He was busted for tax fraud and got packed off to jail. He must have wished the Funz had taken a better swing with his sledge.

I worked days at Tony's putting the finishing touches on the last of the hotel rooms, stocking the bar and kitchen, and just helping around.

Some days when I showed up for work, Tony told me to put down the mop and come with him. Then he took me on his rounds, just like he used to when I was a kid. It was the work-study phase of my education as a mobster.

Sometimes we would ride into the city and he would explain how to set up and run a sports book, or we'd just spend all afternoon at the track and he would teach me how to read the odds and how to loan-shark.

He said the first law of shylocking was the same as the first law of capitalism: Let your money do the work. Everything you earn should be put back in the business, out on the street, loaned to gamblers—you win if they win, you win if they lose.

Tony took me around when he collected, and before long I was doing the collecting for him. I was quick and strong enough to do the job, but Tony also taught me to be smart.

I learned all the tricks of the trade from Uncle Tony. Once, he took me up to the motel roof, where he had a tripod set up and high-power binoculars trained on the tote board a block away at Aqueduct. Tony also had a phone line rigged up that connected him with guys who worked for him in Albany, where track results came in over a Teletype wire. There was a time lapse on the wire feed so Tony could telephone his guys the results before the pari-mutuel board in Albany had them. Brilliant.

On top of the money I was earning at Tony's, I was flush with cash thanks to the $2,000 military severance check that came in the mail. The day after I got it, my father's other brother, Uncle Joe, took me car shopping. I bought a beat-up 1949 Olds for $150.

After work most days I drove over to my sister's, where I got to know little William, whose five-month birthday was just a few days before my twentieth.

Some days I drove to Bay Shore to visit my father. It was great to see my half brother Joe, who was fifteen now, and my dad's other kids with Sarah, my stepmother—Nancy, who was eight, and four-year-old Eddie. They were good kids. But my father still hadn't gone to see Rose's baby, and my stepmother was the same as ever, so I didn't spend much time over there.

I had the radio in my car always tuned to WABC. There were great songs out that year—Sinatra's "It Was a Very Good Year," the Beatles' "Help!" the Stones' "Satisfaction," the old Italian song "Cara Mia" rocked up by Jay Black of Jay and the Americans, and "Bring It on Home to Me" by the Animals.

And then there was the song that said it all that year: "Eve of Destruction."

I was working at the motel one day when Will called. He said Rose was in the hospital with a high fever and a dangerous infection in her pancreas.

I rushed over to Hillcrest General. I expected to find my sister deathly ill. But she was sitting up in bed doing the *New York Times* crossword with Will.

Rose said her condition wasn't serious; she was on medication and she'd be going home soon. We talked about the baby's christening. It was the first weeks of June, and the baptism was scheduled for the end of the month. I gave Rose the money for the white suit the baby would wear for the ceremony. Will's mother and sister were taking care of the baby while Rose was in the hospital. I didn't know anything about Will's family at the time. I wish I'd never found out.

That weekend I drove out to Bay Shore and hung out with some old high school buddies. I met a girl named Cherry at a bar and we danced all night to "Satisfaction."

The next day, Sunday, I called home. My father was in hysterics. Uncle Tony had just called. Will had reached Tony early that morning.

Rose Marie had died in her sleep. My father was crying and wailing and cursing in Italian. My stepmother got on the phone and told me to get home.

It was June 13, 1965.

The day my first life ended.

The next days were a blur of pain and rage. Will followed the Italian custom, and Rose Marie was laid out at the funeral home for three days before the funeral. Our entire family was there; everyone was distraught. My father fainted when he knelt down beside her casket. My aunt Lea loved Rose like a daughter; she took her in for a while after our mother abandoned us. Lea was a trained concert pianist and she taught Rose, who could play a twenty-minute Chopin prelude from memory before she was four years old. Lea was the most religious person in our family, and she tried to hold things together at the viewing, but I think she was hurt the hardest.

I spent the first night at Will's. He sat at the kitchen table all night drinking whiskey and smoking cigarettes. His eyes were watery and red. On the table, he had a picture of Rose holding the baby. Before I went over to Will's, I stopped to see Uncle Tony. He was very matter-of-fact. He said I had to be strong for my sister, that my father was weak and it was up to me to support him. He told me to stand like a man and, above all, show no emotion.

That night at Will's I had to struggle to keep from crying when I looked at the picture of Rose and William. Will's sister Florence came to collect some of the baby's clothes. I had to turn away and not look at her when she said how much her family loved Rose Marie.

That night I prayed for the first and only time in my life. I prayed that our mother would somehow find out what happened and would come to the funeral. I prayed that there was such a place as heaven and that my sister would go there.

The next day Will told me that it was Rose Marie's last wish that she have a funeral mass. That meant that my sister would lie on the high altar and receive the full blessings of the church. The priest—I'll never forget his name; it was Lucchese, like the gang boss—said that because Rose Marie married a divorced man, in the church's eyes, she died in a state of sin. He refused to allow a funeral mass.

I wanted to burn the church to the ground. With Father Lucchese in it. Uncle Tony had a better idea. He knew the Catholic bishop who ran the annual San Gennaro Festival in Little Italy every year. Tony was part owner of an Italian sausage concession. Every year he had to negotiate for space at the festival with the church and with the Gambinos, who controlled the neighborhood and helped sponsor the street festival.

Tony met with the bishop and afterward told me that a $3,000 contribution to the church would get my sister the funeral mass she wanted.

––––––––––

That's when I got my first real introduction to the Mob. Uncle Tony took me back to the old neighborhood in East New York. We went to the same Italian social club that Tony took me to when I was little, where he sat me on the hood of his car and I named all the makes and models that drove by. Back then it was Albert Anastasia's club. Now Charlie Fatico ran the business there.

Fatico was Uncle Tony's age, and he'd been pulling jobs since he was a kid growing up in the neighborhood. He was one of the Mob's original hijackers; he waylaid so many liquor deliveries during Prohibition his Mob name was Charlie Wagons. By the time Albert Anastasia took over Vince Mangano's Family in the early '50s, Charlie was a top capo running the gang's East New York operations, and his crews were hijacking trucks off the waterfront and from Idlewild Airport in Queens.

Tony took me inside and introduced me to Mr. Fatico. He was short and he must've been in his late fifties, but you could tell by looking at him that he was a serious man . . . and deadly. He had on horn-rimmed glasses and he wore his hair in a comb-over that made him look a little like the actor Martin Balsam. I knew he was an important man in the Gambino Family and that he was respected by everyone in the neighborhood, including the legitimate people who came to him for advice, to settle their disputes, and to borrow money when they couldn't pay the rent or had emergency medical bills.

Before our sit-down, Tony coached me on what to say. I told Mr. Fatico about my sister and how she had been refused a mass. I told him that I needed $3,000 to contribute to the church. Mr. Fatico said $3,000 was a lot of money. He said he couldn't give me the money, but he could loan it to me. It would cost me $90 per week. That was the minimum I had to pay him until I paid off the principal. He didn't have to say anything about what would happen if I didn't make the vig payment each week.

Mr. Fatico loaned me the money. I gave it to Uncle Tony, who made the donation to the right people in the archdiocese.

My sister got her funeral mass.

———————

The night before the funeral, Will called me at Uncle Tony's motel. He said he found a sealed letter from Rose Marie that was addressed to me. She had written it the night before she died, while Will was asleep. Will said he would give me the letter on the way to the cemetery.

I sat numb through the funeral, waiting for it to end. It was a forty-five-minute drive from the church in Queens to Pinelawn Cemetery on Long Island. It was a hot and humid day. I rode in the limo with Will; my father and stepmother and the kids rode in another limo.

During the ride, Will gave me the letter. I peeled it open. It was written on soft pink paper. Pink was Rose Marie's favorite color.

Dear Sal,

I want you to know I love you more than anything in this world (except Will and William, Jr.—only because I love my husband and child differently). I just want you to know the last two days I've never felt so much peace. Lord knows that I realize how truly blessed I have been having a wondrous husband and precious baby.

I only want to tell you that I feel life is much too short to be insignificant. Promise me if anything happens to me you'll go and live life with zest. Please take care of yourself and always know how much we loved each other.

Find a nice girl and give her Hershey candy bars-better yet, make it Hershey Kisses. And pay for them!

One special request: Remember how we vowed to each other never to raise our children under a blanket of pain, anguish, torment, and constant threat of total abandonment.

Well, Sal, I know someday you will have children.

Promise me to pray to God to give you the strength to raise your children differently.

Your loving sister,
Rose Marie

CHAPTER THIRTEEN

The Hits Keep on Coming

Uncle Tony encouraged me to live at home after my sister died. I enjoyed hanging out with my half brother Joe when I wasn't working. His sixteenth birthday was coming up, and I had been able to earn enough to buy him a set of Craftsman tools. He was very mechanical and liked to work on cars like I did. On my way to Tony's motel in the mornings, I would drop Joe off at his friend Carmine's house, and they'd spend the afternoon digging for clams in Great South Bay.

I didn't last very long at home. My father was living on cigarettes and coffee. He just seemed to get worse instead of better. He kept blaming Will for Rose's death. He said what a no-good ex-con Will was. By the end of the summer, I had to agree.

I kept calling Will's sister so I could see the baby. His sister finally said Will had gone to California and taken the baby with him. We found out that his family was involved with some sort of cult. They followed the teachings of Nostradamus. His mother was a con artist who bragged about ripping off old-time gangsters in the '30s. She apparently hung out with some of the Murder Incorporated gang in those days. We were never able to find out the details.

We never had the christening for little William, who was supposed to be my godson. I never saw my nephew again after we put my sister in the ground.

I really started hating life at that time.

When I couldn't stand being around the family anymore, I moved into a room at Tony's motel. I was making enough money to pay Charlie Fatico his vig every week but not near enough to pay off my debt. I knew I had to start stealing cars or do something to make money.

I started hanging around with a couple of dopeheads, a guy named Red and his girlfriend Carol. I never liked pot and didn't touch junk, so I didn't have any interest in going into Manhattan with them to hang out with their hippie friends in the Village.

Red and Carol were dopers, but they were also accomplished thieves. They weren't into stealing cars. They broke into them and stole whatever was worth stealing. It was amazing what people left locked in their cars, thinking it was safe.

Red carried a long screwdriver and a small hammer. We were cruising downtown Bay Shore one night when Carol came up with the idea of hitting cars parked in the lot behind a movie theater. Red cracked open the vent of a couple of cars and came back and split the loot; I got a few dollars and a watch.

Now it was my turn. I spotted an Olds convertible. I slit the roof with my pocketknife, got in, and searched the car. I found nothing in the glove box and was about to give up when I felt under the seat.

Somebody must have been afraid of losing his wallet at the movies. I found more than his wallet. In an envelope was his checkbook and a passport.

I got back in their car, and we drove off. I couldn't believe my luck. There was almost $3,000 in cash. Red and Carol took their split and a few of the guy's credit cards and said they were going to the Village to buy drugs.

I said we should find a bank and see what we could get out of the checking account. They thought that was too dangerous. They dropped me off at home and went into the city.

The next day I drove to a bank out on the island, twenty miles east of Bay Shore. I showed the guy's driver's license—they didn't have photos on them in those days—and his gas credit cards. I wrote a check for $3,500. The teller counted out thirty-five $100 bills. A few hours later I hit another branch and then a couple of more. By the end of the day I had close to $11,000 in cash.

The next morning I put aside $3,000 to pay off Charlie Fatico.

Then I went shopping.

I drove around Long Island, writing checks for new shoes, shirts, and suits.

I was writing a check for six bottles of Italian cologne at an Abraham & Straus when a store detective pointed at me and started hurrying my way. I dropped the shopping bags I was holding and ran for it.

Two weeks later I was sweeping up the parking lot at the motel. Uncle Tony was out of town on a piece of work with Sonny Franzese and his crew.

Suddenly out of the corner of my eye I see a big guy with a gun. It was the same cop who'd arrested me on the stolen parts case.

I spent twelve hours at the police station, handcuffed to a chair, denying everything.

After midnight, I was fingerprinted and booked for burglary, grand larceny, and forgery.

I was given a dime to make my one phone call at about 2:00 a.m. With Tony out of town, I called my father. "I should leave you there to rot; it'll teach you a lesson," he said.

I spent the night in the county lockup; the tank was packed with lowlifes and drunks. The next morning I was taken in handcuffs and leg irons to court, where I told the judge I wanted a lawyer. I pled not guilty to all the charges. I spent two more days in the holding pen. I called home, and my stepmother said my uncle was back in town and he was going to bail me out. She told me if they let me out I should look for somewhere else to live. My father didn't want a criminal living with their children.

Tony was waiting for me outside the jail when I got out. I thought he'd tell me I was a jerk for getting caught. Instead he slapped me on the back and said he was proud that I refused to give the police a statement.

He said Red and Carol got busted with two of the credit cards we got out of the wallet. They squealed me out to the cops. Tony said he got a copy of the complaint; a couple who owned the shop where I bought the shoes had filed it. Tony had already been to see them and paid them enough to cover the $80 cost of the shoes and to drop the charges. He said the bank wasn't going to prosecute because they didn't want it out how easy it was to kite their customers' stolen checks.

Tony turned the episode into a lesson. He told me it was never a good idea to work with amateurs. He advised me to learn from the pros. To keep my eyes and ears open at the motel, learn all I could about book-making and gambling. When I went to Brooklyn to pay Charlie Fatico, I should do the same thing, get a feel for that life. "You got to think about the future," Tony said.

––––––––––

It turned out my uncle was wrong about one thing: the bank pressed charges on my check-kiting case after all. I had a hearing on the case that August. Tony got me a lawyer who brought up my psychiatric discharge from the Marines. I was ordered to the VA hospital for evaluation. I played it to the hilt. I talked a lot of bullshit. I walked around babbling to myself and told the doctors I heard voices. When they tranquilized me, I didn't swallow the pills and spit them out when I got the chance. When I saw *One Flew Over the Cuckoo's Nest* years later, I thought, *I did that; yeah, that too.* I even escaped from the hospital in my psycho ward blue pajamas. I called home from a pay phone. My father picked me up and took me back to the hospital.

After that the doctors decided I was nuts, definitely—paranoid schizophrenic with sociopathic tendencies. That's the diagnosis they give serial killers and mass murderers. That worried me at first, but then the prosecutors dropped the fraud charges and I was free.

When I later met Dominic and told him that story, that's when he started calling me Sally Ubatz. The whole Crazy Sally thing was a big act and it paid off big-time.

––––––––––

The hits kept on coming that summer. And one thing happened that made me lose my mind and made me think maybe I really was psycho.

In mid-August, six weeks after Rose Marie died, I got a call at the motel from my father. I could barely understand what he was saying, his voice was so faint. He said Joseph had gone clamming that morning and hadn't come home. Carmine said he was out in the water in Great South Bay. He went under and never came back up.

When I got to Bay Shore, there were two plainclothes sheriff's detectives in the house. The kitchen was filled with cigarette smoke. My father was holding a picture of Joe, just like Will with the picture of Rose Marie and the baby. I couldn't believe this was happening all over again.

The cops said that the sheriff's department had run the search all day with no luck. In the morning the Coast Guard was going to continue it. I walked the cops to their cars. "You know that in cases like this," one said, "it's not unusual for the body never to be found." He told me instead of my father because he could see what awful shape he was in.

For three days we heard nothing. My father and stepmother were in deep shock; they smoked, drank coffee, and ate tranquilizers. The house was in a cloud of death.

Finally, on the morning of the fourth day after Joey went clamming, one of the same detectives came to the house. I thought for a second he had good news. He didn't. He just handed me a business card. It said: SUFFOLK COUNTY MORGUE.

Joe's body had washed up on Fire Island. We had to go to the morgue to identify him.

We were all still in a state of shock and we moved like zombies. I helped my father and stepmother out of the house and into their old Plymouth. I got behind the wheel and we drove to the morgue in silence except for my stepmother's soft weeping.

The same sheriff was there waiting for us. He led us into the building and took us down a long hallway to a pair of wide steel doors.

The room was like a well-lighted tomb. It was empty except for a row of chairs; there was nothing on the walls. My father and Sarah slumped into chairs and huddled together. The doors swung open again and a man in a long white coat pushed the gurney into the room. Joe's body was covered by a white sheet.

The orderly pushed the gurney into the room and stopped. The sheriff motioned for me to stand by it.

The orderly lifted the sheet.

Joe's naked body was unrecognizable. His hair looked like it had been hacked by a knife. There were dime-sized lacerations all over his face, legs, arms, stomach, and chest.

I looked at his dead body and felt nothing but anger and hatred. I clenched my fists and gritted my teeth and made a violent moaning sound like a roar.

I went into some kind of trance or blackout where I don't remember how I got there, but I was on the ground, beating my fists on the floor and howling.

For Joseph, there was no problem with the church. He was given a funeral mass, but in a closed casket.

I gave up caring for anything or anyone after that. I knew my family was cursed. Death owned us, lock, stock, and barrel. Death held dominion over the Polisi family and there was nothing we could do about it. My sister was dead at twenty-one; our half brother wasn't even sixteen. We'd never see the baby again, little William, who Rose Marie loved so and who never got the baptism she wanted, who never became my godson.

I was twenty years old. And death was going to get me too. I knew I wouldn't live to see my twenty-first birthday, much less my thirtieth.

I knew the score from then on.

There really was no tomorrow.

Not even my uncle Tony had an umbrella for the shit storm that year. In October, two FBI guys came to the motel. The Kennedys were gone and the feds were back to ignoring the Families and investigating bank robberies. Their blinders were so good they saw Tony and Sonny strictly as bank robbers. The FBI had to know they were connected—kids playing jacks at the curb outside could have told them that. But those agents just didn't give a shit about "organized crime" in those days—and why would they, since there was nothing in it for them. Hoover would just put the file in the trash and their careers in the toilet. All the two who came to see Uncle Tony cared about was the bank collar.

To get it, they punched and slapped my uncle around—two guys working over a fifty-six-year-old man—asking him what he knew about some jug that got knocked over in Queens back in July. They grilled him about Sonny Franzese and his crew of bank robbers. They must have known they weren't going to get anything out of him; they just wanted to humiliate him. Maybe they got off on beating on a guy old enough to be their own father. They were a couple of brute pricks, and I hated all fedora-wearing federal motherfuckers after that.[7]

Tony told them nothing, of course, but they were all over him from then on. The following year, 1967, Uncle Tony and Sonny were indicted, tried, and convicted. That judge was in nobody's pocket. Tony and Sonny got the maximum—fifteen years in prison. It was a lousy break for Uncle Tony to get hit with that much time behind bars so late in his life. If he did a full stretch, he would be in his seventies when he got out. He was always overweight and was not in the best of health when he went in, and I knew there was a good chance I'd never see him on the outside again.

———

By the time Tony went away, my education was complete. He had taught me how to run a gambling and shylock business and, more important, he taught me the importance of being connected and what it takes to succeed in the Life. He introduced me to all the right people; he got it on record with his friends and associates in the Colombo Family that I was with him and that I was okay, that I was somebody who could be trusted.

After he left for prison, I knew that I had lost someone who was more than just a mentor. I said earlier that when I was a kid I suspected

———

7 Jay Robert Nash, *Citizen Hoover: A Critical Study of the Life and Times of J. Edgar Hoover and His FBI.* Rowman & Littlefield Publishers, 1972. This book came out right after J. Edgar croaked. Uncle Tony's in there; Nash uses his grilling by the feds to show the kind of guy Hoover was— uptight if an agent's hair was out of place or his tie was loose but tolerant as hell when his supposedly squeaky-clean G-men physically abused people and routinely violated their civil rights.

and wished and hoped that Uncle Tony was my real father. After all that had happened in the past couple of years, I was more convinced of it than ever. Whenever I got in trouble with the cops and when I got locked on the psycho ward at St. Albans, it was Tony who came to the rescue. When my sister had her baby, it wasn't my father who telegrammed me the news, it was Tony. When Rose died and the priest refused to give her the funeral mass she wished for, it was Uncle Tony who did something about it.

If Tony was my father, it explained a lot of things—like why our stepmother seemed to hate Rose Marie and me, for one. It also might have been the reason our mother left Frank—because it was Tony she loved. But even if she had grown to hate living the lie and hated living with Frank even more, that didn't explain how she could also leave Rose and me and why she didn't take us with her or ever get in touch with us. That's one hurt I have never gotten over.

All the time I was growing up and all the time we spent together, I never asked Tony straight out if he really was my father.

As it turned out, I would only have one more chance to ask him and find out the truth.

CHAPTER FOURTEEN

Sal's Pizza

UNCLE TONY'S CODEFENDANT, Sonny Franzese, held on to his businesses and most of his wealth when he went to prison. Before he went in, he sold his Cadillac—the one Dominic told the story about the following year at the Fireplace, where I first heard Johnny Boy Gotti's name.

Uncle Tony wasn't so fortunate. For all his wiles when it came to staying out of jail his entire career—thanks mostly to his Family's connections in the New York City criminal justice system—when he was convicted and sent to prison on federal charges, he lost everything.

Part of the reason was that he wasn't a made guy like Sonny. Though Tony had been connected to the Family since the 1930s, Joe Profaci never pinned a button on him because he never clipped anybody—at least not that I know of and not on orders, which is what it took to be made. Where Sonny was a captain in the Family with the juice to hire a criminal attorney who wouldn't dare rip him off, Tony was represented by attorneys who did. They fleeced him for everything he had. Tony had to sell his house and all his cars and property, and he lost his beloved motel and the Diamond Horseshoe, which went into foreclosure.

Despite all his troubles and all he had to go through to dismantle his business and leave the Life he loved, Uncle Tony made sure I was taken care of.

In 1966, a few months before his trial began, Tony set me up in business. He rented a little luncheonette and pizza place on Atlantic Avenue in Ozone Park—it was right down the block from where I opened the Sinatra Club five years later. I called it Sal's Pizza. It had a little kitchen, but the joint was just a cover for my start-up gambling operation. Customers came in, had a slice, and placed a bet on the horses or played the numbers.

Even after he went to prison—first to the federal lockup at Danbury, then to the hard-core pen in Atlanta—Tony looked out for me.

In late 1967, when he was still at Danbury, he ran into an old friend in the visiting room—Sammy Cataldo. Sammy was by then a longtime capo in the Colombo Family, and he was there to see his son Dominic, who was in for counterfeiting and securities fraud. Tony remembered Sammy's son from the old neighborhood but hadn't seen Dominic since he was a kid. Dom was thirty-two years old now and a respected Family member himself.

After getting reacquainted that day in the visiting room, Tony and Dominic spent a lot of time together inside, and before Dom was released from Danbury in the spring of 1968, he promised Tony that he'd look me up.

Dom had grown up in East New York and was about fourteen years old when my family moved out of the neighborhood. I was so young when we left that I didn't remember him or any of the Cataldos even though they remembered me.

"We go back," was the first thing Dominic said when he showed up at Sal's Pizza a few days after his release.

The second I saw him I didn't know who he was, but I knew exactly *what* he was—he was dressed to the nines and he moved across the room to shake my hand with that unmistakable Mob guy swagger, confident as Marciano cutting off the ring.

When he said his name and that our families were from the same neighborhood in Brooklyn, I told him I remembered Uncle Tony telling me about his bootlegging days with Dom's father. Dominic said that Tony had told him all about me and the pizza joint and my sports book and how I was just starting out but was a fast learner. All I needed was the right connections and I'd go places. Uncle Tony said we could do business together.

Dom said he was starting fresh himself and asked if I was interested in expanding my business with him as partner; he wanted to build a big book and shylock business. He said he knew all the right people, and because I had a legacy thanks to Uncle Tony, he'd have no trouble bringing me with him into the Colombo Family. If I went with him, we could build Sal's Pizza into a real operation.

I told him I'd think about it, but I really made up my mind on the spot. It's not every day that opportunity comes waltzing in without even knocking. And when it appears in the form of a gangster who stepped out of a movie, dressed in imported silk and wearing that pinkie ring, it was impossible to resist.

Once we started working together, I found out quickly that Dominic wasn't kidding about his connections. Everywhere we went, guys showed him respect. He wasn't a made member yet, but it was common knowledge in our Family that he had served with honor in the Gallo Wars, and that as soon as the books were opened, he would get his button and be made capo.

Business at Sal's Pizza took off after Dominic came in—and I'm not talking about the sale of slices, though they spiked too with all the players coming in to make a wager or pay up in the back room. Our sports book, our track gambling, and our loan shark operations grew fast—and then, in 1969, everything exploded. That was the year the Miracle Mets won the World Series, Joe Namath's Jets beat the Colts in the Super Bowl, and the Knicks made it all the way to the NBA semifinals. We were taking in so much action that we ended up closing Sal's because running the legitimate side of the shop took too much time away from our real businesses.

We sold our last pizza and soda in 1969 and shuttered the whole place.

It was harder than I thought it would be to walk away from Sal's Pizza. All those memories.

The year before I met Dom, another person walked into Sal's Pizza and changed my life. Hers changed too, but not necessarily for the better.

It was in the fall of 1966, not long after we first opened. I was out of town and my father was working the counter one day when an eighteen-year-old girl with long black hair, pale skin, and beautiful dark eyes came in to buy a soda. My father didn't say a word. He just stood there dumbstruck. And then he burst into tears.

The girl said her name was Angela, but my father would have sworn that it was my sister Rose Marie.

This girl could have been my sister's twin. When he told my stepmother about her, he said, "An angel has been sent down to us from heaven."

My father thought that all his prayers had been answered. Angela not only looked like my sister, but she had a brother named Sal who was in trouble with the police. My father couldn't stop talking about her and kept after me until I asked her out.

At that time I was dating a beautiful blond Irish girl named Carol, whose mother used to work the desk at Uncle Tony's motel. Carol was my first real love, and I thought she was the girl I was destined to be with, like my sister wrote in the note she left for me the night before she died.

Angela had the same sweet disposition as my sister. She had a beautiful smile; she was quiet, not a big talker. She was sexy, even. But we really didn't have much in common. She wasn't into the same music I was. I never talked to her like I did with Carol. I didn't love her. But my father sure did.

We dated that fall and winter, but it was really my father and stepmother who courted her. My father thought he had been given his daughter back. Meanwhile, he openly despised Carol—when she called the pizza place and he was there, he told her not to call or come by anymore.

Angela and I got married on my twenty-second birthday, April 30, 1967. We had a big old-fashioned Italian wedding. We rented an American Legion hall, and a couple hundred people came and everyone brought food and wine. Our wedding song was "Strangers in the Night." That pretty much said it all.

We flew to Louisville, Kentucky, for our honeymoon and went to

Churchill Downs for the Derby. It was pouring rain. I bet the favorite and lost. Angela bet the mudder and won.

But the biggest bet she ever made in her life was on me. And that was a loser. In the husband sweepstakes, my wife took a bath.

After we closed Sal's, Dom and I moved our gambling operation to Ervolino's place in East New York. At the same time, my education as a mobster continued, with Dominic taking over where Uncle Tony had left off.

When Dom first started out with the Family, his mentor was a guy named Freddie "No Nose" DeLucia. Freddie lived right around the corner from Ervolino's place, and Dominic had known him all his life. He now enlisted Freddie's help in mentoring me and showing me the ropes.

Freddie was a longtime Profaci Family hit man who'd earned his place in the history of the New York Mob during the Gallo Wars. He and his partner Sally D'Ambrosio were with Snake Persico when they went after Larry Gallo in 1961. First they whacked Gallo's enforcer, a guy named Joe Gioelli who was called Joe Jelly because he was fat and his belly shook like a bowl of it. They took him fishing and killed him on his own boat out on Sheepshead Bay. They shot Jelly, stripped off his clothes, and chopped up his body. They tossed the body parts overboard, but they kept Jelly's clothes. They stuffed his shirt and pants full of rotting fish and made a Joe Jelly dummy.

Later they took the dummy to Red Hook and dumped it on the street near the Gallos' headquarters. The dummy's message was that the Gallos wouldn't see their triggerman anymore because Joe Jelly was sleeping with the fishes.

But before they left the message, they went to a bar in Brooklyn for an arranged meeting with Larry Gallo, who showed up at the Sahara Lounge in Flatbush all alone because his bodyguard, Jelly, happened to be out fishing on Sheepshead Bay that Sunday.

Because New York State still had blue laws in those days, the bar was closed until 6:00 on Sundays. As Gallo stood at the bar having a drink,

Freddie No Nose, Sally D, and Snake Persico stepped from the shadows behind him. Sally looped a garrote around Gallo's neck and started to strangle him. Luckily for Larry Gallo, somebody absentmindedly left the door ajar behind him when he arrived at the bar. As Larry went limp and fell to the floor, a cop walked into the bar through the partially open side door.

When Persico and his guys ran out the front door, they shot the cop's partner and made their escape. Larry Gallo survived and refused to identify his attackers. Nearly eight years would pass before he got his revenge—but by then Gallo himself was already dead and in his grave.

Freddie was a scary and very weird-looking guy, but nobody called him No Nose to his face. He got that name because he was a boxer who got hit in the schnoz too many times. He had a harelip and his head was lopsided from taking so many hits. He even talked weird, like he was gargling, like he took some shots in the throat too. But you didn't fuck with No Nose. Nobody did.

In a fight, Freddie gave as good as he got. He had a deadly punch. I know because he nearly took my head off with it.

In 1968, when I was a rookie and serving my apprenticeship under Dominic and No Nose, I was arrested on a gun charge. I'd already been popped a bunch of times for bookmaking, and each time Mike Coiro got me off the hook. This one time I was leaving my house on a differ-ent piece of work—a payroll heist—and I was carrying a 9mm auto-matic. Too bad for me, there was a crooked Brooklyn detective named Piccone parked at the curb, laying to earn a little cash by busting me for bookmaking. He figured I'd have some betting slips on me, but he found the gun instead—a felony and a much bigger payoff for him.

Since Freddie No Nose was based in Brooklyn, Dom asked him to find out what it would take to get me off the hook. The word came back that Piccone wanted $5,000. Five g's was a lot of money for me at that time. So when I took the money to Freddie, he opened the envelope and counted the bills. There was only $2,000 in there.

Freddie didn't say a word. He just put the envelope in his pocket and punched me in the mouth. He broke my fucking jaw. I wanted to hit him right back, but I knew better. Freddie was an important man in the Family. I was just a wannabe, an outfielder. Plus, I knew I was wrong. I did a stupid thing. I should have greased that cop the full amount. Uncle Tony taught me always to know who to take care of and I didn't do it. I also should have known better than to think that Freddie No Nose would just sit me down and give me a good talking-to when I fucked up. Instead he gave me a wicked shot in the head.

Freddie's lesson worked. I never made a mistake like that again. That punch didn't exactly change my life, but it sure as hell changed the set of my teeth. I never did go to a doctor to get my jaw fixed, and my bite's still fucked-up.

Thank you, No Nose.

Freddie kept the light envelope for himself, and I was left to go on trial on the gun charge. Mike Coiro got me a few postponements and then, in 1970, the cop who busted me, Piccone, was shot and killed by a rape suspect he and his partner had collared. They were booking the guy and he grabbed Piccone's gun and shot him dead. Piccone's partner killed the rapist right there on the spot, in the middle of the precinct house. The charges against me died with Piccone and I didn't have to go to trial after all.

"Sally Ubatz!" Dom said when he heard about Piccone. "You are one lucky-ass motherfucker!"

As for Freddie No Nose, he didn't live to hear the good news. He and Sally D disappeared at Christmastime in 1969. Their bodies were never found, and it wasn't until years later that Dom found out that they were cornered in a bar just like they cornered Larry Gallo back in '61—only no cop came in to save the day. No Nose and Sally D were tortured and killed, and then they were dismembered and fed to the fishes just like Joe Jelly.

Dom took it hard because he came up with Freddie and loved him like a father.

Me, I wasn't too broke up about it.

No Nose and Sally D were considered the last casualties of the Gallo Wars.

When Joe Colombo got shot two years later, it looked like the war was going to start all over again, but nothing happened.

Then, in the spring of the following year, 1972, not long after Johnny Boy Gotti got out of prison and started hanging out at the Sinatra Club—that's when *Il Vulcano* finally blew.

PART THREE

CHAPTER FIFTEEN

Mob Joint Ventures

FEBRUARY 1972

"THAT'S REAL DOPEY," THE Fox said with a straight face when I told him about the meeting Dominic had with Johnny Boy Gotti. "Stand-up guys in a sit-down."

It had only been a little more than a month since we hosted Gotti's homecoming at the Sinatra Club. When he walked in that night he was flat broke and just one of hundreds of soldiers in his Gambino boss Charlie Fatico's wiseguy army. Now he was in command of Fatico's entire gambling operation, a huge Family enterprise that brought in millions a year from bookmaking, loan sharking, numbers games, and dozens of sports betting, horse, and gambling parlors.

Like most of the Mob's old guard, Fatico was fading. He turned sixty-two right around the time Gotti got out of Lewisburg, and he wasted no time starting to groom Johnny Boy as a future Family leader. Charlie himself was the target of an ongoing federal investigation for tax fraud and facing indictment at any time—for him, the future was now and that's why the hurry. He was putting Gotti through a speeded-up training program and test process, using John to settle beefs and have sit-downs with crews in other Families as well as with the Gambinos.

John was a charismatic tough guy who connected with people instantly, and as much as possible he liked to conduct business in a friendly way. One way to do that was to talk about shared interests, and since every mobster's favorite sport was gambling, that was Wiseguy Water-

cooler Topic #1. And because Johnny was in our club practically every
night we were open, he talked up his new favorite hangout—the Sinatra
Club—as he made his rounds throughout the city on Gambino Family
business.

He bantered with all the gamblers and shylocks and crew guys he
met with and told them about our new after-hours club on Atlantic Avenue in Ozone Park where we had a bar and a jukebox and even pussy
on the house for our high rollers. But best of all, we ran high-stakes card
games that went all night and a lot of times into the next day.

Before we knew it, we had every wiseguy with a bankroll fighting
for a place at the tables, and practically all of them were steered to the
Sinatra Club by the greatest rainmaker any Mob gambling joint ever
had—Johnny Boy Gotti.

That's why Dom and John had the stand-up guys' sit-down I told
Fox about—John had brought so much business to the Sinatra Club, we
made him a partner.

Before the sit-down, Dominic cleared it with his boss, Pegleg Brancato. But that was just a formality. Pegleg was acting boss after Joe Colombo got coma'd back in June, but he was really just a surrogate for the
Family's new chief, Snake Persico, who was still in prison. Dom knew
that when Pegleg okayed Fox and me working together back in December that meant Persico had already given him marching orders—he
wanted increased cooperation between the Colombo and the Gambino
Families.

Gotti likewise had the tacit approval of his Family's boss, Carlo
Gambino, to work with the Colombos; he didn't bother to double-
check it with Charlie Fatico. He accepted Dominic's invitation on the
spot.

Dom told me they sealed the deal with a toast. "None of the old-
time bosses would have believed that a partnership like this, between two
families, could work," Gotti said. "This is the first club in the city that is
a true joint fucking venture. *Salut!*"

John's partnership in the Sinatra Club wasn't the only thing on the
agenda at that sit-down, Dom told me. There was another piece of business Dom and Gotti discussed, and it concerned me and the Fox.

On the first night Johnny Boy came into the club back in January, Dom took him into the back room for a private talk before we started playing cards. Dom told me John broke his balls about us jacking one of Tommy Gambino's IDC trucks. So Gotti knew from the day he got out of prison all about our Colombo-Gambino crime team.

Now, at the partnership sit-down, Dom said, Gotti had some ideas about how to improve our action. First, he said we should start using Jimmy Burke's drop instead of Fatico's own warehouse, which was small compared to Jimmy's. Gotti said that Fatico knew Jimmy's operation was the biggest in the city and that he could move any type of swag and get the best price. Charlie didn't care what drop we used as long as he got his percentage.

Gotti said he already talked to Paul Vario, the Lucchese capo who Jimmy was connected to. When John took the idea to Jimmy Burke, Jimmy agreed right away, but he insisted that because Fox and I were basically untested, we should partner up with his best guy, Tommy DeSimone. What surprised Dom was that Gotti agreed—because Dom and everybody else knew that Gotti hated Tommy's guts. Tommy's brother was a Gambino who ratted on Gotti's Family and got whacked for it. Even though Tommy was with a different Family, the Luccheses, Gotti still didn't trust him. Also, Tommy was a loose cannon with a wild temper. But John also knew that Tommy was a very experienced hijacker and a good man with a gun.

I knew Tommy myself; he and my wife Angela were friends in high school and he'd been coming into the club with Jimmy Burke since we opened. So I was all for teaming up with him.

But I had serious doubts about what Fox would say about it, and not only because he agreed with Gotti on everything and there was no reason to think he didn't hate Tommy just as much as his boss did.

There was more to it than that. I'd gotten to know the Fox pretty well in the past few months—that happens between crime partners when you both depend totally on each other. He and Tommy were as different as morning and midnight.

Except for a shared lust and passion to rob and steal and for the perks of our life of crime, these two were opposites in every way.

Foxy was an easygoing guy who was full of laughs and a blast to be around.

Tommy was wound tighter than a coiled snake. He was the kind of guy who looked for the dis in "How do you do?"

Foxy had style—he dressed with real pizzazz. He was only interested in brunettes, but they had to be bright and have character and upbeat personalities. He courted them and treated them with respect.

Tommy was a good-looking guy too, but he dressed like a slob most of the time and he was a garbage dick—he'd fuck any woman who breathed.

Fox had a neat and nicely decorated apartment in Lindenwood Village, a middle-class neighborhood in Queens, right across the highway from Howard Beach, where John and Victoria Gotti and their kids lived in a big suburban house her parents bought for them.

Tommy lived in a dark, dumpy little apartment above Robert's Lounge on Queens Boulevard.

The Fox was street smart as hell and tough as they come. He was six feet, 210 pounds, and strong as a bull. He was a guy you wanted on your side in a fight. He was a skilled boxer and could knock a bigger guy down with one punch.

Tommy was also six feet tall, but he was skinny and weak, about 150 or 160 pounds. He was always looking for a fight, but he never wanted to brawl. He didn't need to because he always had his guns and that's what made him strong—and feared. Tommy DeSimone wasn't a factor with his fists. But Tommy Two Guns was one dangerous motherfucker.

And that's why Jimmy Burke loved Tommy and why Paul Vario valued him and why Gotti agreed to team him with the Fox, who Gotti loved like a son—because he was good with his guns and an expert, stone-cold killer.

I knew Tommy was dangerous and we'd have to watch him like a hawk, but I wanted him on our team because I knew he'd make us stronger.

When I told Fox we were partnering up with Tommy Two Guns DeSimone, it was my turn to be surprised.

"Sounds nice and dopey," Fox said. He immediately saw the advantages of having Tommy with us and didn't say anything more about it.

Right after that, Fox and I got together with Tommy at Jimmy Burke's drop to seal the deal.

It was the beginning of a beautiful friendship—one that would have lethal consequences.

———————

Thanks to Johnny Boy Gotti, the Sinatra Club had become a regular Magic Kingdom for wiseguys. We were doing business like Disney World, the new theme park that opened in Florida in October, the month before we dealt the first hands at the club.

In the beginning, we ran games just one night a week—on Sundays. That game usually broke up around 3:00 or 4:00 the next morning. Now thanks to all the business our new partner brought in, our weekly Sunday night game usually went into Monday afternoon; we added a Wednesday night game that sometimes went twenty-four hours and didn't break up until the wee hours of Friday. We were closed Friday nights because that was when the bosses had their floating games. We opened on Saturday nights too, but that drew mostly nickel-and-dime players because Saturday was the one night of the week Mob guys traditionally went out with their wives instead of their goombahs or *goomadas*.

It was our high-stakes play that made the Sinatra Club a mecca for wiseguys. Social clubs like Charlie Fatico's new Bergin Hunt and Fish Club—which was also in Ozone Park, a short drive from our joint—all had nickel-and-dime games going where a $100 or $200 pot was a big deal. The kind of $2,000 and $3,000 pots we had routinely were unheard-of in those days.

Because social clubs like the Bergin were registered with the city, they were technically open to the public and anybody could walk through the front door—no legitimate people would, but they could. Also they had to keep regular business hours, so by 5:00 or 6:00 on weekdays they were locked up. At our club we admitted who we wanted only and there was no official time that we closed—if there was action, our joint was rocking around the clock.

We still had the nickel-and-dime table up front. At the second table we played a game called 44, where eleven guys could sit in. It was similar to Texas Hold'em; each player was dealt four cards facedown, then you bet as each card was turned over. Once I added the third table, the $1,000 beauty I ordered from Toronto, we had two high-stakes games going at once.

The third table was for the real serious players; that was mostly five- and seven-card stud and five-card draw. That's the table where Jimmy Burke played. When Jimmy was playing poker and he stayed in the game long enough, you could make a side bet that he would win. Jimmy was another guy who brought in a lot of movers and shakers, some of them legit guys he did business with and also a lot of hard-core crooks, like Henry Hill and Tommy DeSimone.

There were a lot of cutthroats who hung out at the Sinatra Club that spring, a lot of guys who would have a lot of blood on their hands before the decade was done. But out of all those button men—including John Gotti—Jimmy Burke was probably the biggest badass in the room. He didn't look anything like Robert De Niro. Jimmy was a giant, a big brawling Irishman. He was in his forties then and he still did some boxing; he had arms like Popeye and he was quick as a fucking cat. He was also smart as hell and he was funny. But he could be a sweetheart one minute and shoot you in the head the next.

Jimmy had a wicked temper—not like Tommy, who was always flipping out for no reason. Jimmy Burke was your thinking hood's killer. He would weigh the pros and cons like he was making up his mind whether to go out for a bite or order in. Then he'd whack a guy and not give it any more thought.

Jimmy had no remorse; he'd kill you and laugh about it later. He had his own place, Robert's Lounge, the joint in *GoodFellas* where the Tommy DeSimone character shoots the kid Spider (played by Michael Imperioli, who later made it big in *The Sopranos*). We used to play cards in the daytime at Robert's Lounge, but it wasn't commercialized like the Sinatra Club. Jimmy didn't provide food or girls.

Down in the basement was where Jimmy buried some guys when he didn't have any other way to get rid of the bodies. He had a bocce court next door to the club. Guys used to say that Jimmy whacked a guy from our Family, a Colombo named Remo who flipped and became a rat. Remo was a good friend of his, but Jimmy killed him so he couldn't testify against him. Jimmy buried Remo under the bocce court. I guess he preferred it to the bar because he didn't have to keep drilling through the basement floor and pouring fresh cement. It was a lot easier to dig up the bocce court.

Jimmy was like two different people—a sentimental family man who had kids of his own and a guy who tortured children. The way I heard it, if he had a beef or if someone owed him money and he had little kids, Jimmy'd go to the guy's house and stuff the kids in the refrigerator and threaten to leave them there unless the guy paid up. That's some sick shit but it worked—the guy always managed to find a way to pay.

Jimmy was another hoodlum who had a shit childhood. His mother was from Ireland and his father was like Fox's—Jimmy never laid eyes on the guy; he had no idea who or what his old man was. He knew his mother but probably wished he didn't. She dumped him in an orphanage and he never saw her again. Maybe that's why he was Oliver Twisted, from growing up in welfare orphanages and foster homes where the parents wanted the city's money and didn't give a damn about the kids in their care.

Jimmy was known as a methodical killer. He only whacked guys for a reason, but once in a while he'd wig out and you wouldn't want to be around when he did. Just ask Jimmy Breslin.

Burke used to hang out at the Suite, the joint Henry Hill owned on Queens Boulevard. Henry, as all *GoodFellas* fans know, was hijacking truckloads of cigarettes with Tommy D and Jimmy back in the early '60s.

One of the legit regulars at Henry's joint was Breslin, the *Daily News* columnist who wrote a lot about the Mob. He used to stop in at the Suite all the time to have a drink. While he was at it, he'd drink in the atmosphere and pick up tips for stories.

Later on I got to know Breslin a little bit from coaching his kid's football team. He was a good guy. He was also a celebrated character around New York—the classic hard-drinking big-city newspaperman. He ran for mayor of New York with Norman Mailer in 1969, the same year his book about the Gallo Wars, *The Gang That Couldn't Shoot Straight*, came out.

None of that mattered to Jimmy Burke. He didn't care if Breslin was the most famous author alive. I doubt Jimmy read Breslin's book, but he must have followed him in the paper, because one night in 1970 he nearly beat Breslin to death right there at the bar in the Suite.

Henry said Jimmy was pissed about a column Breslin wrote about Paul Vario. But it might have been just because Jimmy didn't like the way Breslin was always making wiseguys look like jerks.

Anyway, nobody was sure what was said exactly; all anybody remembers was Jimmy grabbed Breslin by the neck and put a Kid Twist on him: He held Breslin by one hand and twisted his necktie till Breslin turned red and his whole head looked like it was about to explode. Henry thought he was going to break the guy's neck if he didn't strangle him to death first. Then Jimmy yanked down on the poor fucker's tie and started banging Breslin's face on the top of the bar.

Breslin survived. He told people that he had a concussion, but guys who were there said he must have got a skull fracture at least. Henry said all the guys laughed their asses off afterward. They thought Breslin had it coming. I thought it was a lousy way to treat a guy we read every day in the paper. Mob guys aren't the most literate bunch, but where would they be without writers like Breslin telling their stories?

Henry himself tells a great story about something that happened years before he opened the Suite. He and some guys from Paul Vario's crew were out at Idlewild (now JFK) Airport on February 7, 1964. They were there to encourage TWA to hire workers from one of the unions the Luccheses controlled; they were going to trash a couple of TWA's big jets. They almost gave up the plan because there were too many cops and guards around. Then all of a sudden they heard this weird roar of noise like a crowd yelling and screaming and all the security guys ran over to see what was going on. It was the Beatles arriving at the Pan Am terminal next door. When you see film of the Beatles first trip to America, remember that just out of camera range, Henry and his guys are setting off stink bombs inside two or three TWA passenger jets parked at the next terminal over. Henry likes to say the Beatles were his accomplices on that caper.

There was a whole cast of characters at the Sinatra Club who were only vaguely connected but who used to come in all the time. Most of them were guys whose real names I never knew. We just made up names for them, like we did with connected guys like Roundy.

The whole thing about the weird names guys in the Mob had—most of them were made up just to avoid using a guy's real name. You don't want to be overheard at a bar saying John Gotti did this or that; you say Johnny Boy, and only connected guys are going to know who you're talking about.

One gambler who came in a lot and lost a lot more was a guy we called Steam Roller because he got flattened every night he played. He'd sit down for half an hour, lose all his money, and leave flat broke. He'd come back the next night and the night after that. Every time he'd get up from the table and say, "Well, I made my donation to the Sinatra Club." I loved that line, and every night I'd send him home with a couple of cannolis or whatever the caterer brought that evening. Those cannolis were the most expensive dessert known to man.

Bald Vinny was a guy who pushed funny money. He wasn't even thirty and already he'd lost all his hair. Vinny was into all kinds of counterfeiting. He had a connection to a guy who could make a perfect replica of any document—driver's licenses, checks, even passports and birth certificates. When Fox and I wanted to jack a load of merch one time, Bald Vinny got us a perfect duplicate bill of lading. We showed up at the airport with that and they just handed over the merchandise.

Joe Dellamura told me an amazing story about Vinny's printer. This guy made a set of U.S. Court of Appeals documents that ordered a federal prison to vacate the conviction of a bank robber who was doing time. The documents were mailed to the prison, and they let the guy out!

The printer could also make perfect $20 bills. Vinny was allowed to pass bogus bills anywhere but in Queens. He was connected to Paul Vario and that was Paulie's orders. Still, I always kept an eye on Vinny to make sure he wasn't slipping bogus bills into the pot at the Sinatra Club. He was a great actor, very smooth; he used to pass a lot of his twenties at the porn shops in Times Square.

The reason Bald Vinny sold his counterfeit bills to me even though I was in Queens is a funny story. He wanted $1,800 per thousand twenties. He agreed to sell them to me for a favor, if I'd hook him up with a couple of girls. Afterward, the girls said he was really nice but there was something weird about him. I pressed the girls, and they said he had the strangest cock they ever saw—and they saw a shitload of 'em. One girl held up her pinkie and bent it at a right angle. "His cock is crooked like this," she said.

I broke Bald Vinny's balls about it, and he went nuts; he made me swear I'd never tell a soul. In exchange I got first shot at his best twenties every time he got in a new shipment. He gave me a ridiculous price, like $500 for a bundle worth $20,000. He eventually got nervous about the heat and told me not to spread them around the city. I had a lot of great weekends with my girlfriends, going to Boston or Atlanta or Baltimore and spending bags of bogus bills.

Brownie was a local guy who came in. He wasn't connected, just a shady businessman who did a little fencing on the side; he used to bring in swag merchandise that he'd maybe sell to another guy or use it to pay a debt. Squeaky dealt in stolen watches. Frankie Hole in the Head had a weird scar; he moved hot cars. All these guys would get together at the club and make deals, trade and buy and sell their stuff. A lot of times they fed us tips on trucks we might want to hijack or payroll deliveries guys could stick up.

Another local guy and a big debtor was Tommy Block. He worked for a trucking company that delivered wholesale groceries to markets around the city. He'd swipe cases of food and sell them wherever. Tommy borrowed shylock money from the club; when he didn't have any bread, I took canned food. He started with a case of tuna one week; the next week he lost again and brought in a case of aluminum foil; then he lost more and brought in half a dozen cases of peanut butter and a bunch of canned goods. Pretty soon I had filled up a two-car garage I rented to stash swag. I sent a kid over with some merchandise one day and he came back and said, "Sal, the garage is full. I can't get another case in there."

I eventually opened a deli on the ground floor of a building I bought in my neighborhood. We called it the Parkside Superette. It did a nice little business and everything in it was stolen merchandise I got from Tommy Block and any other debtors who didn't have the cash to pay up.

Another guy who used to gamble at our place was Joe the Mailman. He fed us tips on mail trucks. I stuck up one with Dominic and Donnelly and another with Foxy and Funzi. They both turned out to be disasters. We ended up with trucks full of nothing but mail, which was funny because we thought it would be like Butch and Sundance, who were always robbing the U.S. mail and scoring big treasure—the railroad payroll or whatever. We got nothing but bills and a ton of bullshit. Plus we could get busted for stealing federal property. After that, when Joe the Mailman told us about a big score, we told him to forget about it.

What Joe was really good for was credit card plastic. That was a huge business for us. One of the Gambino guys, Rosie Stabile—he lived in my neighborhood and his kid played with my oldest son—almost all he did was plastic, and he made a good living. He had all kinds of scams going.

Joe the Mailman was our supplier. He was real good at stealing credit cards from the post office and off the mail trucks. The credit card companies used to mail 'em out to customers and Joe would grab 'em and sell 'em to us. We'd have dozens of new cards every week.

The great thing about credit cards in those days was there were no magnetic strips on the back and no computers. Cash registers weren't linked to the banks like now. The only way a merchant could check if a card was stolen or suspended was to check a printed booklet that was sent out by the banks once a month. Sometimes they'd call the bank for authorization, but if you kept the purchase under $50 they wouldn't even do that.

I used to have Stevie, the kid who tended bar and helped out at the club, take orders from our customers. Whatever they wanted—toasters, irons, microwave ovens, toys for the kids, clothing, you name it. One guy had a new baby, and he complained that the kid's formula, Enfamil, was real expensive; he had a standard order for us—one case a week. We'd order it over the phone or go to the store and buy it with phony cards and sell it to him at half price.

Joe the Mailman delivered in more ways than one. He had a son, Joe Jr., on the Queens vice squad. Like practically every other cop in town, Junior was on the take. Junior turned us on to another cop, named Charlie, who in turn had access to DMV records. Charlie gave us truck license plate numbers, names and addresses we might need, you name it. Later, when I got into the stolen car business and ran some chop shops in Queens, he had moved up to senior detective. Charlie and I got a nice little business going together.

When *Serpico* came out, you'd have thought it was tavern owners and the guy at the corner store paying off the cops. That's bullshit. It was the Mob greasing everyone's palms. I can't speak for the other boroughs, but in Queens we owned the police department. That's why we got away with doing the unbelievable shit we were doing all those years. Jimmy Burke used to say he loved living in Queens because it was the best place in the world to commit crimes. That's because Jimmy almost single-handedly turned the blue-collar Queens police force into middle-class suburbanites. It was Jimmy who was paying for all their boats and their mortgages and putting their kids through college. They sure as hell weren't doing that on a policeman's salary.

———————————

Many games at the Sinatra Club ended in wild fashion—with Johnny Boy losing a bunch of big pots along with his cool. But one day they ended in a way I'll never forget.

What went down actually happened in the early morning hours of February 29, 1972, a day that wouldn't have been if it wasn't a leap year.

The fact that he was now partner in our club didn't make John any better a poker player than he was the first night he played there and ended up tearing his cards with his teeth and throwing them across the room. Same with his powerful position as head of Charlie Fatico's gambling empire—even Fox joked that making Gotti gambler in chief was like the strikeout king being named batting coach of the Yankees. John still didn't know when to bet, bluff, or fold.

The last hand that night was a round of seven-card stud that turned into a big-money showdown between John and Dom—with me along for the ride. They both had great cards showing, and the way they kept betting, raising each other $300 and $400, then $500 and $600 at a time, I knew they both had strong bottom cards too.

On the sixth card, Dom counted out a thou. So John borrowed $3,000 from the house. While Stevie counted out his chips and wrote him a marker, I went behind the bar for a Coke. I had a stash behind a loose brick next to the fridge where I kept a bankroll, a gun, usually a little coke to give the hookers a toot, and an emergency bag of *babania* if I had to make a delivery to one of my dealers and didn't have time to get back to the apartment where I kept the kilos. I took the money roll and left the gun and the junk.

When I got back to the table, John was pushing chips into the pot. "I see your thousand," he said, "and raise another thousand."

It cost Dom $1,000 and me $2,000 to see our seventh cards.

It was hard to keep my cool when I lifted the edge of that last down card.

The bet was John's. He didn't hesitate a second. He slapped a grand on the table. Dominic saw it and raised it $1,000. It was $2,000 to me.

"I love this game!" I said, and slowly counted out a hundred $20 bills. Then I counted out a hundred more.

Dom and Johnny looked shocked. Then puzzled. I was showing a pair of 5s and a 2.

"What the fuck, Ubatz!" Gotti said. "You can't have four 5s. Foxy had the 5 of spades."

John might have been careless with his tells, but he had a sharp eye and a killer memory.

We had given up on changing cash for chips by that point, and I pushed $4,000 worth of bills into the pot.

Neither of them could afford to fold. Dom wrote a marker and John wrote his second of the night.

There was more than $20,000 sitting in the middle of the table.

Dom and John called me.

"All I got is two pair . . . of 2s!" I turned over my three down cards—all deuces—that gave me four of a kind, beating their full houses. They both had beautiful hands, just not beautiful enough to win. Dom turned over his first two bottom cards—both kings; Gotti did the same—two aces. They both got dealt sure things that turned out to be losers in the end.

At first, Dom looked disgusted. Then he looked pissed off. Then he looked like he was going to take me on a one-way ride to Boot Hill, his place upstate near Beacon where he planted guys. But all he did was shout, "Ubatz, you fucking fucker! You have one lucky big ass!"

That's when I did something stupid.

"It's only paper," I said. I stood up, and cackling like a madman, I used both hands to rake in my winnings.

John grabbed one of my wrists in a vise grip and locked on me with a deadly stare.

"Don't lose your nice ways, Sally," he said, his voice a cold hiss that chilled my balls and churned my gut.

That was a favorite phrase of his I'd heard him use dozens of times. It was his way of telling guys to watch their ass, that they were bordering on disrespect.

But that night he said it with real menace, in a no-mercy voice hard as prison bars. I knew that guys who heard that voice and saw that dead-souls look in his eyes weren't around now to tell about it.

Nobody made a sound. I glanced at Dom, and he looked like he was ready to kill me if Gotti didn't. He was always telling me to not flaunt my cash; we were always flush with it thanks to our secret business. Dom said we had to be as careful about our drug earnings as we would with loot after any big score. Our fellow wiseguys knew even better than the cops to always follow the money. Bragging that tens of thousands of dollars was only paper was a sure way to arouse lethal suspicions in a guy like John Gotti.

John hated drugs, and Dom and I and everybody else in the room knew it because he said it all the time: "Do the smack, get the whack." (Years later, guys in his own crew forced his hand and he ended up taking control of his Family's drug businesses, but in those days he was as opposed to guys dealing as his own Don Gambino.)

Johnny didn't press it. He let go of my wrist and gave me an angry look that said he was as disgusted with himself for losing as he was with my braggart's display.

"Fucking Ubatz!" he said. Then he picked up a card, chewed the corner off it, and got up from the table. He spat out the card wad and cursed me again as he stomped off to the pisser in the back. "Fucking Ubatz!"

I watched my stupid mouth around John after that night, and in the long run it didn't keep us from becoming pretty close friends.

But even though he didn't consciously know about it, my drug dealing caused an underlying tension that threatened our relationship the whole time I knew John. Because without a doubt if Gotti ever found out, he wouldn't hesitate to break off our friendship—with a bullet.

CHAPTER SIXTEEN

Partners in Crime

MARCH 1972

A GENERATION OR TWO LATER they would have called it Jimmy's Big-Box Drop. Burke moved so much swag he used four or five different warehouses around town, but this one—close by the Brooklyn end of the Williamsburg Bridge—could handle enough merchandise to fill Macy's shelves at Christmas. There was room on the floor to park three or four forty-foot tractor-trailers with plenty of space left over for crews wheeling forklifts to unload and stack the cargo from all the trucks at once.

Jimmy had a very efficient, professional operation. He didn't just have guys wipe the trucks down with a bucket of soap and water after they were unloaded. Jimmy made sure they used bleach so that not the faintest trace of finger- or footprints was left and no dog would want to sniff for evidence. When his warehouse guys were finished with a rig, they dumped it where it looked like it belonged and left a single red rose in the cab as a calling card.

Later, when Jimmy realized that trucking companies were painting big numbers on the top of the trailers so helicopter spotters could track a hijacked truck from the air, Jimmy had his guys pour black tar on the roof to cover the markers.

Jimmy was a fucking criminal mastermind.

When Fox and Tommy and I showed up at his Williamsburg drop to plan our first heist, Jimmy commemorated the occasion—the first meeting of the first on-the-record Three-Families hijack crew the New York Mob ever saw—by giving us a present.

It was a truckload of men's suits and ladies' suede jackets all wrapped up with ribbons and bows. Jimmy must have had one of the largest payrolls in Queens County. Besides half the cops in the borough, he had tipsters in most of the trucking companies and cargo warehouses at JFK Airport on retainer. One of them gave up the garment truck—a big-rig Peterbilt with a forty-foot trailer—and Jimmy presented it to us as a gift.

Normally we'd make a couple of dry runs to track and clock the truck as it made its run from the airport to the Garment District in Manhattan. For our inaugural heist, we didn't have to do that. Jimmy gave us the truck number, the time it would get to the airport, the time it would be loaded, and the time it would leave the airport. He even gave us the exact route it would take into the city—from the cargo loading dock to the main gate, then along the Van Wyck Expressway to the Long Island Expressway and into the city through the Queens Midtown Tunnel.

All we had to do was pick a spot to hit it. Since it was broad daylight—it would have been a lot more considerate of the trucking companies to make their hauls at night, but the dispatchers at the airport were strictly nine-to-five guys—we had to watch out for cops, obviously, and nail the truck where there wasn't much traffic. We weren't really worried about some legitimate slob causing trouble—civilians knew better than to mess with armed gangsters—but there was no sense in making the move right out in the open. That ruled out the tunnel and the LIE. We thought about nailing it inside the airport on one of the access roads, but then we'd be stuck in a restricted area if something went wrong. So we did a quick drive-by the morning of the heist and decided to take the truck on the off-ramp from the Van Wyck. Jimmy also provided another important bit of information: The driver would be making his run alone and there would be no armed security riding shotgun in the cab.

We weren't worried about the driver ID'ing us. Fox had brought along his satchel with all our gear, including ski masks and a set of Smith & Wesson handcuffs. Those were to keep the driver quiet and under control once we moved him to the hotski. It was Fox's idea to explain to any hostages that they were cop cuffs so they didn't panic; we told them that all cops have keys that fit, so they wouldn't have to be sawed off their wrists. It gave them a little hope, which was good so they wouldn't freak out. The drivers had to figure that maybe we weren't going to whack them since we went to the trouble of using Smith & Wessons. But of course they were never sure. It gave them something to think about.

Jimmy's information was dead-on. It couldn't have been better timed if the driver had called us and told us himself when he'd be there. We didn't even have to follow him from the airport. We just drove to the exit ramp and pulled over and waited.

When the truck appeared, we spit gravel and got up right on its tail. We followed it up the overpass, and I cut in front of it on the flat and hit the brakes. The driver blasted his horn, pissed off at the lousy driver in the 327. I waved my arm out the window frantic, like I'm having some problem. He hit the air brakes and nearly rear-ended us.

Tommy and Foxy already had their masks pulled down. They jumped out and ran back to the truck. I'm watching as they spring up on the running boards. Tommy's got the passenger door open and aims the gun at the guy's head; the driver's staring at that while Fox yanks open the driver's side door and shoves him aside. Tommy grabs the guy and shoves the gun in his ribs.

The diesel stalls. But Fox knows trucks from the years he worked in Fatico's drop. He smashes the switch box under the dashboard and crosses the wires. He's got that big rig rolling in less than a minute.

I take the right at the light and lead them four or five blocks. Fox gets in front of me and picks a spot. He pulls the truck over. I pull in front. Tommy and Fox both have their ski masks off now. I see Tommy talking at the driver as he walks him to the hotski. Tommy's got that crazy grin on his face, and I know the driver must be shitting his pants. Tommy shoves him in the backseat, cuffs him, and tapes his mouth. Tommy gets in the front seat and sits sideways. His left arm is draped casual-like over the back of the seat. He's got a gun in his hand pointed at the driver's balls.

"I was just tellin' him something I only tell people who can't ever repeat it," Tommy's saying. "You know why they can't repeat it? Because I make sure they can't."

I catch the guy's eyes in the rearview; I know Tommy told him how many guys he whacked. It's a number even I don't know. "Don't worry, buddy," I say. "Keep cool and you'll be all right." It was the good cop–bad cop schtick we planned. It was an act, but with Tommy you never knew.

We find a phone booth and Tommy calls Jimmy's wife, Mickey. All he says is the pickup has been made. Mickey calls Jimmy at the drop so he'll have everything ready so Fox can pull right into the warehouse without hitting the horn or ringing any bells.

While Fox drives to the drop, Tommy and I spend the next three hours driving around Brooklyn and Queens with the truck driver bound and gagged in the backseat.

Later we stop and buy the guy coffee and cake. Tommy's not trying to scare the driver at this point. He takes off the tape and he even unlocks the cuffs so the guy can drink his coffee.

Our hostage says he's got to pee, so we drive to a park and we walk him into some bushes. He thinks we're going to whack him in there. Tommy reaches into his jacket. The guy is ready to run, but I'm right behind him. I grab his arms and hold him. Tommy pulls out his wallet and takes out a $100 bill and stuffs it in his shirt pocket. The guy's knees buckle and I hold him up.

We tell him we're not going to kill him as long as he doesn't do anything stupid. We tell him to give the cops a description of two guys who look nothing like us. "Who's your favorite ballplayer?" Tommy says. The driver says Willie Mays. "Yeah," Tommy says, "tell him one guy was a spittin' image of Mays. The other guy looked like Shaft."

Finally it's time to get back to Jimmy's drop. We cut the guy loose in Jamaica. There's a tunnel that runs under the Long Island Railroad. We let him off in the middle of the tunnel. He was the happiest man alive. Because that's what he was—alive.

———————

By the time we got back to Jimmy's drop, the truck was unloaded and some of the merch was still in big packing boxes stacked neatly on Jimmy's own forklift pallets. Most of the boxes were open and their contents spread out on long worktables. John Gotti and Charlie Fatico were both there along with Fox and Jimmy, and they were all standing around the worktables that were covered with hundreds of articles of men's clothing. I didn't see any of the high-dollar ladies' suede jackets listed on the bills of lading, so that explained the unopened boxes. Charlie knew he could get a top price for those; the men's clothes were all the latest fashions and he'd get a good price for those too, but there was enough that he wasn't worried about the guys taking a few for themselves. Charlie even picked out a couple of suits himself.

Everything on the tables was made of polyester; there were suit jackets, most with bright patterns, loud-colored shirts, and pants with wide bell-bottoms.

It was crazy the clothes we walked around in those days. The bell-bottoms were all cuffed; the suits were in all kinds of stripes and checks and loud plaids; they had huge wide lapels and pocket flaps with buttons on them.

We were the gang that couldn't dress right.

I knew that Fox wouldn't be caught dead in any of those duds, but Johnny and Charlie and Jimmy each had a pile of clothes in front of him. While I was looking the stuff over, I noticed Tommy picking out a blue suit with a light checked pattern. As soon as he did, Johnny walked over and grabbed it right out of Tommy's hands.

"I already got one a those," Gotti growled. He had the exact same suit on top of his pile of clothes.

Tommy just stood there in shock and watched Gotti carry the suit to the far end of the table. He picked up a pair of metal cutter shears and methodically cut the suit into little pieces.

When he was done, he scooped up the pieces, walked back to Tommy, and dropped them on the floor in front of him. "Nobody wears the same suit as John Gotti," he said.

Then he turned away and started sorting through the clothes, looking to add to his pile.

Tommy just stood there staring at Gotti's back while Fox and Charlie and I fell out laughing.

But we stopped when we realized Tommy was about to blow a gasket.

His face was beet red and he was snarling and trembling with rage. He had his jacket unbuttoned and his hands on the grip of each of the pistols he carried in his waistband.

"Don't fuckin' do it!" Jimmy said.

John finally turned around in time to see Tommy stalking out.

"I was just fuckin' with him," John said, a satisfied smirk on his face.

I don't think any of us had the least bit of doubt that had it been anybody but Gotti, Tommy would have ventilated the guy on the spot.

After that first heist together, Fox and Tommy and I were established as a serious heist crew. The bosses respected us, and we looked forward to making our next move.

The three of us knew we could work together, but we never became true crime partners. As soon as Fox and I started together back in December, we became instant blood brothers. A deeper kind of friendship develops once you become crime partners, one that means you trust the other guy with your life. Everybody knows what it's like to get let down by a friend, but chances are when your crime partner is the friend you're letting down, someone ends up dead.

Fox and I knew we had each other's back. That's what being crime partners was all about. But with Tommy you never knew when you could *turn* your back.

I said before they were night-and-day opposites; I said how Fox was a dandy dresser while Tommy couldn't give a shit how he looked; how Fox had a nice two-bedroom apartment he fixed up and cared a lot about and Tommy lived the low life in a dingy place above Jimmy's bar. But it went way deeper than that.

Fox didn't just dress snappy; he was fanatical about his threads. The second bedroom in his apartment wasn't any kind of guest room; there was no bed, no furniture. It was just an enormous walk-in closet.

He had fifty or sixty suits, and you couldn't count the Egyptian cotton shirts and tailored Italian slacks. He had drawers full of the finest handkerchiefs, drawers full of silk underwear. But what he had more of than anything else was shoes. He had so many that he could wear a different brand-new pair every day of the year and never wear the same ones twice.

He had all that footwear not because he had a fetish but because until he started robbing and stealing, he wore cardboard shoes and stuffed newspaper in them to plug the holes; he started every day with damp socks because he had only one pair when he was a kid and washed them every night. His father pulled a Rose Belviso and walked out on him just like my mother walked out on me, before Fox could get a memory of what he looked like. His mother raised him and his sister on welfare and food stamps and dressed them in rags.

Fox's life was saved by crime. He dropped out of school as soon as he turned sixteen, and he shoplifted and stole cars and did burglaries so he could buy clothes for his sister and put food on his mother's table. The neighborhood he lived in, East New York, was run by the Fulton-Rockaway Boys street gang. It was like a scale model of the Mob. They had their own extortion and shylock businesses; they loaned money and charged vig, and kids who didn't pay on time got the shit beat out of them.

And just like the Mob, they frowned on independent operators on their turf. So Fox joined the gang and soon caught the eye of the Boys' former leader, Johnny Boy Gotti, who was by then working for Charlie Fatico.

John had a shit childhood too. He was one of something like eleven kids and his parents couldn't afford to feed even one. He saw a lot of himself in Fox and took him under his wing and eventually brought him into Charlie's gang at the Club.

That's how Fox got connected and why he revered John Gotti like a father.

Tommy, by contrast, was born connected; he came from a long line of top mobsters. His grandfather and his father's brother succeeded each other as bosses of the Los Angeles Mafia. He had lawyers, doctors, and even a priest in his family, but most of his uncles and brothers went into the Family business. When Angela knew him in high school, Tommy lived in a nice house in Ozone Park and never wanted for anything.

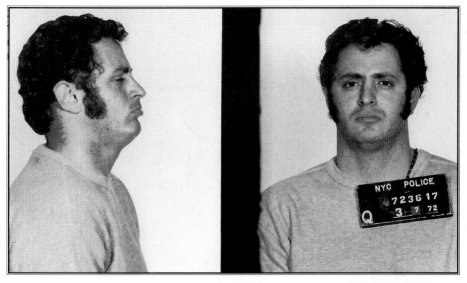

Sally Ubatz, 1972.

I was ring bearer and Rose Marie was flower girl at our father's second wedding.

The only photo I've ever seen of my mother. She's the woman in the background bending over the baby carriage; the newborn she is tending to is me. A former showgirl, she bleached her hair two years later and hoofed it out of my life for good. That's my father, Frank in the foreground, holding my sister, Rose Marie.

Looking very much the tough guy gangster he was, Uncle Tony was in his early forties when he posed with me and Rose Marie and our half brother Bobby—Rose and I weren't the first children our mother abandoned; she dumped Bobby before we were even born.

As far as his neighbors knew, Uncle Tony was just another successful Long Island real estate developer.

My beautiful and gifted sister, Rose Marie, was my angel in life, and in death.

At seventeen, campaigning for Number One in 1963, the year I should have graduated from high school, but didn't.

In 1963 I found myself in Marine boot camp instead of in line to get my diploma. I would later put my Marine muscle to lucrative use as a loan shark.

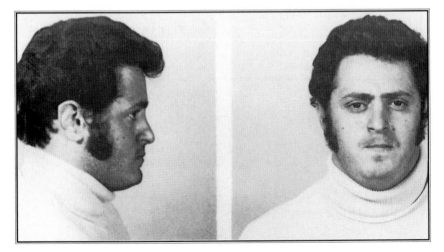

REGENT THEATRE
STUDENT IDENTIFICATION CARD
SCHOOL TERM — 1965-1966

This Is To Certify That The Undersigned
Student
Signature .. Pohisi ....
Is A Student In My Class At

Name of
School ....B.S.J.H..... Age. 14

Teacher's
Signature ....

GOOD ONLY FOR STUDENTS AGES 12 thru 16 YEARS

My half brother Joe's school ID, issued shortly before his body washed up on
Fire Island during my summer of hell in 1965.

Booked for bank robbery in 1972—my taste for white turtlenecks proved my undoing.

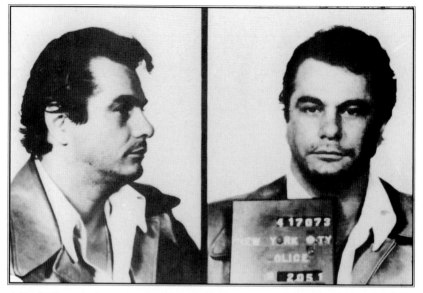

John Gotti, around the time he was arrested for the murder that punched his ticket.

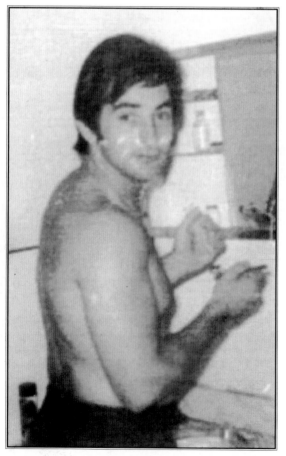

He coulda been a contender: Fox Jerothe, my crime partner, best friend, and blood brother, in 1972.

The Brunetter the Better: The Fox squires one of his beauties from the legitimate world.

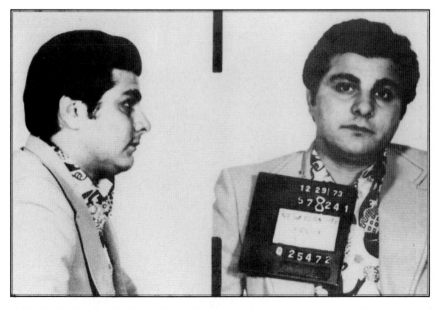

John Gotti's brother Genie—he's the Bergin crew stalwart who introduced me to Fox at the Sinatra Club on Thanksgiving weekend 1971.

Peter Zuccaro test drives one of my motorcycles a few years before a pair of armored car robberies he pulled led prosecutors to launch an investigation that led to John Gotti's first racketeering trial—and ultimately his fall.

Crazy Sally died along with most of my friends from the Sinatra Club. Sal Polisi survived. I'm not sure how or why. Frankie said it best: "That's Life."

Tommy was what today they call entitled. Only Tommy felt entitled to everything he robbed. If anybody got in his way or pissed him off, he felt entitled to blow him away.

But more than their backgrounds and their clothing and lifestyles, the thing that really set Fox and Tommy apart and put them on a collision course—the thing that forged their destinies—was their attitude toward women.

Fox adored all women, and if they were young and pretty and they had a style of their own and—most important—if they were brunette, he would romance and charm and seduce them. Fox wasn't just a ladies' man; he was a true romantic. If he liked someone, he courted her, gave her gifts, made her feel like she was the most beautiful and intriguing woman on earth. Some women fell hard for the Fox, but they all knew what he was—a gangster—and they knew he was never in their bed to stay. But while it lasted they had the time of their lives.

Foxy got his name because that's what all the girls called him when he was a kid. He always had a powerful effect on women of all ages. They either wanted to fuck him or mother him.

Fox loved my wife's mother, who was like the big mama for all the guys. In summer she hosted barbeques at her bar, the Parkside, every weekend for my family and the Cataldos and all our friends. Half the Colombo Family would be there, and all the guys would go to the Parkside after softball games to drink beer.

Fox called Angela's mom Mother-in-Law, and he always brought her a gift when we went to her house. She was twice his age at least, but she was flirting with him one minute and playing mama the next. She worried about what a spendthrift Fox was, how he always blew every cent he stole on clothes and jewelry and presents for his girlfriends.

She used to tell him, "You should save your money for a rainy day, Foxy."

"It's not raining now," he'd say. "And now's all we got."

Tommy's attitude toward women was as far from Fox's as hell was from heaven. Tommy was worse than me. I was a cheating husband, a serial seducer, and a whoremonger—but as much as a guy who pays women to blow him six times a day can be, I was discerning. And I don't just mean a woman had to be blond and she had to be pretty and have a great body to turn me on. That was all true, but if a woman was nasty, foul-mouthed, or rude, if she was a drunk or a junkie or a thief or a liar, I wasn't interested and wouldn't waste my time.

But Tommy, he didn't care. He wanted to fuck any woman who moved—in fact he'd screw them if they couldn't move and were passed out drunk. Tommy also did something I never did and I'm positive Foxy never did either. When Tommy was done fucking a woman, he liked to slap her around

I'm not judging. I'm just saying the way he was and I'm saying it because Tommy's attitude toward women began to disgust and repel Foxy, and Tommy in turn started mocking Fox's spiffy clothes and his boyish grin and his whole every-day-is-Valentine's-Day approach to women, whose purpose in life, as far as Tommy was concerned, was to get guys laid.

Basically Tommy got to seeing the Fox as a big pussy.

Fox and Tommy got along great at first, but once they started to spend a lot of time together, they grated on each other and they both liked to goad the other guy, Tommy especially.

As much as Foxy adored women, there was one he loved above all others—his sister, Patricia. With the exception of his mother, he loved her more than any woman alive. To him she was a precious jewel that by the opposite of a miracle ended up in the shit world they were both born in. She was purity and everything beautiful.

Patricia turned eighteen in 1972, and she was already a strikingly pretty—and dangerously shapely—young woman.

Because he and Patricia never had a father, Fox saw it as his job to do what a father should do for his daughter: protect her and look out for her. Fox knew his world, the world of the Mob, and that Life was no place for his sister. He did everything he could to protect her from it. He wanted for his sister what mine wanted for me. He wanted her to fall in love with a legitimate working stiff nine-to-five guy and live happily ever after.

The last guy on earth Fox would want to see his sister with was Tommy DeSimone.

Somehow Tommy sensed that, and whenever he wanted to wind Fox up, all he had to do was needle him by saying how hot his sister was. Fox took it in stride at first. "Dream on, Tommy," he'd say.

But before too long, Tommy's ball breaking about Patricia began to really get to him.

———————

Soon after the day Tommy came this close to plugging John Gotti for cutting up that suit from our first Three Families crime team heist, Fox and I got another chance to see our new partner practice his anger management skills.

It happened right around the time *The Godfather* premiered in New York, in the middle of March 1972. I remember because the night before we were told that we weren't allowed to see the movie that every mobster in the city had been looking forward to for months. Guys were into it because we all grew up on gangster movies and this was supposed to be the greatest of them all. And this was a gangster movie about *us*—the New York Mob, a movie about Italian gangsters by Italians and starring Italians. We all loved Brando ever since he played the biker gang leader in *The Wild One*. So the fact that the star of the picture wasn't Italian didn't bother us at all.

Tommy, Fox, and I were in the middle of a card game with Gotti and Quack Ruggiero at the Sinatra Club, and we were all talking about the movie when Johnny interrupted and said, "Forget about that flick. Charlie told me to spread the word. From Don Carlo himself. Nobody goes to that fucking movie." He said it was the decision of the whole Commission. "No made guys, no connected guys, nobody in this Life goes."

"Fuck that," Tommy said. "I'm goin'."

"Me too," I said. "What, are they gonna whack us for seeing a fucking movie?"

"Nobody's goin', not you and nobody else. That's it. Period. We ain't talking about it no more."

It sounded like bullshit. When we were growing up, the church announced which movies you could see and which you'd go to hell for seeing. What was this? La Cosa Nostra Legion of Decency?

We bitched and complained but we followed orders and did not see *The Godfather* when it first came out.

That game broke up around 9:00 the next morning. It was freezing cold and I invited Fox and Tommy over to my place. When they got there, Tommy didn't have an overcoat on and his teeth were chattering, but that might not have been just from the cold. We were all popping pills that year. Tommy was into coke even back then, so he was probably snorting that shit too. Fox and I used trucker pills, Dexedrine, to stay up a lot of times. Those were the only drugs I ever took on any kind of regular basis.

I promised the guys hot chocolate to warm up, but I also wanted to show them some new pistols I had just bought.

I had a no-guns policy at home just like at the Sinatra Club. I did keep that one piece stashed in my hiding place behind the bar in case of trouble at the club. We reserved the right to pat guys down, but we didn't make a big deal of it. If they had a piece when they came in, we asked them to stash it in their car while they were in the club. Most guys understood and they respected the rule.

It never occurred to me to pat down Tommy when he came into my house.

I usually kept my own arsenal stashed next door in a locked cabinet in my in-laws' basement, but that morning I had those two new pistols hidden down in my basement.

We had a wood-burning stove in the living room. It was toasty in there, and Tommy and Fox and I were drinking hot chocolate like three ordinary wholesome legitimate guys. I told them about the guns, and I took them down to check them out. Tommy was obsessed with guns. He had a huge collection of them, a lot of throwaway Saturday night specials but also some real fine pieces. He and his brother soundproofed a room in his brother's basement and they had a regular target range down there. Tommy liked to keep his shooting sharp for the day his dreams came true and he got to do a hit on assignment for Paul Vario and get his button with the Luccheses.

The pistols I had were two 9mm Walthers, the automatics that the CIA used. They were great guns, and Tommy wouldn't let go of them. "Sally," he said, "you gotta let me take these to my brother's. Just to try 'em out. I'll bring 'em back."

I made sure he understood that it was just a loan and let him have the pistols. We went back upstairs to the kitchen and he was carrying the guns. I told him to get them the fuck out of sight. Then he opened his coat and I saw he was packing. He had a snub-nose .38 and another automatic. I told him to put that shit out in the car before my wife saw it, and Fox and I went back into the living room while Tommy did as I asked.

A few days later, Fox called when I was in the shower. He left a message with Angela. He said he and Tommy were coming over to pick me up in about an hour.

They got to my house, and Fox had a big box of candy for Angela.

There was always tension in the house between Angela and me, and I liked it whenever Fox came over because Angela would never start in on me in front of him.

But that day she walked into the kitchen right after Fox and Tommy arrived and she didn't say a word and she ignored Fox and his box of candy. She just walked over to the kitchen closet, opened it, grabbed a broom, and started beating Tommy over the head with it.

"You dirty son of a bitch! You thoughtless bastard!" she's screaming as she chases him around the room whacking him with the broom. Tommy doesn't know what the hell is happening.

Fox is laughing his ass off. "That'll teach you to mess with Mrs. Ubatz!" he says.

I stepped between them and got hold of my wife; she was huffing and puffing and shaking with anger.

It turned out that Tommy hadn't put the guns out in the car that day. He put my Walthers in his belt and stashed his own pieces in the broom closet, where Angela found them later.

Tommy was truly apologetic. I never saw him say he was sorry to anybody, and here he was, Tommy Two Guns, a guy who scared the shit out of half the wiseguys in Queens, begging her to forgive him, promising never to go anywhere near her with a gun ever again.

For the second time since we teamed up, Fox and I had seen our crew partner back off from a situation that could have proved deadly. If Tommy had plugged Johnny Boy that day at Jimmy's drop, our Gambino-Colombo-Lucchese partnership would have ended in a Three Families bloodbath, with Fox gunning for Tommy and me having to stop Jimmy from stepping in, which he no doubt would do to prevent Fox from killing his friend.

And if Tommy had struck back at Ange, or—since it was unlikely that he was honoring my no-weapons-in-the-house policy and was probably packing that day too—had he pulled a gun on my wife in her own kitchen, I would have beat him bloody if Fox didn't step in and deck him first.

That Tommy kept his cool bode well for the future of our partnership.

But the happy ending in my kitchen that day was torpedoed by the feeling I got when I saw the ferociousness of Angela's rage and realized that the real source of her anger and frustration wasn't Tommy at all.

The person she really wanted to beat bloody with her broom was me.

CHAPTER SEVENTEEN

Blond Ambitions

THAT COLD SNAP IN mid-March was the last blast of winter we had that year. Spring rolled in before the month was out, and the Fox was eager to celebrate the new season by wining, dining, and banging some hot new hens. All winter we had been spending some of our free nights at Sebastian's, where all the airline stewardesses hung out. Those stews were all young and pretty, most of them were single, and all of them were looking for adventure. For them, a couple of gangsters with money to burn and exciting tales of the big city to tell were irresistible. Sebastian's was a swanky henhouse full of beautiful chicks, and the Fox and I never left there without a couple on our arms.

And that's why Fox couldn't understand it when I begged off a couple of times when he was champing at the bit to drive up to Tommy Argo's place in Forest Hills and see what the evening had to offer. When I told him why, he went ballistic.

The great thing about the stews at Sebastian's for Fox and me was that they all came in one of two flavors—blond and brunette. Fox always said that when it comes to women, "the brunetter the better." Me, I only had eyes for the blondes. That was good because it meant we never fought over the women we met and at the same time we avoided the second biggest source of danger facing any two partners in crime. Number one was violent death; number two was woman trouble.

One of the hottest blondes I ever met at Sebastian's wasn't a stew. The bad news was she was taken. She was Manny Gambino's mistress, Beverly.[8] Manny was Don Carlo's nephew; his father was Gambino's brother Joe. He ran the Family's loan-sharking business in Manhattan. He was rich enough to support his wife and kids and his mistress Beverly, who lived in high style in a house he bought for her. Manny must have had a strong understanding with his wife, since he had dinner with Beverly at Sebastian's practically every night.

Beverly was a stone-cold knockout. She was vivacious and more than pretty, with blond hair and big beautiful eyes and a great smile and an all-in laugh. She was smart as hell, and she was funny, but what got me most was she had long, shapely dancer's legs.

I developed a major crush that turned into a real fixation when I found out she was a professional dancer who worked in the chorus line in big Broadway shows. I didn't need a shrink to figure out that on some level she reminded me of my mother, Rose, who danced with the Rockettes and who was blond and had legs that my Uncle Tony was still rhapsodizing about twenty years after she used them to hoof it right out of my life.

I knew there was no hope for Beverly and me ever hooking up. One reason was that she was no run-around floozy; I think she really loved Manny, and the feeling must have been mutual because I never saw him in Argo's joint with anyone but her.

The other reason was that Beverly seemed to have a crush of her own—on Foxy. She was always flirting with him and telling him he should get over his thing about dark-haired women because blondes were better in bed. She used to give Fox a sexy look and say, "You don't know what you're missing." That drove me nuts because I did know what I was missing—her. Beverly gave Fox endless shit, but she also fixed him up with her girlfriends—she knew a lot of gorgeous brunettes. I actually used to think she knew how I felt about her be-

---

[8] Not her real name.

cause she never once offered to fix me up with any of her blond girl-friends.

I think Fox envied me a little bit because I had a wife and kids at home—and I know he thought the world of Angela. But he had no problem with me messing around with other women. That came with the territory; it's what gangsters do.

But Fox could never understand why I would disrespect Angela and risk losing my kids by banging hookers. The Fox hated whores. He said they dishonor women, and by fucking them I was disrespecting my wife.

That's why Fox went nuts when I told him why I wasn't hitting Sebastian's with him that spring as often as we had been. The reason was I had fallen hard for a blonde, and not just any blonde. Jane was a hooker and the madam—JP—who supplied the girls I had set up in my secret apartment on Liberty Avenue.

"What are you doing with that bitch?" Fox said when I broke the news. "She's nothing but a fucking whore!"

I told Fox I was careful, and what Angela didn't know wouldn't hurt her. He said if I really believed that I was more *upazzo* than he thought.

"They've got six senses, Ubatz, " Fox said. "They've got antennae. She probably already suspects you fuck around on her. That's why she's so pissed off at you all the time. Sooner or later she'll find out for sure about the girls you bang. You can handle that; she knows the score and she'll learn to live with it. But if she finds out you're fucking that rubber hole, that's it, she's gone."

I told Fox he was overreacting, there was no way my wife would ever find out.

"Yeah?" Fox said. "Wait and see."

The only other guy in that Life who hated whores as much as the Fox did was John Gotti, which partly explains Fox's attitude, because he agreed with just about everything Johnny Boy said. Of all the regular high rollers who hung out at the Sinatra Club, Fox, Gotti, and Willie

Boy Johnson were the only ones who didn't dip it at my Liberty Avenue hooker shack.

Fox hated hookers because he was a romantic at heart. I think Johnny hated them because he was a traditionalist when it came to the Mob; he played by the rules because he wanted to get ahead. For the same reason he despised drugs, he despised hookers. Don Carlo Gambino declared both of them off-limits, so that was that as far as Johnny Boy was concerned. Gambino was Sicilian, and he rose in the Mob when Lucky Luciano was boss of bosses. My uncle Tony told me that Luciano was busted on trumped-up charges that he was running a massive prostitution ring; that's the case that got him put away in prison in the 1930s and eventually deported back to Italy. According to Tony, the Mob got out of the prostitution racket after that.

John hated hookers, but he had plenty of ladies on the side. And Fox never had a relationship with a woman that lasted more than a few weeks—and not a day went by in a year that he wasn't seducing or dating or banging one beautiful brunette or another.

But Willie Boy was different from them and every other wiseguy I ever knew. Willie Boy was rarer than a mobster with a PhD—he was a gangster who was also a happily married man who never cheated, never had a girlfriend on the side, and actually loved his wife.

———————

When Fox got on my case about Jane, I told him, "Forget about it. I know what I'm doing. I'm in control here."

But the truth was I wasn't really. I was obsessed. I had fallen head over in heels in love with a bisexual dominatrix whose real name I didn't even know.

When I first met JP that fateful night at the Midtown hotel after Thanksgiving, it was like instant intoxication. The way she moved like a cat in that skintight black dress; the way she talked, deep and slow and ice-cold, with a hint of a Southern accent; the way her perfume smelled like gardenias and the way she coolly looked me over and smiled without a trace of fear, like she knew me and found the fact that I was a gangster only mildly amusing—it didn't make me want her. It made me feel like I had to have her, maybe just to prove I could.

Once JP and I began our business relationship and I started paying her girls to give on-the-house blow jobs to our best regular customers as a perk for doing their gaming at the Sinatra Club, I didn't see or speak to their madam again. All scheduling and payments were made through Lisa, who was the hostess of JP's Manhattan brothel. Once I got to know Lisa, I found out that she was also JP's lover.

That didn't stop Lisa from getting it on with me every chance we got. She loved sex and she had a jones for high-quality heroin and cocaine, which I had plenty of.

Back then coke wasn't anywhere near as popular as it soon became. Dom's suppliers were just starting to bring it in along with smack, and he gave me free samples to spread around. It was a good way to build future business.

I saved some of my coke samples for Lisa and in exchange she gave me all the sex I wanted. She also hooked me up with the hottest girls she knew.

I liked Lisa and we had great sex, but whenever we got together I always managed to steer the conversation around to her boss. When I told Lisa how JP wouldn't give me the time of day when I first met her, she said that was because JP not only owned her business and ran her brothels, she also turned tricks as a dominatrix. Her clients were men, but she didn't fuck them, Lisa said. She humiliated her tricks, had them crawling around on all fours licking her boots, but she wouldn't let them touch her. Her only real sexual relationship was with Lisa.

One night in December, Lisa asked me if I could get JP some ID, a driver's license and birth certificate. Thanks to Bald Vinny, I knew it would be a snap. I also figured it would clear up some of the mystery about JP, but when I asked Lisa what name she wanted on the ID, she told me to make it for "Jane Parker." I had no idea if that was her real name. I still don't know.

Vinny delivered the documents—a full set of absolutely legit-looking IDs, including a driver's license, a birth certificate, and a Social Security card, all in the name of Jane Parker—within a week, but before I gave them to Lisa, Fox and I did another little piece of work for her.

She had told me about this pimp who worked Eighth Avenue near the Port Authority Bus Terminal in Manhattan. She said that he was shaking down some street hookers who were friends of hers. When I told Fox that this guy liked to beat up the girls and torture them by strapping them with the buckle end of a belt and burning them with cigarettes, Fox forgot all about his disdain for hookers. As far as Fox was concerned, anybody who treated women like that deserved the ultimate punishment. "Let's kidnap the fuck and kill him," he said.

I said there was no sense in risking a murder rap. Instead, Fox and I drove into Manhattan one night and went looking for the pimp. Once we spotted him, I got out of the car and put on a drunk act. I stumbled around like I was out of control and told him I needed money to get home. I told him to give me a dollar. He told me to fuck off. "Come on, big shot," I said, "One lousy dollar."

He told me to get my ass out of his sight before he put a boot up it. I started to slouch away, but then I wheeled on him and kicked him square in the balls. He doubled over and dropped to his knees on the sidewalk. I pulled out a set of brass knuckles and I beat the pimp bloody. I got on him so bad Fox had to pull me off him. I told the pimp that we were from Brooklyn and if he ever fucked with any of his girls again we were going to come back and kill him. Then I gave him one last kick, and we left him there bleeding on the curb.

When I called Lisa to tell her I had the ID, she said one of her hooker friends told her that the pimp crawled into the back of a cab after we got through with him and hadn't been seen since.

The next day when I brought over the ID, Lisa had a surprise for me—JP was there to thank me for the ID and for the favor I did for Lisa by taking care of that pimp. She asked what she owed me for the ID.

"You don't have to pay me a dime, and you don't have to consider yourself in my debt," I said. "I did you a favor as a friend of Lisa's. But if you insist, you can repay me by turning me on to as many gorgeous blondes as you've got. All I need is six blow jobs every day."

JP laughed and said that would be no problem.

"One more thing," I said. "If we're going to be friends, I don't want to call you JP all the time. It sounds like something an office schnook calls his boss."

"Call me Jane like it says on the driver's license."

"Is that your real name?"

"It's close enough," she said.

After that, Jane and Lisa and I saw a lot of each other. They both liked the high-quality coke I carried around with me, and they both had a jones for kicks almost as strong as I did.

A typical night started at Jane's apartment on 36th Street—an amazing place with three bedrooms and a fourth she used as an office. The apartment was filled with Tiffany lamps, Wallace Grane Baroque sterling silverware laid out on the dining room table, and Chippendale claw-foot furniture. The bathrooms had gold-plate-framed mirrors, antique bathtubs with claw feet, and black-and-white photos of Jack London framed on the walls. She had walk-in closets with oak shelves and jasmine-scented candles surrounding a golden clock. The master bedroom was like a sultan's chamber—only the sultan in this case was a very successful madam who ran two brothels and a high-end call girl service.

Jane usually made us all drinks and put on music, and the girls would do a few lines of coke. We would sit around the living room for a while talking and maybe dancing. Before long, Lisa and I would start making out, and more often than not we'd end up getting it on right there on the couch. Jane didn't mind that her girlfriend was making it with me; she knew that when Lisa got high she liked a nice hard dick in her mouth. I was the lucky guy who got to put it there.

While Lisa and I were going at it, Jane always kept right on talking or dancing or just sitting there sipping champagne. After we screwed, Lisa and I got dressed and the three of us went out clubbing. One night we took a cab across the George Washington Bridge and Lisa gave me a blow job in the backseat. I don't know if I came in New York or New Jersey.

We had so much fun together I even did a hit of coke with them now and then, but I always made sure I never did enough to lose interest in sex, which is what happens to guys who overdo it. Whenever the girls laid out one line too many, I told them, "No thanks. There's a million limp dicks in the Naked City and I ain't one."

We went on like that for a few weeks until one night in February, when everything changed. The three of us got stone drunk. We were in Jane's living room on this big leather couch and Lisa was giving me head when all of a sudden I realized that she was also playing around with Jane. The next thing I know the three of us have our clothes off and I'm watching Jane and Lisa kissing. Jane reaches out for me and draws me in close. She whispers, "Do you know that when her tongue goes cold, she's about to have an orgasm?"

By now we've moved to the master bedroom, where Jane has this king-size bed bigger than my living room at home. Jane rolled around with us, but I didn't fuck her that night. When Lisa was just about to come, we kissed, and damn if her tongue wasn't ice-cold.

Jane and I started seeing each other regularly after that night. It turned out she loved sex as much as I did. Sometimes it was just the two of us; sometimes it was her and me and Lisa, who could make Jane reach unbelievable orgasms by going down on her. One night when Lisa was working her magic, Jane said, "You gotta do this for me." I said "Uh-uh, no way. Italian guys don't do that shit."

Then Lisa started giving me lessons. She took me right down there with her and showed me how to do it. It took half an hour, maybe forty-five minutes, but it wasn't what you'd call hard work. Jane would reach incredible wild orgasms; she'd yell and scream, and her whole body would shake and tremble in ecstasy. Her climaxes were like massive explosions, and once she came I'd climb aboard and fuck her on top of it.

I got over that Italian Catholic squeamish shit real quick.

———————————

Right around the time Fox and Tommy and I pulled our first score, something happened between Lisa and Jane. I'm not sure what it was exactly, but I started showing up at Jane's and Lisa wasn't there. The first night that happened, Jane told me she didn't want Lisa to get me girls anymore.

A few nights later I arrived at Jane's place, and she said Lisa was coming over but she didn't want me to fuck her or even make out with her. She said she wanted me all to herself. Since I had really only started banging Lisa in the hopes of getting to Jane, that was fine by me.

By the time I told Fox that Jane and I were seeing a lot of each other, Lisa had dropped out of the picture. It was like Jane was having some kind of awakening. After years of making it only with women and hating men who whimpered at her feet like beaten dogs, she had discovered a whole new world of sexuality and she couldn't get enough. Now she wanted sex all the time—the wilder and more spontaneous the better—and she wanted it with me.

Jane got a real charge from having sex where there was a risk of discovery, of being caught fucking in public. I had a van with tinted windows, and a couple of times she had me park it in the middle of Times Square and fuck her in the back. She said she liked listening to what all the legitimate people walking by said when they saw the van rocking and rolling from us fucking inside.

I was as into our escapades as she was. I loved being with a woman who loved sex and getting kicks as much as I did.

I liked the risk taking too. I liked it so much I got careless and risked consequences a whole lot greater than being embarrassed by strangers in a public place.

Just a few weeks after I promised Fox that I knew what I was doing and there was no way Angela would ever find out for sure that her husband—the same guy who had neglected her for years and hadn't so much as kissed her in months—was out fucking around with other women, I discovered the downside of dating only blondes when your wife is a brunette.

———————

It happened the day after Jane and I enjoyed one of our wildest nights of spontaneous sex.

We had found this Chinese restaurant on Mott Street that was open all night. It was after 3:00 in the morning and the place was deserted, just us and the waitress and the cook in the back. We had finished dinner and I ordered another round of drinks. We each took a sip, then Jane put down her glass and said, "Fuck me in the ladies' room."

"Come again?" I didn't mean it as a joke and she wasn't laughing.

"I'm going in there," she said. "You sneak in and get me."

Jane got up and headed to the ladies'. I followed a minute later. I went in and started fucking her in the stall. She had her legs wrapped around me and she was hanging on to the top of the doorjamb and the thing was shaking and rattling. The waitress came in to see what was the commotion, and there we were, me pumping and Jane panting and moaning. The waitress screamed and backpedaled out the door. When we got back to the table we were starving. We ordered a whole new meal.

I got home at dawn, slept all day, and went to the club that night. The game ended early, at around 4:00 a.m. When I got home the house was dark but Angela had left the kitchen light on as usual. There was an envelope on the kitchen table with my name on it.

I figured it was a note asking me to take Sal Jr. to nursery school or something. I tore it open and found a blank piece of typing paper inside. I unfolded it. There was nothing written on it. But in the middle of the page there was a single strand of blond hair stretched between two pieces of Scotch tape.

Maybe I was just paranoid, but I could have sworn I got a faint whiff of perfume. That strand of hair smelled like gardenias.

CHAPTER EIGHTEEN

The Calm

APRIL 1972

"**K**EN IS A NAME, it's not a word."

"Are you challenging me, Sally?"

"You're damn right I'm challenging you."

John Gotti was a bust at cards but he was great at Scrabble. He started playing in the joint, which is where he did a lot of reading, and that's why he usually beat my ass. But I knew I had him this time.

"Three hundred clams says it's a name, a proper fucking noun, and you lose."

"Make it six hundred," Johnny said. He nodded at Fox, who handed me the dictionary.

"You're on."

"Oh, fuck me," I said a minute later. I slammed the book shut and peeled off six hundreds.

"So what's it mean?" Fox said.

"I don't have any ken what it means."

"You just looked it up."

Fox wasn't so swift when it came to word games; he was smart with cards and in a lot of ways, but I'm not sure he ever read a book in his life.

"Don't be a sore loser, Sally. Tell the man what the word means." One of the reasons John and I became friends was that he saw how tight Fox and I were. Still, he didn't like me or anybody else fucking with the Fox.

"It means knowing, to have knowledge about something."

"I don't know why I play this fucking game," Fox said, cracking us all up.

Another guy who played a lot of Scrabble but probably shouldn't have was Roundy. He was great with numbers, but words threw him. One time he came back from the hookers and said he just had the greatest organism of his life.

We also played Monopoly at the Sinatra Club when things were slow. That's one game we didn't bet on. We went one better—we played with real money. All the denominations were the same as the play money except we had to use the fake $500 Monopoly bills. Each player bought two or used an IOU. Fox, me, and Big Funzi used to start with $3,000 each. If we argued over a move, we actually called the Parker Brothers hotline in Massachusetts to get a final ruling.

Chess became a big craze in 1972 because Bobby Fischer and Boris Spassky were getting set to play for the world championship that summer in Iceland. The cold war was still raging and the match was getting big play in all the papers and on television as a face-off between the Russian grand master Spassky and the great American hope Fischer.

Wiseguys got into it like everybody else. We all liked Bobby Fischer. Gotti called him the Al Capone of chess. Big Al was barely thirty when he took over as top guy in the Chicago Mob. Bobby Fischer was still in his twenties and he'd already worked over most of his competition like Capone with a Louisville Slugger. He'd won more tournaments faster than anybody else alive. Gotti used to quote him all the time: "The thing I like most about the game is crushing the other guy's ego."

John knew a lot about the history of the game. Experts are always saying that chess is like war, but Gotti compared it to crime.

He said gangsters who want to get ahead should play chess because it makes you think like a boss. It was a good way to develop your powers of concentration and learn how to see the big picture and think things through. He said chess gave players a way to learn the kind of mental discipline you need when you go out on a score. "You got to always use presence of mind when you rob," was one of Gotti's favorite sayings. He meant keep your focus, don't let the adrenaline control you, don't let fear fuck you up.

John was better at chess than the rest of us. Fox and I were just novices, and Gotti got his only real competition from Charlie Fatico at the Bergin.

I had started hanging out there at the Gambinos' social club with Fox and Johnny, who was busy running things for Charlie Fatico, who more and more was taking a backseat.

And more and more I had my afternoons free because Dom's and my gambling business was beginning to slacken. Off-track betting was only a year old but was already cutting into our day-to-day gambling operations. It wasn't as bad as the next couple of years, 1973 and '74, when the bottom totally dropped out and we stopped bankrolling degenerates at Aqueduct and concentrated exclusively on our own off-track business— loan sharking.

Because Dom and I were spending less and less time at Ervolino's in the mornings and fewer afternoons at the track, I had a lot of free time before our shylock customers showed up at the Sinatra Club to pay their vig and settle their loans.

I used to see a lot of our mouthpiece, Mike Coiro, at the Bergin because he was representing Fatico in his tax fraud case. He said an indictment was a sure thing and it was just a matter of time before Fatico was out of the picture altogether.

The Bergin Hunt and Fish Club was on 101st Avenue in Ozone Park, a little more than ten blocks from the Sinatra Club. Fatico set up his new headquarters there after he moved out of the Club, the Elkin Italian American Social Club where Uncle Tony used to take me when I was a tyke. Guys said he moved because so many blacks were moving into East New York.

The Bergin was a brick storefront with a second identical one next door that was used as an annex. I never went in there; I suspected that's where the Gambinos conducted some of their bloodier after-hours business, and most guys who went in there involuntarily got hauled out the back door in a couple of heavy-duty garbage bags.

There were no windows out front of either storefront. When you walked in the public half of the social club, there was a bar down one side of the front room and card tables scattered around where there were always some old guys who sat all day drinking espresso and playing brisc. The younger guys were usually at the bar or sitting around reading the horse sheets or just hanging out. There was a room in the back where Fatico—and now John Gotti—conducted sit-downs.

Even though Tommy DeSimone was Fox and my heist partner, he never met with us at the Bergin to plan jobs. He stayed away because of the bad blood between him and John Gotti. Tommy also knew better than to set one foot in a Gambino club where the DeSimone name was synonymous with "rat," thanks to Tommy's traitorous brother.

So even after Fox and I teamed up with Tommy, we did a few jobs on our own that we came up with at the Bergin. We were in there one day that spring when we got a tip on a load of sweaters from a cargo guy at JFK. We decided to take it without hijacking the truck. We stole a U-Haul; they were always a piece of cake because all their vans and trucks had a spare key screwed into the grille. U-Haul practically invited us to steal those things.

Our tipster got us some bills of lading, and I got Bald Vinny to make some copies. We filled out the forms for the sweaters and Fox and I drove to the loading dock at the airport a couple of hours before the real truck was supposed to show up. We showed the papers, backed the truck in, loaded it up, dropped the load at one of Jimmy's drops, and returned the truck to the gas station we stole it from before they opened the next morning.

———————

Busy as he was conducting Gambino Family business at the Bergin, John Gotti continued to show up for games at the Sinatra Club. He was still our best customer as well as our partner, and he continued to bring in new players from crews all across the city. Despite his high profile and rising status in the New York Mob, Gotti was still a lousy card player and one of the club's biggest losers.

John was losing $2,000, $3,000, $4,000 a week. That doesn't sound like so much when you know that ten years later he was dropping

30 and 40 grand on Sunday football games alone. But in '72 dollars, 4 g's was a lot of fruit, and his losses were cutting big holes in the club's profits.

The Sinatra Club's take was averaging around $15,000 a week. And every week Gotti ended up owing thousands to the house. That hurt us because we could be putting the money we floated to John back on the street at double the vig he was paying because he was a partner.

Because Fox, Gene Gotti, and Quack Ruggiero were John's silent partners—they were included in the partnership deal to balance Dom's piece, which he split four ways with his brother Joey, Jackie Donnelly, and me—they were as anxious about their boss's IOUs as we were. Because John paid back everything he borrowed at interest and that cash got subtracted from his crew's take, Johnny was gambling away Angelo, Genie, and Fox's end.

To straighten things out, Dom called a meeting to discuss the club's finances. The sit-down was just like any legitimate corporate meeting, except instead of a boardroom, we held ours in a restaurant. We smoked cigars and had a couple of bottles of wine that we didn't wait until the end of the meeting to polish off.

For our sit-down it was just Dom and me and Johnny and his right hand, Quack. We held it at a Gambino joint, the Villa Russo, a great Italian restaurant where I went so often I had my own personal waiter. We met after lunch and had the place to ourselves.

Dom had told me to be sure to bring my black record book. I used it to keep track of all the money that the house loaned to players. On Sunday nights I would settle up all the books; if a player owed money for the week, he would pay on Sunday. If he didn't pay in full, I arranged a shylock loan at a flat 5 percent vig paid weekly. At that time we had about $40,000 in house loans out; that brought in around $2,000 a week on top of the 15 grand we were averaging in house profit.

The first order of business was expenses. I was spending almost two grand a week on booze, catered food ordered from the Villa Russo and the Blue Fountain Diner in Howard Beach, and providing our high rollers with hookers. John didn't like the hookers to begin with and said we should get rid of them. Dom disagreed.

"John, that's why guys come from all over the city to the Sinatra Club," Dom said. "They want to wet their wick."

"Look," John said, "if you want those filthy holes, you guys pay for them. You never see me go near those broads."

Dominic agreed that we'd foot the bill for the hookers from our end.

The next issue was the money that the house loaned players. This was when Dom had me open the book so Johnny could see right there in black and red how much he was borrowing each week. I made sure to refer to the red numbers under Gotti's initials as loans; we might have been acting like corporate execs, but we were all cutthroats, and I was careful to not piss him off by calling his debits in the ledger losses.

John didn't make any promises that he would stop losing and start borrowing less. But he did come up with a good idea. He said to increase profits, the house should simply loan out more cash. Everybody liked that, and we agreed to push money at the club until the shylock book reached 100 grand. I would continue to collect all the vig and keep accurate records of who borrowed what.

We broke up the meeting and that night we all got together again at the Sinatra Club. John didn't play any better or bet any more conservatively or win any more pots than usual. He lost a couple of grand and took out IOUs on two more so he could keep right on gambling—and losing.

There was a hidden reason that Dominic worried about the profit drain that Gotti was causing. By cutting into the club's profits, his losses also threatened to blow the cover right off our secret drug business.

The Sinatra Club's sole reason for being was to trick our captain, Pegleg Brancato—and now, because of our new Family boss Carmine Persico's close ties to Carlo Gambino, the upper echelons of the entire New York Mob—into thinking we were the biggest cash-generating crew in the Colombo Family.

The club, as well as our gambling and loan shark businesses and even our action scores, functioned as a money-laundering operation to disguise our real business as major heroin distributors and dealers. In the same way that smart earners hid their earnings from the tax man by investing in legitimate businesses, we hid our huge drug profits behind the Sinatra Club as well as some legit businesses like Dom's restaurant the Villagio Italia in Ozone Park. The fact that our front itself was an illegal gambling enterprise in the eyes of the law didn't matter to the bosses. In the inverted world of the New York Mob, the Sinatra Club was a legitimate business and provided a perfect cover for operations that the godfathers regarded as a crime deserving the severest punishment.

The summer before we opened the club, Dom and Jackie went on their crime spree and kicked up twice as much tribute to Pegleg as usual; that was how they explained the new houses and Cadillac Fleetwoods that they bought with their first shipment of *babania*. Once the Sinatra Club was up and running, Dom kicked up almost all his slice of the profits from the club to Pegleg so he would go on assuming the club was generating even more fruit than it really was.

So for all practical purposes, John Gotti's losses were doubling Dominic's costs because he was giving Pegleg a taste of all the real profits that John was eating. And that's why Dom was so determined to rein Gotti in. It was all about the drugs, which, if Dom and I had any interest in continuing to breathe (which we did), Pegleg and Gotti and Persico and Don Carlo could never be allowed to find out about.

As profitable as the smack trade was, it was a filthy business—literally.

Besides storing and cutting and dealing the *babania*, one of my jobs was to launder all the cash that came in—and I don't mean hide it. The cash that changed hands between Dom and his suppliers and his distributors like me was all large-denomination banknotes. The money that came back in from our street dealers was all singles and fives and tens and twenties. It was literally dirty money—wrinkled and nasty; a lot of it stank, which is what happens when your customers are low-life junkies.

I always had big shopping bags full of it in the locked room of my apartment on Liberty Avenue. I washed all that cash by hand because it was so badly soiled. Eventually I got a washing machine, but in the beginning I got dishpan hands from scrubbing and drying that shit with a hair dryer.

I sorted it and cleaned it up as best I could, and then I took it around to banks. I used to spend a lot of time in banks. Long before I robbed my first jug, I was into casing them. I used to find any excuse to go in and study a bank, figuring out which ones had the oldest, sleepiest guards, and which ones had the best escapes and looked like there would be the fewest surprises.

Now I had a whole new reason for casing banks. I visited them all over town, but now I was looking for ones that had the hottest tellers. Most of them had at least one or two young good-looking women working behind the teller bars.

When I found a nice friendly-looking teller, I'd take in a couple hundred worth of small bills and change them for new $100 and $50 bills. I'd chat her up and flirt with her, and if she seemed responsive I'd go in the next day with more bills and maybe bring her a present. If that was cool, I'd ask her out on a date.

Pretty soon I had a string of about five or six hot-looking bank tellers who had a taste for coke and sex and didn't ask questions when I brought in a whole shopping bag full of paper money and asked them to change it into crispy new fifties and hundreds.

Plus I was able to fill my daily quota of blow jobs without it costing me more than the price of lunch or a drink after they got off work. So as gross as handling all that nasty money was, I had managed to find an upside.

Dealing drugs allowed me to harvest more fruit on a steady basis and over a longer period of time than any single score ever could. But compared to the challenges and the fun and excitement and the kicks I got from real crimes like truck hijacking, bank robbery, and even loan sharking, which to be good at required excellent people skills, drugs were a bust. Dealing was all riches and no rush. There was no challenge in distributing drugs, and the people you met were degenerates for the most part, low-life street dealers who more often than not were junkies themselves. Worst of all, it was boring because it was so easy.

It really was a piece of cake—and just about as exciting. But the riches—that was another story.

———————

Things at home had settled down for me after Angela and I had it out over that strand of blond hair she found on the jacket I was wearing the night I banged Jane in the bathroom at the Chinese joint on Mott Street. I denied everything, of course. I told her I didn't know where it came from, but I couldn't tell her where the lint on my pants or the grime on my shoes came from either. "It could have come from any one of a million places," I said.

"Yeah? Name one."

That stumped me for a split second, but then I hit on the novel idea of telling her the truth—or at least something that wasn't a lie.

I said Fox and I were at Sebastian's a few nights before and had drinks with Manny Gambino. That was a name I knew would get her attention. I said Manny was with a blonde and I must have picked it up from her— the banquette we were sitting in was fake leather and it was full of static electricity; the blonde's hair was standing on end all night.

She bought it, I think, or at least she pretended to, because she didn't want to face the truth any more than I wanted her to find it out. It was like Fox said—she would go on suspecting me until she found definite proof. And even then she would learn to live with it and accept it because she really had no choice. Her family was Sicilian Catholic, and divorce was forbidden. She never worked a day in her life, and if she left me she'd have no clue how to support the kids. Poor Angela was trapped and she knew it.

And that's why she continued to make my life a living hell at home even after the blond hair crisis passed.

Angela and I fought so much it had gotten to the point where she didn't care that I didn't come home at night and she didn't see me for days on end. I let most of our arguments slide off my back, but when she started in on how I was neglecting our sons as well as her, that got to me.

I felt bad about that and guilty as hell, but that didn't stop me from staying away from home and missing everything from their first haircuts to their first days of school and even their birthdays some years.

I missed seeing my kids grow up and I came to regret it later. But at the time I rationalized it as the price you pay to be in that Life. For me, taking care of my family meant robbing and stealing as much money as I could. I just figured that's the way it was in a family where the breadwinner is a gangster. If my wife and kids couldn't understand that, there was nothing I could do about it.

Whatever the reality of our home life, the Polisis were one big happy family that spring when the weather warmed up and Angela's mother started holding her famous weekend barbeques at the Parkside.

The Sunday gatherings took on a different look that year. In the past the barbeques had always been open to close friends and regulars from the Parkside as well as our friends the Cataldos. Since Dom and I were with the Colombos, we always invited a bunch of friends from the Family, and all the crew guys who played softball with us during the summer were welcome.

That year for the first time guys from other Families attended. Mother-in-Law herself invited Fox, who was the first Gambino who ever attended one of these barbeques. I also told some of the regulars from the Sinatra who were from other Families to drop by later on for the party inside at the Parkside bar after the barbeque. Everybody got along and there was no trouble; but something happened that led to tragedy later on.

Fox brought along his mother and his sister, Patricia. She had just turned eighteen and she still had a childlike sweet shyness about her. Just the same, she put the heads of every guy at the barbeque on swivel mode. I would have stared too if she wasn't Fox's kid sister. She had Black Irish coloring with dark brown hair and long black eyelashes and beautiful pale skin. I made sure I didn't let my eyes wander any farther, but most of the men at the barbeque kept stealing looks at her and checking her out all afternoon. Either Patricia had incredible poise for a teenage kid or she just didn't notice, but all the looks didn't seem to bother her. But once Fox caught on and started seeing guys ogling his sister, he began to get uptight.

Then, after everybody had eaten and Fox was saying his goodbyes, Tommy DeSimone and Gene Gotti and some other guys from the club showed up.

Knowing that Fox was on edge to begin with, I braced for trouble as soon as I saw Tommy walk through the back door of the bar and onto the terrace. But Tommy was on his best behavior, and he very politely thanked Angela's mom for having him over and he introduced himself to Fox's mother and sister.

Patricia hadn't really talked to any of the guys at the party and spent most of the afternoon close by her mother and brother. But when Tommy introduced himself, she struck up a conversation with him. I was standing too far away to hear what they were saying, but whatever it was must have been innocent enough because Fox seemed to relax and he chatted with Mother-in-Law and his mom while Tommy and Patricia carried on their own conversation.

It didn't look like Tommy was in any way hitting on her or making a pass, which is what I would have predicted. Instead he seemed uncharacteristically easygoing. Patricia was smiling as they talked, and instead of acting all cocky and brash and talking loud like he usually did when he was high, Tommy was calm, cool, and confident.

Relieved as I was that Tommy wasn't acting like a jerk and breaking Fox's balls by sweet-talking his sister, I started to get worried when I realized how Tommy must appear in the eyes of an innocent young girl whose older brother—who she looked up to and who was her hero and knight in shining armor—was himself a gangster.

I was used to seeing Tommy in the casual slob threads that were his work uniform on jobs and the polyester suits he usually wore at night to the Sinatra Club. Today he looked sharp and handsome in a metallic blue sharkskin suit and black Italian leather boots.

Tommy in fact looked exactly like a successful New York City gangster should look, and I didn't have to watch Patricia and him for long to realize what the Fox would soon find out.

His kid sister had a city-size crush on Tommy DeSimone.

One of my favorite rites of spring, opening day of the baseball season, didn't happen that year on account of the baseball strike. That cut into our sports betting, and to make up for it we took action on things like golf, which we normally wouldn't touch; I think we even took some bets on the Academy Awards; I was pulling for Gene Hackman to win for *The French Connection* even though he played a cop. And I liked *Klute* because it was about a hooker played by hot actress named Jane (Fonda).

Four nights before the Oscars, on Thursday April 6, 1972, Fox and I had drinks with Manny Gambino and Beverly at Sebastian's. We sat with them at their usual banquette. While we were there, I checked the seats for stray blond hairs and rubbed my jacket sleeve on the back of the booth to see if I could generate any static electricity. I struck out on both counts and made a note to have a prior engagement ready in case Angela ever decided she wanted to meet Manny and his mistress at Sebastian's.

Later Fox and I met a couple of Eastern Airlines stewardesses, and we messed around with them until Tommy Argo closed the place at dawn.

We took the girls out for breakfast and then dropped them at their hotel, and Fox and I went our separate ways.

Driving home, I was about to turn in to my driveway when I saw two guys trying to jimmy the locks on a car I had parked outside. Normally if I see somebody jacking my car, I'll beat the shit out of them. But these guys were in suits and ties and they were both wearing fedoras. They weren't car thieves; they were FBI. I kept driving and found a pay phone. I called home. When Angela heard it was me, she just handed the phone to one of the agents.

"What the fuck are you doing in my house?" I demanded.

He ID'd himself as FBI. He said I knew him. He was the same guy who hassled me at football practice in October. He said agents had arrested a friend of mine, Eddie Pravato, up in Buffalo, and now he was at my house to serve me a warrant for bank robbery. He told me to come home so he could do his job and arrest me. I hung up and called the Mouthpiece.

Mike told me to get lost until the next week. He said the feds always like to bust guys on a Friday so they have to sit in jail all weekend until the courts open on Monday. Mike told me not to worry, and I didn't. I was confident that his and Dominic's connections would get me off.

I knew bank robbery was a federal offense, but I figured that was no problem for Mike.

I was wrong, but a full year would pass before I figured that out.

———————

I drove over to Fox's place in Lindenwood Village, and he said I was welcome to hide out there for as long as I wanted. Fox called Angela, and when she said the coast was clear, he handed me the phone.

She was upset, to say the least. The feds had raided the house when she was home alone with the boys. They did a real number on the place, she said. They were looking for evidence in a bank robbery that I assured her I knew nothing about. She wanted to know why they took one of her wigs. I didn't say so, but I knew they got the wrong wig because I burned the one I used in the incinerator. They also took a machine gun, a .30-caliber rifle with a pistol grip. They missed my weapons stash, which was locked in Mother-in-Law's basement.

When I got home the following week, I found out that the feds also missed about 50 grand's worth of heroin. Before I got the apartment on Liberty Avenue, I needed a place to stash my stash. I had a few cases of peanut butter that Tommy Block paid his vig with one week. I hollowed out a couple dozen jars, leaving a coating of peanut butter on the inside, then I stuffed the bags of *babania* into the jars and screwed on the lids. I stored the cases in the basement at home.

The agents who searched down there must have figured I had a real jones for peanut butter.

———————

I holed up at Fox's place that day and went to the Sinatra Club as usual. There was big news that night.

Right around dawn that day, while Fox and I were partying at Sebastian's with the Eastern ladies, Crazy Joe Gallo was gunned down and died in the street outside Umberto's Clam House in Little Italy.

CHAPTER NINETEEN

The Storm

"HE MUSTA DID SOMETHIN' wrong," Fox said when we got the word. That was a favorite saying of John Gotti's, and everybody cracked up.

There weren't a lot of tears flowing that night at the Sinatra Club. There weren't a lot of guys either, because we were closed on Fridays, but between Fox and Dom and Roundy and me and a couple of guys who came in to place bets on the Masters final that weekend, we had enough for a few hands of seven-card stud.

Everybody was talking about Crazy Joe getting what was coming to him early that morning in Little Italy. Dom sent Stevie out to buy some champagne, and he passed around cigars. Somebody made a joke about Umbertos: "Now he's clammed up for good."

The news was in the afternoon papers and all over the radio and TV. Gallo turned forty-three at midnight, five and a half hours before he turned dead. He was celebrating at the Copacabana with his show-biz friends and his new wife and her daughter, who was in a Broadway show.

Don Rickles was the act at the Copa. He supposedly broke Gallo's balls and Gallo laughed his ass off and invited Rickles over to his table. David Steinberg and Jerry Orbach were there. The papers the next day said that Gallo had a book contract with a big publisher, Viking, to write his memoirs. Orbach's wife was helping him write it. The paper said that

Gallo and his wife got married at the Orbachs' town house in Manhattan a few months before. Steinberg was his best man.

Later we found out that a boss from out of town who was connected to our Family was there that night too. Gallo needled the boss for wearing one of Joe Colombo's Unity buttons. He shouldn't have done that.

After the Copa closed, Joey and his bodyguard, Pete the Greek, and Gallo's family went down to Little Italy for a late dinner. They picked a new place that was open all night on Mulberry Street. Umbertos was owned by a Genovese guy. Maybe Gallo picked it because Umberto was his father's name.

The place was empty except for a few tourists who are probably still going out to dinner on stories about what they saw that night.

Gallo and his group were digging into huge platters of shrimp and scungilli when a guy walked in. One of the tourists said he was tall, handsome, and distinguished looking. The next thing she knew, shots were fired. Pete the Greek was shot in the ass before he could pull out his gun. Gallo jumped up from his seat and upended the table; the papers said he did it to protect his family.

Gallo ran toward the front door. Bullets flew all over the place, and the shooter got Gallo twice in the back as he was going out the door. He staggered out into the middle of the intersection—at Mulberry and Broome.

Pete the Greek got outside in time to fire a round at the shooter's getaway car.

Gallo was dead in the street.

It was a real-life scene right out of *The Godfather*.

A low-level rat in our Family fingered three other Colombo guys, but nobody was ever busted for the hit.

In 2005, *Playboy* ran a story about Frank Sheeran, the Irish button man who claimed he killed Jimmy Hoffa in 1975. He did that job for the same out-of-town boss who was at the Copa that night. Sheeran was a war hero; he was with the American troops that liberated Dachau at the end of World War II. He said Hoffa was his friend, but he killed him on orders because the Mob wanted a less controversial guy running the

Teamsters. He didn't say what they did with the body, whether he's really buried in cement at Giants Stadium like everybody says.

Sheeran said his boss told him to whack Gallo that night because he was the "fresh kid" who insulted him at the Copa.[9]

Another story in the paper that weekend was filled with inside info about the Colombo Family. It said that Snake Persico's brother Allie Boy was running things in the Family until Snake got out of prison. It said the only reason they didn't go after Joey Gallo themselves after Joe Colombo got shot was that Snake's lawyers were in court appealing his sentence and he didn't want to screw that up by launching a gang war against the Gallos.

I showed the article to Dominic and asked him if that's the way it was.

Dom said, "These fucking reporters, where do they get this stuff?"

I took that as a yes.

News crews covered Gallo's funeral a couple of days later. All the showbiz types he hung out with showed up. There were pictures in the paper of guys carrying Gallo's coffin out of Guido's funeral home in Red Hook.

The city was really hyped up; people couldn't get enough about the Mob because of *The Godfather.* All the papers predicted a big gang war; they said it was going to be the Persico crew versus the Gallos. They talked about guys going to the mattresses, a line I knew was lifted straight from the movie script even though I hadn't yet seen the flick myself.

The papers quoted Gallo's sister. Her brother was in an open casket at the funeral. She was crying and screaming. "The streets are going to run red with blood, Joey!" she wailed.

She was right.

Total war broke out the day after the funeral.

———————

I was so eager in those days, I thought the Mob war was some exciting shit. More than that, I thought it was my chance to move up. I had made my rep as a heist guy; the next notch on my résumé would be hit man. I figured Dom would give me an assignment, maybe take me along on a job as a test, see how I handled myself. Then I'd get my own assignment

———————

[9] Charles Brandt, "Who Killed Joey Gallo?" *Playboy,* August 2005.

and I'd make my bones as a button man. When they opened the books, I'd be a made man in the Colombo Family.

It didn't happen that way.

"Forget about it, Sally," Dom said when I told him I was ready—any job he needed done, I was his man. "The feds are on you like flies. You gotta turn yourself in like the Mouthpiece says."

The day after Crazy Joe's funeral, I went to FBI headquarters in Manhattan and turned myself in. They booked me for robbing the Franklin National Bank in Queens the year before. Out of all the strong-arm jobs I pulled in my career, all the hijackings and robberies, that was the only one I got arrested for. All because one of the tellers picked out poor old Eddie Pravato's mug shot—his mask slipped down when he came flying over the bank counter and plowed into me. At least that's the story the feds told me. Years later I found out the real reason they fingered me.

The FBI guys said they showed the tellers my mug because my uncle Tony was a known associate of Eddie's and they figured I was too. I always wondered if it was the head teller who pissed herself who made me. It didn't matter. When I hit a couple more banks with Fox later, I still obeyed my uncle's rule: "Remember Willie Sutton, be polite!"

Mike Coiro represented me. Like I said, I wasn't worried, because he and Dom had a big judge in Queens.[10] He was a friend of Jackie Donnelly's; they used to drink together all the time at Andy Bruno's place, the Pan American Steak Pub on Queens Boulevard. Jackie and the judge were both Irish; they were into hunting and fishing and outdoor stuff. I knew the judge couldn't help with a federal crime, but I figured Mike was a miracle worker. If he could pocket a judge in Queens, he'd know who to get to for this case.

I got bailed out and went home.

The behind-the-scenes star of the Joe Colombo hit was the first casualty in the total war that had been declared on the Gallo gang. Joe

---

[10] New York State Justice William Brennan.

C's bodyguard was ID'd as a guy named Gennaro Ciprio. He played the Jack Ruby role in the hit. He was supposed to be guarding Joe C, but his real assignment was to make sure the shooter didn't talk. He tackled the guy and plugged him before the cops piled on. Then he disappeared.

Three days after the Gallo hit—it was on Oscars night; guys who bet on Hackman and Jane Fonda at the Sinatra Club won—Ciprio walked out of a restaurant he owned in Brooklyn, Gennaro's Feast. A sniper shot him dead from a rooftop hiding place.

You had to figure it was either Persico whacking Ciprio to shut him up, or the Gallos for the same reason, or maybe it was Carlo Gambino who might have had his own reasons to make sure Ciprio never talked. Whodunit was lost in what they call the fog of war.

The bodies started piling up after that. The day after Ciprio got clipped, a Gambino guy named Tommy Ernst got whacked on Staten Island. Another guy named Frank Ferriano, a small-timer with a big belly—the papers said he weighed three hundred pounds—got his head blown away by a shotgun. His body was found behind a shack in a parking lot by the Holland Tunnel.[11]

The same day, a Colombo credit card scam artist named Richard Grossman got the shotgun treatment. His body was found in the trunk of a '61 Dodge Dart in Sheepshead Bay.[12] The cops reportedly got a call telling them where the body was. "This one's for Joey Gallo," the tipster said.[13]

Bruno Carnevale, a Gambino, got whacked in Queens Village. The papers said he died with $1,400 in his pocket.

That seemed to confirm new reports in some of the papers that the Gambinos were siding with Persico's faction against the Gallos. Others had it that Don Carlo was playing both sides against the middle. In an article titled "Blood in the Streets: Subculture of Violence," *Time* magazine claimed that "the Gambinos were deliberately promoting the war,

---

[11] Tom Folsom, *The Mad Ones: Crazy Joe Gallo and the Revolution at the Edge of the Underworld.* Weinstein Books, 2008.
[12] "Blood in the Streets: Subculture of Violence." *Time,* April 24, 1972.
[13] *The Mad Ones.*

approving executions in order to fan the flames and encourage the Colombos and Gallos to kill one another off."

Time had it wrong about that. Fox told me that he had it all figured out.

Johnny Boy called the Sinatra Club the Mob's first "joint venture."

Fox said that the Gallo War was another one, a joint venture of the Gambinos and Colombos.

Like the year before when the papers seemed to have very strong inside information about the Joe C hit, the reporting on the Mob war had to have the top guys on both sides worried. The *Time* article had inside info that only could have come from wiretaps or a rat.

That's the only way to explain how *Time* reported that after Joey Gallo got whacked, the Gambinos "convened their own court of inquiry into Gallo's death." It made it sound like Carlo Gambino was wearing judge's robes and banging a gavel. Don Carlo was pissed because the hit was so sloppy; innocent bystanders could have been killed, and that would have brought down a shit storm of heat. Supposedly he let it go because Gallo was killed and no legitimate people got hurt. It goes to show there's no argument better than success.

If the magazine got that from a rat, via the cops, there must have been more than one feeding information from deep inside the war councils of the fighting Families. *Time* published their hit lists like box scores. They said the Gallos "put out contracts for the deaths of three enemies": Allie Boy Persico; Nick Biano, a Gallo who was suspected of being a rat; and Joe Yacovelli, Dom's friend who was a Colombo capo.

On the Colombo hit list were the Gallos' top two guys, Kid Blast and Punchy Illiano.

If anybody wanted to see the action up close, the magazine directed them to the Gallos' bunker on President Street. They said Kid Blast covered the windows with chicken wire to stop hand grenades.

The Colombos were holed up in an apartment building on Fifth Avenue in Brooklyn, *Time* said.

They made it sound like an episode of *Combat.* They said both armies stationed sentries and sent out guys on patrol, on search-and-destroy missions.

The killing came close to home a little while later when one of our guys from the Sinatra Club, Rosie Stabile, got whacked. Rosie was a master at credit card scams. He was the guy from my block whose kid and my kid were buddies.

A lot of guys get hit and their bodies are never found. Or they're dumped somewhere out of the way. Rosie was one of those hits that were made to send a message. They didn't just whack him. They shot his eyes out: two bullets, one in each peeper. That was an old Murder Incorporated technique. The message was, *This guy was a rat.*

Just to make sure nobody missed the message, they dumped Rosie's body in the trunk of a car and parked it in Prospect Park, which is like leaving it in Times Square. Then they set the car on fire.

Because Dominic and Donnelly were with Persico, they were probably in on the hits, but Dom would never in a million years talk about it. I think he was secretly glad about the war because of all the heat it would bring down on the Families. He figured the war was good cover for his drug business because it kept the bosses distracted.

Dom even used the war to cover a hit of his own.

The word on the wire was that the Westies, the Irish gang from Hell's Kitchen, were doing contract work for both sides in the new Gallo War. They were carrying out hits and they were also using the war to promote their side business, which was kidnapping connected guys. Normally they would just hold them for ransom and whack them if nobody paid up. With the war, they could grab a guy and sell him to the highest bidder—either let him go for a ransom or, if the enemy Family offered more, whack him.

The balls those guys had! Even before the war started, the Westies were kidnapping Gambino bookmakers and loan sharks. The going ransom rate was around $20,000. They were also kidnapping drug dealers, which made Dom very paranoid. He warned me to be extra careful because these Irish guys were snatching guys off the street.

I remember it was right around the time another rocketload of

Apollo astronauts landed on the moon,[14] that Dominic got Fox and me to do a dirty piece of work.

Three or four days before, Dom and Donnelly had whacked a guy I never heard of, probably over a drug deal, but they made it look to the Family like it was a legitimate hit on an informant. Dom said the guy had a stash of cash and jewelry that he wanted to get his hands on. The loot was in the apartment the unfortunate dealer shared with his girlfriend. The girlfriend didn't know the guy was dead, just that her boyfriend hadn't been home in a few days. Dom said there was 10 to 15 g's in it for Fox and me and no chance of getting ratted out to the cops.

Fox and I came up with a plan.

The next night, a Sunday, I called the girlfriend and said her guy was in trouble and he needed her help. I tried to sound frightened because Fox was supposedly holding a gun to my head.

She was frantic. "What's this all about?" she said. I told her I couldn't tell her over the phone, but she better scrape together whatever cash she had because if she didn't, her boyfriend's life and my life were on the line. She was crying when I hung up the phone.

The girl's apartment was a nice prewar place in Forest Hills, where you didn't live unless you had money. The place was gated and I rang the front bell. There was an intercom but no camera, and she buzzed me in, with Fox right behind me. We took the elevator up to her floor. Fox pulled a heater and stood to the side when I knocked. She opened the door and Fox pushed me inside ahead of him.

"Jerkoff, get on the floor!" he told me. He pointed the gun at the girl. "Sit there next to him. Your boyfriend and this asshole here stole a lot of money and I'm here to collect."

The girl was terrified, and Fox was such a good actor I would have been too if I didn't know better.

Fox said he knew there was 100 grand stashed in the apartment. "Now where the fuck is it?" he demanded.

The girl sputtered and said she only had about 20 grand in the

---

[14] Apollo 16, the second to last moon landing, April 20, 1972.

house. There was more in the bank, in a safe-deposit box, but it was Sunday.

She led us into the bedroom and pulled a shoe box down from a shelf in the closet. Fox ordered her to put it on the dresser next to a wooden jewelry box. She opened the shoe box. It was double-long, the size used to package boots, and was stuffed full with stacks of mixed bills in $1,000 bundles. Because it was all different denominations, that told us it was drug money. While she counted out the bundles and transferred them to a duffel bag, Fox cleaned out her jewelry box and a gold watch on the dresser top. He stuffed them in his pockets.

"Could you leave those small earrings?" the girl pleaded. "They were my grandmother's." She was hyperventilating, hysterical.

Fox dug the jewelry out of his pocket and picked out the earrings. He gave them to her and she calmed down a little.

We already had more than the 10 or 15 grand Dom promised. But Fox surprised me.

"We're going to stay here 'til morning. Then we'll all take a ride to your bank."

The girl and I sat on the couch. Fox sat in a chair with the duffel bag in his lap and watched television all night. I pretended to sleep, but I knew if Fox fell asleep she'd try to escape. The girl stayed awake all night too.

In the morning, Fox had her make a pot of coffee. She was composed by then, resigned or determined to do what she had to do to save her boyfriend's life. She was a helluva girl. Too bad her boyfriend was dead and gone.

Fox didn't want to scare her any more than we already had. When she said they didn't have 100 grand in the bank, they only had about $30,000, Fox was almost gentle.

"Okay," he said. "That will be enough to get your boyfriend back."

She drove us to her bank on Jamaica Avenue in Richmond Hill. I went in with the girl. She presented her safe-deposit key to the manager. He took us to the vault in the back, then left, and she opened the box.

It was all crisp and clean, stacks of brand-new $100 bills.

She drove back to her building. Fox told her to stop around the corner. He had the duffel with all the cash in one hand, and his other hand was on the gun in his pocket. He told the girl he was taking me and the money back to the safe house where he had her boyfriend. He told her to keep her mouth shut and her guy would be home later that day.

I called Dom, and he told us to meet him and Donnelly at the Sinatra Club. We got there and piled the cash and the jewelry on the bar. Dom and Jackie hardly looked at the cash. Dom picked up the gold watch and handed it to Donnelly. On the back of it was inscribed: "From your friend, Jackie."

All they cared about was the watch because it could have tied them to the hit.

"What about the cash?" I said.

"Keep it, it's yours," Dom said.

We made more than 40 g's on that score, but it was good fruit that left a bad taste. It was a goddamned rotten thing we did to that girl.

CHAPTER TWENTY

The Reel Mob

FOX LIKED THE SCENE where Sonny was banging the bridesmaid in the bathroom.

Tommy Guns cheered when Pacino gave the NYPD captain one right between the eyes.

I loved the whole damn thing, start to finish, all three hours of it.

The Godfather was a celebration of this Life of ours. So we celebrated it by doing what we did best—we committed a crime.

We finally went to see the movie everybody was talking about almost two months after it premiered. We went even though John Gotti told us that the real godfather ordered us not to.

The theater was on Queens Boulevard in Rego Park, and the joint was packed. We sat in the last row. We were riveted right from the start.

When the theater let out, everybody around us was buzzed. We heard people saying what a great movie it was, how exciting, how cool it must be to be in that Life. We were like kids ourselves. We walked out of there like we were ten feet tall.

We piled into Tommy's car—he was driving a big Lincoln Mark. The Sinatra Club was closed that night, and we went back there to have a few drinks. We couldn't stop talking about the movie.

It was a like a stew of true stuff about the Mob mixed up with fiction. We sat around for hours that night matching scenes and characters in the movie to their real-life sources.

Everybody knows the obvious ones, that Moe Green was based on Bugsy Siegel and that Al Martino's character, Johnny Fontane, the singer who lands a big movie deal with help from Don Corleone and sings at the Family's Vegas casino, was based on Frank Sinatra, who supposedly used Mob ties to get his Oscar-winning part in *From Here to Eternity* and who sang at Mob-owned casinos in Vegas throughout his career.

But if you want to hear some real *Godfather* trivia, hang out with three gangster-movie-obsessed Mob guys sometime.

That night we took it from the top and agreed that even though they filmed the opening wedding scene at a walled estate on Staten Island—the one they used was on Todt Hill near where Big Paul Castellano lived—the model for the Corleones' Long Island compound had to have been Joe Bonanno's walled estate out in Hempstead. And though Johnny Fontane was modeled on Sinatra, it was Tony Bennett who sang at the wedding of Joe Profaci's daughter and Joe Bonanno's son at the Hotel Astor in 1956.

When Don Corleone's bodyguard, Luca Brasi, gets garroted at the closed hotel bar and his bulletproof vest is delivered to James Caan's character with a dead fish wrapped inside it, we knew that was based on two incidents during the Gallo Wars—when Larry Gallo got garroted at the Sahara Lounge and when Joe Jelly got whacked and the rotting fish dummy was delivered to the Gallos as a message that Jelly "sleeps with the fishes." (The botched murder at the Sahara turned up again two years later in *Godfather II*, when the hit on Frankie Pentangeli is interrupted by a cop.)

The great scene in *The Godfather* where the movie director wakes up with a severed horse's head in his bed must have been based on the judge in the Bonanno boss Lilo Galante's trial in the 1960s. The judge got up one morning and there on his front porch was the severed head of his family dog. Lilo left it to suggest that the judge might meet a similar fate if the case ended in a guilty verdict. It didn't work and Galante went to prison.

The story line about Michael Corleone taking over after the attempted hit on his father seemed based on Joe Bonanno's son Bill, who ran the Family while his father was on the run to avoid getting whacked by Carlo Gambino in the 1960s.

The climactic scene where Pacino's character goes to the bathroom at the restaurant in the Bronx and comes out with a gun was based on the 1931 hit on Joe "the Boss" Masseria in a Coney Island seafood restaurant that my uncle Tony told me about. But when Lucky Luciano excused himself and went to the head, he didn't come out shooting like Michael does in the movie. Instead, a squad of Bugsy Siegel's and Meyer Lansky's triggermen walked in and did the job for Luciano. Joe the Boss died with his lobster bib on, like Sterling Hayden's cop in the movie.

There never was a massacre of four Family bosses like the one Pacino's character orchestrates at the end of *The Godfather*. Joe Bonanno and Joe Profaci did plot to whack Carlo Gambino and the two other New York bosses so they could take over the Commission in the '60s, but they weren't able to pull it off. And in 1931, when the New York Mob was just two Families run by Joe the Boss and Little Caesar Maranzano, Luciano rubbed them both out, but not at the same time.

We finally left the Sinatra Club around 2:00, but we were still jazzed from the movie, so we found another bar. After a drink or two we called it a night. It was like 3:00 a.m. and Tommy was about to drop me off at home when I said, "You know, we should celebrate the movie. Let's go nail a truck." Fox was all for it, and I knew Tommy would be.

We stopped a few blocks from my house on a dark street where I had stashed a hotski. We parked Tommy's Lincoln and took off in the hotski. After we stopped by Fox's place to pick up the gear, Tommy said, "Let's go to Staten Island—we'll take a truck when it comes over the Verrazano." For the hell of it, we all agreed the truck had to have a red cab; the first red eighteen-wheeler that came over the bridge—we'd nail it.

Before we got to the bridge, we stopped at a pay phone. Tommy called Jimmy Burke and talked in code: "Jimmy, my two cousins and my aunt, they just moved up from Florida. They got a lotta furniture. They'll need a big place to store it till their new place is ready." That meant the three of us were about to make a move and we needed a big warehouse for a big truck. Tommy said as soon the furniture arrived—as soon as we nailed the truck—we'd call him back.

So thirty minutes later, we're parked on the Staten Island end of the Verrazano, the beautiful suspension bridge that connects the island to Brooklyn. We're sitting there for close to an hour waiting for the right truck. We're watching all sorts of eighteen-wheelers roll over the bridge. Then finally we spot a shiny red White Freightliner with a chrome trailer. We know our trucks. The big semis come in two sizes. This is a big one, a forty-footer.

Tommy's in the front seat with me. Foxy's in the back with his satchel, handing out the masks, the duct tape, the handcuffs.

We follow the truck across the bridge, and I say, "Okay, as soon as he stops, I'll cut him off." The truck exits the bridge and stops at the light. I cut in front of the truck. Tommy and Fox hit it from both sides. The guy's alone, nobody riding shotgun, no alarm, no resistance, a piece of cake.

We work the usual routine—Fox drives the truck to Jimmy's drop while Tommy and I ride around for a couple of hours with the driver bound and gagged in the backseat.

We stop at a Dunkin' Donuts at dawn and remove the duct tape gag. The driver's from South Carolina. He says his name is Junior. I ask him how he likes his coffee and what kind of doughnuts. He says, "Black, no sugar," and that he loves jelly doughnuts.

Junior tells us we've just jacked ourselves a high-dollar load of commercial carpet. It's going to the Bankers Trust building downtown on Wall Street.

"Not anymore it's not," Tommy says.

We cut the guy loose, give him $50, and drive to the drop. Tommy bangs the code on the steel door—three quick bangs, pause, three more—and one of Jimmy's guys opens up. Jimmy looks grim. He gives us the good news first. He's got the paperwork for the truck. We've got a great load of carpet. The bad news is he needs a special forklift with a "big dick"—a twelve- or fourteen-foot steel rod—to unload the carpet rolls. He tells us he's trying to locate one.

Jimmy's a killer. He's been whacking guys for twenty years. Nobody makes the joke about him not having a big enough dick.

He tells us to go home and meet him later that day at Robert's Lounge.

It turns out Jimmy can't find the right kind of forklift. Two days later, he dumps the truck fully loaded somewhere near JFK.

Bankers Trust got their carpet. And we got a good laugh—for years we told the story about *The Godfather* celebration heist.

———————

The year 1972 was one of the most tumultuous in the long history of the New York Mob. The Families were at the height of their glory, but the signs of their future demise were flashing all around. For guys like Fox and Tommy and me—and for John Gotti especially—it was the best of times. But for Carlo Gambino, 1972 was the year the shit really hit the fan. That would happen later during the summer, his season in hell. But the beautiful month of May had to be one of the most miserable in Don Carlo's long, eventful life.

Bad enough that a hit movie that exposed the secret underworld doings of a crime lord a lot like him who ran a vast criminal enterprise a lot like his was still playing to sold-out audiences two months after its release.

And that the secretive don who had determinedly kept his name out of the papers since 1959 when he and his first cousin and brother-in-law Big Paulie Castellano got busted at the Apalachin Commission meeting could not now pick up a newspaper or newsmagazine without reading speculation that he was somehow behind two of the most spectacular murders and the bloodiest Mob war in recent memory.

Even coming as they did on the heels of headlines he made the year before—"Gambino: Quiet Man in Spotlight," read a *New York Times* feature in July 1971—after an embarrassing arrest for drug trafficking (charges that miraculously disappeared) and deportation proceedings that ended when he conveniently had a heart attack, the news reports were overshadowed by a series of catastrophes that rocked Don Carlo's world in ways he never experienced before and the legitimate world never knew.

The first bomb dropped on May 2 when he and practically everyone else alive learned that J. Edgar Hoover had croaked. Few, however, knew as Don Carlo did so well that with his death the Mob lost the firewall that had protected and allowed it to flourish for most of the past half century.

J. Edgar wasn't yet cold in his casket when his friend Roy Cohn delivered the next body blow and informed Gambino that there'd been a rat gnawing away at the very heart of his empire and spitting up Family secrets for six straight years. Now that Hoover was dead, the secret reports from the rat inside Charlie Fatico's crew at the Bergin Hunt and Fish Club, the largest and most important in the entire Gambino Family operation, would be secret no more.

Gambino got more bad news when the Bergin crew's wise, trusted, and ruthless captain, Charlie Fatico, was finally arrested, indicted, and ordered to stand trial on federal income tax evasion charges. Desperate as the don was to ferret out the rat in his Family, he would now have to trust the task to the new and untested acting boss of the Bergin crew—John Gotti.

But it was a final, unthinkable event that must have rattled Gambino more than all the rest. While he was still pacing in his Massapequa home in mourning for Hoover and figuring out how to trap a rat, he learned that his brother Joe's son Manny—Fox's and my pal from Sebastian's—had been kidnapped.

At first everybody assumed it was an act of war, but then word went out that Manny got snatched as he was leaving the office in Manhattan where he ran his shylock operation, and the Westies who grabbed him were demanding $200,000 for his safe return, ten times the going rate.

Fox and I knew that negotiations for Manny's release must have stalled because he wasn't in his usual booth at Sebastian's whenever we went in there, and we didn't see Beverly, his beautiful blond dancer mistress, anymore either.

For Gambino, the kidnapping was more than an insult. That a bunch of Irish barbarians from Hell's Kitchen would dare snatch a blood relative of the most powerful Mafia emperor in America was a direct challenge to his power and authority. It meant that maybe the godfather—and the Mob itself—wasn't so invincible after all. *Don't fuck with us* was our motto, and nobody ever did. Until these fucking Westies came along.

If it came down to a battle between the Westies and the Gambinos, there's no doubt that the superior manpower of the Mob would crush the renegade Irish gang. But no commander wants to fight a war on two fronts, and an all-out assault on the Westies would open a third. It would bring more heat from the press and the public, not to mention the law, than Don Carlo was certain his Family could handle.

So instead of loosing his legions, Gambino prepared for a surgical strike.

He would continue to negotiate for his nephew's release but at the same time launch an investigation to find out who made the snatch. Then, once Manny Gambino was home safe, he would dispatch a hit team to kidnap the kidnapper and teach him a lesson he would immediately forget. He wouldn't be able to remember being tortured and forced to confess his crimes for a simple reason—he'd be dead.

The man Don Carlo chose to carry out the investigation and, when the time came, the hit, was the same one he was entrusting to finger, trap, and exterminate the Bergin's rat—John Gotti.

Even before Gambino gave John the job that would make his career, there were obvious signs that Gotti's status in the Family was soaring.

For one thing, guys in his crew didn't use his old Rockaway Boys name much anymore. Even when he wasn't around, it was John or Johnny but rarely Johnny Boy. And lately when he arrived at the Sinatra Club, he wasn't in the street gang leather he wore when he was fresh out of Lewisburg five months before. These days he looked sharp in a light summer suit, and Quack Ruggiero or one of his other guys held his raincoat for him and lit his cigar.

For me the capper came when I ran into John at the Rainbow Room in Rockefeller Center. Sarah Vaughan was doing a string of nightclub appearances around town that May, and her show at the Rainbow Room, the swankiest joint in the city, was a very tough—and expensive—ticket to get. I was flush with drug cash as usual, and I got Jane and me a great table right up front.

Because he was busy running Fatico's gambling operations and now the entire Bergin crew, Gotti wasn't hijacking trucks anymore or pulling big scores. His sole source of income was the taste of the profits he got from the guys below him—and a big chunk of that change he was blowing nights at the Sinatra Club.

So when I ran into John in the men's room after the show at the Rainbow Room, I was surprised. He was wearing a beautiful tailored Italian silk suit and tie. He said he was there with Victoria and his brother Gene and his wife. I knew what I paid for Jane's and my table; I could only guess what it cost him for the four of them.

"That nigger's sure got some pipes," Gotti said as he washed his hands at the sink. I knew he wasn't real enlightened when it came to race relations, and I guessed then he wasn't overly reverent about one of the true greats of jazz either. But I also knew from seeing him in there that a lot more top earners throughout the Family were paying him tribute, because he never could have afforded to be at that show if it was just our friends in his old street crew kicking up to him.

One result of Gotti's growing power, prestige, and bankroll was that instead of reporting to Fatico at the Bergin like he used to, he now drove into the city every weekend for one-on-one meetings with his friend Quack's uncle, Neil Dellacroce, who had served as Carlo Gambino's underboss since 1957 and who remained the number two man in the Family, directly under Don Carlo himself.

Uncle Neil's headquarters at the Ravenite on Mulberry Street was like sacred ground in the legends of the Mob. It's where Lucky Luciano plotted his war against the Mustache Petes in 1931. During the San Gennaro Festival every September, thousands of tourists flocked to Little Italy, and few of them had any idea what the innocuous-looking brick tenement building was and what schemes and crimes were being hatched inside it as they strolled by the Ravenite, munching Italian sausage sandwiches and cannoli from Ferrara's.

And that May not even the guys inside the club knew that before the year was out there would be a new prince running Uncle Neil's fiefdom.

———————

A few weeks after Manny Gambino disappeared, Johnny came to Fox with what at first looked to my partner like a routine piece of business.

John knew that Fox and I had a guy in the Queens PD who ran plates for us; it was the detective, Charlie, who was a friend of Joe the Mailman's kid, the vice cop. Every week or two, Fox and I met with Charlie and gave him plate numbers we got from tipsters on trucks or gamblers either of us needed to track down. We talked about which came from what tipster and what degenerates needed reminding they were behind on their payments.

When John asked Fox to run one particular plate number for him, Fox said sure. But then John instructed him not to let me or anyone else know about it. He told Fox that when he got the results from Charlie, he was not to show anyone the name and address, including me, and to bring it directly to John and nobody else.

That was the way the crew chiefs and top guys did everything: If you were in on a piece of work for them, you knew only as many details as you needed to get the job done. That way if anything went wrong, if you got busted, the boss was protected.

So when we gave Charlie our plate numbers that week, I noticed there was one on there we hadn't talked about. I didn't think anything about it; I assumed it was a number Fox added at the last minute for one of his own shylock customers.

Then when we got the list back from Charlie, the added result had no special significance. After I copied down the names and addresses I needed, I gave the list to Fox and forgot all about it.

It turned out that the plate number Fox ran for John was connected to Manny's kidnapping. Another Gambino guy had been snatched on Staten Island right around the time Manny got grabbed. Some good citizen got the plate number of the car used in that snatch. He didn't call the cops; he did the right thing and called the Gambinos.

Fox didn't realize at the time that Johnny was working on special assignment for Carlo Gambino and that he was running the Family's investigation into Manny's kidnapping. Neither did he know that the plate number had anything to do with it.

Fox just gave Gotti the name and address and didn't hear anything more about it until almost a year later.

But when he did, he found out that John used that plate number as the fuse that launched his rocket to fame and ultimate misfortune.

CHAPTER TWENTY-ONE

Love During Wartime

JUNE 1972

I WAS MORE OF A Casanova than a Romeo. And Jane for sure was a harlot. But our relationship, perverse and fucked-up as it was, was a love story. It was even a kind of tragedy.

Which might not come as much of a surprise, all things considered. Jane was a bisexual dominatrix who had never let a man into her bed or even kiss her on the lips. I was a thug who robbed banks and beat up people for a living. She fell for a guy who cheated on his wife, fucked whores on a regular basis, and treated women like a betting slip—buy it, use it, crumple it up, and throw it away. I fell for a woman who made her living tormenting and humiliating men. I guess we were made for each other.

I'm not sure exactly how it turned from lust to love for Jane and me. It happened gradually over a period of time, and neither of us were even aware that we were falling in love. A year would pass before it did for real, and when it happened it was like nothing I ever experienced before. Intimacy and love were as foreign to me as voting and paying taxes—or having sex with my wife.

Jane's and my feelings for each other started to change on a night that began with us both pissed off. I had glommed a pair of tickets to the Majestic Theater on Broadway to see *Grease*, which was a big hit musical that opened the year before.

Our plans were scotched by a bitch killer of a storm, Hurricane Agnes, which turned out to be one of the worst that had ever hit the city. Except for the Sarah Vaughan concert a few weeks before, Jane and I never went on actual dates where we planned something ahead of time. We just got together whenever we could and fucked, then we went out on the town, hit some clubs and maybe a restaurant for dinner, and then it was back to her place for more sex.

But this night was a real date where I got the tickets ahead of time and we planned on seeing the show and then having dinner at Gallagher's, our favorite steak house on West 52nd Street, across from Roseland Ballroom. Jane was jazzed about the night ahead, and she was all dolled up in a black satin sheath when I arrived—only to tell her that the show was canceled because fucking Agnes was barreling up the coast and the city was braced for a direct hit.

Jane was disappointed at first, then she got mad, and I got mad at her for getting pissed off about something there wasn't a damn thing we could do anything about.

"Now what?" she said. "We're stuck here doing the same shit."

I looked around her apartment all lit up brighter than a Broadway stage; everything glittered gold like the jewelry counters at Bergdorf's.

"Yeah, stuck here in this crappy penthouse, going out and doing the same old shit every night, fucking in Times Square like everybody else."

For a split second Jane thought I was serious and couldn't think of what to say. Then she burst out laughing.

We did end up doing something we never did before that night.

We kept our clothes on. For a while anyway.

And we talked. Not about that Life, not about my heists and her johns, but about our real lives.

We sat in the living room with the hurricane winds howling and the windows rattling, and I told her things I never told Dom or anybody in that Life outside of Fox. I told her about my mother abandoning us because she didn't like the straight life and about my sister and how much I loved her and about her dying on me and my half brother Joe drowning and Rose Marie's baby vanishing all in one fucked-up summer.

Then she told me about her own life, which made mine look like Pleasant Valley Sunday.

She said she grew up in a little town in North Carolina. Her mother was a whore, her stepfather abused her, a neighbor sexually assaulted her when she was seven or eight. She was put in an orphanage, where the female attendants fondled her and a male aide started fucking her when she was twelve.

When she turned sixteen, she ran away. She tried to hitchhike to New York. The first guy who picked her up was a trucker in his thirties who seemed nice and said his father was a preacher. The first night on the road he pulled off the interstate, tied her up, and raped her. He kept her captive in the cab of his truck, tied up behind the seats, when he wasn't fucking her.

He drove around with her for a few days, then stopped at an out-of-the-way Laundromat outside Washington and told her to wash his clothes. He thought he had his own little sex slave on wheels. She found a bottle of bleach in there and squirted it in his eyes.

She took off, leaving her suitcase and everything but her pocket-book. She was close enough to New York to afford a bus ticket. She got off the bus at Port Authority and blew a couple of guys for money.

From there she did tricks on the street and moved up to a whore-house on the west side. She didn't blow her money on drugs like the other girls and avoided the rip-off pimps like the guy I beat up for her friend Lisa.

She saved enough to rent a nice apartment, and before she knew it, she had two apartments on 36th Street—one for her and one for business—and a second brothel out in Rego Park. She got into being a dominatrix so she didn't have to fuck guys anymore. By the time I met her, she was one of the top madams in the city. She was a regular New York success story, just like me.

Usually Jane did lines before, during, and after sex, but that night there was nothing working inside her but champagne—and me. For once we weren't the stallion and the mare racing frantic to the finish. We were both giving, not taking, and for the first time we did it slow and easy, not wild.

We were so tender it felt almost chaste, like innocent kids.

That's why when Angela found another blond hair the next day, it was almost funny—because I felt like for once I didn't do anything wrong.

Angela didn't bother saving the blond strand and putting it an envelope for me to find.

She didn't yell and scream or beat me with her broom; she didn't even wait to listen to my lies.

She just said I disgusted her.

CHAPTER TWENTY-TWO

The Bergin All-Stars

JULY 1972

WE WEREN'T THE MOST patriotic guys in the world—that was for the legitimate slobs. We didn't care for Uncle Sam—we didn't pay his taxes and we didn't fight his wars. But we did celebrate his birthday at the annual Bergin Hunt and Fish Club Fourth of July Barbeque and Fireworks bash.

And every year, like all legitimate red-blooded Americans, we played softball on July 4th. Only ours was an all-wiseguys softball game.

And the starting lineup was a for-real Murderers Row.

The badasses who crowded around the first base line while Charlie Fatico and his brother Danny chose up teams included: the Bergin crew's enforcer Willie Boy Johnson; Tony Roach Rampino, the feared hit man; Angelo Quack Ruggiero, Johnny Boy's chief lieutenant and a killer in his own right; Charles Carneglia, a serial killer who dissolved victims' bodies in acid; Mark Reiter, who later became a major heroin dealer and brought a lot of shit down on the Bergin; Sal DeVita, whose daughter later married Tommy DeSimone; and of course the Gotti brothers, John and Genie.

I wish I had filmed it. None of these guys wore softball T-shirts or baseball shoes; everybody was in street clothes. We were all dressed in Bally shoes and silk socks, Armani pants and Italian knit shirts; everybody wore pinkie rings and Saint Christopher medals and sprayed-up hairdos.

Charlie won the toss, and the first guy he picked was Tony Roach, the Frankenstein's monster–looking guy and the best ballplayer at the park by my house where the game was played. Out of all those gangsters, Tony was the only real athlete. He was about six one and muscular. He could play any position with Cal Ripken fielding ability—and he had an arm like a rocket. Everybody there was good with a bat, but they couldn't hit a softball to save their lives. Except Tony—he hit it a mile every time up.

I got on Tony's team with Johnny Boy and the Fox. I was an okay fielder and I could hit, but nothing like Tony. Except for him, none of us could play for shit, but we all followed baseball. Most guys were from Queens and they liked the Mets; they were jazzed because the Mets traded for Willie Mays that season. I was a Yankees fan. Johnny Boy didn't care; he bet on any team he thought might win. When they had the baseball strike that year, Johnny bet on when it would end. He bet on our team in the softball game, and because of Tony Roach, we won.

Johnny, Quack Ruggiero, Fox, and I spent a lot of the game talking about a heist we were planning for a few days later. Quack had a tipster who told them about a load of mink pelts that were being shipped in an armored truck from a fur-dressing plant in the Bronx. Because the truck was armored and there would be an armed guard riding shotgun and possibly a second guard in the back, the job would require a four-man team.

This was one of the first high-dollar heists under Gotti's new command, and he didn't want any fuckups. He considered it a job for his old Bergin crew, and he was including me because I was partners with Fox, but he didn't want Tommy DeSimone in on it as the fourth.

Quack wanted John to use the tipster. The problem was this tipster was from Staten Island and connected to the Bonannos, and he wanted in on the action. Quack wanted to let him in because he was in a position to bring a lot of rich scores to the Bergin in the future. So even though everybody but Quack was against using the guy, a small-time thief with no balls who had never been on a real piece of work before, John relented.

All this was discussed as we were running bases and fielding plays and waiting for our turns at bat. It wasn't settled until the third or fourth inning, when Quack vouched for the guy as he stepped to the plate. Quack got a hit and John gave the okay.

After the game, we all went over to the Bergin for the barbeque.

———————

A couple days later we jacked the fur truck. It was pretty much a disaster from the get-go. We hit the truck in the middle of the afternoon rush hour on Bruckner Boulevard in the Bronx. Fox and I worked up front with Quack as backup and the tipster in the follow car. Taking the truck looked like a piece of cake. The driver was alone in the cab and it turned out there was no guard in the back either. But as soon as Fox and I jumped on the running board, the truck alarm went off.

And that's when the comedy started. It was like something out of the Keystone Kops, only it was gangsters doing the slapstick.

The driver unlocked the doors as soon as he saw our guns, and Fox got under the dash to smash the box, but that didn't shut off the alarm. I was about to get under there with him when I looked up and saw the fucking tipster running away down the block. I had to go after him and drag him back to the truck.

Once we got the alarm off and Fox put the truck in gear, the engine overheated and the truck stalled out. I sent the tipster to get some bottled water from a deli. I promised he would die if he tried to run away again. He went for the water and came back in five minutes.

Damn if that dumb motherfucker didn't buy a six-pack of seltzer.

That was the end of the comedy show. We got out of there and made it back to Charlie Fatico's drop with a truckload of mink worth 100 grand easy.

Charlie had handed the reins to Gotti, but he still kept his hand in and he still got a taste from any scores that he fenced. I ended up wishing that Gotti hadn't insisted we use Fatico for the score. He gave us a fraction of what Jimmy Burke would have paid for those minks.

We all wanted to murder Quack's tipster, Gotti most of all. He was furious about the fuckups because he knew it made him look bad. A lot of eyes were on him as the new Bergin boss, and he had to know the old guard would say that back in the day that tipster would have been executed on the spot for cowardice and for deserting his post in the face of the enemy. The fact that he was with the Bonannos made it all the worse.

Quack took the blame, and because he was so close to John and because the score was a success—plus the fact that the guy was supposedly good for future pieces of work—Gotti let the guy live.

So Quack slapped him around and then got me and Fox to give him a real working over. We beat the hell out of him and half choked him to death and sent him back to the rock on Staten Island he crawled out from under. He knew better than to set foot in Brooklyn or Queens again anytime soon.

We heard later that the tipster was busted for shooting his wife and dumping her body on the Long Island Expressway. A guy like that was an embarrassment. In the old days, nobody even remotely connected would have gotten away with the shit he did.

Later, back at the Bergin one day, Gotti and I had a long talk about that heist. He said guys like that tipster were a symptom of the rot at the heart of the Mob. He said that guys like John himself and like me, guys who were not only 100 percent Italian but who also had brains and balls and who respected the traditions, were getting hard to find.

I didn't realize at the time, but John was getting ready to make me an offer that I would have no choice but to refuse.

CHAPTER TWENTY-THREE

The Syrian

THREE MONTHS AFTER Joey Gallo ate at Umbertos and more than a year after Joe Colombo celebrated being Italian in Columbus Circle, the Second Gallo War was still raging in the streets. The body count was already close to twenty when some guy on a kamikaze mission went into the Ravenite in Little Italy and opened up with an automatic. Talk about a gangster who couldn't shoot straight. This for-shit hit man fired six shots at point-blank range. His target was a table full of Neil Dellacroce's guys playing cards, and he missed them all. Nobody was hit, but everybody must have been in shock because the shooter got out of the club alive.

Neil put his best investigators on the case; his guys made the cops and FBI look like pikers. They didn't use high-tech stuff. Their tools and tactics were simple: They stuck the barrel of a gun down a witness's throat and listened to him sing. It didn't take the Gambino detective squad long to solve the crime and track down the Ravenite shooter. He was charged, tried, convicted, sentenced, and executed in about ten seconds.

The legitimate world loved reading about the Mob war as long as it was like in *The Godfather*—which was still in theaters five months after it came out—and no "pain-in-the-ass innocent bystanders" got hurt.

The cheers stopped on Friday, August 11, 1972. That's when a couple of legitimate kosher beef wholesalers met two friends for drinks at the Neapolitan Noodle restaurant on the Upper East Side of Manhattan.

The Noodle was a little Italian place on East 79th Street. It was one of those below-the-sidewalk, semibasement kind of joints; you went down a few steps to go in. You couldn't get a good look at who was in there from the sidewalk. And if you were inside, Marilyn Monroe could stand out front with her dress blowing up over her head and you'd never know it.

That's probably why Allie Boy Persico picked the Neapolitan, so nobody would spot him when he had a meeting of his war council to figure out how to put the Gallos down once and for all.

Persico and his son, Little Allie Boy, and two of Dominic's friends, Jerry Langella and Pete Iocavelli, were having drinks at the bar while waiting for a table to open up. The four of them represented the top leadership of the Colombo Family since Joe C started vegetating somewhere and Snake Persico was doing the same thing in prison.

Right around 9:00 p.m., the maître d' told Allie Boy that his party's table was ready. As they left the crowded bar, their seats were immediately taken by the kosher beef guys and their two friends who had come to celebrate one of their kids' wedding engagement.

Moments after the businessmen ordered drinks, a guy walked in who looked like he came to the wrong restaurant. All the other men in the place, including Allie Boy's group and the businessmen at the bar, were wearing suits and ties. This character off the street was wearing shades and a long black wig that looked like something Cher would wear at the flea market. He squeezed in next to the businessmen at the bar and ordered a scotch. He took one sip and put his glass down. Then he took a step back from the bar and pulled out two long-barreled revolvers.

The man in the wig with the guns was a button imported from Vegas called the Syrian. He was brought in by Kid Blast Gallo because Allie Boy and his guys wouldn't recognize him when he walked into the restaurant. The trouble was, the Syrian didn't recognize Allie Boy either.

The Gallo tipster assigned to follow the enemy faction had reported that Allie Boy and his war council were wearing suits and sitting shoulder to shoulder at the bar of the Neapolitan Noodle. When the Syrian arrived, he immediately saw four sizable guys in suits at the bar. He leaned in close enough to hear New York accents. That was good enough for the Syrian.

He opened up on the kosher guys with both barrels. Allie Boy and his party saw the whole thing from their table, twenty feet across the dining room.

The Syrian walked out and left two dead and two wounded and a city full of legitimate people who didn't think it was so fun and exciting to have innocent civilians killed in the crossfire between warring Mafia families, even if they were shooting it out just like in *The Godfather*.

The next day the until-then universally praised hit movie got its first bad reviews. Jimmy Breslin wrote that to the widow of one of the dead innocent bystanders, *The Godfather* was like "hard-core pornography."

New York mayor John Lindsay held a news conference and demanded "that the romanticization of the mob must be stopped and the gangsters run out of town."[5]

There hadn't been any real public outrage against the Mob since 1952, when a kid named Arnold Schuster spotted Willie Sutton, a wanted fugitive, on the subway and called the cops. Schuster was hailed as a hero in the press, but he was rewarded by the Mob with a bullet in his balls and one more in each of his eyes. That brought a lot of heat down on the Families, and Albert Anastasia's poor judgment in ordering the hit was one of the reasons Carlo Gambino later used to justify whacking his boss.

Now, twenty years after the Schuster debacle, the fatal fiasco at the Neapolitan Noodle brought a firestorm down on Gambino himself. He became the target of public wrath because he was the most prominent of the real-life godfathers and was widely thought to be the puppet master behind the Mob war that had just cost the lives of two innocent bystanders.

Those dead businessmen caused Don Carlo way more than just a pain in the ass.

Outraged newspaper editors not only put Gambino's picture in the

---

[5] "Run Gangsters Out of Town Angry Mayor Tells Police," *New York Times*, August 17, 1972.

paper—they also published the addresses of his office in Brooklyn and his home on Long Island.

The ink was still wet when reporters started staking out the Don's office at 2230 Ocean Parkway and crawling around his estate at 34 Club Drive in Massapequa. While reporters grilled Gambino's neighbors and asked questions about the Mafia chieftain, carloads of tourists and gawkers flocked to see where the real-life godfather lived and where he made offers that could not be refused.

The papers also identified the Don's next-door neighbor, Ettore Zappi, as a Gambino capo, and for the first time, members of the reading public saw a name that would make headlines thirteen years later—Paul Castellano was identified as a close adviser of the first cousin, brother-in-law, and boss he would one day succeed.

Bad enough that the great Gambino had for the first time in his life become tabloid fodder and that his personal privacy had been disrespectfully violated. The real danger for Don Carlo came from the Manhattan district attorney, who announced that he was going to empanel a grand jury and subpoena six hundred Mob members to appear before it.

At that point Gambino and every connected guy in New York understood that the Syrian's stupidity at the Neapolitan Noodle had caused collateral damage that not only took the lives of two civilians but also threatened their own existence.

To reach a peace and to protect his own Family and to strengthen the New York Mob itself, Gambino began work on a blueprint to restructure the Families and to promote cooperation instead of war between them.

To implement his plan, he turned to trusted underlings, including one of his Family's promising young leaders, who in the eight months since his release from prison as a low-ranking soldier in Charlie Fatico's crew had risen to become its de facto boss and a relied-upon adviser to Neil Dellacroce, the number-two man in the whole Gambino empire— John Gotti.

CHAPTER TWENTY-FOUR

One Big Mob

SEPTEMBER 1972

A MONTH AFTER THE SHOOT-OUT at the Noodle, Johnny Gotti and I attended the wedding of our friend Big Funzi's son with our wives and kids. My son Sal Jr. was the ring bearer. He and John's son Frankie were the same age, four. It was a real Families affair. Dom and all the guys from our crew were there because Funz was with us. Johnny and his Gambino guys from the Bergin were there because we all hung out together, but also because John wanted to make a statement. After the ceremony, he spelled out what it was.

John pulled me aside for a talk during the reception. He started out like it was any other bullshit session. He said how much he liked the Sinatra Club and all the good times we had there and what made it a special place was that it wasn't all guys from one crew but from all the different Families that played cards there and just came by to hang out together.

Then Gotti got down to business.

"The Sinatra's like the All-Families Social Club," John said. He said that all the bosses should take a lesson from the club. Instead of war between the families, there ought to be more cooperation. That's when he told me that Carlo Gambino himself knew all about the Sinatra Club and he wanted to see more joint ventures like we had between our two Families.

Then John said that he had good reason to believe that the Commission was going to reopen the membership books within a year or two, and that young guys would be getting their buttons. That was good news for both him and me, he said.

The next thing he said wasn't such good news for somebody. At the same time that the bosses wanted to strengthen the families by bringing in good young guys, they also wanted to cut dead wood and, while they were at it, hunt for rats.

There were too many members in all the Families who weren't true *amici nostra*, friends of ours, John said. There were a lot of useless guys in the crews, made guys and associated guys both who had been around for years but who had to go. The Families had gotten fat and corrupt because too many guys were weak and undisciplined, he said. Too many guys were dealing heroin, and that was poisoning the Families. When John said the word *babania*, his lips curled and he said it with unmistakable hatred.

"There's a lotta garbage in the crews," he said. "And what happens with garbage—you get rats." That word he spoke like he was spitting it out of his mouth.

OCTOBER 1972

A month after the wedding, John returned to that same theme when I met with him at the Bergin to talk about a score Roundy tipped Fox and me to. We wanted to hit S. H. Pomerance, a very high-end custom brokerage warehouse at JFK that I knew about because Dominic and Jackie Donnelly and Big Funzi hijacked a truck out of there in 1969.

Roundy told Fox and me that Swiss Air used Pomerance for huge shipments of watches from all the best Swiss manufacturers. Fox and I thought at first that we'd hijack one of their trucks, like usual. But we had a problem with the drop. Jimmy Burke and Henry Hill lost their case—they were tried for extortion that year—and they were going away to Lewisburg. Jimmy was shutting down his warehouse until he got out. So we decided that instead of jacking one of the armored trucks Pomerance used, we'd go in there and help ourselves.

When I told Dom about it, he said no way. The idea was nuts. He knew because he'd cased the Pomerance warehouse himself. He said it was in a secure freight area inside the airport. I told him I was sure it would work, but to pull it off we'd need some inside help.

That's when I went to meet with John. I told him that Fox and I decided to shelve the heist until we found somebody inside. John gave his okay for Fox to work the score, and he even promised to give us another guy in his crew to help out.

John had been running Charlie Fatico's crew for just a few months. Now he was on the verge of getting another big bump up. Just like Fatico, his and John's boss Neil Dellacroce was having legal problems of his own. He had been indicted for tax evasion earlier in the year, and his case was set to go to trial in December. He was already starting to prepare for it by turning some of his operations over to John. That meant that come December, John would be officer in charge of the Family's legions at both the Bergin and the Ravenite—and that from then on he would be meeting directly with the emperor himself, Carlo Gambino.

That day at the Bergin made me think he already was.

As we talked, John touched on some of the things we discussed at Funzi's kid's wedding and again got to talking about the future of the Gambino Family and how his bosses—he didn't say the names, but I knew they were Neil and Don Carlo—wanted to fold the smaller Families into the bigger ones. They wanted to make the Mob smaller, leaner, and stronger, he said.

Everything he said was confirmed a couple of months later by a story in the *New York Times*. When I read the article,[16] I thought it sounded like Gotti could have written it. It said that Gambino wanted to reduce the number of Families to two or three "and ultimately one." He wanted to purge hundreds of made guys "who were a risk to security." That meant rats and guys who were dealing—guys like me.

The article said Gambino wanted to open the membership books "to allow the initiation of selected young men of proved strength and ability." I loved the way they put shit like that.

The paper also said "one boss was overheard grumbling"—the article

---

[16] "Gambino Believed Seeking Single Mafia Family Here," *New York Times*, December 8, 1972.

didn't mention that it was a rat or a bug who overheard the unnamed boss—that "Carlo wants to swallow up everybody."

That was pretty much Dominic's take on Gambino's vision for "One Big Mob" too. After the story came out and I talked to Dom about it, he said, "I know one guy who ain't goin' along with that bullshit—Carmine Persico. Don Carlo can swallow this"—Dom grabbed his joint—"before he swallows the Colombo Family."

I made sure I never told Johnny how my boss felt about Gambino's new order.

And I also made sure never to tell Dom how my conversation with John ended that day in October at the Bergin.

———————

John was saying that the problem with bringing in new members was that there wasn't a lot of good fresh blood out there. He said he wanted to build an army of loyal soldiers, but the talent pool was running dry. Even in the old neighborhood you couldn't find any 100 percent Italians, at least not any that had both brains and balls. He said you find a guy with an Italian last name, he's got an Irish mother; a guy looks Italian and his last name's O'Shaughnessy. "All we got's a bunch of mutts, Sally," he said.

That's when Gotti dropped the bomb on me.

He invited me to join his crew.

For one thing, he said, I was 100 percent Italian. Plus I spent half my time at the Bergin, I played cards with his guys at the Sinatra, and when I wasn't at either of those places, I was running around with Fox. He said I should go ahead and make it official.

I was flattered that he was taking me into his confidence in the first place and was proud to be asked to join him, and I told him so. But I also said that I was with Dominic and that my uncle had brought me into the Colombo Family, and I would dishonor him by switching my loyalties to the Gambinos. Besides, I said, I was an action junkie; I needed excitement. Robbing banks was one of my favorite things to do, but they brought too much federal heat for Don Carlo. I'd have to stop if I went with the Gambinos.

John said he admired my loyalty to my Family and that there were no hard feelings. Then he said that it was an open invitation, that things change. Who knows, he said, when the books finally do open, I might change my mind and want to join his Family. Left unsaid was the hint that by that time, there might not even be a Colombo Family.

Also left unsaid was the real reason *why* I said no to my friend, who in ten months' time had risen from the lower ranks of the Gambino Family to its very highest echelon—and who, as his power increased, became more and more of a danger to anyone who crossed him.

CHAPTER TWENTY-FIVE

Junk Dealers

NOVEMBER 1972

A S UNDERSTANDING AS John Gotti said he was when I turned him
down, I knew he was not the kind of Mob boss-on-the-rise who
liked to have his offers refused. But unwise as it might prove for me to
say no, I really had no choice. And the reason was I was making more
money dealing drugs than I knew what to do with. I had trouble doing
enough robbing and stealing and gambling and loan sharking to explain
where I was getting all the cash as it was.

Even if I thought I could continue to deal under John, which was out
of the question to begin with, I would have to kick up to him, which is
something I did not have to do with Dominic. Every other guy in the
Mob has to pay tribute to his crew captain; you have to pay a certain
percentage of your earnings to your boss. If you don't, if you fail to earn
enough or if you're light on your payments or chronically late, that can
be a capital offense.

So if I went with John I could get whacked if I earned too little, and
I could get whacked if I earned too much, because he'd know I must be
dealing.

Because my boss Dominic was also my drug business partner, I had
some protection. But dealing was a dangerous game to begin with. And
with Johnny now talking about purging the families of drug dealers, it
was all the more dangerous. Dom and I were exactly the guys Johnny and
Gambino were worried about; we were the guys who were poisoning the

talent pool; we were the guys who were corrupting and weakening the Families from within.

———————————

There were a lot of downsides to dealing besides the fatal consequences of getting caught. One was that it was boring; it provided zero kicks and excitement, which is what I lived for. Also, you were surrounded by low-lifes and oilers, which is what we called the users of the junk we sold.

One of my main dealers was a construction worker named Donnie, who was an oiler himself. He showed no outward signs of being a junkie, but he'd disappear for days at a time and I knew he was shooting himself.

Donnie introduced me to a guy everybody called Carmine the Tail. He was a big six-footer who got his name because he had a protruding ass bone. I made a business deal with Carmine because he had a lot of street customers. Before we sealed the deal, I gave him a sample of my *babania*. He brought a junkie along with him and had him shoot it up on the spot. Even though I had stepped on the pure six times, the kid almost OD'd on it. Carmine couldn't care less that the guy nearly died; he said he'd take all the smack I could supply him with. He agreed never to speak my name to anybody he dealt with; he kept his word and I made a ton of money with him. I didn't find out until later that he was hooked on the junk himself. But I knew he was a nasty and vicious piece of work right from the start.

I also had a husband-and-wife team working for me. Ozzie was an out-of-work short-order cook and small-time thief who dealt the stuff to support his own habit. Irene was a lifelong addict who would fuck you, steal from you, or do whatever she could to put another bang in her arm.

When I met an Italian kid named Victor, I thought I finally had a clean dealer working for me. He was a muscular tough guy who'd done a stretch in Sing Sing for robbery. I hired him to deliver my product to some of my other dealers. One day I met Ozzie and Irene to collect a payment, and they told me that the last bag Victor delivered was half a gram short. It turned out Victor was dipping; he holed up in a hotel somewhere and shot up the dope he was supposed to deliver.

I knew I couldn't take Ozzie and Irene's word for it; they might easily have ripped off the bag themselves. I had to crack Victor on the head a couple of times before he admitted it.

I was making enough money to buy a nice stand-alone two-story town house in Ozone Park. I paid $17,000 for it and put it in my father-in-law's name, like everything else I owned. I was getting rich on my dealing, but it was nothing compared to the wealth Dom and Jackie Donnelly were amassing.

Dom bought a new Cadillac every couple of months. He got an expensive forty-foot boat and spent a fortune on clothes and fancy jewelry. He loved playing the horses and thought nothing of dropping 3 or 4 g's on a single race.

He and Jackie were also branching out their business. They got into importing pot and expanding their drug business to Florida. They found an engineer down there who they got to design and manufacture silencers for machine guns; there was a big wartime demand for them in New York back then. The guy was a toy inventor Dom knew from childhood. When he got busted and took a plea for possession of silencers and machine guns, he was smart enough to keep his mouth shut about who he was making the silencers for. I met him in prison later on. He was a very straight guy who wasn't cut out for prison, and after being inside just a few weeks, he tried to kill himself. They sent him to a hospital and he got early release. He got out of the Life and was never heard from again.

Along with his wealth, Dom was beginning to develop a bad case of paranoia. It was well-founded considering that he had to worry about getting busted by the cops and whacked by the Mob.

He was also convinced that his friends were jealous of his money and his enemies were trying to rip him off or that he might be kidnapped by the Westies like Manny Gambino.

When a couple of other made guys who were also big-time suppliers got ripped off, Dom even accused me and Fox of being in on it.

He had a pretty good reason.

I kept my drug business a secret from Fox, but when I got a tip on a score that involved ripping off dealers, I knew he'd be up for it.

One of my street dealers told me about a house in Bedford-Stuyvesant where a gang of smack dealers bagged their dope. Every Sunday night, the place was loaded with cash.

Fox and I cased the place; we sat low in an old Chevy on a Sunday night and watched the house. The next week we figured out our plan. We went to Times Square and bought a couple of bogus NYPD detective badges.

The next Sunday we parked outside the place at around 11:00 p.m. We pinned our badges on our jackets and waited. Five minutes later, a tall black guy with a purple hat came down the block and turned into the house. Fox and I jumped out of the car and grabbed the guy. Fox shoved his 9mm automatic in the guy's back.

"You make a sound, you're deader than the Kennedys," he said.

We walked the guy to the front door and rang the bell, and they buzzed him in. At the end of the short hallway, a door opened. There were eight or ten girls in there wearing surgical masks and bagging the smack, and two guys counting money. We pushed our escort in ahead of us. "Police!" I shouted. "Make one fucking move and you're all dead. Everybody on the floor."

Fox covered me while I grabbed a bag and scooped up the money on the table. I grabbed a box full of bundled cash, and we were out of there in about two minutes. Another piece of cake.

We got back to Fox's apartment and counted the money. It was all small bills and it smelled like shit, but it was a sweet number—$42,000. The next day Fox spent a few thousand on new shoes and suits. I bought Angela a new Chevy Malibu; I paid the dealer $3,880 in cash.

I didn't breathe a word to anybody about our score, but Fox had to give Gotti 5 g's for his taste. Fox was loyal and would never think of cheating Johnny. John would have whacked even Fox for dealing drugs, but ripping them off was a different story.

Unfortunately for both of us, John told Dominic about our drug score. Dom wouldn't have cared except that just before this, a couple of his friends got ripped off by one of my tipsters, a sometime junkie called Nips. He was a tall, skinny guy with rotten teeth. Nips used to move quarter kilos and half kilos for Dom and Jackie. He started using again and became part of a vicious gang of junkies who ripped off other drug dealers.

Nips's gang made the mistake of stealing close to $1 million from two connected guys, Colombos who were friends of Dom's.

Dom and I were out drinking one night, and he asked me if I'd seen Nips around lately. I hadn't and I said so. Then he told me the story. He said Nips and two other guys raided the house of a capo from our Family. The capo's mother was home, and she had a stroke and dropped dead on the spot.

When Dom started telling me the story, he was calm, but by the time he got to the part about the guy's dead mother, his face was twitching he was so pissed off.

He took a long drag on his Camel and blew the smoke in my face. "I know you and your partner just took down a black motherfucker in Brooklyn." He looked hot enough to kill me right there, but his voice was ice-cold.

"Dominic, I swear on my kids. Yeah, we nailed that guy, but that's it. We haven't done anybody else like that."

Dom didn't say anything for a few minutes. Then he said, "We'll have to wait and see what Nips has to say."

For the next two weeks I didn't hear anything more from Dominic. I was starting to get in a panic. Nips might say anything to save his own ass; he might tell Dom that Fox and I were the other two guys so in case Dom let him go he wouldn't get whacked by his real partners.

When Dom called me in for a meet—at Sebastian's, no less—I didn't know what to expect. My only hope was that if Nips had dropped the dime on us, I'd already be digging my own grave on Boot Hill or taking one of Charlie Carneglia's acid baths.

Dom ordered us a couple of steaks. When we finished, we had a few drinks and he finally got to the point.

"We got Nips last week," he said. "We tortured him, and before we killed him he opened up. He finally told us who the other two guys were."

He let me spin for a minute, and then he said, "For a while there I thought you and Fox were in on the robbery."

"Dom, you know me better than that," I said. I tried to laugh it off, but he could tell how relieved I was. He said he and his capo friend tracked down the other two guys and took care of them. I knew Dom enjoyed killing, and it showed when he said it.

In November 1972, a huge scandal broke over what was said to be the biggest drug rip-off in history. And it wasn't dealers who got ripped off. It was the cops.

When the police broke the famous 1960 French Connection case that the movie was based on, they confiscated a shipment of *babania* worth something like $30 million. The junk was stored in the NYPD's property clerk's office on Broome Street, along with hundreds of pounds of other confiscated coke and heroin shipments and all kinds of stolen property. Altogether the NYPD stash was worth about $73 million. Because of all the publicity about the case after the movie won the Oscar, somebody thought it might be interesting to find out whatever happened to all the drugs.

The cops opened up the storage bin. The French Connection drugs had been stored in three giant suitcases for ten years. They opened the suitcases . . . which now contained a couple hundred pounds of cornstarch and flour. The entire property clerk's drug stash was gone.

It turned out that the guy who stole it was an old friend of Dom's, a Lucchese guy named Vincent Pappa. Vince had found a cop who worked at the property clerk's office and did what wise guys do best: Vince bought the cop and the cop helped him steal the smack.

One of Vince's main partners was a guy named Fat Gigi Iglese, who was part of the Purple Gang uptown and one of the biggest dealers in New York. I got to know Fat Gigi in prison; he was one of two guys I got close to inside who showed me a way out of that Life. But back then, in 1972, that never crossed my mind. I was living in a world where wiseguys were selling smack that they stole from the cops who took it from other wiseguys. Who would ever want to leave a world like that?

Another guy who Vince supplied vast quantities of stolen NYPD smack to was his friend Dominic Cataldo. Besides the Marseilles connection that continued to bring in kilos of smack by sea and air, Dom and Jackie had had a pipeline to the NYPD property clerk's junk from the beginning.

When I realized that all this time I'd been cutting and bagging and selling some of the junk that won Gene Hackman an Academy Award, I laughed my ass off.

CHAPTER TWENTY-SIX

A Heist of the Heart

DECEMBER 1972

Like a lot of successful young executives with several businesses to run and a wife and kids at home, I didn't have as much time as I would have liked to spend with my mistress.

Business was booming at the Sinatra Club, which meant I worked nights and into the next day on Sundays, Wednesdays, and Thursdays. Monday nights were spent at the club taking care of our shylock businesses, meeting with customers, and balancing the club's books as well as our loan ledgers. On Saturday nights, even I obeyed the Mob rule most of the time and spent at least part of it with my wife, taking her out to dinner or a movie.

That left Tuesdays and Fridays for Jane, and a lot of time she was busy with the demands of running two brothels and an out-call service, and seeing to the needs of those customers who paid to lick her boots and feel the sting of her whip.

Because we had to carve time out of our busy schedules to see each other, we tried to fill those nights with as much action and excitement as possible. That meant lots of wild nights out on the town and all kinds of kinky sex.

We still banged in the back of the van in Times Square, and we even did it under the blankets in the back of a horse-drawn carriage clip-clopping through Central Park one night.

Jane liked me to tie her to the bed and fuck her. Because she loved jewelry, she liked it even better when I tied her up with gold belts and silver chains. One night I had a big gym bag full of hot jewels that I was meeting with a fence the next morning to sell. I took the bag with me to Jane's, undressed her, and tied her wrists and ankles to the bedposts with belts made of solid gold braid. Then I covered her body in emeralds and rubies and sapphires, diamond necklaces and gold bracelets. We had a great time that night.

Whenever I was with Jane, I always showered before I went home and I always checked out my clothes to make sure there were no telltale strands of hair. I kept a clothes brush in my car and gave myself a quick going over before I walked in the door at home.

But Angela had the forensic skills of a CSI investigator. Despite all my precautions, she compiled a whole shitload of fiber evidence—all in the form of strands of hair and all of it pointing to the conclusion that I was seeing another woman who was blond and possibly wore gardenia-scented perfume.

Angela was a one-woman court of law, but for whatever reason she refused to convict without incontestable eyewitness proof. It was almost like I told Fox—what she didn't see didn't hurt her. And as her actions told me after I came home that morning and found the envelope with the hair in it, if I didn't shove it in her face, she could and would live with it.

I had been seeing Jane for almost a year and so far managed to avoid any situation that offered the slightest possibility of a chance encounter with Angela when I was out with Jane.

As it happened, I had less than a year remaining before my luck ran out.

All that is not to say that Angela was even a little bit happy knowing I was fucking around on her or that she was giving me a pass. In fact she made me pay for my sins daily. My punishment came in the form of endless nagging and bitching and complaining about what a shit husband I was.

And Angela was never afraid to use the one dagger that never failed to hit home, the one thing that hurt the most—my neglect of my sons.

Years later I would turn my life upside down for them and try to make up for the shit hand they were dealt when they were little and their father was basically on the lam. Back then I was a virtual stranger to them; I wasn't home enough to really even get to know them. I felt tremendous guilt about it, but I never did a damn thing to change the way I treated them.

I used to buy their affection with toys and gifts. And that Christmas of 1972 I came up with a surprise that helped ease my guilt.

But before that I got a nice little gift of my own.

———————————

Earlier that year, Dom and I got caught in an FBI gambling sweep. Along with a dozen other mobsters, we were charged with interstate gambling. The government had a solid case and we were all found guilty. Before the sentencing hearing, Mike Coiro told me to go to the VA hospital instead and check myself into the psycho ward.

When I didn't show up at the sentencing, the Mouthpiece apologized for my absence. He told the judge that I had a history of psychiatric problems. He said I was mentally disturbed and that I was seeking professional care.

Everybody else got slapped with $7,000 and $8,000 fines. For Dominic, the fine was no hardship; to him that much money wasn't fruit, it was crumbs.

I finally appeared in court a few weeks before Christmas. The judge looked over my medical sheet and let me go with a $1,000 fine.

Dom couldn't believe it. "Sally Ubatz," he said, "you crazy motherfucker. It pays to be sick in the head."

———————————

On Christmas morning, I had all kinds of toys and presents wrapped under the tree for my sons but no time to give them. I barely stuck around long enough for them to open all their gifts.

Christmas was on a Monday that year, and I had to meet Bald Vinny to pick up a shopping bag full of spanking new $20 bills.

After that I had to go to the Sinatra Club to settle up with customers, since the successful shylock never misses a payday, even when it falls on Christmas.

On the way from Vinny's to the club, I had an idea that hit me like a vision on the road to fucking Damascus. It was like a score with two ends where you get rich coming and going, like Vince Pappa stealing stolen goods from the cops and selling them again.

Only my idea had nothing to do with smack or swag of any kind. It was a heist of the heart.

I had been planning to fly down to Atlanta that week to spread Vinny's bills around. In the car on Christmas Day, I decided to drive instead and take four-year-old Sal Jr. with me. We would have a blast on the drive down, we'd have some quality time together, and then I'd show him the sights in Hotlanta.

When I got home and sprung the surprise and told Little Sal we were leaving in the morning on a road trip, he started jumping up and down. Even Angela thought it was a great idea. And when I told him we'd be staying in a fancy hotel in Atlanta, he got even more excited.

I didn't tell him or his mother, of course, that I had already booked an adjoining room at the hotel and that Jane was going to fly down and meet us in Atlanta.

I was damn well pleased with myself for cooking up a plan that eased my guilt for neglecting my kids and simultaneously gave me a chance to spend time with the woman I neglected them for.

And there was an unexpected bonus to taking Little Sal along to Atlanta. Having a cute little boy along with me made spreading counterfeit paper as easy as the smile on Sal's face when I bought him goodies in every candy and toy store, five-and-dime, grocery, and deli in downtown Atlanta. Not one clerk in any of stores even looked at the $20 I gave them before handing over the change.

We were all back in New York by the following Saturday. The night after that was New Year's Eve, and Angela and I had dinner with Mike Coiro and Dominic and his wife and Joey and Louise Cataldo at the Pan American Steak Pub where we always saw in the New Year together. I had a date set up with Jane for after that.

Fox and I were also celebrating our first year together as crime partners, and Jane said she had no problem with me bringing him along when we went out carousing after midnight.

On Sunday afternoon before the fun started, I went over to Fox's pad in Lindenwood Village where we still had milk crates full of stinking dollar bills from our Bed-Stuy drug score.

We were sitting around with nothing to do when I had an idea. I got a pair of scissors and grabbed a bunch of bills and started cutting them in half. "What the fuck are you doing?" Fox screamed. He never got over being poor as a kid, and what I was doing was the ultimate sin.

"We're gonna have some fun tonight," I said.

After our family New Year's Eve party at the Pan American, I dropped Angela off at home. When she asked where the fuck I was going, I gave her the line that only pissed her off all the more since it was so obviously a lie. I told her I had business to take care of and it wasn't any business of hers.

Fox had spent some of his loot on a new Lincoln Continental with a moonroof. We picked up Jane and bought a case of Dom Pérignon. Then I told Fox to drive us to Times Square.

There were still thousands of drunks stumbling around on the streets two hours after the ball dropped. The cops had reopened the streets to traffic by then, and I had Fox motor slow down Broadway.

I had a big bag full of cut-up bills in the back of the Lincoln, and I told Jane to grab a handful. We stood up through the moonroof and started throwing the cut-up bills to the crowds outside.

The drunks fell all over themselves scrambling for the bills; they'd grab a bunch and start searching for the matching half. They went crazy scooping up the money. Fox was honking the horn and Jane and I got hysterical from laughing and yelling and screaming out the moonroof.

After that, Jane dared Fox to streak down Broadway. He chugged half a bottle of champagne, took off all his clothes, and ran down 42nd Street while Jane and I fucked in the backseat.

We rang in the New Year in a big way.

We didn't know it, but 1973 was going to be the last good year we would have before everything went to hell for all three of us.

PART FOUR

PART FOUR

CHAPTER TWENTY-SEVEN

Stealing Time

JANUARY 1973

FOX AND I WERE at the Bergin, talking over our plans to hit the Swiss Air watches shipment at S. H. Pomerance, when we heard about Manny Gambino.

They found his body in a dump out in Jersey. Manny's not-so-final resting place was on the site of an abandoned World War II navy base and ammo depot in Sandy Hook. It was swampy ground, and it wasn't totally frozen even though it was the middle of winter.

The guys who dug Manny up out of the muck said it was eerie because he was buried straight up in a sitting position, like the stiffs buried alive in Pompeii almost two thousand years before. Manny was dressed in a suit and tie, and he was just sitting there upright under the ground like he was in his favorite booth at Sebastian's.

Manny's car had been found at the airport; his kidnappers must have whacked him in the car and left him there where he sat. Rigor mortis set in by the time they got around to burying him and dumping the car at the airport.

The whole time the Gambinos were negotiating with the Westies for Manny's release, Don Carlo's nephew was already dead. The Gambinos paid those Irish bastards 100 g's for Manny's safe return—five times what the Westies would get for any other loan shark they snatched.

You could bet a kilo of pure smack that Gambino would have launched an all-out attack and burned the Westies' Hell's Kitchen headquarters to the ground and killed every double-dealing Irish thug in it if he could. The gang had made Gambino look vulnerable by kidnapping his nephew in the first place. By killing him and then shaking down his uncle for 100 g's made the great godfather look like a chump.

But the Syrian had already brought so much heat down on Don Carlo by his botched hit at the Neapolitan Noodle that Gambino had to not only resist launching an all-out offensive, he also was forced to order John Gotti to delay his surgical strike against the guy who, according to Gotti's own investigation, had kidnapped Manny.

Almost four months would pass before the Don felt it was safe enough to dispatch Gotti, now the trusted lieutenant who was running the Gambino Family's two largest crews, to exact revenge for his nephew's murder.

———

Fox and I both were a little busted up about Manny, who we got to be pretty good friends with from all the nights we spent with him and Beverly at Tommy Argo's joint. Now that we knew for sure that Manny wasn't just being held for ransom somewhere, we knew we weren't going to be seeing Beverly at Sebastian's anymore either. That's the way it was in the Mob: Once a guy was gone, that meant any mistresses or side chicks were dead too, as far as his Family was concerned. Same with his other family—in Manny's case the Gambinos were both. We knew Beverly would have to move out of the house Manny bought for her and disappear. She didn't exist in any way as far as both his families were concerned. She wouldn't even be allowed to go to the funeral; the girlfriends and mistresses never were.

———

Right before we heard about Manny, I met a kid at Club 93, a pothead who lived upstairs from the bar. We got to talking and—what do you know?—it turned out that he worked at S. H. Pomerance at JFK. And not only did he work at the brokerage, his job was in the secure customs warehouse, the place where Fox and I had been clocking the armored trucks full of high-dollar Swiss watches.

I hung out with the kid and got him a couple ounces of some high-grade weed, gratis. He couldn't believe his good luck. I was his new best friend. I told him I had colitis, which I didn't, but I gave it as the reason I wasn't getting high with him, and he bought it. I guess he could tell from everything about me that I was no kind of cop.

From this kid I learned the whole operation that Roundy tipped us to: Swiss Air made the delivery on Tuesdays; the freight was delivered to Pomerance, where it was stored in their secure freight cargo area overnight; the next morning at 10:00, federal customs agents arrived, checked the freight, stamped it, and released it for shipment. The kid was stoned as Saint Stephen, but everything he said was on the money, right down to the special chrome American brand padlock used on the outside security door. I also got the kid to tell me his own schedule. We were in luck. He was off on Wednesday mornings when the customs guys arrived.

Fox's cousin drove for a trucking company that hauled cargo in and out of the airport. The cousin let Fox have some of his paperwork. I got Bald Vinny's man to make a perfect copy, filled it out to Pomerance, and dated it for the Wednesday we chose for the score. We stole a truck, and Vin got us registration papers to match the hot plates we put on the truck.

On the day of the heist, I rode up front with Fox; in the back of the truck were Big Funzi and Charlie, a good heist guy who was one of the old-time hit men Gotti inherited from Fatico. Charlie's nephews ran a record label that had a lot of teenybopper hits; this was the time when there weren't a lot of singers acting like bullshit gangsters; actual gangstas ran a lot of the music business in those days.

Fox drove the truck to the rear gate at the airport. He showed the bogus documents, and the security guy checked the plates; it all looked good and he waved us through. The pothead's directions from the gate to the warehouse were perfect. It took us five minutes to get there and back up to the dock.

Next to the big padlocked garage doors was a regular steel door. I rang the bell, and somebody buzzed us in without even looking. Fox and Charlie and I were standing with our backs to the door. We pulled down our ski masks and walked right in—we left Funz in the truck as backup because he was a giant and stuck out in a crowd. When Funzi helped

Dom hijack the Pomerance truck in 1969, they got found out because witnesses described a six-foot-four hijacker, and that was enough to finger Funzi because there weren't many guys that size in the truck-stealing business. There still weren't, and that's why we didn't want Funz working up front for us now. Another result of that earlier Pomerance score is an interesting story that I'll get to later.

Inside the warehouse, we had the entire shift taped and cuffed and sitting in a windowless office by 9:05. We got their keys to the storage area and the outside padlock. We had fifty-five minutes before customs arrived, but we figured we'd be out of there in fifteen. We figured wrong.

Watches are one of Switzerland's biggest exports. They must've shipped every high-end watch they made that month to New York. We were looking at stacks and stacks of crates filled with the best watches in the world—*fifty-six thousand of them.*

We thought about untying some of the workers and getting them to load the truck. We got it done ourselves, but we cut it close. We had a long drive to the drop—with Jimmy's operation shut down, we were using a funeral home owned by someone in Dom's family out in the Hamptons. It was almost 10:00 by the time we were loaded. The customs inspectors would be there at any minute.

Luckily, I had brought along my own chrome American padlock, and we put that on the loading dock doors. We hoped that might delay things so we could get a good head start.

We got all the way out to the Hamptons no problem. We made sure the tank was topped. It was during the gas shortage and there were long lines at all the stations; it would not have been cool to have the cops on our ass and we're sitting in line at some gas pump with a hot truck full of hot merchandise.

What we hadn't figured on was somebody croaking. We pulled up in the truck and there was a funeral service going on. We drove around back and parked next to the hearse. We were hurrying to unload before they brought the stiff out the back and loaded it into the hearse.

Finally we got the crates down to the basement. Funzi and Charlie ditched the truck while Fox and I started opening the crates. We couldn't believe it. There were tens of thousands of the best watches made by man: gold watches, silver watches, Omegas, Piagets, Movados. Even after Funzi and Charlie got back, it took us hours to count and sort the watches. It was dark down in the basement, and at one point Charlie asked what time it was. All the watches were set in Switzerland, five or six time zones ahead. We all fell out laughing. We had fifty-six thousand fucking watches and *nobody's got the right time*.

We divided the watches into four equal shares, fourteen thousand for each of us. We each negotiated our own deals. Fox and Funzi and Charlie all used Charlie Fatico's fence, who paid them 40 grand each for their ends. Dominic sent his fence out to look at my stash. I put aside a few thousand of the best gold watches; he still paid out $55,000 for my end.

The night after the score, I went into Club 93. The pothead was in there and was all excited about the big robbery at Pomerance. He got the whole story from the guys on the morning shift. He told me all about it, including my favorite part where the customs agents arrived and their key didn't work in the American padlock. They had to get a torch some-where and cut it off. It was after 11:00 a.m. before they even started look-ing for whoever pulled the score.

The kid had no idea it was me who stole the watches. But somebody ratted us out. We found that out three days after the robbery, when our mouthpiece, Mike Coiro, called and told me an amazing story.

He said that back in '69, when Dom and Jackie jacked the Pomer-ance truck and Funzi got ID'd, Mike made a deal to return the merch before it was fenced. The deal was set up by some of Mike's contacts in the Queens robbery division and Lloyd's of London, the big insurance company that covered Pomerance.

The cops agreed to bury the case, so Dom and Jackie moved the merch to a U-Haul and parked it somewhere in Queens to be picked up. They hid out and watched when two detectives came for the truck. They opened the back and took their own piece of the pie. They went through the shipment and stashed a bunch of the loot in their own car before they drove off with the truck. The return to Pomerance went smooth and nothing was said, even though the shipment was short. Funzi was never charged and everybody moved on.

Now, four years later, the same Queens detective who set it up in
'69 called Mike and said Lloyd's of London knew we pulled the watches
score and they would pay 300 g's for the return of our entire load, no
questions asked.

We told Mike to tell the cop we didn't know what the fuck he was
talking about. We didn't take the deal because we'd already divided the
merch and agreed to prices. But we couldn't figure out how the Queens
cop knew we pulled down the score. Nobody ID'd any of us and it was a
mystery how they fingered us. The cop never would have gone to Lloyd's
just on a hunch that it was Funzi—or me just because I was connected to
Coiro and Dom.

It wasn't until Fox told John about the cops acting as go-between
with Lloyd's of London that we found out the answer. John told Fox that
the only way they could have learned was from a rat loose in the crew.
Then he let Fox in on the secret: Carlo Gambino himself had warned
him that there was a traitor inside the Bergin.

When Fox told me about it, he said that John did everything he
could to find the rat and that a couple of suspects had been taken care
of. I didn't say anything, but that made me think that maybe some of the
Gambino casualties of the new Gallo War were actually victims of John
Gotti's own war on rats.

We would all have to wait thirteen years before we found out that the
suspected rats who got whacked were innocent. And then, when the real
traitor was finally exposed in 1986, it turned out to be a guy in the crew who
Gotti ordered to find the leak in the Bergin and plug it. So the hunter and
his prey were one and the same—the rat himself.

CHAPTER TWENTY-EIGHT

Woman Trouble

MAY 1973

THE IDEA FOR OUR road trip began as a joke, a funny line Jane had picked up from one of her girls: "Hey, hey, first of May, outdoor fucking begins today!"

It ended with Jane, who never allowed a man to kiss her on the lips, and me, the king of pay 'em, fuck 'em, and forget 'em, finding a kind of religion—one where we felt reborn and vowed to make our new-bloomed love last. For a couple of criminals for whom the word "fidelity" was as foreign as a chaste hooker in a whorehouse, that was a pretty big step.

Our transformation occurred the day after my twenty-eighth birthday. May Day fell on a Tuesday that year, and because our track-gambling business was slowing to a crawl and because I had worked alone on my birthday at the club, doing the books and collecting from our shy-lock customers while Dom took care of some smack shipment, he told me to take the day off.

I picked up Jane that morning and we set off on our road trip. We planned to drive up into the Catskill Mountains and find a meadow somewhere and do some outdoor fucking. It was a beautiful spring day in the sixties, but we never rolled in the hay—not outdoors, anyway.

Jane said she wanted to stop at the Mohonk Mountain House and buy me lunch as a birthday present. The Mohonk is a big, beautiful inn built in the late 1800s on a lake outside New Paltz. We took one look at the place and checked in. We had a big lunch and spent the afternoon walking around the lake. We had a couple of bottles of wine at dinner and went up to our room.

Jane brought a little coke and champagne. She did a line, and we were just sitting on a little love seat in our room when she started crying. When I asked her what was the matter, she couldn't talk. She was sobbing and hyperventilating. I was afraid she was having some kind of hysterical breakdown, but she finally caught her breath and calmed down a little. She kept on crying and the tears were pouring from her eyes, but she managed to tell me about something that happened when we were down in Atlanta between Christmas and New Year's.

Because I didn't want Sal Jr. telling Angela all about the pretty blond lady who stayed in the room next door, he never knew Jane was there. Sal and I spent all day spreading paper and Jane did her own thing. At night, once I put him to bed and he was asleep, then we opened the connecting door to her room.

Every once in a while I got up to check on Sal. I went into the other room to make sure he was warm enough and hadn't kicked off his covers.

Jane started sobbing as she told me how she got up and followed me to the door and peeked in a couple of times. She said that seeing me with him broke her heart, that it reminded her of her own child.

Then she told me something that she'd left out of the story back in June when we had that long talk during the hurricane. She said that she got pregnant in 1968, which was the year Sal was born. She wanted to have the baby but changed her mind and had an abortion because she was a whore and didn't want to raise a kid in that life.

She said that now she was glad that she had the abortion because she was still a whore and it would have been cruel to bring a child into a world like hers—and mine.

"That's why you have to get out of this Life," she said. "You don't belong in this Life." She said that over and over that night.

Jane kept talking, and all the emotion she kept jailed up inside her tough-as-leather-madam-with-a-whip exterior kept pouring out. She said how empty she felt, how she hated herself for living the way she did, how lonely she was at Christmas when I was home with my family and how everyone she knew, even her customers, were home with their families—while she was all alone in her fabulous apartment full of things she didn't give a shit about.

She broke down again, wailing how ashamed she was of her life.

It broke my fucking heart seeing her like that, and I tried to tell her that she wasn't an evil person, that she made guys feel good, she play-acted with them, she didn't beat them up and break their heads with a baseball bat and con a girl out of the loot in her dead boyfriend's safe-deposit box.

Jane said how tender I was with my little boy and that I had to get out of the Life so he wouldn't follow in my footsteps. All of a sudden, I was crying too. That's something I never did before, not in front of anybody, and for sure not in front of a woman. I was way too macho for that, but here I was crying like a baby right along with her.

Then she said something that sounded from the way she said it like it was as big a surprise to her as it was to me.

"I love you," she said. "I mean it. It's insane, but I do. I love you."

Then something even more unbelievable happened.

I said it too. "I love you."

That night we made love. It wasn't anything like any of the sex we usually had. It was tender like the night of Hurricane Agnes only even more intense, with some kind of spiritual trance we both went into. I remember touching her lips with my fingertips and feeling her heartbeat and looking into her eyes until she changed into some other kind of being, a spirit. As we made love, we kept looking into each other's eyes and grinning in amazement, like we were possessed by some other-worldly kind of energy. I felt like I was in the arms of God—and She was the hottest damn woman who ever lived.

Afterward I told Jane I wasn't sure what just happened, but whatever it was I didn't ever want to lose it.

Jane said we were in the presence of a higher power, and if we didn't keep it alive it would be a sin. "It would be like an abortion," she said. "Not for any kind of bullshit moral reason but because we would regret it the rest of our lives like I regret not having my baby."

I never heard anybody say anything that heavy in all my life before or since. When she said it, I believed it totally—that our love was some kind of divine power and we'd be struck down and suffer if we didn't honor and obey it.

We vowed that night to keep it alive at all costs.

It was a vow that turned into a curse.

The next morning the spirit was as alive between us and as strong as it was the night before.

After we made love, we renewed the vow, and we each made a pledge.

Jane promised me that she would close her brothels and stop seeing her dominatrix customers and all other men. She would get out of that life totally and start anew in the legitimate world.

I promised Jane that I would tell Angela about our love, and that whatever it took I had to have Jane in my life. I would ask Angela to accept Jane as part of our family, and if she refused, I would leave her.

"And promise me," Jane said, "that you'll get out of the Life too, for the sake of your sons, so they don't get trapped too."

"I will," I said.

That afternoon I dropped her off in the city and drove to the Sinatra Club to get ready for that night's games. On the way, I imagined our life together. I pictured Jane and me living in a big Dutch Colonial like Dominic's out in Valley Stream and right next door Angela in an identical house and the kids playing on the big green lawn between.

The part about getting out of the Life and joining the legitimate world—I didn't give that another thought.

Jane and I hadn't gotten much sleep the night before, and I had to pop trucker pills to make it through work at the club because that night's game didn't break up until noon the next day.

Because I crashed out that afternoon and slept right through dinner and into the night, it saved the Fox's life. Otherwise I wouldn't have been home when Joey Cataldo called to raise the alarm that Fox's lust for women who were the "brunetter the better" was about to get him killed.

While I was sleeping, Fox and Joey were out carousing. Fox talked Joey into going to a club in Brooklyn that was the hangout of some Colombian drug gang. Fox wanted to go there because he knew it would be full of Colombian women. Of all the dark-haired women in the city, he loved South American chicks the most. He knew every bar in Manhattan and the boroughs where you could find hot women from south of the border. Unfortunately for Fox, the bar he and Joey went into was owned by a drug dealer whose Colombian girlfriend Fox had been banging. The owner wasn't there but his crew was, and they recognized Fox and cornered him in the bar.

Joey slipped out of the place and found a pay phone. He called me at 3:00 in the morning. If I had been at Jane's or out somewhere on my own, which would have been the case every other night of the year, Joey would have been out of luck. But he got me on the phone and said these guys have got Fox at their club and they're waiting until it closes at 4:00 and then they're going to kill him.

I got out of bed, got dressed, and got the two everyday Walthers that by then I was keeping in a new locked stash in the basement. I was out of the house two minutes after Joey called. I jumped in the car and I was doing a hundred on Grand Central Parkway.

Joey said if I got there late, he didn't know how I was going to slip in like he slipped out. Slip? My balls. I got there and the doors were closed but they hadn't locked up yet. I kicked the doors open and charged in with both guns out. I didn't give a fuck what customers were there.

I saw Fox in the back at the bar. I shouted, "Don't anybody fucking move!" I almost hoped they did. I kept my eye on the bartender to make sure he wasn't reaching for a piece.

Fox grinned and got up from the bar and walked over and stood behind me.

We backed out of there like Butch and fucking Sundance.

Fox steered clear of Colombian bars after that.

But Fox had another kind of woman trouble. It was a lot closer to home and would prove even more dangerous than a crew of pissed-off Colombian drug dealers.

———————

Tommy DeSimone had been on his best behavior and acted like a real gentleman the previous spring when he met Fox's sister Patricia at Mother-in-Law's barbeque. And because Fox was so protective of his sister and watched Tommy like a hawk, he didn't notice what I saw that day. Patricia was totally charmed by Tommy, and Fox's worst fear—that she would fall for a gangster and be lured into that Life herself—might be coming true.

It was easy to see—for anybody but Fox—what the kid sister of a dashing New York City gangster would see in Tommy DeSimone. He was a good-looking guy with an exciting life. Everywhere he went he was treated with what must have looked to her like respect even if it was, in fact, fear.

More than anything else Tommy had going for him in Patricia's eyes was the fact that not only was he friends with her brother, who she worshipped, he also was his business partner.

At the same time, she might have been attracted to Tommy *because* Fox was always telling her to find a legitimate guy. Every kid wants to rebel, and since Patricia didn't have a father, maybe she was rebelling against Fox a little bit when she flirted with Tommy.

Patricia always went to Mother-in-Law's barbeques with her own mom and Fox. But she was old enough to drink now, and a few times she went into the Parkside on her own or for a beer with her friends.

It was on a night like that that she ran into Tommy at the Parkside, and this time Fox wasn't around to chaperone. She and Tommy talked like any girl and guy might. Patricia was still a teenager, but it's not like Tommy was robbing the cradle—even though he was already a heavy hitter in the Mob, he was only twenty-three years old in 1973.

Tommy asked Patricia out that night, and they went on a few dates during the summer. Patricia knew better than to tell Fox, and Tommy sure as hell wasn't going to tell him. I don't know what happened between them, and Tommy never said, but somehow Fox found out that they were going out. By the time he did, I don't think they were really seeing each other anymore, but that didn't stop Fox from forbidding his sister from ever seeing Tommy Two Guns again.

The next time Fox saw Tommy at the Sinatra Club, they nearly got into a fight about him dating Patricia. Fox was cool at first; he told Tommy he didn't want his sister involved in our Life and asked him to respect that. Tommy said sure, but being the way he was and because there were a lot of the guys around, Tommy made some crack about how he tried to stop her but she just couldn't keep her hands off him.

Fox blew up. I had to grab him from the back in a bear hug before he slugged Tommy and took his head off with that killer right fist. I thought Tommy was lucky Gotti wasn't there that night or he would have helped Fox beat the shit out of him.

Consorting without permission with the women in a connected guy's family—mothers, sisters, daughters, wives—was a whackable offense. Guys have been fighting vendettas and wars over women since time began—that's why the old Sicilians made fucking another guy's woman a capital offense; they wanted to nip that shit in the bud before it could blow up into a war. John Gotti believed in those traditions and wouldn't think twice about whacking a guy who violated Mob law.

There was no evidence at all that Tommy was screwing Fox's sister. And there was nothing that Gotti or Fox could do about it if there was, because under that same Mob law, Tommy was Lucchese and they couldn't whack him without Paul Vario's okay. But Gotti hated Tommy to begin with, and he didn't need permission to pound the living shit out of him for messing with the sister of one of his favorite guys.

That night at the club, Fox told Tommy to stay away from Patricia. Tommy told him to keep his shirt on. Fox didn't have anything to worry about anyway, Tommy said, because he was seeing somebody else.

They left it at that, but from then on there was real tension between my two heist partners. Tommy always got a kick out of breaking everybody's balls, not just Fox's. He loved jabbing people to see how far he could push them. He started needling Fox by just saying things in passing. He'd point out a woman in a club who had a gorgeous body and say she reminded him of Patricia. He'd always pick out someone who *did* look a little like her so there was nothing Fox could really say. But Tommy got under his skin with that shit, to the point that Fox became convinced that Tommy and Patricia were sneaking around behind his back.

Early the next year, Fox's paranoia about Tommy and his sister almost torpedoed the richest score our crew ever pulled.

CHAPTER TWENTY-NINE

Whack Job

MAY 22, 1973

A FULL YEAR AFTER MANNY Gambino was kidnapped and five months after his body was dug up in Jersey, John Gotti and his boyhood buddy Angelo Quack Ruggiero and a Bergin guy named Ralphie Gallione drove to a bar on Staten Island. The bar was a dive with a cute name, Snoope's. I guess Charles Shulz didn't want them using the dog's name so they spelled it with an "e." Anyway, they didn't go there looking for Charlie Brown.

The Gambinos were looking for the guy whose name came up on the plate number Fox ran for Gotti the year before. John, Quack, and Ralphie went to Snoope's because they had a tip that the guy—James McBratney—was in there having a drink at the bar.

And that's right where they found him, sipping a sixty-five-cent glass of crème de menthe when the crew from the Bergin walked in.

It turned out that McBratney knew the Gambinos were looking for him, and in case of trouble he never left home without a loaded machine gun. Unfortunately for him, he left it in the trunk of his car when he went into Snoope's that night.

Gotti and his guys were carrying handcuffs, and they announced that they were cops come to arrest Jimmy McBratney, but nobody in the bar bought it. John and the two gorillas didn't look much like cops. Some guy in the bar demanded to see their badges. They didn't have no stinking badges, so Ralphie pulled his gun instead. He fired a shot into the ceiling to shut the guy up, but the cops charade was over as soon as he did.

The plan was to haul McBratney out of there and take him somewhere to torture him and give up the other Westies who kidnapped Manny Gambino, but when Quack tried to cuff him, McBratney put up a fight.

He was a big Irish guy, bigger even than Angelo, and he made it halfway to the door with Fat Ange and Gotti both on his back. Ralphie put a stop to it by shooting McBratney in the head at point-blank range.

The McBratney murder was one of the sloppiest hits in Mob memory. Witnesses ID'd both Angelo and Ralphie, but nobody at the bar recognized Gotti.

Two months later, in July, Quack and Ralphie were arrested.

Soon after that, Ralphie got whacked.

Everybody thought the Westies killed him to avenge Jimmy McBratney, but something happened at the same time that later made me wonder.

Days before Ralphie bought it, John came to Fox with another mysterious assignment. He told Fox to rent a car in his real name and leave the keys with one of the guys in the crew. Then he told him to take a vacation in Florida. He told Fox to take me along and have a good time, stay in a pricey hotel and register under our real names. I don't think I even told Angela that we were going out of town. She was used to not seeing me for days on end, and when I showed up later she didn't say a word about it.

John gave Fox a few thousand bucks to blow on the trip. Fox figured it was a reward for having our man in the Queens PD run McBratney's plate number. But John didn't say anything more about it. He just told us to have a good time, which we did.

When we got back to the city, Fox was arrested for murder. The cops had found an unidentified body in the trunk of the car Fox rented before we left. Mike Coiro represented Fox at his arraignment. He had Fox's and my airline tickets and our receipts from the hotel. He had me as a witness who could vouch for Fox's every move that weekend. The judge told the cops to stop jerking off the court, and Fox was released without charges.

When we heard later that Gallione got whacked, we wondered if that was Ralphie in the trunk of Fox's car. We could have found out easy enough, but we knew that the secret to happiness and a long life was that sometimes it's best not to know.

———————

A month or so after his arrest, Angelo went on trial, but with Ralphie out of the picture, the prosecutors had no case. They had apparently based it on the hope that Ralphie would flip and testify against Quack, which is why it might have been Ralphie's body that was found in the trunk of Fox's car while we were enjoying our all-expenses-paid trip to Florida.

Angelo got a hung jury, but he wasn't off the hook.

In mid-October, a grand jury indicted John Gotti, and a warrant was issued for his arrest. He and Angelo Ruggiero would be tried together for the murder of James McBratney. Instead of waiting for the cops to show up at his house in Howard Beach, Johnny disappeared himself.

John would remain on the lam for eight months before he was arrested in June 1974. He stopped going to the Bergin altogether, but throughout the time he was in hiding, he continued to show up at the Sinatra Club. It wasn't until years later that it was learned that the cops finally caught up with Gotti only because the Bergin crew's rat told them where to find him. And that's when I realized that John had been able to go to the Sinatra Club all that time with no problems because the rat was gambling there too and didn't want the place raided and shut down by the cops.

OCTOBER 1973

Two weeks before John went on the lam, he and his brother Genie and Mike Coiro and I attended the opening home game of the 1973 World Series at Shea Stadium. We had front-row box seats on the first base line. It was like the pictures of Al Capone in his box at Wrigley Field, only nobody outside the Mob knew who John was then; there were no ballplayers lined up to get his autograph.

That was the series against the great Oakland A's team with Reggie Jackson, Catfish Hunter, Vida Blue, and Rollie Fingers. Tom Seaver pitched against Catfish in the opener. The A's won in eleven innings and went on to beat the Mets in seven games. The game we saw was the last one Willie Mays ever played.

During the game, John and I got talking about our kids. I said I wanted my sons to grow up to be athletes. I didn't want them to follow in my footsteps. I wanted them to have the kind of lives my sister wanted for me.

I told John that I didn't want my boys to grow up with a father who was dead or in prison like my uncle Tony. It was beginning to look like that would be my fate too. Mike Coiro hadn't been able to get my bank robbery case thrown out and he told me to prepare to go on trial in a few months. I told John that I wanted a legitimate life for my sons.

John, though, saw things totally different. He said that this Life of ours was the best there was. Nothing would make him more proud than to see his boys grow up to be made men.

That day watching the game, it seemed like a sick thing to me, to want your own children to have a life of violence and death.

And while I was talking to John, I realized I was saying almost the exact same thing—and using the very same words—that Jane said to me that night at the Mohonk.

Everything about that night had seemed so right.

And it all turned out so wrong.

CHAPTER THIRTY

Hearth, Home, and Hellfire

November 1973

EVEN THOUGH I KNEW plenty of guys who torched joints, it was a corrupt cop who taught me an important trick of the arson trade: Never use gasoline if you want the victim or the insurance company to suspect it was a shorted-out wire or spontaneous combustion of a bunch of paint rags in the basement or whatever. Gasoline, the cop told me, leaves a residue that will tell the tale.

Being a motor head and an auto-racing fanatic, I used pure alcohol for racing fuel when I wanted high performance. Alcohol isn't a petroleum product; it comes from plants, and when it burns, it leaves no residue at all.

I loaded five gallons of the stuff in the trunk of my car, along with a piece of sheet metal that I had shaped into a large flat-nose funnel.

I drove into the city and found the building in the Financial District. It was a typical five-story tenement that had been converted into offices. The basement apartment housed a different kind of operation from the law offices above. It was a brothel.

Jane was still running her main joint uptown, but she had closed the one in Rego Park and reopened downtown in this building near the South Street Seaport.

That part of town wasn't anything like it is today; except for the Fulton Fish Market a few blocks away, the Financial District was totally deserted after business hours. Jane's downtown place catered to a Wall Street clientele who dropped in for a quickie at lunch or right after work. The place was locked up by 9:00 at the latest, and the offices upstairs were empty long before that.

There was a short staircase leading to the building entrance on the first floor. Under the staircase was the door to the brothel. It was perfect for my purposes because it provided a good cover.

I parked around the corner and made sure nobody saw me carrying the five-gallon can and the sheet metal funnel downstairs to the basement door. I pushed the flat end of the funnel under the door and poured in the racing fuel. When I was finished, I took the can and the funnel back to the car and went for a ride down Broadway to the Battery and back up Church Street. I drove around for about forty-five minutes. By then I figured the fuel would have spread out and soaked the rugs and the place would be filled with fumes.

I went back to the building and tossed the match and *KA-BOOM!* I had no idea the type of explosion that racing fuel would ignite. Flames shot up two stories instantly. If anybody had been in there, they'd have had no chance. The fire trucks arrived in minutes and quickly got it under control so the building wasn't totaled.

The next day Jane called me at the club and told me her place was destroyed in a fire. I expressed to her how shocked I was.

———————

The reason Jane and I went from a state of bliss and pure ecstasy in May to me burning down her brothel in November—and that was just the beginning of the story of how our love went up in flames that fall—was simple: We were both obsessed. Everything we did—our sex, our wild times, our love—was intense and over the top. When making the switch from sinners to saints proved easy to promise and impossible to deliver, we both went wild with jealousy and possessiveness.

When she heard that one of the hookers she supplied the Sinatra Club with was giving me blow jobs on the side—no surprise, but she heard right—Jane put a knife to the girl's throat and told her she'd die if she ever went near me again.

I couldn't stand her being with another man—even if he was crawling around like an animal at her feet. When she didn't close her operations, I burned down her brothel in a jealous rage.

But Jane stayed in business after I torched her downtown place. She still had her whorehouse in the East 30s and her out-call service, and she kept on turning no-touch tricks for her customers, wealthy guys with sick fetishes who got off on her treating them like dogs, only you'd never do to your own dog what she did to them.

And since Jane kept hookin' and I kept on crookin', we continued to partner up on crimes.

Her customers liked to confess stuff about their businesses to her. Some wanted to impress her, but a lot of them assumed that because she was in business she must be protected by the Mob and they thought they could pass along information through her to somebody like me if they wanted to fuck with a competitor or one of their own business partners. When they did, Jane passed along the information to me.

Thanks to Jane, Fox and I made a specialty of robbing couriers and jewelry shop owners in the Diamond District, on 47th Street in Manhattan. That only worked if you had a give-up, somebody on the inside who tipped you on a score. Sometimes Tommy worked the district with us, but most of the scores were two-man jobs.

Those were brazen daylight robberies with the sidewalks crowded and all the gold and silver and diamond stores open for business. Fox and I had our own UPS uniforms and we'd just follow a courier into a shop when one of Jane's give-ups told us a delivery was going to be made. One morning I followed Fox on a motorcycle while he tailed a Hasid with a briefcase full of diamonds down the sidewalk. Fox got right behind the guy, pulled down his ski mask, and grabbed the briefcase. I pulled up at the curb, Fox hopped on, and we took off.

We made a lot of fruit on those scores, and we never would have had them without Jane's help.

Back in May when Jane and I declared our undying love and each made our promises, one of mine was that I would tell Angela that Jane and I were in love and that I would leave her if we couldn't work it out any other way.

Now it was six months later and I still hadn't breathed a word to Angela about Jane or confessed anything that would confirm my wife's suspicions that I was fucking around on her with anybody at all.

I didn't because I knew my fantasy that we could all live together with the kids in some kind of suburban three-way was crazy shit, and I would have laughed in the face of any fool who told me with a straight face that he was going to set up that kind of arrangement with his wife and girlfriend.

But more important, I couldn't bear the thought of my two little boys growing up with a sick-minded stepparent like my sister Rose and I had. I knew that the minute I told Angela that Jane even existed, much less that I was in love with her, she'd be out the door and in a lawyer's office in a heartbeat. She wouldn't care what the Catholic church had to say about it—she'd get a fucking divorce. And I never heard of any Family man who had a family court judge in his pocket, and it's doubtful that even a Mobbed-up judge would award custody of two small children to a violent criminal like me instead of to Angela.

Jane was just as jealous and possessive of me as I was of her, and when I kept leading her on, promising I was going to tell Angela about us but never actually doing it, she got more and more crazed and emotionally wound up.

Finally, all hell exploded one morning.

I had spent the night at Jane's and for some reason I didn't have my car, so we decided to take hers. I drove, and the plan was that I'd get out a few blocks from home and Jane would return to the city. We always avoided going to Queens together for fear of a chance encounter with Angela, and I had a bad feeling the whole way over.

Sure enough, we were stopped at a light and there was Angela driving our custom van. She had just dropped Sal at school and Joe at day care.

For more than a year she had been collecting blond hairs, and when she eyeballed me in a strange car with a blonde, she went berserk.

I floored it, and Angela came after us in a hot chase. I stopped at a light, and Angela skidded her van and plowed into the back of Jane's car. Then it was Jane's turn to start yelling and screaming. I took off again, and I could see Angela driving wildly behind us. Finally I pulled over and ran back. Jane was shouting and Angela was screaming at me. I yelled at her to go home before she got herself and us killed. I told her it's not what she thinks. Angela broke down crying and put the car in gear and drove home.

I went back to Jane's car, and she's furious—not at Angela for slamming into her car but at me. She accused me of never having any intention of telling Angela the real score.

If I was smart, I would have tried that novel approach and leveled with Jane right there, but I kept on lying and said I would go home right then and tell Angela everything. I told Jane to go home and I'd call her later.

Angela screamed at me as soon as I walked in the door. She started throwing dinner plates and coffee cups at me and yelling the whole time. I shouted more lies, telling her the blonde was just the wife of one of the guys at the club who gave me a ride home. I told her to calm the fuck down and I'd explain everything.

The second those words were out of my mouth, we heard an enormous bang. Jane had driven over the curb and *crashed her car into the front of the house!*

Before I could say *What the fuck?* here comes Jane charging through the front door. She barged right in and attacked Angela; she went for her throat and started choking her. Angela fought back like a banshee, and the two of them were on the floor, pulling hair and scratching and kicking. I couldn't believe my fucking eyes, and all of a sudden I realized I was laughing hysterically. *My wife and my* goomad *fighting it out over me!*

I finally came to my senses and pulled them apart. Jane had a bloody nose; Angela gave her a real working over. It was a side of her I'd never seen before. She was fighting for her family, protecting what she thought was hers—*me*.

I told Jane to get the fuck out of the house. I told her she was out of control and I never wanted to see her again.

She left and I told Angela that she was right all along, that I'd been seeing Jane, but it was all over now.

Of course I couldn't be totally truthful. I did not tell Angela that Jane was a whore and that I loved her like I never loved anyone in my life.

I even threw in one last lie for good measure.

I told Angela that when she saw us in the car that morning, I was telling Jane that we were through and that I was going home where I belonged—with my wife and kids.

———————————

I don't know if it was the excitement of seeing my wife fight for me or what it was, but Angela and I went upstairs and made love for the first time in recent memory.

In the following days we had long heart-to-heart talks. I apologized for the way I treated her and I promised to mend my ways and be a better father to the boys.

Angela, bless her, did her best to make herself attractive to me so I wouldn't stray, and for the first time since we'd been together we had what felt like a real marriage.

That was a really nice time in our lives.

It lasted until about three weeks later, when Fox and I went to Sebastian's and I picked up a hot young blond stewardess from Oklahoma City who begged me to give her a gangster's tour of Manhattan.

She even promised to make me an offer I couldn't refuse.

CHAPTER THIRTY-ONE

The Five-Families Heist

JANUARY 1974

JOHN WAS ON THE lam, but that didn't stop him from organizing the score that would make Carlo Gambino think his dreams of creating One Big Mob had come true.

The funny thing was, John never would have run with it if he knew I got the tip from a whore.

In October, before the big blowup, Jane told me about a give-up with a rich piece of information. One of her customers was a coin dealer in Midtown. He told her about a company called the Metropolitan Coin Exchange on 57th Street that received large shipments of silver bullion delivered from JFK by armored trucks once a week. I asked her if she could find out the color and make of the truck and get the license number if possible.

A couple of weeks later, we were having what turned out to be one of our last dinners together. Before the waiter delivered our meals, Jane slid a folded piece of notepaper across the table to me. Written on it were a plate number and the words "Blue armored van," and under that "Wednesday, a.m."

I parked outside the main exit from the JFK cargo area the following Wednesday morning but never saw the van. The next week I had better luck.

I saw the truck—and I also saw a problem. There was a second man in the cab with the driver, a guard riding shotgun. I couldn't see the weapon, but chances were that's exactly what he was carrying—a shotgun. To pull off this score we would need four guys instead of three.

I followed the truck, and it took the same route that most of the trucks we targeted took from the airport to the city—the Van Wyck Expressway to the Long Island Expressway. As this one crawled slow up the ramp to the overpass, it was so heavily loaded that the rear bumper nearly scraped the asphalt. The driver took the expressway to the Midtown Tunnel and up Third Avenue to 57th Street.

After I clocked it again the following Wednesday, this time with Fox, I told Dom about the bullion truck, but he wasn't interested in getting in on it. He and Jackie weren't into nailing trucks anymore. He told me to take it to Gotti; Dom would get it on record with Pegleg because this looked to be a big score and he'd want his taste.

Fox and I then had a sit-down with Gotti. I told him the setup and about the guard riding shotgun and said we'd need a fourth man for the heist.

Gotti was a high school dropout like me, but he was a very smart guy. When I read books about him where the cops say what a dumb fuck he was, I knew better. Back then in 1974 he had a police scanner set up way out in the Beach Channel in Jamaica Bay that monitored FBI transmissions. In those days, the FBI used the World Trade Center rooftop to transmit on a special frequency; John's crew could monitor all the FBI's radio traffic. I guess their rat inside his crew must have been so top secret they never mentioned it over the radio. But every other move the feds made, Gotti knew about it.

Right away, as soon as he heard me out that day, he came up with his visionary plan to turn the silver bullion heist into the first All-Families score. He said that since Fox and Tommy and I were from three different Families, and since the heist would require four guys minimum to pull off, he wanted us to bring in not one, but two more experienced guys, and he told us to make sure that one of the extra guys was a Bonanno and one a Genovese.

He said a heist using members of all the Five Families would help to finally end the war that was still going on with sporadic hits happening every few months.

"This is what we got now." John raised up his hand with all five fingers spread out. "Five Families fighting each other. Put 'em together and
whattya got?"

He balled his hand into a fist and banged it on the table.

"*Power.*"

———————

John took his plan straight to the top. He had a sit-down with Carlo
Gambino and Paul Castellano, who was his acting underboss with Neil
Dellacroce in prison.[7] John knew that this score would be perfect for
what he and Don Carlo had already talked over a number of times and
he knew that Gambino would go for it, But Castellano's presence com-
plicated things, so John laid it out from the top.

Gotti told the bosses that a Colombo guy brought him the idea
for a score, to nail an armored truck carrying a load of silver bullion
from JFK to Manhattan. The truck was loaded with rare silver coins
and hundred-ounce bars of solid silver. He said the heist would require
a minimum of four guys to pull off, so why not add a fifth and bring
in one heist guy from each of the Five Families. With all five pulling
the score together—and sharing the riches—it would promote peace
and harmony at a time when war was creating more heat than anybody
wanted.

Sure enough, Big Paul thought it was a horseshit idea and said
so. He said it was ridiculous to even suggest it to the other Families.
It would make the Gambinos look weak. And if anything went
wrong it would embarrass everybody.

Big Paul knew that Gotti belonged to Neil Dellacroce, who was
Castellano's main Family rival. Paul had no interest in okaying any plan
that might make Gotti and Neil look good.

Don Carlo didn't want to disrespect Castellano, so he heard him out
and then made the call. He said he liked Gotti's idea. He understood his
cousin's argument, but he had to overrule him, he said. He gave John the
green light.

———————

[7] He was convicted of tax evasion and sent up in March 1973.

With one condition: If anything went wrong, if the job was botched, Big Paul would have John's head on a platter.

———————

Since John was still in hiding, we met at the Sinatra Club—Dominic, me, Fox, Charlie Fatico, Gotti, and Quack. We went over my plan to nail the truck. John named the five guys who would do the score.

Dom already cleared me with Pegleg. Fox was the Gambino on the heist. Tommy Guns was the Lucchese; Roundy, whose uncle Carmine Galante, the Bonanno boss, was in prison, would have to be cleared by his acting boss, Rusty Rastelli. A guy named Rocky from the Genovese Family was somebody we all played cards with, so we all agreed on him. John asked Charlie, who all the bosses knew, to talk to Rastelli and the Genoveses. Fatico said he would.

We agreed that the shipment would be split evenly among the Five Families immediately after the score. Each guy in on the job would sell or stash or do whatever he wanted with his share or however he decided with his Family.

We all drank a toast to the score. John said it was good we were meeting at the Sinatra Club, which was our first joint venture between the Families. "Here's to many more," John said. "*Alla Nostra Salute!*"

Then he looked at me and said, "Don't fuck this up!"

———————

Fatico got the okays, and all five of us clocked the truck together the next week. We followed it into the city and agreed to hit it on the down-ramp from the overpass between the Van Wyck and the LIE.

On the night before the score, Rocky and I went out and got a couple of hotskis. The Sinatra Club was closed that night, so we used it for a final meeting. When I got back to the club after jacking the car, there was a big problem.

———————

Fox had just got off the phone with his mother. She was frantic—Patricia had been out all night and still hadn't come home. Fox was sure she was with Tommy. "I'm gonna kill that rat bastard!" he swore, and ran out of the club.

As far as I knew, Tommy hadn't gone out with or even seen Patricia since Fox found out they'd been dating back in the spring. Fox almost slugged him then, and Tommy wasn't even seeing her anymore. Now, if Tommy spent the night with Patricia and Fox confronted him in the state he was in, I knew there was no way Tommy would give a shit about a fair fight. He'd pull his guns and ten to one he'd be the only man standing.

All I could do was hope that Tommy wasn't banging Fox's sister. But Fox was so paranoid about Patricia he might not even bother to find out. He'd been waiting all year to catch Tommy fucking around with her, and the way he left the club, saying he was going to kill the bastard, he might do it as soon as he found him and ask questions later.

If Fox and Tommy got into it tonight, of all nights, it could sink our All-Families heist. And if that happened and John's head ended up on Big Paul's platter, he'd make sure I didn't live to hear about it.

Half an hour after Fox ran out to find him, Tommy strolled in like he didn't have a care in the world. He really didn't have a clue what was going on. I played it cool and asked Tommy what was up. Before he could say anything, Fox came back into the club all sheepish. He didn't say anything to Tommy. He just pulled me aside and told me that his mother had freaked out for no reason. His sister had a babysitting job the night before and had stayed over because the mother of the kid got home so late. The woman paid her extra to take care of the kid all day and drove her home right when Fox got over to his mother's place. Fox apologized to me for freaking out.

Relieved as I was, tensions between them were already sky-high before that night, and I dreaded to think what would happen if Tommy were to start plowing Fox's sister for real.

We met at our rendezvous early the next morning. Fox, Tommy, and I were in the lead car, Rocky and Roundy in the backup. Rolling out of there, we were like the fucking United Nations on wheels, all Five Families present and accounted for.

The truck showed up right on time, riding low like when we clocked it. Before I passed to get in front, I thought I saw sparks where the rear bumper scraped the asphalt. The truck was moving even slower than when I first clocked it. I had to crawl to stay close enough in front of him. The backup car's job was to slow traffic behind us as we exited the Van Wyck. When we got across the overpass and started down the ramp, I let us get a little ahead. Tommy and Fox had their ski masks pulled down and Tommy had his sawed-off out. I checked the mirror, the truck was closing in. "Get ready," I said, "I'm gonna hit the brakes." Tommy was leaning forward, checking the .38 in his ankle holster, when I jammed on the brakes. He banged his head hard against the front dash. The truck was too close; it slammed into the back of our car. Tommy jumped out of the car, pissed off about smacking his head. He leveled both barrels at the front of the driver's side windshield. The armed guard in the passenger seat didn't go for his gun. He pressed both palms against the windshield, and Fox yanked open the door and shoved the driver over.

Fox got behind the wheel of the truck with the two truckers smashed between him and Tommy. I happened to look over the guardrail on the exit ramp. There, stuck in traffic at the light on the service road, was an NYPD cop watching the whole thing go down. He didn't make any kind of move. I guess he was so surprised, he was paralyzed with shock. That or he didn't want to get shot. This being Queens, more likely he was on the payroll.

I led us onto the LIE. We exited on 108th Street in Elmhurst, where we found a quiet street and switched the drivers to the chase car. Roundy followed the truck to the drop, a big warehouse Fatico lined up in Queens. Rocky and I took the drivers on a joyride and dropped them off in Jamaica with a $100 bill each.

When we got back to the drop two hours later, Fox and Tommy were still high-fiving each other. Gotti and Fatico and Roundy were divvying up the take.

All the silver coins were in shiny one-gallon paint cans. The bullion bars were stacked inside black five-gallon drums. It was a beautiful sight.

I'm not sure what the other guys did, but Fox sold his share to Gotti at 25 percent of the face value; it came out to 100 grand for Fox. I had the bars melted down and sold it for 98 percent value. I walked away with close to half a million dollars on our historic Five-Families Score.

———————

Thirty-five years later I met the guy whose shipment got jacked. He told me that the man I sold it to was a competitor; they hated each other. The silver merchant who got ripped off said the heist nearly ruined him. He had to pay back every coin dealer and investor who lost money, because he wasn't insured. But he said he had no hard feelings. The score made him work harder, and he eventually recouped his losses and went on to make a fortune.

CHAPTER THIRTY-TWO

The Law Won

APRIL 1974

MY FIRST SURPRISE WAS that my bank robbery case made it to trial at all. A full year had passed since my arrest, but after Mike Coiro won me delay after delay I finally got my unwanted day in court. I thought all along that in the end my mouthpiece would find somebody to pay off, but federal cases were tough, and Mike couldn't do anything to bury mine before trial.

My next surprise was that the prosecutors had a still photo from a surveillance camera of me in the Franklin National Bank. Mike held the picture up in front of the jury and showed them the picture close up. It showed somebody wearing a fake wig and a fake mustache and a white Damon knit turtleneck sweater.

Mike argued that there was no solid ID; all they had was the head teller, who was so distraught she relieved herself right there at her booth. That's the first I knew that it was the lady I tried to be polite to, like Willie Sutton.

My biggest surprise came when the DA jumped out of his seat and pointed at me. "Look!" he cried, "he's wearing the same sweater today." Sure enough, me, the smart guy, wore the same sweater to court that I was wearing the day of the robbery and that I was wearing in the surveillance photo my attorney had just waved in front of the jurors.

After that, the jury took twenty minutes to convict me, which was no surprise at all.

The judge gave me eight years in the federal pen at Lewisburg, the same joint John Gotti got out of the night he walked into the Sinatra Club for the first time.

Before I went in I was to report to the VA hospital on First Avenue in Manhattan for psychiatric tests while the court considered Mike's motion that I was bonkers and shouldn't be subjected to a prison environment.

I figured that since the Ubatz defense had served me so well in the past, it would work once again. I left there feeling good about my chances. But I was in for another surprise.

Mike Coiro couldn't work his usual wonders in my bank robbery case, but he helped pull off a beauty for Johnny Boy and Angelo, who had murdered a guy in cold blood in front of a barroom full of witnesses.

John was still on the lam, but he knew the cops would find him sooner or later, and when they did, he and Angelo would be put on trial for the McBratney hit. They were both looking at twenty-five years to life in prison for murder.

Carlo Gambino might have wanted to pay John back for avenging the murder of his nephew, or maybe he just didn't want to lose one of his Family's great young hopes for twenty-five years. Whatever the reason, he saved John's ass. Gambino got one of the most famous attorneys in the country, Roy Cohn, who was Don Carlo's and Neil Dellacroce's mouthpiece, to look into John and Angelo's case.

Cohn worked out a deal two months before the cops even arrested John, who was still in hiding when Cohn contacted Mike Coiro to set up a meeting.

Just a few days after my trial ended and before I checked into the VA hospital, Mike asked me to drive him and Angelo to a secret meeting with Johnny in Manhattan. John might have been in hiding from the cops but not from us. We saw him practically every day, so I wondered why all the secrecy.

I picked Mike and Ange up in my big Lincoln Mark IV—it had to be big to hold Fat Angelo's three hundred pounds. I had got to know

Quack real well, and I could tell when he was anxious about something. He was a chain-smoker, and when he was relaxed, he held his Camel like most people, in between his first two fingers. When he was uptight, he held it between his thumb and forefinger and took deep drags, and when he did, his pinkie stood straight up like a little pink pecker. On the way into the city, Angelo was puffing away on his Camel and his pinkie was pointing at the sunroof, so I knew something was up.

On the way in, Mike told me what was going on. We were going to pick up Johnny and take him to a meeting with Roy Cohn at his town house on Sutton Place. This meeting with Cohn was big stuff, Mike said. Cohn was the famous lawyer who prosecuted the Rosenbergs, the Commie spies who got fried back in the '50s. Mike knew him because Cohn was friends with Mike's former boss at the Waterfront Commission.

We got into Manhattan and headed uptown on First Avenue. Somewhere in the 50s, Angelo directed me to take a right and then pull over. He got out, and before he closed the door, he leaned in and pointed his pinkie at me. "Sally, hey, whatever you do, we get inside, you don't look at me. I know you. Just don't fuckin' look at me."

I didn't know what the fuck he was talking about. Quack closed the door and waddled across the street and disappeared around the corner. Mike and I got out and walked slow down the block. When we got to the end, around the corner came Angelo with John Gotti. He was wearing a fishing hat. He hadn't shaved in three days. He was wearing a blue polyester leisure suit. He looked like a tourist from Florida who had been left behind when the bus pulled out.

The block where Cohn lived was one of the ritziest in the city. The town houses had stone gargoyles and carved oak doors. Cohn's building had a little staircase leading up to an oak door with a stained-glass window set into it.

We climbed the stairs and Mike rang the bell. You could hear the sound of chimes inside. I never knew a doorbell could sound like a million bucks.

While we waited, Quack shot me another stern look and pointed his pinkie at me. Quack was a big scary-looking guy. If you knew him, he was funny, but if you didn't, you'd run the other way. Here he was wagging his pinkie like a three-hundred-pound schoolmarm.

I expected that paying a visit on Gambino's lawyer would be like dropping in on the Don himself. We'd be frisked by bodyguards before we stepped across the threshold. When the door finally opened, the person standing there was like no bodyguard I ever saw. He was tall and thin and pale, and he was wearing a golden kimono. His legs were bare and he had little black-and-gold slippers on his feet. He had a long skinny neck, a buzz cut, and big, surprised-looking eyes. He fixed them on Coiro and didn't dare look at the rest of us. You could knock this guy over with a feather, no joke. He looked like a fucking orchid.

I thought maybe that's why Quack was so nervous—he was afraid this guy *would* frisk us.

Our greeter introduced himself as Pierre. "Mr. Cohn is expecting you," he said. "Please follow me."

He walked ahead of us like he was going to break with every step. Mike and John followed close behind. Ange and I trailed.

I took a few prancing steps and let my wrist go limp. Ange shot me a look like he was going to break my legs, but that just made it all the funnier. Here we were, big tough guys, and we were supposed to be on our best behavior and show respect to a guy in a kimono. What can I tell you? We were gangsters.

The Gambino godfather's lawyer did all right for himself. Pierre led us down a hallway with a marble floor, fourteen-foot ceilings, and antique crystal chandeliers. Oil paintings in fancy frames lined the walls. The whole place smelled like perfume. There were flowers everywhere. The smell stuck in my nostrils. I wrinkled my nose at Quack, trying to bust him up. The hallway led to a set of bronze doors.

"Mr. Cohn is up in his study," Pierre said in a breathy whisper. He opened the doors and ushered us into a small oak-paneled elevator.

Pierre looked awful thin and fragile squeezed into the tiny elevator with the four of us. But John and Angelo acted like they were being taken upstairs by the deadliest enforcer in New York. It hit me in the elevator why Gotti seemed so different that day: He was humbled. Roy Cohn was one guy he couldn't intimidate. He was so powerful even his houseboy was somebody Gotti didn't want to offend.

The doors opened and I was face-to-face with Roy Cohn. He was short, no more than five five. He was completely bald. His skull shined. He smiled, and his teeth were beautiful, ultrawhite. I guessed they were capped.

He greeted Mike Coiro with a hug and a kiss on the cheek. Mike introduced John and Angelo and me, and then the two mouthpieces chatted briefly about old times.

Cohn's study was dominated by an enormous oak desk. There were floor-to-ceiling bookcases crammed with law books and photos of famous people everywhere—among the most prominently displayed was a signed picture of J. Edgar Hoover.

Cohn sat behind his desk while John and Mike sat in a couple of Queen Anne chairs facing him and Angelo and I sat on a leather couch off to one side. Cohn got right down to business.

"Okay," he said, "I did what had to be done over in Staten Island. John, you and Angelo will take a manslaughter plea. You'll both get four years. That's it. Don't talk about the case to anybody."

Manslaughter. That's what you get when you kill somebody accidentally or in the heat of an argument. Somehow Roy Cohn—or a lot of Carlo Gambino's money—convinced the state's attorney's office that John and Angelo just happened to drop in at Snoope's and a gun just happened to go off and the bullets just happened to hit Jimmy McBratney in the face. Funny how accidents happen.

Cohn stood up and we followed suit. Mike handed a manila envelope to Cohn. Cohn smiled and placed the envelope gently on top of his desk.

That was it. Meeting over. We weren't in his office for more than five minutes tops.

Cohn himself walked us to the door. We took the staircase instead of the elevator. When we got to the foyer, Cohn again kissed Mike. He gave John a hug and a kiss on the cheek. I noticed Angelo inching closer to the door.

"Take care of your buddy John," Roy said to Angelo. "And don't worry. We'll get your state time to run concurrent with your federal time when you take your plea in Brooklyn." Angelo looked relieved when Cohn gave him a pat on the back.

Once we got outside, Ange finally cracked up, saying something about John making a fix with a fag. Gotti lit up one of his De Nobili cigars.

"Who gives a fuck?" he said. "That happy little homo just saved our asses. We can do four years standing on our heads. Fuhgeddaboudit."

MAY 1974

At the VA, I did my whole *Cuckoo's Nest* routine. I jabbered gibberish; I told the docs I heard voices; I twitched and squirmed during interviews with the evaluators. I thought I did a pretty good job of convincing them, but it wasn't good enough. Two weeks after my sentencing, the judge read the headshrinkers' report and banged the gavel. I was going to Lewisburg with room and board for eight fucking years.

I was ordered to surrender in July, two days after the Fourth.

CHAPTER THIRTY-THREE

Goodbye to All That

MAY 1974

ONE OF THE MOST momentous events of my life happened and I didn't even know it.

The last game at the Sinatra Club was played two nights before my trial judge decided that I wasn't *upazzo* enough to stay out of prison. I was so certain the Ubatz defense would get me off the hook once again, it never occurred to me that that last night would be just that and there would never be another.

That final night at the club was like the Life itself—routine. We had no reason to think we wouldn't be back there two nights later and two nights after that—playing cards, telling stories, planning heists, whooping with laughter, scooping up ridiculous pots one minute and cursing Lady Fucking Luck the next, and going all in on just another great good time at the Sinatra Club. We never for a second thought to stop and appreciate what we'd had going there three and four nights a week for the past two and a half years—just like nobody in that Life ever thought we wouldn't go on gambling and looting and pulling rich scores—*and getting away with it*—forever.

We knew we were having the time of our lives, but not for a minute did we think they'd ever end, that these were the glory days and sometime in the future it would be all over and—if we survived long enough—we'd be looking back in wonder and a whole lot of disbelief at the way we were and the shit we pulled back then.

I wish now we'd had one last blowout at the club, that we'd gotten all the regulars back for a marathon game and a party to celebrate the place and all the amazing times we had there. But once I knew I was going away and I only had a month and a half left before they locked me in chains, I told Dom he'd better look for somebody else to run the day-to-day. But Dom said he had no interest in keeping the place going except as office space to run our shylock business.

In fact the club had pretty much outlived its usefulness as a cover for our drug business by then. In the beginning, the profits from the Sinatra Club combined with our other gambling operations generated enough cash to explain our earnings to Pegleg and the other bosses. But off-track betting had really taken off in the past year, and that wiped out a big share of our gambling operation. Without that cash coming in, the club didn't generate enough profit to make up for it. Our sports book was our strongest gambling business now, and Dom said he was going to concentrate on that. He'd also begun to invest a lot of money in operations he had going in Florida, and not long after that he got in with the Pizza Connection syndicate that hit on the genius idea of using pizza joints as the perfect front. They were both the money laundry and the distribution points for the supply of drugs that generated the cash that needed laundering. The Sinatra Club could never compete with a sweet setup like that.

The day after my psychiatric evaluation came down, I went to the club to shut it down. Big Funzi was going to take over management of my gambling and loan shark operations while I was gone, so I left some of the chairs and couches and the bar, which we used as a desk in the afternoons. But most everything else I cleared out. I took down the travel posters and my Marilyn Monroe photos and the Salvador Dalí painting of the nude with the head of a rose—my tribute to my guardian angel, Rose Marie. I left the fishnets and the seashells and buoys, as well as the bamboo partitioning—no sense in leaving Dom and Funzi with nothing but bare walls and exposed wiring and heating ducts to look at all day.

I gave one of our beautiful felt-covered Vegas regulation–size poker tables to the guys at the Bergin and sold the others. The toughest thing to figure out was what to do with the Wurlitzer Statesman jukebox that my burglar friend had boosted for me and stocked with all the Frankie records that gave the Sinatra Club its name. To this day, when I hear some of the songs that got a lot of plays on that juke— Dion's "The Wanderer," "Runaway" by Del Shannon, and just about everything Old Blue Eyes sings—it brings back memory flashes from that time when we were young and wild and living large and the Sinatra Club was our home.

The jukebox was a kind of symbol; it contained the spirit of our place and I didn't want it to fall into the wrong hands. I didn't want it to end up someplace it would get abused, like a Westies watering hole or—worse—a cops' bar.

I was about to haul it over to my house and store it in the basement when I ran into Jerry, one of the nickel-and-dime players, a legitimate guy who always played the jukebox when he came in. He was a Jewish guy—and Mob guys being what they are, we all called him Jerry the Jew. He took no offense. Jerry loved everything Italian, us Mob guys included, and his favorite singer was Frank Sinatra. He'd play nothing but Sinatra songs on the juke.

Jerry told me he was opening a bar out in Far Rockaway. He was call- ing it A Wing and a Prayer because that's what it was. Jerry didn't have a lot of money, but he got a good deal on a place and he told me to come by and check it out.

I gave the Wurlitzer to Jerry to put in his new bar and he came back with a truck the next day to pick it up. He asked me if I wanted any of the records in there. I told him it wouldn't be a jukebox without them and he should take them all.

Jerry said he might change out some of the other records, but the Frank songs he would never touch.

So I knew a little piece of the Sinatra Club would live on at A Wing and a Prayer every time a Frank song played on the jukebox.

But that didn't really make it any easier to turn out the lights and walk away. It was like when I padlocked the door on Sal's Pizza. I left an awful lot of memories locked up in there.

There was something else about shutting the place down. The Sinatra Club represented the action, the fun, and the excitement of that Life of ours. When I turned out the lights, it felt like the fun times were over.

JUNE 1974

With the Sinatra Club closed, I spent a lot of time during my last month of freedom at the Bergin with Fox. We started to see John Gotti there again too. His life on the lam ended in early June when he was busted one afternoon in a bar in Maspeth that he used for meetings. Years later it was learned that the Bergin's resident rat tipped the feds that John was at the bar. The feds told the cops who had been looking for him for nearly a year, and they arrested him there in the middle of a sit-down with Tony Roach. Victoria put up their house in Howard Beach, and John was out on bail in a few days and back in business at the Bergin.

The clock was ticking on my freedom, and I think somehow Fox sensed that he was on borrowed time himself. We went on a good times rampage together and had a lot of spur-of-the-moment adventures. One night we went into Sebastian's and met a couple of stews. We stayed up all night, and in the morning we all went to the airport and flew down to the Bahamas. Another time we flew down to Florida in the afternoon, met some girls that night, and flew home the next day.

Things between Angela and me had improved ever since I stopped seeing Jane, and as long as I kept it that way she didn't hassle me too much about staying out all night. Plus I had a ready reason: I told her I was busy earning so she and the kids wouldn't suffer when I was gone.

The truth was I had enough loot stashed away that they wouldn't have any worries about money. I cashed in a bunch of the Krugerrands I'd saved from the silver bullion heist, and it was more than enough to take care of expenses while I was gone. I gave Angela that money and I told Fox where the rest of my stash was. If Angela ever needed money, she was supposed to see Fox and he'd get it for her.

One day in the middle of the month, Fox called me with a message. It was from Jane. Her car was stalled somewhere in Queens and she didn't have any cash for a tow. She knew better than to try me at home, so she called Fox and gave him her location.

I found her pulled over on the access road on Queens Boulevard. It was a little after noon and Jane was dressed like always—ready for nighttime escapades. She looked as burning hot as the first time I saw her three years before.

There was nothing wrong with Jane's car. She had found out from one of the girls she supplied the club with that I was going to prison and the Sinatra Club was closed. She said she left the message with Fox because she wasn't sure I'd show if she didn't give me a good reason, even a bogus one.

Other than that brief exchange, we didn't do a lot of catching up.

We raced back to her place, and I didn't come up for air until the next afternoon.

We hadn't seen seen each other since the day she crashed the car into my house. That was six months ago. In all that time I hadn't lost even a little bit of love and lust for her. I stayed away because things got so crazy. If they did again now, I didn't really care.

——————

One afternoon in the last weeks of June, Fox and I were lying around his apartment, bored out of our minds.

"We need some kicks, Fox," I said. "I need an excitement fix."

"Something audacious," Fox said.

"Yeah, audacious."

"Take a look at this." He opened the sliding doors and stepped out on the balcony. He pointed down at the street. There through the branches of the trees was a sign on the side of the building across the way: COLUMBIA NATIONAL BANK.

"Let's hit that jug right there," Fox said. "I watch them make deliveries every morning. I see them carrying all that fruit. We'll go downstairs, walk in nice and dopey, and help ourselves. Is that audacious enough for you?"

We talked it over and came up with a totally *upazzo* plan. We decided to rob the bank and make our getaway on bicycles.

Fox's apartment was in an isolated little neighborhood. It was wedged in between Howard Beach and the Belt Parkway on one side and the Cross State on the other. There was only one way in and one way out. But there was also a pedestrian bridge over the Cross State Parkway.

The golden rule of bank robbery I learned from the Geriatric Twins, Eddie and Joe: Get off the street and disappear as quickly as possible.

We stole a couple of bikes and timed it. It took ninety seconds to ride from the bank to the pedestrian bridge. The usual response time for the cops was two to three minutes. We knew exactly what road they would have to take to come after us.

We stole a U-Haul and put the bikes in it. We stole a hotski and parked it on the far side of the bridge. I put on workman overalls over my street clothes, and Fox wore a long raincoat that went all the way to his ankles.

We put on ski masks that look like knit caps until you pull them down. Fox had a sawed-off shotgun under his raincoat. I had my favorite bank-robbing tool: a couple of plastic shopping bags with I ♥ NY printed on them.

We parked the van down the block and around the corner. We strolled up to the bank, pulled down our masks, and hit it. Fox walked in like he'd hit a hundred banks. He stood next to the front doors, whipped out his shotgun, pumped it, and said, "Everybody freeze!"

I did my thing. I vaulted over the counter and cleaned out the drawers, leaving the bottom bills like Eddie and Joe taught me. We were out of there in ninety seconds. We walked slow out of the bank. We got to the van and went in through the front, shed our masks and outerwear, grabbed the bikes, and went out the back. Three minutes after we hit the bank, we were pedaling down the road.

We saw the cops speeding by. They didn't look twice at a couple of bicyclists out for a spin. We rode across the pedestrian bridge and ditched the bikes in some bushes by the hotski. We were back at my hideout apartment in Ozone Park, counting the fruit, ten minutes after I cleaned out the last drawer.

We had 14 grand in cash spread out on the bed. "Not bad for a dopey stroll across the street," Fox said.

I knew that would be the last heist we'd pull for a while.

I had no idea that for Fox it was the last ever.

JULY 3, 1974

Jane and I had the chance to get together only a few more times after the day her car didn't break down.

We talked about the same things we did up at Mohonk the year before—only without the fireworks accompaniment.

Jane said I messed up her world. She planned from the day she got off the bus at the Port Authority and pulled her first trick to pile up enough money to get out of New York one day, to get out of the Life. And now she'd done the one thing she promised herself would never happen: She got emotionally involved with a man. And not just that, but a married man who was also married to the Life. And who was now going away about as far as you could get for the next eight years

I didn't take the idea of getting out of the Life as anything even remotely realistic back when Jane said I should do it for the sake of my kids. But on top of what John Gotti said at the World Series about wanting his sons to follow in his footsteps and how sick I thought that was, the idea must have taken seed somewhere in my brain.

So when Jane brought it up again, I took it a little more seriously, like it was something that *could* happen. And now that I was going to prison, her idea that we both get out of the Life and find a place upstate somewhere around the Mohonk and settle down into a nice ordinary legitimate life sounded pretty fucking appealing.

Our sex on the last night we were together was a lot more like it was in the early days, hot and wild, maybe desperate, not so tender and vulnerable like the night we made love during Hurricane Agnes and then at the Mohonk when we had our ecstatic rebirth as love gods.

I saw her one more time—on the day before the Fourth of July. I told Jane I had something I wanted to give her, and we met for an early dinner at Bill Hong's, a high-end Chinese place we liked in Midtown.

I gave her a box of Godiva chocolates and two Hershey Kisses. She knew what they meant—just like the ones I used to give Rose Marie.

Jane promised to visit me in prison. I asked her to wait for me, and she said she would.

We got carried away a little and talked about how when I got out we would run away and get a place upstate in the country and live a different kind of life together and maybe have kids of our own.

It was a beautiful dream. But that's all it would be.

JULY 4, 1974

The Bergin's annual Fourth of July barbeque and softball game wasn't anywhere near the fun it had been the past couple of years.

For the first time since my summer of hell in 1965, I felt really down. It was hard not to be depressed when you were looking at eight years in the slammer. It would be 1982 by the time I got out. I'd be thirty-seven years old. Sal Jr. would be in his teens, baby boy Joseph would be eleven.

I'd been an at-home absentee father all their lives so far, and now I was abandoning them for real. The only difference between the way my mother walked out on me and my leaving them now was that she left in heels and I'd be going in cuffs. The guilt I felt for neglecting them was something I kept buried and only acknowledged when Angela threw it in my face—and when Jane made me see that my sons were going to turn out just like me if I didn't do something about it. Now I was going to have eight years to think about it.

The thought that once I did get out, my boys were going to have a jailbird, an ex-con, for a father didn't make me feel any better. Maybe that's why I told them a lie so they wouldn't have to start telling their teacher Daddy's in the joint. I told the kids I had to leave home because I was going to the hospital. I said it was something to do with the heart infection I had in the Marines. I figured I'd tell them the truth when they got older. But I probably wouldn't have to. One visit to the penitentiary would tell them that place was no hospital.

And as for Angela, who I treated like shit throughout our seven years of marriage, who I cheated on almost daily, neglected in bed and lavished on her nothing but lies, I couldn't help but think she was secretly planning to hire a brass band to see me off to jail and then throw a party *after*

I was out of the house, out of her hair, and out of her life. Eight years of me gone had to be better than the seven of hell I'd given her.

But instead of tormenting me for my failures and cursing me for being such a loser that the feds were carting me off to jail, she was nothing but supportive in those final days. She promised to wait for me and to take good care of the kids until I got out. I loved her for that. I promised her I'd change and make it all up to her.

And as I said that I was thinking about Jane and how I'd better make sure that she didn't show up at the same time Angela and the kids visited me in prison.

After the softball game, Fox and I didn't stick around for the barbeque and fireworks. He went with me to Mother-in-Law's, where she was hosting her own family picnic.

Dominic and his brother Joey and all the Cataldos were there. Dom loved to school me, and he had a lot of advice on how to survive prison. The main thing he said was to say I was with him, Little Dom; that would be enough to get me transferred to the Mafia cellblock at Lewisburg. There were guys in there who would look out for me. He said I should never sell anything to anybody because that was a sure way to set yourself up for a shiv in the ribs. He said I should always offer to share food and any goods I had smuggled with the Italians but nobody else.

Fox's family was his mother and sister. He loved my family like they were his own because everybody treated him like he was part of it. He knew that Angela and I had no kind of real marriage, but he loved her too, and my kids and in-laws.

Before the party broke up, Fox and I took a walk. He had just watched me playing with the boys, and he said the same thing Jane and I talked about. He said I should get out of that Life, I should do it for my kids. He said he didn't see any other kind of life for himself, but he did for me. He said I should use the time in prison to change my life and get out of this one. Then he said he probably wouldn't be here in eight years when I got out. I said, "Whattya talkin' about? Sure you will."

"No tomorrow, remember," he said. "Eight years is nothin' but a whole shitload of tomorrows."

I don't remember when Fox left that night. We didn't get a chance to say goodbye.

That day was the last time I would ever see him.

CHAPTER THIRTY-FOUR

The Big House

1974

L EWISBURG WAS RIGHT OUTSIDE of Nowhere, Pennsylvania, off Route 15 and not far from Williamsport, where they have the Little League World Series every year.

Lewisburg held about a thousand big-league bad guys.

It was a nasty-looking place, a giant Gothic fortress that was built around 1930. There were towers with hacks manning machine guns, floodlights, and barbed wire. It looked exactly like the kind of joints they threw Cagney and Edward G. into, in all the old movies.

Lewisburg was high security on the outside, but inside it was a country club ... if you happened to be connected. For the other inmates, especially the black guys who were in the majority even back then, it was a shit hole.

But for us, the prison was like Queens all over again: We owned it. Mob guys had the judges and cops in the pocket back home; they had everybody from the warden down to the hacks in there. Even the prison priest was on the take. That guy ran hookers out of his office; his secretaries were specially chosen for skills besides filing papers and taking shorthand.

Most of the Mob guys had at least three or four hits to their credit; Jimmy Burke, who was there when I arrived, had to have more than twenty-five or thirty. These guys were the biggest serial killers in the country; they made Ted Bundy look like a beginner. But not one of those hit men was in for murder.

When I first got there, I was in a holding section of the prison called Admission and Orientation. There was another new arrival in there with me; he had done a lot of time and was being transferred to Lewisburg. He seemed like all the other long-timers, resigned to his fate. A few days after I met him, he slit his throat in the bathroom with his own Gillette Blue Blade. Bled to death on the tiles. That made me wonder where the Mafia cellblock Dom told me about was and when the hell I was going to get in there.

It wasn't long before I was moved to J Block, Mafia Row. It only existed because the prison was totally segregated. Martin Luther King would have shut down the joint. There were separate cellblocks for blacks, Hispanics, Irish, gays, you name it. It definitely paid to be born Italian if you had to do time at Lewisburg.

It was like Henry Hill said in *Wiseguy*. Mob guys gambled, broiled steaks, and drank scotch. You could get girls, drugs, whatever you wanted from a hack on the take.

The top Mob guy inside was Johnny Dio—Johnny Dioguardi. He was behind the sulfuric acid attack that blinded the labor reformer Victor Riesel back in the '50s. That was the hit that sickened me when I read about it when I was a kid. By the time I went to Lewisburg, I had met plenty of vicious, old-style gangsters. None of them were as nasty a piece of work as Johnny Dio.

He came up at the same time as my uncle Tony. But where Tony was charming and had a light on inside him, Dio was pure darkness.

He was the devil who Jimmy Hoffa sold his soul to and went from being a friend of the working man to the guy who let the Mob fuck them royally. The irony about the Mob's control of the unions is that the old Sicilian and Jewish gangs in the 1920s hired themselves out as strikebreakers; they broke the legs of workers who even dared think about forming a union. After Prohibition, the Mob needed new monopolies, and guys like Johnny Dio got them by terrorizing labor and management both. Before Dio ordered the hit on Riesel in 1956 because he exposed the Mob's control of the Teamsters, he had already taken over the garment industry and autoworkers' unions in New York.

Johnny Dio was with the Luccheses, but by the time Johnny Gotti met him in Lewisburg, Tommy Lucchese, whose daughter was married to one of Carlo Gambino's sons, was dead and the Gambinos controlled Dio's Family.

When Gotti was in Lewisburg, both Johnny Dio and Hoffa were in with him. When I got there, Hoffa was gone but Dio was back in on another beef, and he would die in prison. But he still had a lot of power on the outside, which I later found out the hard way.

When I got to J Block, Johnny Dio knew I was with Little Dom Cataldo, and he got me transferred from the machine shop to yard detail, an easy job that was basically gardening. After I got out, I wished I'd never met Johnny Dio, but at the time I was thankful he helped me out.

The joint was full of characters. And a lot of them you've heard of. Lewisburg was a Hollywood producer's wet dream. I can name four or five movies that came out of the can. The *Dog Day Afternoon* bank robber was in there. Henry Hill and Jimmy Burke were there, and so were Paul Vario of *GoodFellas* fame and Frank Lucas, whom Denzel Washington played in *American Gangster*.

Then there was Fat Gigi, Louis Inglese. He was connected to two movies. He was doing time at Lewisburg for tax evasion when he was convicted in the French Connection case. He was Vince Pappa's partner; they orchestrated the swipe of the heroin from the NYPD evidence storage place downtown. Gigi's also the guy Chazz Palminteri based *A Bronx Tale* on. Gigi himself was one of the best storytellers I ever met. I used to get a hack to smuggle in his favorite cigars so I could sit for hours and listen while he spun tales.

Gigi was always trying to convince me there were better ways to make a living than robbing banks, hijacking trucks, and muscling guys for loan sharks. "Ubatz," he'd say, "you want to have fun—steal. You want to get rich—push junk." Or he'd say, "Ubatz, when you leave here, give up that gun. I made more money with a spoon and a strainer than you can ever make with a gun."

Gigi made his fortune in smack, but he knew that cocaine was the coming thing and he gave me some valuable career advice: Sell coke, don't do it. Guys who did wrecked their lives, not just their noses.

I never told Gigi that I'd been dealing heroin for years. There were guys from all the Families in the joint with us. If word got around inside that I was dealing, it would reach the outside in no time.

Another amazing Damon Runyon–type character in with me was Harry the Hump—Harry Riccobene, a little hunchback guy from Philadelphia. He was practically a midget, four foot something, and he was bald on top with a big bushy white beard. He looked like a cross between Santa Claus and the troll who lives under the bridge in the fairy tale, Harry was a famous gangster in Angelo Bruno's Family in Philadelphia. He got his button when he was just seventeen. Harry was pushing smack before I knew what that shit was.

After he got out, he made headlines during the Philadelphia Mob wars. Some guy tried to whack him the same way Mad Dog Coll got it—in a phone booth. The button man fired six shots and hit Harry with five of them. After the sixth shot, Harry got out of the booth and beat the shit out of the guy and took his gun. The guy ran away and Harry collapsed on the street. He refused to tell the cops who the hitter was. Harry the Hump was a true hero among Mob guys.

Another was Richard McCoy. He was in the joint for skyjacking. He parachuted out of a 727 with half a million in cash a year after D. B. Cooper got away with a quarter of a million. A lot of us thought McCoy *was* D. B. Cooper. McCoy escaped from Lewisburg after I left. I believe he was the only inmate who ever escaped from that pen.

There were a lot of guys I knew from back home in there too, including Joe Vitale and Eddie Pravato. We were all in on the same beef, hitting the Franklin National Bank. While we were in the joint, the Franklin National collapsed. Fourteen years later, Michele Sindona— the Italian Mafia banker who engineered the Franklin takeover for the Mob—supposedly committed suicide. He found an unusual way of doing it: drinking a cup of coffee laced with cyanide.

I knew John Carneglia, the older brother of Charles, the body disposal expert, from the Bergin, but we spent a lot more time together inside than we had on the outside. When we both got out, we went into the car business together.

The top-ranking Bergin guy inside was Angelo Ruggiero. Quack was in Lewisburg on an interstate hijacking beef. That was the federal case

Roy Cohn talked about that day at his palace on Sutton Place. Under the plea bargain Cohn negotiated—or bought, depending on how you looked at it—Ruggiero would serve the two sentences concurrently.

That meant that when John Gotti started serving his sentence at Green Haven in upstate New York in August 1975, Quack would almost be ready to get out.

A week after my wife and kids came to visit for the first time—I was right, the boys didn't buy the lie that the joint was a hospital with bars on the windows and guards instead of doctors—Jane came to see me. That was a sight I'll never forget. She walked in there on high heels with her blond hair and tight black sweater and leather skirt, and the whole joint went gaga. Even the other wives and girlfriends in the visiting room stopped talking and stared when she crossed the room to the soda machine.

Jimmy Burke and I played cards together in the joint just like we did at the Sinatra. When I told him about my case and how the judge had rejected Mike's motion for a full psychiatric hearing, he said I had good grounds for appeal. He told me about this whiz mouthpiece he had working on his own case, Gerald Shargel.

Shargel later became famous for getting John Gotti off in the 1990 case where a union official was shot after busting up a Gambino restaurant, Bankers and Brokers in Battery Park City.

Back then he was just a very sharp attorney, and Jimmy arranged a meeting with him for me at Lewisburg a week before Christmas.

I left that meeting with real hope. He said that the judge was out of line denying Mike's motion. He said there was a good chance my Ubatz defense would work on appeal.

That was the good news.

I got back to J Block to hear the worst news I got since my father called to tell me my sister Rose Marie was dead.

CHAPTER THIRTY-FIVE

No Tomorrow

DECEMBER 18, 1974

I GOT THE DETAILS LATER. All I knew that day came from Angelo Ruggiero. Quack was in touch by phone every day with John Gotti, who was still free and running things at the Bergin and the Ravenite and taking orders from Carlo Gambino. Because there was no pay phone for prisoners at Lewisburg, Quack and Gotti conducted their business in the prison priest's office. Connected guys were the only inmates that the holy father let use his phone.

On that Wednesday, after my meeting with Gerald Shargel, I ran into Quack as he was coming up from the priest's office. He had a sick look on his face.

He pulled me aside, said he had something he had to tell me. But then he just stood there; whatever it was, he didn't know how to say it. Quack of course knew how close Fox was to Johnny and to me. Quack loved Fox as much as we did. He'd known him almost as long as John had, since Fox was a kid on the streets in the old neighborhood and running with the Rockaway Boys. They were crewmates at the Bergin, they played cards at the Sinatra Club every night we were open, and all of us spent so much time together we were like family.

That's why Quack was having such a hard time delivering the message he'd just gotten from John.

Fox was dead.

Tommy DeSimone shot him once in the eye with a .38, then pumped three more rounds in Fox's head for good measure.

All Quack could tell me was that it happened at Fox's sister, Patricia's, apartment and that they fought because Fox found out Tommy had fucked his sister and then beat her with his fists.

———————

Looking back, what happened between Fox and Tommy was in the cards from the beginning. It was like those two were destined for trouble from the day in 1972 when Dominic Cataldo and John Gotti agreed in that sit-down to partner me and Fox up with Tommy to form the Three-Families Heist team.

Tommy was always trying to prove himself when he was around other gangsters who were suspicious of him because his brother was a rat and that made him insecure. So did the fact that he couldn't fight his way out of a cab. He acted like a tough guy, but he was nothing without his guns.

He was erratic and unpredictable and half psycho, and that made him dangerous to be around. There were guys who wouldn't work with Tommy or even play cards with him because they didn't trust him. This was a guy who bragged about shooting and killing some kid on the street he didn't even know just for kicks.

Tommy had no trouble getting women, but he was insecure with them too. He had a mean streak that turned a lot of women off, especially the ones he beat up.

Tommy looked at Fox and saw a guy who was everything he wasn't. To Tommy, Fox had it all: He made friends easily; he was loyal to them, and they'd trust him with their lives. Fox was a real tough guy who would never back down from a fight but was smart enough to avoid one when he could. But the biggest thing that set Tommy and Fox apart was Fox's way with women—they were scared of Tommy but they adored Fox.

Tommy only chased women who were in the Life, who knew he was a gangster and who were turned on by that. The Fox romanced only women who were from outside our world, who were attracted to him not *because* he was a gangster but because of who he was, which was a really rockin' hot guy who was a blast to be around. A lot of women fell for the Fox *even though* he was gangster, not because he was.

No doubt there was underlying friction between Tommy and Fox from the beginning because Fox was a Gambino, the Family that Tommy's brother betrayed, but they started out as friends. And different as they were, nothing would have come of it if not for the fact that Fox had a tragic flaw—his love for his sister.

Everybody knew how Fox felt about Patricia. She was Fox's angel, like my sister Rose Marie was for me. And Fox wanted for her what my sister wanted for me and what I was only beginning to realize I wanted for my own sons—a normal, happy life that had nothing to do with this Life. Ours was a world of deceit and violence and death, and as much as Fox loved living that Life, he would die—or kill—to protect his sister from it.

Tommy DeSimone was a walking stick of dynamite, and he embodied everything about our world that Fox saw as a danger and a threat to his sister.

Fox became so incensed and obsessed when he found out Tommy was dating Patricia that he went over the edge. He became so fanatical and paranoid that he convinced himself that Tommy was plowing his sister when he really wasn't. He let Tommy's ball busting get to him so deep that he flipped out over nothing the night before the Five Families silver bullion heist and nearly wrecked the whole operation.

Tommy might have been crazy, but he wasn't stupid; he knew John Gotti thought he was a rat bastard and that if ever given cause would whack Tommy in a heartbeat. Fucking Gotti's favorite son's sister would have been suicide for Tommy, and he knew it.

That's why I was sure Tommy never laid a hand on Patricia. But then I went away to prison, and things changed.

In the days to come, Quack filled me in on what happened between Tommy and Fox.

According to Quack, who got it from John Gotti, Fox was drinking in some joint a night or two before the shooting, and somebody told him he heard about Tommy slapping his sister. He said it assuming Fox knew all about it—it had gotten around that much. But this was news to Fox, and he went wild and shouted at the guy that he was going to find Tommy and kill him with his bare hands.

But before he went hunting for Tommy, Fox drove to Patricia's apartment. When he got there, he took one look at his sister and knew that this time he wasn't being paranoid. Patricia had a black eye and her face was swollen from Tommy beating on her. Patricia told Fox that they had started seeing each other again and it had gone too far. Fox charged out the door and got in his car and raced all over the city, looking for Tommy.

Finally he went back to Patricia's apartment and stood guard all night, hoping Tommy would show up so he could take him apart and put him back together dead.

Then it was Tommy who went looking for Fox. Quack said that Tommy had gone out to two or three different bars that night and at each one he heard the same thing—that Fox had been in there looking for him and saying he was going to kill him once he found him.

Hearing that sent Tommy into a rage of his own. Tommy looked for Fox at his apartment and hit some other joints but couldn't find him. The next day he drove over to Patricia's apartment in Queens.

The rest of the story Quack said Gotti got from Patricia, who knew John all her life.

There was a knock on the door and Fox answered it.

There was Tommy.

Neither of them said a word. Fox hauled off and punched Tommy in the face. Tommy staggered backward, and the next thing Patricia knew there were gunshots and Fox was dead from four slugs to the head.

Fox's sister refused to tell the cops anything. She said she didn't know who the guy at the door was or why he shot her brother.

But she told John Gotti everything.

———

When Quack first told me the bare bones of what went down, I felt nothing but numb. I didn't say anything for a full minute or more. When I finally did, my voice felt like it was coming from somebody else. There was no anger, no emotion, just simple dumb logic, as if Quack had told me there was a package at the post office for me.

"Then I'm going to have kill Tommy," I said. "Fox is my crime partner. Tommy will pay."

Angelo said I had to forget about it. He said Fox was with John and Gotti was going to take care of Tommy.

I played it cool. In that Life, when somebody got whacked, it was part of the landscape. You always had to expect it; it was always a possibility.

I thanked Ange for telling me. We all had our own one-man cells in the J Block. I went back to mine that night. I tried to go to sleep for hours but I kept thinking about Fox.

I cried myself to sleep. I never told a soul, ever, until now.

Fox was only twenty-seven years old.

CHAPTER THIRTY-SIX

Patron Saint

FEBRUARY 1975

WHEN A BIG BLIZZARD socked Pennsylvania during my first winter at Lewisburg, traffic on the interstate highways came to a standstill. Most snowbirds traveling south through the state were able to find motels for the night. But one busload of passengers traveling north wasn't so lucky. That bus and all its passengers—convicts from the high-security, hard-time federal penitentiary in Atlanta who were being transported to New York for court hearings—was rerouted to Lewisburg and put up at our No Comfort Inn.

I'll always be thankful for that blizzard, because one of the passengers on that bus was the man who changed my life.

He was a guy named Dave Iacovetti who was very high up in the Gambino hierarchy. He ran the Family business in Miami.

When Johnny Dio heard Dave was in Lewisburg for a few days, he pulled some strings and got him out of the holding pen and up to our cellblock. Dave and Johnny had known each other for years.

Dave was professorial looking; you'd never take him for a mobster. He had soft features and a round face and a big warm smile. He was very smart, and everyone on the block treated him with great respect.

I only saw him to say hi those few days he was at Lewisburg. But a couple of months later, I was bused back to New York for hearings on the appeal that Gerald Shargel, Jimmy Burke's mouthpiece, was making for me. I was put in the West Street Detention Center, which was a lockup for guys going in or out of prison and where they put you if you were on trial or making appearances in court. I spent my thirtieth birthday in that place.

APRIL 1975

When I got to West Street, Dave still was in there while his case was being appealed. He was serving a five-year sentence for stock fraud. Because we were bused back and forth to court and held in waiting rooms together every day, we got to know each other. Somebody back in Lewisburg had told me that Dave was good friends with Frank Sinatra.

Since Sinatra was the patron saint of my gambling club, I asked Dave about Frank. He didn't say a lot and I didn't press him, and because I didn't he later started to open up to me a little. And Dave was a guy I knew right away I wanted to know better because he was the kind of gangster I always wanted to be—one with wealth, power, and a whole lot of class.

He was in his fifties and a really cultured and sophisticated man, not like any other Mob guy I ever met. He grew up on the streets in Brooklyn, but you'd never know it. He read everything he could get his hands on and loved books and especially anything to do with American history. He loved fine art, music, and wine. He had homes in Miami Beach and in Trumbull, a wealthy suburb off the Merritt Parkway in Connecticut, where his wife and family lived. His wife, Nan, owned a restaurant there and his daughter Judy was married to a state trooper.

I wanted to get to know Dave because here was a guy who had gone far in the Life. I thought by getting to know him I could learn how to get ahead in the Mob. But what he ended up teaching me was that the smartest play of all was getting out of it.

JULY 1975

Dave and I got to know each other a lot better in July when they closed the Detention Center and moved everybody to the brand-new Metropolitan Correctional Center on Park Row next to the federal courthouse on Foley Square. Dave and I were shackled together when they moved us, and we were both put up on the seventh floor.

At the MCC, Dave and I were pinochle partners. Pinochle is a team card game and a pretty good betting game, but we didn't play for money; the losers had to do push-ups. When Dave and I lost, I did Dave's push-ups for him.

Dave and I ended up playing against one guy I knew well—Jimmy Burke, whose case was on appeal at the same time mine was and was being argued by the same lawyer, Gerald Shargel. Jimmy played pinochle like he played poker at the Sinatra Club—he was unbeatable. I did a lot of push-ups when Jimmy was playing.

Seeing Jimmy at MCC was a nice surprise.

When another regular from the Sinatra Club showed up on the seventh floor that summer, it was a big shock.

It was Tommy DeSimone. When I saw him I almost said, "I thought you were dead!" I sure as hell wished he was. But Tommy swaggered in big as life, cocky as ever, and grinning like I'd be glad to see him. He greeted me like the friend and heist partner I used to be, and I acted like I still was. But I wanted nothing more than to take a bat to his fucking skull.

It had been nine months since Tommy shot Fox in the face. For a long time I checked every newspaper I could get my hands on for the story about Tommy's body being found in the trunk of a car with his balls shot off and a rat stuck in his mouth.

When Quack told me I wasn't going to be the one who avenged Fox's death, that John would take care of it, I figured Tommy didn't have more than a few days to breathe. When weeks and then months passed, I couldn't guess what the fuck Gotti was waiting for. John loved the Fox as much as I did, and he'd hated Tommy a lot longer than I had. For me, wanting to see Tommy dead was a whole new experience.

Eventually I came up with a few explanations of why John let Tommy live, none of them good enough for me. For one thing, John was about to start the sweet sentence Roy Cohn got him for McBratney; he was a lot luckier on that one that he ever was at cards. So it was understandable that he wanted to lie low and not bring any further heat on himself or his crew—or on his boss, Carlo Gambino.

More important, John couldn't whack Tommy no matter how much he wanted to without permission. And the okay to kill Tommy had to come from Paul Vario. Paulie hated Tommy, but Paulie's biggest earner was Jimmy Burke, and Jimmy loved Tommy like a doting father loves his most fucked-up son. If Paulie okayed a hit on Tommy, Paulie would go broke, so Paulie protected Tommy for Jimmy.

I didn't find out until years later, from Henry Hill, that the whole reason Tommy was at the MCC in the first place was that Paul Vario was in the joint and Tommy was scared shitless that without Paulie in town to protect him, the Bergin crew would find some way to whack him and say it was an accident.

Tommy was out on bail on a hijacking charge, and he actually got his bail revoked on purpose so he could get off the streets. Tommy must have been damn desperate to use a jail as a hiding place, and he must have known if it ever got out he'd be a laughingstock because it's a no-balls thing any gangster would be ashamed to admit.

I wasn't a Gambino, but Fox was my partner and I hung out at the Bergin often enough that I might as well have been. So Tommy must have shit when he went to jail to escape the Gambinos and found me in there on the same floor as him. He didn't let on if he did, and I played it cool, but I'm sure he didn't sleep so sound at night knowing I was a few cells away thinking of ways to outsmart the system and whack him myself.

I think Dave Iacovetti must have heard about my beef with Tommy. Either that or he was some kind of mind reader. Because a little after Tommy showed up at MCC and I started thinking about strangling him in his sleep or drowning him in the shitter—or doing it right and waiting until I got out and maybe even getting my button for it—Dave gave me a warning.

He said he just wanted to have a talk about my future. But the first thing he said was something I'll never forget. He told me to think long and hard about taking part in a killing. "Once you pull that trigger," he said, "you can't take it back."

My hair actually stood on end when he said that, and I almost asked him if he knew about Tommy and Fox and me. I kept my mouth shut, and his warning didn't change my mind about wanting to kill Tommy. But as it sank in, I began to think that my lifelong goal—to get my button and become a made man—might not be the golden path I always thought it was.

Dave said a lot of other things that day that down the line had a big effect on my thinking. One was that there were a lot of legit ways to make very good money on the outside. He told me about a small company based in the Bahamas that was about to explode. He said I should think about investing in Resorts International; this was in 1975, three or four years before Resorts opened the first legal gambling casino in Atlantic City.

Then he started talking about the future of the Mob. He predicted its eventual demise because so many wiseguys were not only dealing drugs, they also were doing them, and that was causing a real breakdown in the structure of the Families. He went on about how the feds were determined to break the Families, and the Mob's own members were helping them do it.

I thought a lot about what Dave said. His words poured a little more water on the seeds that first Jane and then Fox had planted in my head.

Instead of thinking about getting made, I started thinking seriously about getting out.

It would be a long time coming, but I eventually followed Iacovetti's advice. Too bad that the years between when he gave it to me and when I did something about it turned into one long nightmare.

AUGUST 1975

A month later, my court hearings had ended and I was back in Lewisburg when the unbelievable happened. The warden notified me that I was being sent back to New York to appear before the judge who'd sentenced me. I was going to be held at the MCC for a few weeks and released before the end of September. *Shargel had won my case!* The 2nd U.S. Court of Appeals had overturned my sentence. It became some kind of landmark ruling. After serving less than fourteen months of my eight-year bid, I was getting out. I went to the priest's office to call my wife, but the reverend father wouldn't let me use the phone. Johnny Dio happened to be in there, and he said, "Let the kid make his call." The priest didn't say another word. I called home with the good news.

As I left, I thanked Dio. He told me to think nothing of it. Maybe I'd be able to do him a favor some day, he said.

When I got to the MCC in New York a few days later, I made a call from the pay phone that prisoners were allowed to use. I didn't call home. I dialed Jane's number. I got a recording: "This number is no longer in service." I went into some kind of shock. I realized it had been two months since I got a letter from Jane. A few days later I received a package forwarded to the MCC from Lewisburg. In it were the letters I had written to her. They had all been stamped with the words from the Elvis song: "Return to Sender, Address Unknown."

I didn't know what to think. I couldn't believe she'd leave town without a word. Something must have happened to her. I began to imagine that she'd been killed by one of her sicko johns or she'd been arrested. I didn't allow myself to think that she had left me, abandoned me like my mother, deserted me like my sister and Fox.

All the elation and excitement I felt evaporated. I was as depressed now when I was about to get out of prison as I had been going in. Only this was worse.

Now I had nothing. With Fox dead and Jane vanished, the old Life we had didn't seem worth living.

Down as I was during my last days at the MCC, when I got out and went home and saw my kids again, it hit me. Thanks to Jimmy Burke for showing me the way and hooking me up with Gerald Shargel, I had played the Ubatz card and won the biggest pot of my life—*seven fucking years*. Now I didn't have to miss the best years of my kids' lives after all, and I wasn't going to be aged and stooped like Eddie Pravato and Joe Dellamura were after prison sucked the life out of them.

I was thirty years old and had my whole life ahead of me. And I wasn't going to spend the next thirty feeling guilty about neglecting my boys. I'd been given another chance to be a real father to them, to get to know them and become a real part of their lives, and I wasn't going to blow it this time. If I learned anything in prison, it was how empty and alone you feel the instant those cell doors slam. And as soon as I got home and saw my sons, I felt nothing but joy.

As for Angela and me, we did our best. I tried to let her know how grateful I was that she put on a brave face when she came to visit me in prison, which was her worst nightmare come true of what being married to a criminal would come down to. I loved her for that and for showing me nothing but support and for taking care of our boys and our home. But at bottom I think she knew deep down the same thing I knew—that I didn't love her, not in the real sense of a couple, a man and wife loving and being there for each other. Terrible as it is to say even all these years later, it was the truth.

The first chance I got I went out looking for the woman I did love. I tracked down Lisa, Jane's old girlfriend who had quit working as her hostess and brothel manager back when things lit up between Jane and me. Lisa had been in touch with some of the other girls who used to work for Jane, and they all said the same thing. Jane had suddenly disappeared back in the spring. Her girls showed up for work one day and the one joint Jane had left, the place in Midtown, was closed. She'd shut down her call service, and none of them heard from her or of her again.

My first thought was that her vanishing act was no accident. Jane operated independently of the Mob, but she might have been muscled out by a competitor who was connected. I asked around but got zilch.

I had Charlie the Queens detective run her name through police arrest records and missing persons. He came back with zip. The doorman at Jane's apartment on 36th Street said a new tenant had moved in months ago. He had no forwarding address, no nothing.

I visited all the old places we used to hang out, Jack Dempsey's, Gallagher's, Elmer's, Hong's, our Chinese place downtown, the Rainbow

Room, Jilly's. I went to Zabar's where she liked to shop. A blonde would catch my eye and I'd be hopeful for a second, but no.

I spent months hunting and just hoping I'd run into her but never turned up a clue. All I could think was that she had got out of the Life like we talked about. And she got out without me.

Eventually, though it broke my heart, I stopped looking.

Two full years would pass before I found out what became of the whore who hooked my heart.

In the meantime, Angela and I settled back into our old routines and me into my old habits. I started going out nights on business when I didn't really have any—unless you count chasing down as many blondes as I could bang business.

Jane Parker left a gaping hole in my life, and it took a shitload of blondes to fill her place.

PART FIVE

CHAPTER THIRTY-SEVEN

Highway to Hell

1975–1977

Two cursed years, ten years apart. When my sister and half brother died in 1965 and my godson disappeared forever, that was my impetus to get into the Life. When I lost Fox and Jane ten years later, it was my impetus to get out. It took me almost another ten years to do it. Those years in between were a nightmare: a decade of drugs, depravity, and death.

After prison I went straight . . . back into the Life. Only it wasn't anything like it had been. No bank robberies, no hijacks, no crime partner, no fun and excitement. All I cared about at that point was making money and getting rich.

It was all scams and schemes and dealing drugs.

The month before I got out of the joint, Johnny went in. While he was away, his crew got into the drug play big time. Angelo's brother Sal Ruggiero became one of the biggest, wealthiest cocaine dealers in the country. When Quack got out of the joint, he went into business with him. Even Johnny's driver Tony Roach and John's brother Genie started dealing. The whole country turned on to coke in the '70s and '80s; there was so much money involved it was impossible for guys to resist. The harm it was doing to the Families nobody cared about; as long as it wasn't discovered and we kept breathing, we kept dealing.

I did a lot of business with two Bergin guys. One was one of John's oldest friends in the crew, Willie Boy Johnson, the Indian. The other was a slick young Jewish guy who played softball with us back in 1972, Mark Reiter. Mark got his stuff the way Dominic did, from France and Italy. Willie Boy had a smack connection with Frank Lucas's guys up in Harlem and the Italian Pleasant Avenue Mob. Those guys had more money than God.

I had a dealer who was also a chemist. I put him together with Mark and Willie Boy. My chemist tested their stuff for them. Mark's product tested at 99 percent pure; Willie Boy's was good stuff too at 75 percent. Willie Boy always brought me his *babania* for testing because he could never be sure how much his suppliers were stepping on it before they sold it to him. When I'd test his shit, he paid me by giving me six or seven grams; I'd turn that into a full ounce. I was making 10 g's a month just testing Willie Boy's stuff.

I knew Willie Boy from the old days at the Sinatra Club and at the Bergin, of course, but I got to know him a lot better when we were in business together. The Bergin crew always talked about Willie Boy like he wasn't there, like he was a muscle with no brain, a guy who would do whatever he was told to do, threaten guys, beat a guy near to death, whack him, whatever the boss ordered, but never had a thought in his head. But I got to know another side of Willie Boy, and I knew he had something going on up there; he wasn't the dumb beast everybody took him for.

Two other Bergin guys, John and Charles Carneglia, got into drugs and a lot of other nasty shit. When John got out of Lewisburg, he started dealing heroin, cocaine, and pot. John shipped weed in to Jamaica Bay on freighters, just like Joe Profaci brought booze in from Canada back in my father and Uncle Tony's day. John Carneglia moved such huge quantities he once lost a forty-ton shipment to the Coast Guard. That was a big loss, but John's business made so much money it didn't hurt him too bad.

John and his brother were also in the car business. They owned Fountain Avenue Auto Parts, a garage repair lot in Queens. They did a big business selling American cars overseas to places like Saudi Arabia and Kuwait. They were new-car dealers—only their cars were all newly stolen. John ran the car business.

Charles used the lot for his own business, which was gun for hire. He was a hit man, and he disposed of bodies for all his hit man friends. He's the one who gave guys acid baths in a steel barrel at the auto parts lot. He'd dissolve bodies in acid and then dump the barrel in the ocean. If he didn't have time for that, he just put the body in the trunk of a car and drove it over to a junkyard called Industrial. It was run by a guy named Joe; Joe would cube the car, body and all.

The Carneglia brothers used to hang out at the Blue Fountain Diner near the lot. One night an off-duty court bailiff and his girlfriend were in there. Charles Carneglia scared the shit out of her; she saw he had a gun on him, and her boyfriend arrested him for carrying an illegal weapon. Maybe he was being his girl's knight in shining armor, but this wasn't the days of fucking olde. He should never have done that.

The knight's name was Arthur Gelb. A year later Charles was put on trial on the gun charge. A couple of nights before Gelb was supposed to testify, John followed him home from his job in Brooklyn Night Court, cut him off in traffic, and shot him four times as he sat at the wheel of his car. The knight's shining armor didn't protect him. He was dead, and the case against Charles was dropped.

John Carneglia was okay, but his brother was a vicious prick and a cokehead. He fed blow to every waitress at the Blue Fountain. Then he took them somewhere and fucked them and tortured them; he tied them up and burned them with cigarettes. He told them he'd whack them if they ever said a word. They didn't dare tell the other waitresses, so they all dated Charles and lived to regret it.

Charles was a sick fuck and I never liked him much. I liked him less when I found out that two months after Fox was shot, Charles was an usher at Tommy Guns's wedding. I never asked Patricia what she thought when she heard about Tommy's nuptials. But I'm sure she didn't like the idea of Tommy walking down the aisle or anywhere else any more than I did.

My dislike of Charles Carneglia didn't stop me from going into the auto business with his brother. I opened my own car business. I called it Classic Cars. We specialized in Corvettes and other old cars, refurbishing them and selling them. That's what I was doing on paper. In reality it was a chop shop. I ran a gang of car thieves who stole cars for me; I chopped them up for parts and sold them to John. We also specialized in new cars, which my guys would jack off the streets; we'd switch out the Vehicle Identification Numbers from wrecks and sell the new ones to legit dealers. Then I'd get the plate numbers and have my crooked detective friend Charlie trace the new owners. I'd wait a little while, then send my guys out to steal the cars back before the DMV reported they had fake VINs. Then I'd tag them with different VINs and sell them all over again.

We did pretty good and I liked the work, but I got into it because I needed a new cover for my drug business now that the Sinatra Club was closed and I had sold my gambling and shylock business to Big Funzi. He had been running it while I was away. He bought it for 60 g's, which he paid off weekly. I gave him all my gambling and shylock customers and introduced him to each one.

One guy named Stanley was a New York City bus driver and a nickel-and-dime horse degenerate. I explained to Funzi that he shouldn't get too rough with Stanley or even threaten to; he was a delicate kind of guy. Also he had a cousin who was an FBI agent. Funzi didn't listen to me. Stanley fell behind on his payments and Funzi lost his cool. He threatened Stanley. Stanley got scared and called his cousin. My old friend Big Funzi ended up convicted in federal court and went away for five years.

My jewelry business also was only partly legit. It served as an excellent fencing operation and as a second cover for my drug dealing. I was able to launder my drug money and protect it from both the IRS and the new, official head of our Family.

I should say "heads" of the Colombo Family because Allie Boy was standing in for the Commission-approved godfather, Carmine Persico, who was still in prison. The Gallos were kaput by then. Carlo Gambino had given Kid Blast a choice—get whacked or leave the Colombo Family and become a Genovese, which is what Blast did. That was the peace arrangement that finally ended the Gallo Wars after almost twenty-five years.

I bought and sold gold and silver as well as jewelry. My uncle Tony taught me a long time ago that there was big money in money. I started learning about coins way back when I was running Tony and my sports book out of Sal's Pizza. Silver was $1.29 per ounce then. I had a sign in the window: PAYING CASH FOR SILVER COINS AND SILVER CERTIFICATES. You could get one ounce of silver for a silver certificate dollar bill. I studied the coin books, learned about low-mintage coins. I memorized all the key and semi-key dates of Indian head pennies, Lincoln pennies, Buffalo nickels, Mercury dimes, standard Liberty coins, and Seated dollars, Morgan dollars, and Peace dollars.

Silver shot up from $1.60 an ounce in 1970 to more than $50 an ounce ten years later. I memorized the coin dealers' newsletter, the Greysheet they called it. I knew all the mint marks; the rarest are CC—for Carson City—minted in 1878, '79, '80.

In one of the only robberies I pulled after I got out of prison, I hit the jackpot. I'd gotten a tip that a rich gambler out on Long Island had a big stash of rare coins. I nailed it. He had boxes of uncirculated Morgan silver dollars, worth about $800,000 then. I don't want to even think what they'd be worth today. The price of silver is skyrocketing now that the economy has gone to hell, and the coins themselves have gone up in value twenty times over the years.

Within a few years I owned three jewelry stores in Queens. I advertised on television. They were all semilegit. I bought and sold and traded. I also stole and fenced and bought stolen property, melted down the metal, and put the gems in new settings.

I was also working bank and insurance scams. One time I ran a scam within a scam and ripped off half a million dollars in diamonds in my own store by faking a robbery and getting the insurance company to pay up.

That was a good score, but in terms of kicks and excitement, it just didn't do it for me like in the old days.

1976

I saw my uncle Tony for the last time during the summer of the bicentennial. He got out of prison after serving ten of the fifteen years he was sent away for. He was sixty-seven years old, and prison had taken a lot out of him. He looked frail and sickly. He was dressed great in a summer suit and straw Sam Snead hat, but his clothes looked a size too big for him. I don't think I ever saw him drive a car that wasn't a Cadillac. Now he was driving a rented Ford sedan, a car that he never would have been caught dead in when I was a kid. He came to see me at my Classic Cars lot on Liberty Avenue.

He said he was living up in Connecticut, near Danbury, where the prison was. He was living with a good woman, but not Kitty, the Marilyn Monroe beauty he was with when he went in back in 1966. He was back in business buying and selling houses like before, but I knew it wasn't going too good because he asked me if I had a decent legit car I could let him have on loan. He'd pay me when his cash flow got better.

I kept legit cars on the lot for show, including a beautiful Corvette. He sat in it for a minute, then got out and took the station wagon. That was a car my father would drive, not my uncle Tony. I told him he could have it, no loan, it was his. I thought about asking if he needed money. I had plenty of it, but I knew he would take that as an insult.

He said I looked like I was doing all right. He asked me how the gambling business with Dominic was doing. I told him I wasn't working the track anymore and that I sold the business he started me out in. I told him my real business was supplying heroin to dealers. I should never have told him that. He had a disgusted look on his face. I got uptight and told him how I was making more money than I could ever make running a sports book and shylocking at the track. I said he wouldn't believe the money.

Tony said he would believe it, all right. He said half the guys in the joint, connected guys, were drug dealers and junkies; vicious scum, he called them. He said he thought he showed me how to act in the life, that he taught me the code, all his stories about the history of the Mob weren't just hot air, they were meant to teach me the traditions and how to live and act with honor, how to be smart. Dealing drugs wasn't smart, he said. It was the stupidest fucking thing he ever heard of. He said guys like me were the reason the Mob was finished. He said if I was really smart, I'd get out.

He gave me the keys to the rented car and told me where to return it. Then he got in the station wagon and drove away. I never saw him again.

I was pissed off. Fuck him, I thought. It took a while for it to sink in. Tony driving out of my life was one loss I could have done something about. I couldn't save my sister or Fox, but losing Tony, who had been the most important person in my life all the time I was growing up, that could have been prevented. I hated myself for that.

We lost all contact with each other, just like Jane and me. I think he died up there in Connecticut. I'm not sure when.

I never did ask him if he was my real father.

Everything Tony said about the Mob came true. Carlo Gambino died of a heart attack that October. Just before he kicked, the Commission opened the books for new members for the first time in twenty years. Right away guys started selling buttons—Albert Anastasia did the same thing in the 1950s and got whacked by Gambino for it.

In the old days, getting made was like a baptism, a sacred ceremony. To qualify, you had to be sponsored by two made men, you had to be 100 percent Italian, and you had to take part in a murder. Now made guys got rich selling buttons for $250,000. They'd pass half up to their captain and the captain would get another made guy to be the second sponsor. When inflation kicked up to double digits, the price of a button soared to half a million.

The month after Don Carlo died, Big Paul Castellano became boss. He lived on Todt Hill on Staten Island in the same neighborhood where they shot the wedding scenes at the opening of *The Godfather*. *Todt* means "death." That the old Dutch settlers named the hill Todt was a bad omen for Big Paul. Castellano was a wealthy guy who lived like a king, but he was different from the old dons. Dave Iacovetti said he wasn't a real gangster. He didn't like to get his hands dirty; he saw himself as a straight-up businessman. He was treacherous, and you didn't know where you stood with him. And he was afraid of drugs because he was afraid of guys flipping.

Big Paul split the Family up into two factions. He ran the business side, the white-collar rackets, and left the traditional stuff—the gambling, the shylocking, the heists, and all the strong-arm stuff—to Gambino's underboss, Neil Dellacroce, who was out of prison by then and back running operations at the Ravenite. Castellano pretty much left Neil alone, except for ordering him to make sure no Gambinos got involved with drugs. But it was already too late for that.

When Johnny got out of prison the next year—he ended up doing just half of his four-year sentence—he got his button and he was made captain. Charlie Fatico was still alive and his legal problems were settled, but he took a backseat. John had been running things before he went into prison, and now it was made official. Gotti was the acting boss of the Bergin crew and he was Neil's right hand.

Carlo Gambino's dream of One Big Family was buried with him. Instead of uniting all the Families into one strong and powerful organization, Castellano divided his own Family in two. There was Neil and Johnny on one side and Castellano on the other. One of Big Paul's top guys was a thug named Sammy Gravano. He could have been on either side. He was a hit man and he was a businessman. He would also turn out to be the most treacherous Mob guy alive.

The split between the two gangs was going to prove deadly—for Big Paul and for the Gambino Family, and in the end, for Johnny Boy and for the New York Mob itself.

When John Gotti left prison, the inmates gave him a going-away present—a plaque they hung on the wall at the Bergin—and the guys gave him a welcome-home present—a new Lincoln.

I was on probation for two years and wasn't supposed to hang out with known hoodlums. I stayed away from the Bergin for the first few months. I didn't have the Sinatra Club anymore and, of course, no Fox to keep me informed about what guys were doing and what kind of scores were going down. Most of the stuff I heard I got from the guys I dealt with in my auto and drug businesses, John Carneglia and Willie Boy and Mark Reiter. By the time John got out, I had probation pretty well figured out.

My probation officer was a thoughtful guy. He called before he came to see me so I could always start doing some kind of legit busy-work when he showed up. He coveted my Corvettes and we talked about wheels more than anything else.

Anyway, John's status had changed so much, and he was so busy running a lot of operations for Neil and meeting with him at the Ravenite in Manhattan, that I didn't see a whole lot of him. He still gambled—to say the least. So I'd see him around wherever there was action. I'd see him at the track and at clubs and bars some, but not like before.

1977

John got out of the cement in July, the famous summer of '77 when the Bronx was burning. It was the year of punk rock and the headline in the *Daily News* when the city went bankrupt and the president told the mayor he wasn't going to bail him out: "Ford to City: Drop Dead!"

It was also the summer of the Son of Sam, David Berkowitz, the fruitcake from the Bronx who started whacking brunettes. Fox would have found that guy and crucified him. There's no excuse for that shit, shooting girls. Wiseguys had no tolerance for that. I never heard of any contract put out on a woman. That was one of the worst sins you could commit.

Guys got pissed when he made the mistake of hunting girls in Queens. The Bergin crew formed a posse and went out looking for that coward. One of the detectives on the Son of Sam squad knew that Gotti owned the disco where the killer stalked his last victim, Stacy Moskowitz. It was a club up on Northern Boulevard.

The detective contacted the Bergin through some corrupt cop—those weren't hard to find—and asked John's crew to look for the shooter. They called him the .44 Caliber Killer, because he used a gun that would bring down an elephant to blow some poor girl's head off while she was necking in a car. Guys got together and said let's find this fuck and whack him. Berkowitz was lucky the cops got him before those guys did.

John came home to a different world. Practically everybody in his crew was into drugs. He made a lot of noise about what Castellano told Neil. He said he'd have the first guy he caught dealing whacked. But John was a hypocrite about drugs. He had to be. He needed the money to cover his huge gambling debts. He could never let Neil, or especially Big Paul, find out. He'd wake up at the bottom of Jamaica Bay if he did.

But there was nothing really he could do to stop it. He would have had to whack his whole crew including his own brothers; both Genie and Peter Gotti were into it deep, and his little brother Vince was a junkie himself.

His oldest friends in the crew, Angelo and Willie Boy, were dealing; so were the Carneglias, who also grew up with Johnny. Angelo's brother Sal was a multimillionaire drug dealer; he had his own fucking plane. He was under indictment for dealing, and when he heard he was going to be arrested he went on the lam. He went into the wind, Ange said.

Johnny knew Sal from way back. They were busted together in the early '60s for stealing that Avis car. John also knew about Sal's millions and shook him down for a big piece. What could Sal do?

Even the Mouthpiece, Mike Coiro, got into it. John had made him house counsel at the Bergin. Mike still represented Charlie Fatico and guys in the crew, but he functioned as John's adviser and consigliore. Mike loved it. He was tired of being a lawyer by then. He wanted to be a gangster himself, to be a wiseguy like his clients. I remember John sent him to pick up a ton of blow from Sal Ruggiero's stash after Sal was killed in a plane crash. Mike was driving a big motor home full of drugs and loving every minute of it. I thought if only his old pals on the Waterfront Commission could see him now.

This was all happening years before the public ever heard of John Gotti. But he was already dressing like the Mob star he later became. The days when he wore those polyester checked suits we jacked were long gone. He started wearing very expensive tailored suits. They must've fallen off some very high-end trucks. He was already living large. When John went to Florida, he had somebody like Tony Roach chauffeur him.

The public didn't know him, but every connected guy in the city and every wannabe knew who he was.

John was closer than ever to Neil Dellacroce. He was going to the Ravenite two or three times a week to meet with his boss. Neil was probably the best-known Mob guy in the city at that time. The papers ID'd him as the boss of the Gambino Family. They never mentioned Paul Castellano. If Neil had been made boss instead of Castellano—everybody I knew thought he should have been—I think John would have eventually been his second in command. He would have been Neil's underboss.

When Neil got indicted for ordering some murder down in Florida a couple of years after John got out of the can, John and Willie Boy and Tony and Angelo, all the guys who used to hang out at the Sinatra, they went down and whacked the witness against Neil. Neil got off and he never forgot the service the Bergin crew did for him.

Right around then, the *Midnight Cowboy* star Jon Voight, Angelina Jolie's father, had an audience with John at the Bergin. He had just won the Oscar for the Jane Fonda movie *Coming Home*, and he was doing research for a film about a connected guy.

That was just five years after Gotti was a nobody who walked broke into the Sinatra Club and borrowed a few thou so he could play cards. If anybody placed a bet back then that when the hottest star in Hollywood wanted to meet a top guy in the Mafia, he would seek out Johnny Boy Gotti, everybody in the joint would have laughed in his face and taken his money.

Powerful as he was by 1977, it looked like Gotti still didn't have the juice to settle an old score. Three years after he shot Gotti's favorite son in the face, Tommy DeSimone still hadn't paid for his sins. Despite the fact that Fox was my crime partner and closest friend, John had even more reason to kill Tommy than I did. Everybody knew Fox was John's fair-haired boy and a longtime and loyal member of the Bergin crew, not to mention a friend he loved like a son. It seemed to me, and I'm sure to a lot of other guys, that for Gotti, Tommy's very existence was a slap in the face and a sign of weakness.

All I could think was that for Tommy to be alive three years after he shot Fox in the eye in front of his own sister, he must be bringing down some awfully big scores for Jimmy Burke and Paul Vario. And now, as everybody who saw *GoodFellas* knows, that's exactly what Tommy was doing. His success as a hijacker and killer was all that was keeping him from getting his own eyes put out with a bullet.

There was another ghost haunting me from the past that I did get some closure on that year. Charlie, my good old corrupt friend from Queens detectives, finally got a line on Jane that fall. She was living in the country like she always dreamed, but not in some funky old village in the Catskills. She was up in big-money country in one of the wealthiest towns in America, right over the Connecticut line from New Canaan.

I assumed that because Charlie provided his services to wiseguys all over the city, whoever Jane had hooked must be connected. Charlie had called me at my Classic Cars office and I was already rummaging through the drawers for a map. As soon as I hung up the phone I was going to drive up to Westchester and find the bitch. She left the city but she didn't leave the life. I was going to go up there and demand to know what the fuck she was doing after she promised me that she'd wait for me and we'd start a new life together in a nice little house in a quiet little town and have kids and raise a family. Now she had just found some other bad-ass gangster and she was still living the life and in high fucking style. Jane had pulled off a heist that hurt like hell—she stole our dream.

But then Charlie told me that she wasn't shacking up with some Mob version of a sugar daddy. This guy she was with was the son of a megarich business tycoon. Charlie told me something else that made me stop looking for a map.

Jane and this guy were married. And they had a kid.

And I was right back where I was two years before when Jane followed in my mother's footsteps and walked right out of my life.

She was gone, and I had to get over her all over again.

I didn't know it yet, but losing Jane for the second time was just a taste of the shit storm that was right around the corner, a long evil season when the Life I loved went to hell. But before the lights went out and the real nightmares began, I had some last blasts with Dominic. He and Jackie were making so much money they were living like kings, and the treatment we got in nightclubs and restaurants and from all the women who loved all that money was addicting. All of us lived like Fox said—"no tomorrow"—but the times we had in those years also let me live like there was no yesterday. And no Jane.

Just before Gambino died, Dave Iacovetti sent me tickets to see

Frank Sinatra at the Westchester Premier Theater, the Mob-owned place in Tarrytown where the famous picture of Sinatra was taken with Carlo Gambino, his brother Joe, Big Paul Castellano, and a cast of other wiseguys, including Jimmy "the Weasel" Frattiano, the guy who later ratted out the Mob's casino business in Vegas. Gambino had a heart attack and died right after that. It was one of the only photographs most people ever saw of Don Carlo. I guess he thought hanging with Frank was worth blowing his cover for.

Dom was a huge Sinatra fan, and a few years later his friend Jilly Rizzo set Dom up for a meeting with the man at his restaurant in Midtown. Jilly was very protective but Frank loved hanging out with wiseguys, and if a top made guy wanted to meet him, Jilly would set it up. When the date was set, Dom invited me to come along. Dave Iacovetti was out by then and I visited him up in Connecticut. He told me that Frank liked the color orange on women, so I made sure my date wore an orange miniskirt.

Frank was at the bar with Dom and some other guys; I was in a booth drinking with my date. Frank ogled her all night long. She loved slinking by him on the way past the bar as he twisted his neck to watch her ass. I thought the skirt looked like something a hooker would wear, but it gave this chick such a kick I got a great blow job on the way home in the car thanks to Frank's love of orange.

Dom and Jackie had carte blanche at the Vegas casinos that the Mob ran—which was most of them in those days. The New York Families had their own travel agent, a guy named Big Julie Weintraub who ran junkets for wiseguys to Vegas. We used to go see Big Julie in his New York office, give him 25 g's each, and fly to Vegas where that deposit gave us $50,000 credit at the casino of our choice. Our boss Pegleg had a hold on Big Julie; together they skimmed millions from the Vegas casinos.

Julie worked for all the Families. Most wiseguys who used his pipeline were assigned a certain casino hotel where they were supposed to spend their credit. Top guys like Dom had their pick. We always stayed at the Sands. We had luxury suites and showgirls provided. We even had our own pit boss who was assigned to get us anything we wanted.

Dom had a blackjack dealer at one of the big hotels who was also a *babania* and coke dealer. Dom sent him a package of street goods every few weeks to deal. On one of our trips to Vegas, Dom needed an out-of-the-way place off the strip where we could bag a special shipment of powder he had sent in. We just happened to pick the Hilton. We had no idea when we booked the room that Elvis was playing there that week.

Dom and I were down in the casino at around 4:00 in the morning playing blackjack when we saw a huge crowd around the craps table. Sure enough, bigger than life, there's the King himself.

Just as I squeezed through the crowd to place a bet, the dice were passed to Elvis. At craps I always bet the hard 4, the box with 2 and 2. I bet $200 and Elvis rolled a bunch of times without crapping out. Each time he rolled a 4, I got $1,400. When I placed a $2,000 bet on the 4, even Elvis took notice. He rolled, and *bam*, he hit the hard 4 and I had $14,000. Five minutes later, he hit it again—another 14 g's. Now Elvis and I are laughing our asses off. I walked out of there with $60,000 and singing "Viva Las Vegas," never dreaming that Elvis would be dead eight months later.

That summer I made a bet that later saved my life. I bet on my kids. My older son turned eight that year and he started playing Pop Warner football. Before then I had taught him the basics of the game—it was one of the things we started doing together after I got my early release from prison. When he started Pop Warner, I helped out with the coaching like I did back in 1971 with my brother-in-law Lenny's team. When my younger son started later on, I did the same thing. They were both talented athletes, and both grew up to be star players in high school and college.

But I would have loved coaching them even if they warmed the bench every game. Football gave me a chance to really be a dad for the first time. I bonded with my boys like I never had when they were little, when I was so deep into the Life that I hardly gave them any time at all. When we were at practice or just across the street in the park throwing the ball around, I'd remind myself that by all rights I'd still be in the joint, still serving my sentence, and the boys would be growing up without me.

Getting to share my love for football with my boys and be there on the sidelines when they played felt like a gift from God, like I'd been on death row waiting for a date in the chair and I won a reprieve I never saw coming.

A lot of guys I knew from the Sinatra Club and the Bergin had kids in Pop Warner. There were so many wiseguys' kids in the league they called it Little Grid Fellas. I used to sit on the sidelines with some of the other dads, and we'd plan heists and set up deals while we watched the kids play. I used to carry grams in my gym bag in case I had to meet a dealer in the parking lot during the game. Dominic had meetings with me at games. Mike Coiro didn't have a kid, but he came to games with Peter Gotti and his kid.

John Gotti's son Frankie played on my older son's team. He was a great kid; he had a weight problem but he was quick and he could throw a mean block. He and Sal Jr. became pretty good friends.

Back in 1973 when John and I attended that World Series game, we talked about our kids and what kind of men they would become when they grew up. With Frankie, John never got the chance to find out.

CHAPTER THIRTY-EIGHT

Dead Ends

1978

JOHNNY DIO DID ME a couple of favors at Lewisburg. He got me out of the prison factory and onto the yard detail, and he got that priest to let me make a call on the prison parish phone.

Three years after I got out, Dio called in those favors. I don't know if it was because I said something he didn't like or I didn't pay him respect or maybe he could sense that I thought he was a vicious prick. Whatever the reason, he gave me the kind of assignment you'd give your worst enemy. It made me wish I never heard of Johnny Dio.

He was inside the joint, but he still had power and influence in both the Lucchese and Gambino Families. The son of a capo in Florida was sleeping with the wife of another made guy. If the kid had been made himself, he would have been whacked for messing with the man's wife. The old dons back in Sicily knew that's how family feuds began. It's how the Trojan War and every bloodbath before and since started, with some guy in one tribe fucking the woman of a guy in the next tribe over. The Sicilians figured kill the guy right away and you'll save yourself a lot of carnage.

The Family involved—I don't know if the capo's kid and the guy whose wife he was fucking were in the same Family or not; I was never told and I knew better than to ask—they consulted Dio in prison and asked him what to do. He suggested they use the old Murder Incorporated punishment: Instead of killing the fucker, they should cut his balls off. Dio said he knew just the man for the job, an ex-con who owed him—me.

I'll spare you and me the details, but I did it. And after I did I wished to Christ I'd listened to Jane and Fox and Dave Iacovetti and my uncle Tony and got the hell out before I did.

———

Things sicker even than that were going down that year. There was an orgy of off-the-books killing like the Mob had never seen before. Traditionally all Mob hits had to be approved by a boss, and approval was granted only if there was good reason to perform the murder. Killings to settle personal scores or those motivated purely by greed were forbidden. By the late 1970s, those rules were forgotten or ignored. Guys started doing unsanctioned hits over drugs and money left and right.

My own boss and friend Dominic Cataldo was one of the worst offenders. He'd been whacking drug business partners without permission for years. The richer he got, the more paranoid and bloodthirsty he got. He got his button when the Commission opened the books; he was made a capo. That didn't stop him; in fact it seemed to make him worse. Now he had money and power, and he started doing coke. When guys with guns start doing that shit, get out of the way.

Dom used to do hits on guys right in the back room of his restaurant, the Villagio Italia, then he put them in the trunk of his car and drove them up to Boot Hill. Now he started planting guys up there faster than they could dig their own graves. Which was Dominic's idea of a good joke.

Boot Hill was upstate off the Taconic Parkway near Beacon, New York. He told me how he got a guy to help him take a body up there one day. He got the guy to dig the hole and they threw the body in. Then Dom said, Oh, shit, he forgot to see what the stiff had on him. So he got his helper to get down in the hole and see what he could find. The guy searched the body and handed a wallet, a wad of cash, a watch, a ring, and a gold chain up to Dom. Dom said, "Thanks," and shot him in the head. Then he shoveled in dirt on top of both dead guys.

Dom thought that was a fucking hoot.

He saw killing as the solution to every problem. He told me he was having trouble at home and his wife threatened to leave him. He said to her go ahead, get the fuck out, but if you do I'm going to kill your parents. That was Dom's way to solve his domestic problems—whack the whole family.

Dom was just one of many homicidal maniacs in the Mob at that time. There was a total breakdown of order. The killings were not about power struggles between families, weren't turf wars, weren't even about revenge. There was no plan or strategy. It was just a bloodbath. There was nothing like it before in the whole history of the Five Families. I guess it was the death throes of the Mob.

You had crews like Roy DeMeo's that performed hits like Murder Incorporated, only they did them with or without contracts. DeMeo's crew were Gambinos under Nino Gaggi. They did a lot of business with the Carneglias, whacking guys connected to their auto-exporting business and using Charles's acid drums to get rid of the bodies. They also killed indiscriminately. They'd whack the guy delivering pizza if he couldn't break a $20.

They turned killing into some kind of blood orgy where they shot victims and drained the blood, and then stripped naked and cut up the bodies. They got naked so they didn't get guts and brains and gore on their clothes. But a bunch of naked Mob guys drenched in blood? That's some sick shit.

It was during that time when the Mob was on a blood rampage that Dom started making noise that it was time I got my button. I think in his coke-eaten brain he was getting more and more paranoid and suspicious of everybody around him, including me. He was starting to worry that I might flip on him or rip him off like he thought I had that time when he tortured the truth out of Nips.

My entire career as a hoodlum, I expected that sooner or later I'd kill on order and get my button. But for one reason or another it never happened. I never had to make that decision Dave Iacovetti talked about when he said that once you pull the trigger you can't stop the bullet, you can't take it back.

By the time my getting made became an issue, I wasn't interested anymore. I had grown sick of the Life and sick of the death and the killing.

I think Dominic sensed that, because when he finally gave the order that would make my bones, it wasn't to whack a guy but simply to participate in a murder. That was enough to hold over me if I ever tried to betray him, which was the whole point. Once you killed for the Mob or took part in a hit, that was it. Cops would let you flip on any crime but murder. Of course that was about to change too.

For my initiation into the Colombo Family, I was ordered to dig a grave. I drove out to the Hamptons on the east end of Long Island and found a spot along a deserted stretch of beach. The soil was sandy, but it still took me most of the night to dig a hole six feet long, three feet wide, and six feet deep. I finished and went to meet Dominic back in Ozone Park. When I got there, he said the deal was off. The guy he was going to whack had won a reprieve. I drove back to the beach and filled in the hole before dawn.

Later that day I went to watch one of my sons' Pop Warner games. I was standing on the sidelines, and I looked down and saw that I still had sand on my shoes from grave digging. I stamped the sand off my feet. It felt like something filthy, that I had brought something from that world of death and violence there to the playing field where my son and all those other boys were playing.

It made me realize that I didn't want any part of that world anymore. Burying a body wasn't exactly pulling the trigger like Dave Iacovetti said, but if I had done it, if Dominic had killed the guy and I had shoveled sand over the corpse, I wouldn't have been able to take that back either.

DECEMBER 1978

It was the kind of golden opportunity every mobster wishes for but rarely receives: a chance to get my button—and to earn it for a piece of work that isn't just an assignment but a meaningful hit that fulfills a promise and puts a bitter beef to final rest.

The boss who gave me that shot to become a made man by settling an old score was not Dominic Cataldo—it was John Gotti. And the hit was on a target who once consumed me with hatred and that I had spent years itching to carry out—Tommy DeSimone.

I hadn't seen John since a couple months before at a Pop Warner football game. The coach had cut his son Frankie from the starting lineup because he was overweight. John drove out to the game and raised hell about it. It was hard to believe that the coach didn't know who John was, but he didn't back down. He said Frankie was a good player, but he was out of shape and huffing and puffing in practice. The coach said he'd put Frankie back in, but he needed to trim down first. The coach stuck to his guns and Frankie stayed on the bench.

John was furious. He pulled me aside and said he was going to take care of that fucking coach. He was dead serious. He wanted to whack the Pop Warner football coach. I realized he was just like Dominic. He thought whacking guys was the solution to any problem.

On December 11, 1978, my old Sinatra Club friends Jimmy Burke and Tommy DeSimone, along with a crew of other thieves, pulled off the richest heist in the history of the New York Mob, if you didn't count Vince Pappa's NYPD French Connection score. The Lufthansa heist at JFK was the biggest cash robbery in American history up to then. It was the kind of heist Uncle Tony would have loved because they stole $6 million and got away with it.

Before the Lufthansa score, Tommy invited me in on it. I think after all those years he was finally trying to atone for Fox. I told Tommy no thanks, I wasn't doing robberies anymore. That was true. But if I was to start again it sure as shit wouldn't be with the guy who whacked my best friend. Later, when I read about the heist in the papers, I thought even Fox would have wanted me to get an end of a score that big. I thought that heist would make Tommy's career. Paul Vario's taste would be a feast. It looked like all Tommy's dreams of becoming a made guy with the Luccheses were about to come true at last.

A day or two after the robbery, I was working at one of my stores when John Gotti drove up in his Lincoln. I went outside and we had a brief chat. He said it was time Tommy was taken care of for killing Fox, and he wanted me in on it.

I was shocked by John's timing. After four years of *expecting* him to whack Tommy, he decides to do it when I least expect it, after a heist so big all the Families including the Gambinos were sure to get a taste.

There was a lot I wanted to say to John, but you didn't explain yourself in the Mob. I had to give him a yes or no on the spot. I told him no. He didn't say another word. He just got in his car and drove away.

I would have liked to tell John that I loved Fox as much as he did and that I hated Tommy for what he did, but a lot had changed since then. I wasn't interested in becoming a made guy anymore. But more than that, I no longer really held Tommy responsible. A lot of time had passed, and I felt like it was the Life that killed Fox. If it hadn't been Tommy, it would have been some cop or an armed guard on a truck or a hothead Colombian drug dealer whose girlfriend Fox was fucking. I always more or less liked Tommy. So did Fox, up until Tommy messed with his sister. Killing Tommy now seemed to me like another fucking waste, just like him killing Fox was a waste.

1979

In January, a month after Johnny paid me that visit and offered me a chance to avenge Fox's death and get in on a hit that would have earned me my button, Tommy "Two Guns" DeSimone disappeared.

For a long time I didn't know how it went down for Tommy. There were a lot of conflicting stories at the time, and the *GoodFellas* movie fudged the details and didn't make clear what exactly happened or who did it.

The full story comes from Henry Hill, who was good friends with Tommy, and he made it a point to find out what happened as best he could.

The way Henry tells the story: Tommy was whacked by Gotti's crew for killing Billy Batts, a made Gambino guy, back in 1970, and for Fox, who wasn't made but was with John and the crew at the Bergin. Henry says that it was Paul Vario—who always hated Tommy himself but protected him because he was with Jimmy Burke, and Jimmy was his biggest earner—who gave Tommy to the Gambinos.

Henry's explanation of why Paulie gave Tommy up has to be believed. He says Paulie was having an affair with Henry's wife Karen while Henry was in prison. At the same time, Tommy got wasted on coke and put the moves on Karen too. She told him to fuck off and he beat the shit out of her. That enraged Paulie, who not only gave Tommy up to Gotti, he also drove Tommy to the fake induction ceremony himself.

The part in the movie where Jimmy bangs down the phone and cries when he finds out what happened was true, Henry says. Only he and Burke were in Florida when they made the call, not outside a diner in New York.

When Tommy got to the house where he thought he was going to be made, there really was a ceremony planned—only it wasn't the one he hoped for. John was there. And instead of me, so was Tommy Argo, the Gambino guy who owned Sebastian's. Argo also whacked one of Tommy's brothers, the one who was the rat and who was the reason Gotti always hated Tommy.

One thing Henry says makes me glad I turned down John's offer to lend a hand avenging Fox's death: Gotti and Argo didn't just whack Tommy. They tortured him and they killed him slowly. Henry says that John made sure Tommy's death "took a long time."

That was just one of the sickening things that happened back then. And there was more yet to come.

Fox's death in 1974 hit me hard. The shock of it numbed me at first and then sank in and left me with a kind of sick feeling of hopelessness and dread, a form of depression that lasted for years. When I closed the Sinatra Club, I had a vague feeling that it was the end of an era. Fox's murder seven months later left no doubt that the good times were over. My love of that Life died when Fox did. By the time Gotti said it was time for Tommy to pay for killing Fox, I knew that it was that Life itself that killed him. Tommy pulled the trigger, but Fox was a victim of the world of violence and death that we were both a part of. I didn't consciously realize until Tommy met the same fate Fox did that I if I stayed in that

Life, it would kill me too. From that point on, getting out stopped being a vague notion and became an urgent need.

───────────

Another long-ago Mob killing that sent me into a state of shock and unsettled my mind and left me with a sick feeling that haunted me for years was in the news in 1979. Congress released its watered-down report on the results of its reinvestigation of the Kennedy assassination sixteen years before. The report pussyfooted around and said there *might* have been a conspiracy and there *might* have been Mob involvement and left it at that. But enough came out about Hoover suppressing wiretaps and witnesses coming forward with information the FBI wasn't interested in hearing in 1963 to convince anybody who bothered to read between the lines. Not many people did, apparently, because the assassination remained a mystery—it still does in most people's mind.

Mob guys like me might have been the only people in the country who ever got closure about Kennedy because for us it was not an unsolved crime.

After I got into the Life and knew the score and the idea sank in that the assassination was a hit, I understood just how all-powerful and indestructible the Mob really was. That they could pull off something like that, whack the president of the United States of America like he was a boss in the barber's chair and get away with it—that meant that they weren't just bigger than U.S. Steel; they were stronger and deadlier than the whole damn U.S. government.[18]

1980

The next year, the days when the Mob was invincible began to seem like ancient history. Pressures had been building inside the Families that threatened to crack the old structures wide open, and it looked like the city Uncle Tony called the Volcano was about to erupt and bury the whole Mob.

In April 1980, Henry Hill was busted. Soon after, that, Mike Coiro

───────────

[18] In the years since the 1968 murder of Robert F. Kennedy, investigators have turned up no evidence indicating that RFK's assassination was a Mob clip job like his brother's—as I assumed back in 1968.

came to me and told me that Henry had flipped. Mike said that Henry was giving up Jimmy Burke and Paul Vario and who knows who else. Even before Tommy was killed, Jimmy had begun to systematically bump off everybody connected to the Lufthansa heist. Henry wasn't in on the score, but he had helped set it up and thought he might be next on Jimmy's hit list. So he got Jimmy before Jimmy could get him.

Mike was scared shitless because he had been Henry and Jimmy's lawyer; plus Henry knew that Mike was now working as house counsel for Gotti and the Bergin crew. Mike found out real quick that being a gangster maybe wasn't such a good career move after all.

Henry could drop a dime on Mike that could send him to prison along with a bunch of his clients. And if Mike were to flip in order to avoid prison himself, the whole house of cards could tumble. Mike could bring down Dominic and me as well as Johnny and the entire Bergin crew and just about every major drug dealer in the city, which by then was practically every connected guy in every Family.

Mike had branched out so far from his humble beginnings as Dom's mouthpiece back in the 1960s, his flip would cause shocks all the way to Washington.

In early 1980, Dom called me and told me to get 5,000 g's in new crispy $100 bills and bring them over to a Mob-owned joint in Queens. It was an election year and a candidate in a statewide race for national office was holding a fund-raiser there. I got to the place and gave the cash envelope to Dom, who was there with our mouthpiece. Dom handed the envelope to Mike. Then they both introduced me to the candidate, who was there with his wife and family and his brother, who was also a lawyer.

Before I left, Mike pulled me aside. He asked if I had the key to my secret apartment on Liberty Avenue. Mike used it all the time to shack up with his girlfriend. I gave him the key, figuring he had a hookup. But then he asked if I could fix the candidate up with a couple of young girls. He specified there be two of them—young and *hot*. Mike didn't say so, but I knew he was setting the candidate up so he and Dom would have a guy in Washington in their pocket. If the guy won, they'd have him over a barrel.

I had a couple of gorgeous coke whores who specialized in three-somes. I arranged it with Mike and sent them to the apartment. The girls told me after that the candidate had them do each other while he watched. I don't think he fucked them, but the three of them emptied most of a case of my best wine—Château Petrus that went for a few hundred a bottle; they sell for a couple of thousand today.

I couldn't believe the election results in November—the guy won. Around the same time, I got busted for tagging hot cars and running my chop shop. Mike got me out of that by buying off a judge, the Irish guy who was a friend of Jackie Donnelly's. That cost me 35 grand. But because of that arrest, the feds wanted to nail me for a parole violation. When I went to court for that the next year, guess who Mike got to represent me? The politician's brother. And it just so happened that the judge who was hearing my case was a friend of my new lawyer's brother, the politician. The judge gave me a postponement and the case lingered and I never was sent back to Lewisburg for probation violation.

It was like Uncle Tony always said: You got to know who to take care of.

Another thing happened that year involved my car business. It was something I hardly took notice of at the time, but it caused ripple effects that ultimately resulted in the earthquake that would one day bury John Gotti.

I had two vicious young cokehead car thieves named Pete Zuccaro and Andy Curro working for me. They were the new breed of Mob wannabes Uncle Tony warned me about, guys who did enough drugs that they thought they could get away with anything. They stole the cars that I in turn sold to John Carneglia, who exported them through his own Fountain Avenue operation to the Arab Gulf states.

Zuccaro and Curro came to me one day and asked if I ever hit an armored car. I told them about the silver heist. I said it was armored, but it wasn't the kind of armored car they were talking about. Those things were bad news because they were steel-plated, they had bulletproof windows, and most of them had a heavily armed guy riding shotgun in the cab with the driver and another guy in the back where the money was. You couldn't get into the back without taking care of the third guard.

They said they were going to show me it could be done.

I advised them to go on record with Carneglia's boss, John Gotti, which they did.

John and Victoria Gotti suffered a tragedy that year that you wouldn't wish on anybody. It had nothing to do with that Life of ours, but the repercussions had everything to do with my getting out of that Life for good.

The Gottis' neighborhood in Howard Beach provided a peaceful enclave for connected guys like John and Quack Ruggiero who lived nearby as well as for ordinary people like Gotti's close neighbor John Favara. Howard Beach was a place where the two worlds—Mob and legitimate—lived side by side.

In March 1980, those worlds collided in a tragic way.

The Gottis' middle son, Frankie, who played on my son Sal Jr.'s Pop Warner team, was known as Frankie Boy. John's two other sons were Johnny Boy, just like his dad used to be, and Peter Boy, who was named after John's older brother. Back when John and I went to that Series game in 1973, he said how proud he'd be if his sons followed in his footsteps. I didn't realize how sure he was that they would until I learned from Sal Jr. that all John's sons had nicknames like everybody in his old East New York street gang, the Rockaway Boys.

On the day after St. Patrick's Day, Frankie Boy borrowed a friend's minibike, a kind of motorized bicycle, and went for a ride around the neighborhood. Minibikes don't have a lot of power but enough that if you don't know how to drive them, they drive you. Frankie Boy, who was twelve, had never driven one before.

John Favara lived in the house directly behind the Gottis and his own son was a friend of the Gottis' oldest, Johnny Boy, and they used to have sleepovers at each other's houses. Favara worked at a Castro Convertible sofa factory and he was driving home from work that afternoon. He was on a westbound street and driving directly into the setting sun when, a block from the street he lived on, a minibike darted out from a construction Dumpster parked at the curb directly in front of Favara's car. A collision was unavoidable, and Frankie Boy Gotti was dead at the scene.

When Frankie Boy died, John and his family went into shock and then mourning for their precious son. They built a shrine to him in their home. They ran funeral notices in the *Daily News* wishing Frankie Boy a happy birthday in heaven.

Favara and his family went into mourning too. And when they started to receive telephone death threats, they didn't go into hiding but kept to themselves even after somebody spray-painted MURDERER on Favara's car, still dented from the accident.

Favara was a legit guy, but he grew up in Brooklyn and knew some people who were connected. He contacted one, a Gambino, and asked for his advice. His friend gave it to him straight: Get the hell out of Dodge. He told him not to wait to sell the house. He should pack up and leave. And he told him to get rid of the goddamned car too, because Victoria Gotti was telling her friends how it tormented her seeing it in the driveway out back every day.

Favara didn't listen. He didn't do anything. Until one day he knocked on the Gottis' door. I guess he was trying to reach out, to make amends. But Victoria wasn't in a forgiving mood. She grabbed one of John's favorite weapons, a baseball bat, and took a swing at Favara with it. That's when he finally got the message and put his home up for sale.

The house didn't sell fast enough. On July 28, while John and Victoria and their surviving kids were on vacation in Florida, Favara left work and headed toward a diner next door, where he parked his car. The diner's manager and some of his customers watched in shock as a gorilla walked up to Favara, clubbed him on the head, and threw him into a van. The van and a follow car full of other tough guys drove off, and John Favara hasn't been seen since.

When the story got in the papers, the whole city was shocked. People naturally sympathized with anybody who lost a child so young, but nobody could believe that even a gangster would take revenge for something that was so obviously a tragic accident.

People wanted to believe that Frankie Boy's father was as outraged as the next guy and that John Favara got vanished by some wannabe trying to curry favor with the boss.

But when reporters asked the parents how they felt about their missing neighbor, Victoria said she was glad the guy got what he deserved. "I don't know what happened," John Gotti said. "I am not sorry if something did happen. He killed my kid."

I knew John was a bad motherfucker, but I never thought he was stupid enough to say something like that.

My twelve-year-old son was upset when he heard about Frankie Boy. But when he read John's quotes in the paper, even *he* knew that Gotti himself had the guy whacked.

I half expected John to get whacked himself, for giving the Mob a bad name like Anastasia did when he sent two gorillas to kill the guy who fingered Willie Sutton.

When I heard what actually happened to Favara, I was ashamed that I counted John and his guys from the Bergin as my good friends. It was sickening that the same guys I played cards with at the Sinatra Club and hung out with and whose kids played with my kids were the same guys who kidnapped John Favara and made sure he was never seen again.

The way I heard it, my friend Quack Ruggiero was the gorilla who clubbed Favara over the head. Genie Gotti and Tony Roach were both in on it, and so were the Carneglia brothers. The crew killed Favara and dumped the body in one of Charles's steel drums full of acid. They dissolved the body and took the drum out on one of the guys' boats and dumped it in the bay. They then drove Favara's car to Industrial and it got it cubed.

John was my friend, and in a way he was even my mentor. I learned from him like I learned from Uncle Tony and from Dominic.

But what I learned from John in 1980 was that I was finished. That was it for me. I was done with madness and killing and death. I was done with the Mob.

That year I drove upstate, to a little town outside Port Jervis. I shopped around for a house and bought a big piece of property outside town. I started to fix it up so when the time was right I could move my family up there and get my kids as far away from that Life as I could go.

On July 29, the day after John Favara was kidnapped, my two car thieves, Peter Zuccaro and Andy Curro, hit an IBI Security armored car. It turned out there was no guard in the back as I had warned, and they scored 300 g's. Five months later, they hit a second truck from the same company for a big pot—$750,000.

I had to give them credit for pulling it off. But then they showed they were just as stupid and vicious as I thought they were. A few months later, Curro had a fight with his girlfriend. In the middle of a screaming match, she threatened to tell the cops about the IBI heists. Curro waited until she cooled down and then he sweet-talked her into meeting him at a motel to do some blow. When she got there they snorted coke and then he raped her, tied her up, tortured her, and strangled her. Then he cut her body up with a machete. He didn't know what to do with the parts, so he set them on fire.

This was the kind of guy John Gotti used to complain about, the scum that was rising to the top of the Mob's gene pool.

Zuccaro and Curro were busted for the IBI heists less than three months after they pulled them. Curro was also indicted for the murder of his girlfriend.

The DA who prosecuted Zuccaro and won a conviction was an Italian woman from Ozone Park named Diane Giacalone. The judge who sentenced Zuccaro to twelve years was Eugene Nickerson.

During the investigation of the IBI heist, Giacalone's detectives followed some of the robbery money to the Bergin and from there to the Ravenite Social Club in Little Italy.

Giacalone found that interesting because she used to walk past the Bergin and see all the wiseguys hanging out in front of it when she was in high school in the early '70s.

She instructed her staff to start looking into the operations at both clubs and to begin an investigation of their bosses, John Gotti and Neil Dellacroce.

Five years to the month after Frankie Gotti died, John and Neil would be indicted on charges resulting from that investigation. Representing them and pleading them not guilty was Mike Coiro.

A year after that, Giacalone and Gotti would fight it out in Judge Nickerson's courtroom.

And I would have a front-row box seat.

PART SIX

PART SIX

CHAPTER THIRTY-NINE

Day of Reckoning

1986

I WAS LOOKING AT HALF the starting lineup of the Bergin Hunt and Fish Club's Fourth of July softball team. The same Murderers Row was shoulder to shoulder at the defense table: John Gotti and his brother Genie, Quack Ruggiero, Willie Boy Johnson, John Carneglia, and Tony Roach.

Just ten months before, on December 16, 1985, those Bergin All-Stars scored their first major league hit when they knocked Big Paul Castellano out of the park in front of Sparks Steak House.

There was no question who the MVP was on that spectacular play, but that's not why John Gotti and his wrecking crew were in Courtroom 11 of the federal courthouse in Brooklyn.

And it's not why I was in the witness box.

It was October 2, 1986, and I was there to testify against my old partners in crime. John and the rest of the guys from the softball team, plus a couple of John's flunkies named Nicky and Jo Jo,[19] were all on trial, charged with racketeering under the federal RICO statute that basically makes it a crime to be in a crime family. Among the crimes John was accused of committing in order to advance the Family enterprise was the murder of Jimmy McBratney in Snoope's bar on Staten Island thirteen years before.

The prosecution had a guy from a Westies kidnap gang there to testify about the McBratney hit. I was there to establish the fact that

---

[19] Nick Corozzo and Lenny DiMaria.

John's Bergin crew was a criminal gang and not a hunting and fishing club.

My old pal had come a long way since Tony Roach drove him to the Sinatra Club the night he got out of prison in 1972. The guy who couldn't win a hand of poker to save his life in those days was now the very wealthy boss of the Gambino Family, the biggest criminal enterprise there was.

The Big Paul hit had made him both rich and famous. He was the most celebrated gangster in America. In March, after the only witness against John in an assault trial took the stand and said he couldn't remember who beat him up, a headline about John's acquittal made headlines. The *New York Post*'s front-page story about the accuser who got cold feet was headlined: "I FORGOTTI!"

John was soon on the cover of *Time*; instead of a photo, they got Andy Warhol to paint his portrait. Just before his trial started in August—it had been postponed when John's new underboss, Frank DiCicco, had an untimely meeting with a car bomb—*New York* magazine introduced him on its cover as the "New Godfather." In court he was dressed the part, in a silvery tailored Italian silk suit and tie.

From where I sat, the prosecutor, Diane Giacalone, the same assistant U.S. attorney who put my old cokehead armored car thief Peter Zuccaro away for twelve years in 1981, had a slam-dunk case. But for a guy who was looking at a twenty-year stretch in prison, millions in fines, and the confiscation of any of his wealth that he had come by illegally, which meant all of it, John looked like he didn't have a care in the world.

When I first walked into the courtroom, he gave me a cold stare that said when this was all over he would do to me what he did to Paul Castellano and Jimmy McBratney and Tommy Guns and Frank Favara and a lot of other very dead guys.

Now as Giacalone signaled me to begin my testimony, John had a knowing smirk on his face that gave me a bad feeling, like he had something up the sleeve of his thousand-dollar suit.

––––––––––––––

It had taken me two years to leave the Life, to move my family out of Ozone Park and settle in that small town upstate. It was a hundred miles and thousands of crimes away from the world I grew up in. There were things up there you just don't find a lot of in Brooklyn and Queens, like trees and pastures and barns and cattle and small-town people who had never seen a numbers chit or a betting slip and wouldn't know what to do with one if they did.

They thought baseball bats were only used to whack a ball and they thought a wiseguy was Eddie Haskell teasing the Beav.

They probably never met an actual hoodlum before, one who robbed banks and hijacked trucks and shylocked loans and broke legs and ran a squad of coke whores who sold soul-sucking, human-debasing drugs for a living. They sure wouldn't like to know a guy like that was up there living among them.

My neighbors had never heard of John Gotti or the Bergin Hunt and Fish Club. They didn't even want to know there were people like Dominic Cataldo shooting guys and burying them in Boot Hill and Charles Carneglia torturing women and chopping up bodies and dissolving them in acid.

The good folk of our town and of every town in America grew up on gangster movies and TV shows about romantic Robin Hoods who stole from the rich and gave to their poor widowed mothers, who acted nobly when it mattered most, and whose life of crime always ended in jail or the chair.

They didn't want to believe that real godfathers commanded large gangs of criminals who brazenly committed the most vicious crimes imaginable and were allowed to get away with it by the very people everyday folks paid to protect them. The mobsters simply paid the cops and judges and their city fathers more than the taxpayers ever could. In exchange, the gangs were allowed to do whatever they wanted, even when the corruption and thievery and mayhem and violence harmed the citizenry they were sworn to serve.

Angela and the kids and I lived in a converted barn, and we tried to make a go of the go-kart track and restaurant that came with the fifty-acre property and that I sunk hundreds of thousands of stolen dollars into fixing up. Angela got a job and made good friends; my kids starred on their school sports teams, had buddies and nice girlfriends and fit right in; my family became part of a sweet little community and we built happy new lives for ourselves.

I was a first-rate thief and I was an expert at administrating a drug and gambling and hot car business. But a legit trade? I bombed out big time—the track went broke and I got back in the drug business.

I drove back into the Volcano and looked up John Carneglia, and he fronted me 50 grand and I became a coke dealer. I thought I'd do it long enough to recoup my losses, then try again with the track.

In the short time I'd been away, the hammer was coming down hard on organized crime. Wiseguys were getting busted and flipping left and right. Even the bosses were on the run; Johnny Boy's old friend Joe Massino, who was in charge of the Bonannos at that time, had gone into hiding. The feds planted bugs in the Bergin and the Ravenite and even in Big Paul's own kitchen.

As soon as I got back into the Life, I realized how much I had missed it. Like most guys, I couldn't read the writing on the wall.

After a year or so of commuting between country and city with bags of cash and cocaine, I got busted when one of my coke whores set me up, making sure I sold her just enough blow—four ounces—to guarantee I'd be sent away for twenty-five years to life as an ex-con and career felony offender.

––––––––––––

I was raised right. I was taught to hate and despise rats, and I was trained to recognize one when I saw one—and I sure as hell never thought I'd ever see one in the mirror. Just like soldiers who were trained to know the enemy it was their job to kill, we were trained to hunt and kill the one enemy there was no real defense against—the enemy within.

I wasn't born a rat, but I became one when the only alternative was to scurry around in a cage for the next twenty-five years. I'd gone to the joint facing a term less than a third of that amount of time. I was given a reprieve and got to enjoy my freedom, and I was given a chance to try to build a life with my kids. I didn't want to lose my freedom, and I didn't want to rot in brick and bars until I was ready for Medicaid and adult Depends.

So I did exactly what the feds hoped and Carlo Gambino and the rest of the old dons feared when they made their own antidrug laws: I flipped.

When I was offered a deal by the government, I was already determined to get out of the Life. I'd blown the chance of making the break on my own by getting busted. That made becoming a rat the only ticket out.

Growing up in the Mob, I always assumed that any rat who would turn on his friends and Family felt tremendous shame and guilt. But I didn't, because I had grown to hate and despise that Life as much as I had been taught to hate and despise anyone who would betray it.

I didn't want to simply jump off the wagon and run; I also wanted to do something to end the madness that killed Fox and Tommy and made John Gotti think that it was just and reasonable to avenge the death of his son by taking the life of the poor fuck who from no fault of his own caused Gotti to lose something precious to him.

I wanted to stick an iron bar in the spokes and help end the Mob's long sweet ride.

And the feds gave me a chance to do that.

I wore a wire. I looked up old friends and helped put away the corrupt judge who bought my car case. And I set up a low-life wannabe who sold bombs and hand grenades to a Colombian coke gang. I did all that and I didn't feel a twinge of remorse. I was happy to do it. Most of it, anyway.

I had to use my old mouthpiece, Mike Coiro, and my onetime best buddy Joey Cataldo to help me help the feds bust that judge. I felt bad about those two but not at all about the judge.

To John Gotti and everyone else I knew in that Life, I was now the lowest form of life and did not deserve to live. I knew that not even Dominic would hesitate to exterminate me if he could, and he wouldn't lose any more sleep over it than Jimmy Burke did about his old friend who lay dead and buried under his bocce court.

The surprising thing was, none of that bothered me. I didn't lose any sleep either. Once I became a rat, I actually enjoyed it—and I was good at it. It was a hell of a lot more exciting than drug dealing, which is what being in the Mob became all about in the end. Wearing a wire and being a spy in the enemy camp took a lot of scheming, and you had to be totally alert. It put me back on the edge, where I liked it, like pulling off a heist.

I was still an excitement junkie, and wearing a wire gave me a real good fix. My adrenaline hadn't kicked like that since I used to vault over bank counters.

I had no qualms about it. I'd grown so disgusted with that Life, so sick of the killing and treachery, I was happy to stick it to the Mob.

But when they asked me to wear a wire on a guy I revered and respected, that I couldn't do.

I was down in Florida, working the case against the judge, when the head of the FBI office down there came into a meeting.

"I hear you're close pals with one of the biggest Mob guys we've got around here."

"Yeah?" I said. "Who might that be?"

"Dave Iacovetti."

I would kill myself before I wore a wire on Dave. Of all the made guys, the career mobsters I met in that Life, Iacovetti was the one true mafioso, a man of honor. The kind of gentleman gangster my uncle Tony talked about when he told me his history stories about the Mob. He was the last of a dead tradition and I told the feds I'd walk right then and there if they insisted I go after Dave Iacovetti.

"He never did nothin' to me," I said. "He was nothing but a father to me."

CHAPTER FORTY

Rat Trap

BY DECEMBER 1985, my family was already in the Witness Protection Program, living under new names and starting new lives down in Dixie when I heard about the Paul Castellano rubout at Sparks, his favorite restaurant. I used to go there, but the steaks weren't nearly as good as at Peter Luger's.

The minute I heard the news, I knew it was John. He and Paul had hated each other ever since our silver heist. Paul saw John as a power and a threat. That hit—at the height of the rush hour, with Christmas shoppers everywhere, Santa Clauses on the street corners, in front of a popular restaurant that got a happy hour crowd at the bar—it was just so blatant and brazen I knew John planned it and the Bergin crew did it.

He thought he was fucking invincible by then. He whacked that poor bastard neighbor of his, then practically announced in the newspapers that he was the guy who did it and he'd do it again if anybody dared fuck with him. The Castellano hit was the same thing.

Neil Dellacroce died two weeks before that. Instead of making Gotti his next in command, Big Paul not only appointed another guy, a nobody named Tommy Bilotti, as underboss, he told John he was going to split up Neil's old crew, which should have gone to John; Paul said he was going to put his guys with other captains. He basically said fuck you to John, and that was Big Paul's death warrant.

If I was Castellano, I wouldn't have stepped foot outside my house without an army of guys around me. He had to know Johnny was gunning for him. What does Paul do? He sets up a sit-down with John at Sparks to smooth over bad feelings. Then he pulls up outside the joint in his Lincoln and he doesn't even have a gun on him. The old bosses used to drive around in armored cars with machine guns mounted on swivels. This guy steps into a shooting gallery with nothing but a cigar in his hand. His bodyguard, Tommy Bilotti, was useless. He had no gun, not even a peashooter; all he was carrying was his car keys when they whacked him.

The other thing about John: He might as well have had his crew wear name tags. I was a thousand miles away and I knew the shooters had to include Quack, John Carneglia, and Tony Roach—John would only trust his closest guys with a job like that.

The feds had to know it too. They had John's crew wrapped in more wires than a chicken coop. They had the phones tapped at the Bergin and Ravenite; they had both those places bugged and wired for sound and under constant surveillance. When the crew started using the phone next door to the Bergin, they tapped that too. The feds even had bugs in guys' cars.

The worst thing, though, was Angelo Ruggiero and his big mouth. Diane Giacalone had had a tap on his phone since 1981 when her investigators found out that Ange was John's best friend and Neil's nephew. When they did, they also found out how much Ange liked to quack—Giacalone turned him into a big fat pigeon.

Angelo quacked up a storm about all the crew's drug deals. The feds not only tapped his home phone, they also pulled a B&E and wired his whole house. They could listen to practically every word that came out of his mouth, and that was a shitload. Ange quacked himself and Genie Gotti and John Carneglia and a bunch of Bergin guys, including our old mouthpiece Mike Coiro, right into a federal indictment for heroin dealing in 1983. When the feds announced they had the tapes to prove it, that's when Big Paul threw a big shit fit. He ordered Neil to make his nephew hand over the tapes, and of course Ange refused because he knew one listen and Big Paul would whack him before he could say another word. That started the whole standoff among Big Paul and Neil and John.

With half his crew already charged for dealing smack, Giacalone hit John with the federal racketeering indictment. Nine months before the Sparks hit, John and Genie and Willie Boy were arrested at 4:00 in the morning at the Bergin. The cops busted them as they were playing poker, just like old times at the Sinatra Club. Even though he was under indictment himself in the heroin case, good old Mike Coiro was there first thing the next morning to plead them out.

So with all that heat on him, Gotti still went ahead and whacked Castellano on 46th Street. That's the way John was. Just like the New York Mob itself, he got away with so much for so long, he thought nobody could ever touch him. He was one of the smartest guys I ever met; his problem was he thought so too. He had grown so overconfident I was sure he was headed for a big fall.

I thought so because when I heard about the hit, I was already flying up north to a secret location outside Detroit to meet with Diane Giacalone and prep for my day in court with the New Godfather.

I was certain John's goose was plucked, boiled, and cooked when Giacalone briefed me and I finally found out who the rat inside the Bergin was.

Even now, after twenty-five years, I have trouble believing it.

Ever since 1972, when the dying J. Edgar Hoover let Roy Cohn in on the FBI's big secret, and Cohn passed it on to Don Carlo who then tipped Charlie Fatico, the elephant in the room at the Bergin was a rat the size of a gorilla.

First Charlie and then John looked everywhere to find it and exterminate it, and the whole time it was one of his most loyal soldiers and best friends.

Letting a rat get that close to him, for that long, was a whackable offense. And it showed very bad leadership qualities. When the Bonannos came this close to making an undercover FBI agent, Donnie Brasco,[20] a made man in that Family, the guy he suckered, Sonny Black, got whacked. Before they shot him, they chopped his hands off.

---

[20] Special Agent Joe Pistone infiltrated the Bonannos in 1976 and spied on them from the inside for six years. When it got found out, there was a half-million-dollar contract on Pistone's head, collectable by any connected guy from any Family.

John still had a nice shiny pinkie ring on his hand after his rat was exposed. And he was still sitting with the rat at the defense table and having lunch with him during recesses, and at night they were locked up in cells next to each other at the MCC, where they were held throughout the trial.

In March of '85, when John and Genie and Willie Boy were arrested at the Bergin and Mike Coiro pleaded them out, they were all charged with committing certain specific crimes. Giacalone's idea was that by proving the crimes, she could make her RICO case that they were all conspiring together in a criminal enterprise. John and Angelo were also charged once again for the McBratney hit. They had no double indemnity protection because they'd never been tried for it before, thanks to Roy Cohn's plea deal. The crime Willie Boy was charged with was for whacking the guy down in Florida who was supposed to testify against Neil Dellacroce.

The rest of the Bergin guys in the indictment were rounded up at the same time and brought before the judge, who set bail for everybody but Tony Roach and one other guy. Tony was locked up in a hospital to detox from his heroin habit. The other guy was Willie Boy Johnson.

The judge was Eugene Nickerson, the same who sent Zuccaro away and who presided at the trial I was set to testify in. Nickerson just about choked on his gavel when Diane Giacalone told him why Willie Boy shouldn't get bail—because he was a secret FBI informant who for twenty years had been ratting on Charlie Fatico's and then John Gotti's crew.

Willie Boy.

When that bomb dropped, nobody could believe it, least of all John, who'd known the man practically his entire life.

Willie Boy knew what was coming as soon as they were all arrested at the Bergin because Giacalone had been pressuring him to testify and threatened to out him if he didn't. As they were driven in handcuffs to the courthouse for arraignment, Willie Boy told John that the feds were going to say he was a rat but it was bullshit. John believed him at first because it was impossible for him to accept that Willie Boy, of all people, was the rat Cohn had warned about back in 1972.

It turned out that in 1966, the year Johnny Boy joined Fatico's crew, Willie Boy got busted and sent away. Willie Boy got Fatico to promise to take care of his family while he was in the joint. Fatico said he would, but he didn't do shit for them. That pissed Willie Boy off so much that he vowed to get even. And when he got busted by the feds for something else, he made a deal with them: If they promised to never reveal his identity, and he would never be asked to testify in court, he would feed them info on everything Fatico and his crew did.

When John took over the crew, even though they were old friends, Willie Boy felt like a second-class citizen. He felt like he never got the respect he should. He knew guys called him Half-Breed behind his back. He never knew that his handlers at the FBI weren't any better. Their code name for him was Source Wahoo. Whoever came up with that must have been a Cleveland Indians fan—Chief Wahoo was the name of the grinning brave on their ball caps.

He also knew everyone thought he was slow, John included. So Willie Boy kept on informing after John took over. He gave the feds everything—they knew about every heist and hijacking we did, every score we made. The reason Lloyd's of London knew it was us who pulled the watches score was that Willie Boy told them. He even told them about our All-Families silver heist. The feds never did anything about any of it because they didn't want to blow Willie Boy's cover. When John and Angelo whacked McBratney, Willie Boy fingered them for that and then told the FBI where to find John when he was in hiding.

At the same time, the FBI never knew that Willie Boy also started ratting out the crew to the NYPD after he got popped by the cops for something in the '70s.

Willie Boy had to be the greatest actor who ever lived, full-on Oscar-worthy. He was playing three sides to the middle: He was working for the Mob, the FBI, and the cops all at the same time, and not one of them knew about the others. The bottom line is that *everybody* underestimated him.

He had to remember exactly what he said and to whom and everything he did and when in order to keep it all straight—the whole time knowing that one slipup and he was done.

He got away with it for twenty years and he probably still would have if Diane Giacalone didn't out him like she did.

Her plan didn't work. Willie Boy refused to testify or even admit that he was a rat. That's why he was being tried along with the rest of the guys in the crew.

When he told Giacalone he wouldn't testify, she put him in a cell right next to Gotti in the MCC. She figured that was like putting cats in a bag; John would threaten him and Willie Boy would flip.

Instead, John and Willie Boy came to an agreement. Even though Willie Boy still denied it and he would sit beside Gotti at the defense table throughout the trial, John now knew despite Willie Boy's protests of innocence that it was the Indian who had been the rat all along. John told Willie Boy that as a reward for doing the right thing and not testifying for the prosecution, he was going to be allowed to live. John promised Willie Boy that he would not whack him for being the rat, but he said that once the trial was over he was never going to speak to him again. As long as Willie Boy did the right thing, John promised no harm would come to him and his family.

Willie Boy took John at his word. And John kept it. For the time being.

Giacalone went ahead and prosecuted Willie Boy, hoping that he'd still flip and testify, but he never did. Anyway, she could introduce as evidence everything in his Source Wahoo file. That's why I thought she had a strong case when it was my turn to testify.

CHAPTER FORTY-ONE

Brucified

WHEN MY TURN FINALLY arrived, I was flown to New Jersey and put up under tight security in a hotel across the river from the city. I had followed Gotti's case in the papers and watched all the trial coverage on CNN. But I didn't know how big a story it was until I rolled by the courthouse in Cadman Plaza in an unmarked U.S. Marshals van. There were dozens of TV satellite news trucks lining the street and crowds of people milling around the courthouse.

The van drove around back and down a ramp to the basement, where there were a bunch of limousines lined up. I figured they must belong to John's team of expensive lawyers.

The marshals were my bodyguards and they escorted me into the building and up to the private witness waiting room. There I met the marshal assigned to take care of me, an Italian woman who came on like a hardnose, like she'd met plenty of wiseguys back there and wasn't taking any shit from me. It was her job to keep me company, feed me, and escort me in and out of the courtroom. I ended up spending seven days on the witness stand, but because of all the stops and starts and days off, it was almost a month before it was over.

When I walked into the courtroom for the first time, it was like walking out onto a stage. The place was packed; there were rows of seats up front crammed with reporters and sketch artists. Behind them were the wives and relatives of the Bergin guys I knew and wiseguys against the wall in back I recognized. There were all sorts of other people in there, all craning their necks for a look at the rat who was going to testify against the New Godfather.

Stepping out in front of the audience was one of the greatest adrenaline rushes I ever had. My blood was boiling with excitement like it did when I hit my first jug with Eddie Pravato. I wasn't scared or nervous, even; there was no fear at all. I was on center stage and I loved it.

When I stepped up into the witness chair, I looked directly at John. He just sat there motionless, with that strange smirk on his face, like he was omnipotent. I scanned down the table. There was his brother Genie, Angelo, Carneglia, Tony Roach, Nicky, and Jo Jo, and in the last seat at the end of the table to the far left, Willie Boy.

They were all dressed up in suits and ties. Giacalone told me to go casual, so I had on a striped sweater and slacks, and all the guys laughed at me like I was a schlub dressed for a day at the track.

They all smirked like John and whispered and laughed throughout my time on the stand, but the only time it bothered me was once when John caught my eye when the lawyers were having a sidebar. He had his hand under the edge of the table so nobody else saw him do it. For a few seconds he held his hand like a gun with the first finger pointed at me and his thumb cocked, and then he pulled the imaginary trigger.

Giacalone and her assistant, a sharp young guy named John Gleeson, spent days prepping me and going over my testimony, which was basically just me telling the story of my life of crime. They wanted me to tell it from the beginning. We went over it so many times I was sick of hearing myself talk. Giacalone said the most important thing was not to lose my cool. So to prepare me, she kept pushing and prodding me until I finally did blow up. After that I refused to talk about it anymore so I guess she was a little anxious about how I'd do on the stand.

Giacalone walked me through it, and I did like she said, I told my whole story, starting with how I felt like I was destined for the Mob and that Life from the time I was a little kid and heard stories about how my father and Uncle Tony and Dominic Cataldo's father Sammy smuggled booze from Jamaica Bay for the Brooklyn bootleggers during Prohibition. I told them how Uncle Tony taught me the fine points of gambling from age four, how my first crime was stealing candy kisses for my sister and I how I moved up to shoplifting and stealing cars and breaking into that racing supply auto shop and getting busted when the guy I was with turned me in so his father wouldn't go back to prison on a parole violation.

I told them how I got sick in the Marines and discharged for acting *upazzo* after they put me on the psycho ward for punching that male nurse. I said that's how I got my name Sally Ubatz, by acting crazy when I needed to.

I told them how I got shylock money from Charlie Fatico to pay off that crooked priest and how Uncle Tony set me up in Sal's Pizza and we ran a sports book and how he introduced me to the gang of bank robbers that hung out at his hotel by the track.

I said how Dominic met Tony in prison and came out and we went into business together. I described hitting the Franklin National with Eddie and Joe Vitale and what a rush it was. I told them about how I got shot by that cop and while I was laid up we opened the Sinatra Club.

I said how our gambling and shylock business and the club itself were all covers for our drug business, and how we were pushing heroin before most other connected guys got into it in a big way. I laid it all out in detail, how huge the money was and what a blast we had spending it.

I told them about meeting the guys from the Bergin and how Gene Gotti brought in Fox one day and we became best friends and crime partners, how we hijacked trucks and pulled jobs in the Diamond District and how we once robbed a bank on bicycles. I think I got that far the first day and the court recessed.

We got in the van but had to wait while the limos parked down there pulled in front of us. The doors opened from the courthouse and out walked all the jurors. They got in the limos and drove off to wherever they were sequestered.

The jurors were all anonymous. I read later that the defense gave them all made-up names; the jury foreman they called Larry King because he had big glasses, and one of the black jurors they called Willie Mays.

When I got a minute alone with Giacalone the next day, I told her they were crazy to drive the jury around in those limos. What was stopping the crew from following them and finding out where they were staying? She said I was being paranoid. I said she was nuts if she didn't think they'd try to fix the jury. She laughed at me and said it was impossible; there was no way that could be done. I told her she didn't know how these guys worked.

After that I was sure of it because of the way John looked like he wasn't even paying attention half the time. I kept after Giacalone about it, but she never listened.

———————

On the second day, I picked up where I left off and described how Johnny got out of prison and the first thing he did was have Tony Roach drive him over to the Sinatra Club. I said how much John loved to gamble but he wasn't any good at it. That's one of the times he looked at me like he was going to enjoy popping one in my bonnet. I added that he was good at Scrabble, and maybe that made him feel better.

I talked about the kind of charisma and gangster swagger John had and how right away you could tell he was going places. I said how we got to be good friends and how our kids played Pop Warner football together. I said how he rose to become acting head of the Bergin when Charlie Fatico took a backseat because he was under indictment.

I said I got busted for that Franklin National robbery and how for the first time Dominic's mouthpiece couldn't get me out of it.

That's when I laid it all out about how crooked the so-called good guys were; how, thanks in part to Mike Coiro, Dom and Jimmy Burke and the whole Bergin crew had the entire Queens courthouse in their pockets, from the DAs to the top judges; how it was hard to find a cop or a detective who wasn't on the take. I thought that might get a big reaction from the crowd, but I guess I was just stating the obvious.

I talked about what it was like hanging out at the Bergin and mentioned all the guys who were sitting there ten feet away at the defense table. That got a lot of scowls and cold stares.

I said how I closed down the Sinatra Club before I went away to prison and how I was saved once again by being *upazzo*.

Then I told them about how Tommy shot Fox in the face and how it all went down the tubes from there; how everybody and their brother got into importing, distributing, and selling smack and coke and killing each other to keep guys from going to the cops or ratting them out to their bosses. How the money made them crazy with greed and everybody started whacking everybody else and how vicious and shitty that Life became.

I told them about Boot Hill and the Carneglias' acid baths and about guys who dismembered and burned the bodies of their girlfriends and all the shit that made me sick to my stomach and made me want to get out.

I gave it all to them, every dirty detail, until I felt like it was a disease in my gut and the only way I could get rid of it was by puking it up and that's what I was doing on the witness stand.

My second day's testimony ended with me talking about my chop shops and jewelry business and some of my scams and schemes. Then I said how I tried to make a break and moved up to Port Jervis but then got back into dealing. I said how Carneglia fronted me the loan for the coke and I got back into the Life until I was busted. I said twenty-five years to life looked like death to me and I flipped. I wore a wire and here I am now.

Then it was the defense's turn. Each guy's lawyer took a crack at me. But it didn't get rough until John's lawyer, Bruce Cutler, took over. He was like an attack dog. He tried to intimidate everybody in the courtroom.

He looked more like a gangster than any of the guys in there besides Gotti. His head was big and bald and shiny; he looked like Mussolini in a three-piece suit.

The reporters said that witnesses were afraid of him. They said he "Brucified" anybody who got on the stand.

Cutler pretty much ran that trial. Giacalone was definitely intimidated by him, and he even dominated the judge. The only one on the prosecution side who really handled him was John Gleeson. He was tougher and smarter than Cutler or any of the other million-dollar lawyers lined up against him.

But Giacalone was the lead prosecutor and she did the best she could. She was real smart and well organized, but she was naïve. And Judge Nickerson let Cutler run all over her. He mocked her and broke her balls every chance he got. He called her the Lady in Red because she wore a red suit on the first day of the trial. He got witnesses to call her a bitch and a whore on the stand, and Nickerson didn't do anything to stop the attacks on her.

Cutler's whole thing was to put stuff he wanted the jury to hear into a question, and there it was, even if the judge said it was inadmissible.

Cutler had hired a private investigator to dig up dirt on me, which must have been the easiest dollars that guy ever earned. Most of what he threw at me was absolutely true. He said that I dealt tons of drugs and stole tons of money and lived my life as a low-life whoremonger who beat up people for a living. I couldn't argue any of it.

Other stuff he twisted around or just made up. There were a few black jurors, and he played to them. His investigator found out about Fox and me ripping off the drug dealers in Bed-Stuy and about me beating that pimp half to death on Eighth Avenue. He asked me why I hated black people. I said I was a dumb Wop and that I grew up prejudiced against blacks and anybody else who wasn't Italian.

He tried to intimidate me, but Giacalone and Gleeson had prepared me so I didn't lose my cool. They told me to answer every question *yes* or *no* or *correct* or *incorrect*, and that's what I did.

I was glad when it was over, but in a way I was also glad that I went through it. It was like a trial by fire and I felt like I passed.

Talking about it all, telling my story and then getting Brucified by Cutler, made me feel good in a weird kind of way.

I felt like I had finally purged and expunged all that evil shit from my soul.

On my last day in the courthouse, I said goodbye to Rose, the marshal I spent hours with every day I was there during those three weeks. She said she felt like she had gotten to know me and thought I was a very bright guy and I could have done something better with my life. She said she hoped that maybe now I would try. She asked me what I was going to do next.

I said I was going to California and start all over again.

She looked at me kind of startled-like, and I laughed.

"I'm going to start a new life," I said, "not *the* Life."

Epilogue

I HEARD THE NEWS ON the way to a NASCAR race in North Carolina. The jury in John Gotti's racketeering case found him and the other Bergin guys not guilty on all counts.

It was Friday the 13th, 1987, and it looked like bad luck for me.

Johnny Boy became a folk hero, the Teflon Don—none of the shit everybody knew he was guilty of stuck to him.

I was still convinced there was only one way he beat that case. He didn't win because of Bruce Cutler's tactics or Giacalone's failures; at the very least she had proved he was the boss of the Gambino Family, the criminal enterprise that the case was all about in the first place.

I was sure he fixed the jury.

And later I would be proved right.

A month after John walked, I did too—I was given five years' probation on my drug case for cooperating with the FBI.

One of the reasons John didn't post a Sal Polisi Wanted Dead or Alive poster in the Bergin back then in 1987 was that half his shooters, including Carneglia, Genie, and Angelo, went on trial in the heroin case two weeks after I got probation. Two other old pals of mine, Mike Coiro and Mark Reiter, the dealer whose Bergin *babania* I used to test, were on the docket with Quack and the rest. When John's good friend Tony

Roach got busted for smack himself, John wanted him whacked. Gravano testified later that John loved the guy, but what could he do? He couldn't risk the Roach turning rat.

Tony survived for the same reason I did—John was already drowning in a rising sea of shit.

———————

Four years later, John was on trial again—for the last time.

Sammy "the Bull" Gravano made everybody see that the Dapper Don's Teflon was no more real than his innocence. Sammy put the nails in Johnny Boy's coffin. And the whole New York Mob was buried with him.

It was a story as old as the Mob itself. Gravano was the trusted lieutenant who betrayed first one boss and then another, just like Lucky Luciano set up the two old Mustache Petes sixty years before. But instead of eliminating Gotti to become boss as Luciano and Vito Genovese and Carlo Gambino and Gotti himself did before him, Gravano flipped to save his own neck and set up his godfather to get whacked by the government.

The New York papers called Sammy "King Rat." When he flipped, it caused an earthquake. Sammy gave up every secret the secret society ever had. He got on the stand at John's trial and told all, right down to who put the bullets in Big Paul—it was our old friend from the Sinatra Club, John Carneglia. Along with all the hits and high crimes he hung on John, one of them was jury fixing. Gravano testified that Gotti bought a juror in the Giacalone trial for 60 g's, guaranteeing his acquittal.

There was no J. Edgar Hoover around anymore to protect the most powerful Mafia leader in America. A guy named Rudolph Giuliani put together a team of prosecutors who decided the days when the Mob could get away with murder were over. They were sick of John flaunting his power. They made the don's Teflon their number one target. And when they were ready, they threw the book at him.

John didn't know it at the time, but Friday the 13th, 1987, wasn't his lucky day after all. After the jury found him and the whole crew not guilty, his guys danced in the aisles, and John pointed at Diane Giacalone and John Gleeson and said, "Shame on them! I'd like to see the verdict on them."

But they got the last laugh. Gleeson, Giacalone's assistant in that trial, got burned by Gotti once, but not again. He was lead prosecutor in 1992 when the verdict went against Johnny Boy, and he was sentenced to life in prison without possibility of parole. The jury found the don guilty of five counts of murder, conspiracy to murder, loan sharking, illegal gambling, bribery, and tax evasion.

John died a miserable death from cancer ten years later. When I read it about I thought about the great good times we had, the all-night games at the Sinatra Club, the heists and the hijinks. Oh, did we laugh in that Life. But John died like he lived—Cosa Nostra to the end. Lucky Luciano said when you went into that Life, the only way out was in a coffin. John was the King of Death and he died a king.

———

Things didn't go any better for the rest of my friends from the Sinatra Club. Genie Gotti and John Carneglia got fifty years in the heroin case. Angelo Ruggiero died of cancer before that verdict came down. In the last days of his life he pleaded with his old friend Johnny Boy to visit him on his deathbed. Gotti refused. Ange's quacking had caused him so many problems that John had forsaken him in the end.

My Family friend and mentor and unindicted serial killer Dominic Cataldo was convicted in the famous Pizza Connection case in 1987—he was part of the Italian and New York Mob–run drug gang that imported more than $1 billion worth of heroin over a ten-year period. He also died a painful death from cancer ten years later.

Our mouthpiece Mike Coiro, the former Waterfront Commission investigator who decided to become a gangster himself, was convicted in the heroin case along with Ange and Genie and the rest. He got fifteen years and served eight. He died in Las Vegas in 2003.

Jimmy Burke, the Sinatra Club's all-time cards king, the hijacking genius who had all the cops in Queens in his pocket, and who had more hits on his belt than any mass murderer you've ever heard about—he got dealt his first losing hand when Henry Hill flipped on him back in 1980.

Jimmy went to prison for fixing Boston College basketball games, then he was convicted for one of the murders he loved doing. Jimmy had an excruciating death too—he died of lung cancer in the joint in 1996. He was sixty-four years old.

The only real tragic character in the whole drama was Willie Boy Johnson.

In 1988, Willie Boy was out of the Life and living in peace with his wife and kids in Brooklyn. He left his house one morning and was walking to his car when two Bonanno guys with a contract signed in blood by John Gotti shot Willie Boy in the legs. Willie Boy fell on his face and they shot him in the back. Then they shot him in the head. It was a hit in broad daylight on a quiet residential block. It was a hit like the glory days of the Mob—brazen, right out in the open. The killers used machine guns like it was the St. Valentine's Day Massacre. They threw six-point spikes on the street to slow ambulances and cops, and drove away.

Henry Hill, whose life story became a hit movie in 1990, ten years after he flipped on Jimmy and the rest of the goodfellas, is one of the last Sinatra Club regulars still breathing. Henry and I see each other now and then. We've had some laughs remembering the old days. But he's like me—what I feel most when I think about my life in that Life isn't remorse, really; it's more like disgust at the things I did and the person I was.

I got my own fifteen minutes of fame after the trial when Nick Taylor published a cover story in *New York* magazine about my kids and how they suffered for my sins. Three years later, he published it as a book titled *Sins of the Father*. I met Nick through his wife, Barbara Nevins, who covered the Gotti trial for CBS-TV. She did one piece on me that was funny. She got my Mob name wrong—she called me Sally Ugatz instead of Ubatz. The Mob guys I testified against must have loved that—*ugatz* means "prick" in Italian.

The year after the trial, Angela and I split up. After twenty-one years of my lousy husbanding, we finally got the idea the marriage wasn't working. The price she paid for my sins I can never make up to her. The one blessing is our kids, who grew up a whole lot smarter and healthier than I ever was. That was one thing I did right that Johnny Boy did not—I made sure my footsteps never led my boys into that

Life. They have wives and kids of their own now, and their children have something their grandfather's kids never had—full-time dads who aren't hoodlums.

My ex and my kids have managed to build happy lives for themselves out from under the shadows of my past. They even gave me a gift way beyond any I deserved.

I remarried in 1991, and now I have two more wonderful kids. They're teenagers, and my sons love them like the sister and brother they are. The gift my children gave me is a family—the kind that's got nothing to do with Colombos and Gambinos and all the rest.

———————

Before I did what I told Rose the courthouse marshal I was going to do— move to California and start a new life—I committed one last crime.

It was 1989 and I was making TV appearances to build interest in Nick's book, and I did something I never thought would happen if I lived a thousand lifetimes. I gave the keynote address at graduation ceremonies at the FBI Academy in Quantico, Virginia. After a lifetime spent despising cops and prosecutors, I now counted them among my best friends. I even hit it off with the cop who busted me back in 1984, Remo Franceschini. He was not only one of the first honest cops I ever met; he also was one of the first New York cops who made it his mission in life to bring down the Mob. He was taking down wiseguys when everybody else in the NYPD was on the take. The FBI guy who flipped me, Dan Russo, became a good friend too. When I first told him about John and the Bergin crew, he spelled his name Gotty. Ed McDonald's another one; he's the guy who brought Henry Hill over and got him in Witness Protection. Ed did the same for me. He got me doing seminars with law enforcement so they could figure out ways to put guys like me away.

Remo and Dan and Ed will probably be pissed off to find out that after I made an appearance on Geraldo Rivera's old talk show, I drove up to Port Jervis and dug up a couple of steel ammo boxes I'd buried on my old property in 1984. Those boxes are indestructible, and the cocaine I'd stashed in them was as pure as it was the day I buried them.

I managed to find a Colombian coke dealer in Fort Lee, New Jersey, who was still in business. I sold him the coke and stashed the loot in the back of the motor home I bought with part of the proceeds.

I had maybe 80 grand left. I figured that would be more than enough to get me started out in California. I vowed that score would be my last, and it was.

It was exhilarating driving across country in that motor home. I drove away from the city, the Volcano where I'd spent most of my life, and never looked back. I had committed my last crimes and I had finished doing my bit for the government. I was still living under an assumed name, but I had left Witness Protection—I had to when I started making TV appearances. I was driving west to California, the land of new beginnings.

I had nothing but time, so I went the long way. I took the most southern route you can take—along the Rio Grande River in Texas. For the hell of it, I crossed the river into Mexico.

The whole time I'd been driving, the money I had stashed in the rear interior wheel housing kept eating at me. I guess it was some kind of mixture of guilt and fear. Guilt for having committed a crime after I had convinced everybody I knew that I turned over a new leaf—my family; Nick Taylor, who was writing a whole book about me going straight; and the federal guys who made it possible for me to get out of that Life without going to prison.

The money meant that all I had really turned over was the rock I had the coke buried under. The fear was the one every criminal has—if I was caught with a bag full of drug money, it would be so long new life, hello twenty-five to life.

As I drove, the money took on a life of its own; it was like something out of Edgar Allan Poe and the pounding of the telltale heart.

The Mexico side of the river near El Paso was piss-poor in those days. It's the first time I ever saw young mothers with babies begging in the streets. It's the first time I saw children alone and standing in rags begging cigarette butts from passersby. I didn't see any houses that weren't slums; the towns had no city services at all, not even traffic lights. There was just poverty everywhere. I saw a huge garbage dump, a stinking mountain of trash and rotting garbage, and it had that smell of death like burning tires and burning flesh. It looked like something from the pits of hell, and there were kids swarming all over it, looking for food or anything of value, of which there was none.

I pulled over and watched those kids and thought about my own kids and about all the wealth in America and about the millions of dollars I stole and that I wasted in my life. I thought about the greed that fed the machine the gangs of New York ran on, the greed that made the dollar the almighty so it didn't matter how you got it. Money was everybody's god, not just us guys in the Mob. That's why the cops let us get away with murder. And the feds? They let us get away with assassinating the president of the United States. All because J. Edgar Hoover's greed and fear of being outed as a degenerate gambler and a closeted homosexual who blackmailed others for their own sexual preferences had to protect his friends in the Mob at all costs.

Greed is part of the reason why the public cheered us on in the movies: "Tell Mike it was only business." They liked us because we got rich, and maybe they could too. All it takes is a gun and a dream.

Those kids on the garbage heap didn't even have a dream. Their life was garbage, a mountain of it.

Watching them, I remembered going to Times Square with Jane and Fox and we cut up all those bills and watched the dumb slobs fight over the worthless halves. I thought what evil bastards we were, laughing at people who might have been just as greedy as we were, but they didn't commit crimes to make their dreams come true.

I walked into the back of the motor home and pulled out the drug money. I had it stashed in a duffel bag along with the only other things from my past that I brought with me: the letter from my sister, written on her deathbed and begging me to do something useful with my life; my Mickey Mantle baseball cards were in there, the only other possessions I had that weren't tainted by my past life. In there too were the letters Jane wrote me in prison. I'd saved them as the only evidence I had that our love was real, but it wasn't real. Our love was a mirage; our relationship wasn't even that—it was an obsession. I left the baseball cards and my letter from Rose Marie along with 20 grand that I owed to a legitimate guy who had helped me out when I was first in the relocation program. I also left enough cash to send monthly payments to my ex and to get my kids through college And I left enough for me to live on for a year or more.

I had a big steel bucket in the back that I used for tailgate parties. I took out the scrub brush and the cleaning rags I had stored in there and I stuffed it full of cash—5, maybe 10 grand in fifties and twenties and tens. I put the letters from Jane on the top and carried the bucket back up front.

I opened the door of the motor home and tossed the letters out onto a pile of broken bottles and other trash. The letters were written by a ghost that I didn't want haunting me anymore.

Then I set the bucket down and reached in with both hands and scooped up a pile of bills and heaved them out the door. They fluttered in the air for a second, then settled on the ground. None of the kids even saw me throw them out. I set the bucket on the floor by the driver's seat. I got behind the wheel and started the rig. I rolled down the window. Then I leaned on the horn and started to drive away. I went slow at first, and I reached into the bucket and grabbed cash by the fistful and started throwing it out the window. The breeze picked it up and it swirled in the air. I kept honking the horn and throwing money out the window and the kids came running.

I threw cash out the window until the bucket was empty. The breeze carried it all over that mountain of garbage. I could hear the kids yelling and shouting and screaming as they raced around picking up the bills.

I looked in the rearview and I could see kids waving their arms with bunches of bills clenched in their fists.

There were still bills floating in the air, like manna from heaven.

Acknowledgments

⚞ SAL POLISI ⚟

To my oldest son, Sal Jr., who lives under his Federal Witness Protection name furnished by the U.S. Government. I thank him for his unconditional support and his amazing memory of details from the 1970s and '80s.

To #2 son, Joe, who has become the godly man, loyal husband, and dedicated father. He has always listened to his dad the dreamer and given unconditional support.

To #3 son, Sergio, who was so proud of his dad that he traded in his witness protection name to become Sergio Polisi. Intrepid and loving.

To my daughter, Summer, who was born a strong-willed child. She has a piece of her dad. Summer calls it as she sees it.

To Nick Taylor, author of the 1989 Simon & Schuster book *Sins of the Father*. Thank you for introducing me to Steve Dougherty.

To the entire Gallery Books/Simon & Schuster team: Louise Burke, Anthony Ziccardi, Ed Schlesinger. Thank you for all your dedicated and hard work.

Last but not least to my agent, BJ Robbins. I met BJ twenty-two years ago, and several times we talked about a follow-up book. This book would not have been published without her brilliant and creative input. She has managed to bring me back to reality throughout the entire process. My heartfelt thanks to you, BJ.

✍ STEVE DOUGHERTY ✍

THANKS TO NICK TAYLOR, who introduced me to an amazing character—Sal Polisi—and launched me on this adventure. I am also indebted to a host of brilliant reporters and writers whose books were an invaluable guide and inspiration, and without which *The Sinatra Club* could not have been written; among them are Selwyn Raab, Gay Talese, Nick Pileggi, Mike Dash, John H. Davis, Gene Mustain and Jerry Capeci, Tom Folsom, Jimmy Breslin, and two mobsters who took pen in hand themselves—Henry Hill and Joseph Bonanno. And, of course, to Sal, who is *upazzo* like *la volpe*.